Strategy and the Sea

John B. Hattendorf

Strategy and the Sea

Essays in Honour of John B. Hattendorf

Edited by
N.A.M. Rodger, J. Ross Dancy,
Benjamin Darnell and Evan Wilson

THE BOYDELL PRESS

© Contributors 2016

All Rights Reserved. Except as permitted under current legislation
no part of this work may be photocopied, stored in a retrieval system,
published, performed in public, adapted, broadcast,
transmitted, recorded or reproduced in any form or by any means,
without the prior permission of the copyright owner

First published 2016
The Boydell Press, Woodbridge

ISBN 978 1 78327 098 9

The Boydell Press is an imprint of Boydell & Brewer Ltd
PO Box 9, Woodbridge, Suffolk IP12 3DF, UK
and of Boydell & Brewer Inc.
668 Mt Hope Avenue, Rochester, NY 14620–2731, USA
website: www.boydellandbrewer.com

A catalogue record for this book is available
from the British Library

The publisher has no responsibility for the continued existence or accuracy of URLs for
external or third-party internet websites referred to in this book, and does not guarantee that
any content on such websites is, or will remain, accurate or appropriate

This publication is printed on acid-free paper

Contents

List of Illustrations vii
List of Abbreviations viii
List of Contributors ix

John B. Hattendorf – A Transatlantic Tribute
N.A.M. Rodger 1

Introduction
Evan Wilson, Benjamin Darnell and J. Ross Dancy 5

1. Spanish Noblemen as Galley Captains: A Problematical Social History
   Carla Rahn Phillips 9

2. Strategy Seen from the Quarterdeck in the Eighteenth-Century French Navy
   Olivier Chaline 19

3. Danish and Swedish Flag Disputes with the British in the Channel
   Jakob Seerup 28

4. Reconsidering the *Guerre de Course* under Louis XIV: Naval Policy and Strategic Downsizing in an Era of Fiscal Overextension
   Benjamin Darnell 37

5. British Naval Administration and the Lower Deck Manpower Problem in the Eighteenth Century
   J. Ross Dancy 49

6. British Naval Administration and the Quarterdeck Manpower Problem in the Eighteenth Century
   Evan Wilson 64

7. The Raison d'Être and the Actual Employment of the Dutch Navy in Early Modern Times
   Jaap R. Bruijn 76

8. British Defensive Strategy at Sea in the War against Napoleon
   Roger Knight 88

9. The Offensive Strategy of the Spanish Navy, 1763–1808
   Agustín Guimerá 98

10. The Influence of Sea Power upon Three Great Global Wars, 1793–1815, 1914–1918, 1939–1945: A Comparative Analysis
    Paul Kennedy   109

11. The Evolution of a Warship Type: The Role and Function of the Battlecruiser in Admiralty Plans on the Eve of the First World War
    Matthew S. Seligmann   138

12. The Royal Navy and Grand Strategy, 1937–1941
    George C. Peden   148

13. The Atlantic in the Strategic Perspective of Hitler and his Admirals, 1939–1944
    Werner Rahn   159

14. The Capital Ship, the Royal Navy and British Strategy from the Second World War to the 1950s
    Tim Benbow   169

15. 'No Scope for Arms Control': Strategy, Geography and Naval Limitations in the Indian Ocean in the 1970s
    Peter John Brobst   179

16. Sir Julian Corbett, Naval History and the Development of Sea Power Theory
    Andrew D. Lambert   190

17. The Influence of Identity on Sea Power
    Duncan Redford   201

18. Professor Spenser Wilkinson, Admiral William Sims and the Teaching of Strategy and Sea Power at the University of Oxford and the United States Naval War College, 1909–1927
    Paul M. Ramsey   213

19. Naval Intellectualism and the Imperial Japanese Navy
    Keizo Kitagawa   226

20. History and Navies: Defining a Dialogue
    James Goldrick   236

21. Teaching Navies Their History
    Geoffrey Till   242

Afterword
N.A.M. Rodger   252

A Bibliography of Books, Articles and Reviews Authored, Co-authored, Edited or Co-edited by John B. Hattendorf, 1960–2015   255

Index   285

Tabula Gratulatoria   305

Illustrations

Frontispiece: John B. Hattendorf. Photograph by John W. Corbett

Figures

5.1	Royal Navy manpower in the eighteenth century	52
5.2	Factored seamen and petty officer recruitment	55
5.3	Seamen and petty officer ratings	57
5.4	Volunteer seamen ages and rating	59
5.5	Ages of pressed men	60
6.1	Lieutenants' commissions and successful exams, 1775–1805	69
6.2	Ratio of number of officers to positions available	72
12.1	Percentage shares of total defence expenditure in financial years	149
12.2	Expenditure (£ 000s) in financial years	153

Tables

6.1	Estimate of lieutenants' positions by rate	71
7.1	The numerical strength of leading navies in the seventeenth and eighteenth centuries	80
12.1	DRC and New Standard fleets compared	156
12.2	New construction programme for New Standard Fleet	156

Abbreviations

AMN	Archivo del Museo Naval
ANM	Archives nationales de France
BNE	Biblioteca Nacional de España
CCC	Churchill College, Cambridge
CID	Committee of Imperial Defence
DNI	Director of Naval Intelligence
DRC	Defence Requirements Sub-Committee of the Imperial Defence
FCO	Foreign and Commonwealth Office
FRUS	*Foreign Relations of the United States* (see ch. 15, n. 5)
IWM	Imperial War Museum
KTB/Skl	*Kriegstagebuch der Seekriegsleitung 1939–1945, Teil A*, ed. W. Rahn and G. Schreiber (Herford and Bonn, 1990)
LHCMA	Liddell-Hart Centre for Military Archives, King's College, London
MoD	Ministry of Defence
NID	Naval Intelligence Department
NMM	National Maritime Museum
NMRN	National Museum of the Royal Navy
NWC	Naval War College
PME	Professional Military Education
RAF	Royal Air Force
RN	Royal Navy
TNA	The National Archives, Kew

Contributors

Tim Benbow is Senior Lecturer in Defence Studies at King's College London. His work focuses on the development of naval aviation, and he has published a number of articles and chapters on that theme. He is in the process of completing a book for the US Naval Institute Press entitled *The Royal Navy, the Carrier Question and British Defence Policy 1945–1963*.

Peter John Brobst is Associate Professor of History at Ohio University. He has published a number of works on the Great Game and strategy in the context of the Indian Ocean. He is in the process of completing a book entitled *Indian Ocean Strategy, 1957–1977: Sea Power and Globalism in the Era of Decolonization*.

Jaap R. Bruijn is Professor Emeritus of Maritime History at Leiden University and one of the world's leading experts on Dutch maritime history in the seventeenth and eighteenth centuries. His most recent book is *Zeegang: Zeevarend Nederland in de achttiende* (Zutphen, 2016).

Olivier Chaline is Professeur d'histoire moderne at Université de Paris IV – Sorbonne. He is the head of the Laboratoire d'histoire et d'archéologie maritimes and co-director of the *Revue d'histoire maritime* and the collection *Histoire maritime* at the Presses universitaires de Paris Sorbonne.

J. Ross Dancy is Assistant Professor of Military History at Sam Houston State University in Texas. He received his DPhil from the University of Oxford, where his research examined British naval manning at the end of the eighteenth century. His book, *The Myth of the Press Gang*, was published by Boydell in 2015. He holds a BA in history from Appalachian State University, and an MA in Naval History from the University of Exeter. He served as a US Marine for four years, and was deployed throughout the Western Pacific and Indian Oceans.

Benjamin Darnell is a DPhil Candidate at New College, Oxford under the direction of Dr David Parrott. His research investigates the administration of the French Navy under Louis XIV during the War of the Spanish Succession (1701–14). He is interested in naval finance and the role of private enterprise in resource mobilisation.

Rear Admiral **James Goldrick** recently retired from the Royal Australian Navy. He has held multiple seaborne commands. From 2003 to 2012, he commanded the Australian Defence Force Academy, Australia's Border Protection Command and the Australian Defence College. He was made Officer of the Order of Australia for his leadership in defence education and training.

Agustín Guimerá-Ravina is a Research Fellow of the CSIC (Spanish Council of Scientific Research), Madrid. He has published extensively on the maritime and naval history of the eighteenth century Atlantic world, and he has edited several international books in naval history.

Paul Kennedy is J. Richardson Dilworth Professor of History and the Director of International Security Studies at Yale. He is the author or editor of nineteen books, including *The Rise and Fall of British Naval Mastery*, *The Rise of the Anglo-German Antagonism* and, most famously, the bestselling *The Rise and Fall of the Great Powers*. His most recent book, *Engineers of Victory*, was published in 2013.

Captain **Keizo Kitagawa** is the Defence Attaché at the Japanese Embassy in London. He was commissioned in 1994 and has spent the last two decades in a variety of command and staff positions in the Japanese Maritime Self-Defence Force.

Roger Knight spent the majority of his career at the National Maritime Museum, which he left in 2000 as Deputy Director. In 2005, he published a critically acclaimed biography of Nelson and was appointed Professor of Naval History at the University of Greenwich. His most recent book is *Britain Against Napoleon: The Organization of Victory, 1793–1815*, published in 2013.

Andrew D. Lambert is Laughton Professor of Naval History in the Department of War Studies at King's College London. He is a Fellow of the Royal Historical Society and Director of the Laughton Naval History Unit. His most recent book, *The Challenge: America, Britain and the War of 1812*, was published in 2012.

George C. Peden is Emeritus Professor of History at the University of Stirling. He has published extensively on British public finance, mainly in the twentieth century, and the economic aspects of defence and foreign policy. His most recent book, entitled *Arms, Economics and British Strategy: From Dreadnoughts to Hydrogen Bombs*, was published in 2007 in the Cambridge Military History series.

Carla Rahn Phillips, Emerita Professor of History at the University of Minnesota, has published extensively in the economic, social and maritime history of Spain. Her most recent book, *The Treasure of the San José: Death at Sea in the War of the Spanish Succession*, appeared in 2007.

Contributors

Werner Rahn spent his career in the German Navy, reaching the rank of Captain and serving as director of the German Armed Forces Military History Research Office from 1995 to 1997. He has published a number of important works on German naval history, with a particular focus on the Second World War.

Paul M. Ramsey is completing his doctorate at the University of Calgary. He recently held the Edward S. Miller Research Fellowship in Naval History at the US Naval War College.

Duncan Redford was Senior Research Fellow in Modern Naval History at the National Museum of the Royal Navy in Portsmouth. He served as a submarine officer in the Royal Navy for a decade before completing his doctorate. He is editing a multi-volume history of the Royal Navy.

Nicholas Rodger is a Senior Research Fellow at All Souls College, Oxford and the leading historian of the British Navy. He is in the process of completing the third volume of his critically acclaimed *Naval History of Britain*.

Jakob Seerup is a curator at the Royal Danish Naval Museum in Copenhagen, and he also teaches naval history at the Royal Danish Naval Academy. Most of his work has been published in Danish and explores the history of the Danish Navy in the eighteenth century, but he has also published an article about the Danish Naval Academy in the *Mariner's Mirror* and an article about officers' early careers in the *Journal for Maritime Research*.

Matthew S. Seligmann is Professor of Naval History at Brunel University. His work focuses mostly on Anglo-German relations and the causes of wars and he has authored or co-authored nine books and numerous articles on these topics.

Geoffrey Till is Emeritus Professor of Maritime Studies and Chairman of the Corbett Centre for Maritime Policy Studies at King's College London. Since 2009 he has been a Visiting Professor and Senior Research Fellow at the Rajaratnam School of International Studies, Singapore. His *Understanding Victory: Naval Operations from Trafalgar to the Falklands* was published by ABC-Clio in 2014 and he is currently working on a fourth edition of his *Seapower: A guide for the 21st Century*.

Evan Wilson is the Caird Senior Research Fellow at the National Maritime Museum. He completed his doctorate at the University of Oxford in 2015. He has published a number of articles on naval officers' careers and social backgrounds in the late eighteenth century. His first book, *A Social History of British Naval Officers, 1775–1815*, will be published by Boydell & Brewer later this year.

John B. Hattendorf – A Transatlantic Tribute

John Hattendorf was born in Hinsdale, Illinois on 22 December 1941, a fortnight after the Imperial Japanese Navy had flung the United States abruptly into the Second World War. The next few years were to contribute a great deal of naval history to the United States and the world, but few would have searched for a future naval historian in the outer suburbs of Chicago, nor in Gambier, the small town amidst the peaceful Ohio cornfields where John studied as an undergraduate at Kenyon College. But Kenyon, though far from the sea, was not isolated from the wider world, and certainly not from the scholarly world. Charles Ritcheson, the noted historian of the American Revolution, was then a professor at Kenyon. His experience included wartime service in the US Navy, and a DPhil at Oxford, while his private interests ranged from the Paris Opera to the Beefsteak Club. John also had close contact with the distinguished German medievalist Richard G. Salomon, driven from his chair in Hamburg in 1934, who retired from Kenyon in 1962 aged seventy-eight but remained an active scholar. At one period when he was housebound after a fall, John fetched books for him from the library: a new parcel every week, a book for every day, each in a different language. Salomon introduced John to the scholarly tradition of the *Monumenta Germaniae Historica*, and aroused in him an enthusiasm for archives highly unusual in an undergraduate. Over two years' voluntary work, John listed and organised the college archives, and he edited *A Dusty Path*, an anthology of documents and photographs drawn from them.[1] Salomon almost lured him into medieval church history – but not quite.

Instead, on leaving Kenyon in 1964, John joined the US Navy, and the following day, as he remembers, 'someone started a war in a place called Viet Nam'.[2] In February 1965 he was commissioned as an ensign, and before the end of the year he was at sea off that coast as an officer of the destroyer USS *O'Brien*. In 1967 he was mentioned in despatches for his 'skill and judgement' under fire. From the *O'Brien* he went to the Naval History Division in Washington, where he found himself in danger of a different sort. The USS *Constellation*, then as now preserved at Baltimore, was widely identified as the frigate of 1797 rather than the sloop of 1854 which she in fact is. Much emotional and political capital had been invested in the 'frigate *Constellation*' by the US Navy and the city of Baltimore, on the basis of wishful thinking and what subsequently proved to be

---

[1] T.B. Greenslade, *Kenyon College: Its Third Half Century* (Gambier, OH, 1975), pp. 188–9 and 202–3. *Kenyon College Alumni Bulletin*, xx, no. 1 (1997), pp. 12–13 and 55, printing John's speech on accepting an honorary doctorate in 1997.
[2] 1997 speech cited in n. 1 above.

forged documents; Rear Admiral Ernest M. Eller, the Director of Naval History, was a warm partisan of the theory. Looking for something else in the archives, John found the log of the yard which had built the sloop: conclusive evidence, but not what the admiral wanted to hear. All John's characteristic combination of rigorous integrity and emollient diplomacy was needed to get out of this awkward position.[3]

After the Naval History Division, John spent a summer studying at the Munson Institute of Mystic Seaport under the great maritime historian Robert G. Albion, and then was released for two years (1969–71) to do an MA in History at Brown University under the noted historian of science and technology A. Hunter Dupree. His subject was 'Technology and Strategy: A Study in the Professional Thought of the US Navy, 1900–1916'; he had to fight to get the Brown faculty to accept that warfare could be a legitimate subject of scholarly research, and indeed (the emotions generated by the Vietnam War then running high) that a serving officer could be an acceptable student. Returning to active service, John studied at the Naval Destroyer School and then became Operations Officer of the destroyer USS *Fiske*, based at Newport (and by coincidence named after a noted naval reformer of the late nineteenth century). For his next job John moved across the harbour (as it now seems inevitable he would) to join the staff of the Naval War College as research assistant to the President, the former Rhodes Scholar Vice Admiral Stansfield Turner. Few Lieutenants work directly for a vice admiral, and very few indeed can have been recommended for immediate promotion on the grounds of being 'superbly qualified for independent historical research'. The admiral hoped indeed that the navy would send John to Oxford to do a doctorate, but to Turner's dismay the Washington bureaucracy was prepared to approve only a 'useful' subject such as nuclear physics. 'He is an outstanding officer,' Turner wrote, 'who has the potential of becoming an outstanding naval historian, and I regret that he cannot continue to be both officer and historian, in the tradition of our own Admiral Alfred Thayer Mahan and of the Royal Navy's Admiral Sir Herbert Richmond.'[4]

So the die was cast, John resigned his commission and in Michaelmas 1973 started at Pembroke College, Oxford, as a DPhil student, supervised by Norman Gibbs, Chichele Professor of the History of War at All Souls. His subject was 'England in the War of the Spanish Succession: A Study of the English View and Conduct of Grand Strategy, 1701–12'. It was entirely characteristic that he at once rejected any narrowly naval or narrowly English view of the war, but considered allied grand strategy as a whole from the sources of all the participants. Since Gibbs was no specialist in the subject, John had much to do with Professor Ragnhild Hatton, who encouraged him to read widely in foreign languages, and

---

[3] The tortuous story of the *Constellation* affair is explored by D.M. Wegner et al., 'Fouled Anchors: The Constellation Question Answered' (Bethesda, MD, 1991), available at http://www.navsea.navy.mil/nswc/carderock/docs/fouled_anchors.pdf.

[4] Quoting John's official 'Report on the Fitness of Officers' for 1972–73, written by Turner himself.

interested him particularly in Swedish history. He also profited greatly from the friendship and counsel of the military historian Dr Piers Mackesy of Pembroke. The thesis was submitted in 1979, passed and subsequently published. By then John was already back at the Naval War College as Assistant and then Associate Professor of Strategy between 1977 and 1981. He then spent two years as Visiting Professor of Military and Naval History at the National University of Singapore, returning to Newport as Professor of Naval History in 1983. He has been there ever since, apart from a year on exchange with the Militärgeschichtliche Forschungsamt (the German armed forces historical office) in 1990–91. In 1984 he was appointed to the chair named after Fleet Admiral Ernest J. King – linking him, somewhat incongruously, with one of the US Navy's less intellectual and least likeable senior officers. He also served first as Director of the College's Advanced Research Department, and then Chairman of the Maritime History Department and Director of the Naval War College Museum. In all this he has been supported by Berit Sundell, whom he married in 1978 on his return to Newport. With their three daughters and six grandchildren all living within five miles, the Hattendorf family forms a united core, surrounded by the widespread circles of John's professional friends, colleagues and associates all over the world.

John's distinguished career in the service of the US Navy and the worldwide intellectual community of naval historians and strategists has now lasted fifty years and shows no signs of running out yet. His list of publications is all the more extraordinary coming from someone who did not start academic life until his mid-thirties, and has never enjoyed the research opportunities available to university post-holders. John's unusual career has been shaped by his experience of the sea and sea fighting, his unshakeable commitment to the highest standards of research, and his skilful adaptation to the situation of the Naval War College, which has given him the opportunity to produce numerous smaller pieces of work, but not the big books which he could have written so well. In a military establishment somewhat outside the usual academic circuits, John has avoided isolation by organising a notable series of international conferences which brought together leading historians from all over the world. 'The Influence of History on Mahan', held at the College in 1991; followed in 1992 by 'Mahan is not Enough' on Sir Julian Corbett and Sir Herbert Richmond; 'Ubi Sumus? The State of Naval and Maritime History', held at Yale in 1993; and 'Doing Naval History', also at Yale the following year, were particularly influential in drawing together diverse viewpoints and setting research agendas. As a natural diplomat, discreet, efficient, calm under pressure, a skilful navigator of naval bureaucracy, John has repeatedly found himself at the centre of international collaborative ventures, interpreting the navy to the scholarly world and vice versa. He was one of the authors of the massive single volume *America and the Sea: A Maritime History* of 1998, and editor-in-chief of the four-volume *Oxford Encyclopedia of Maritime History* in 2007. He made numerous contributions to other historical dictionaries and encylopedias, including twenty-two biographies for the *Oxford Dictionary of National Biography*. He has edited the proceedings of all but one of the US Navy's biennial International Seapower Symposia between 1991 and

2011. Following the example of Salomon, he has made notable contributions to scholarly infrastructure by editing documentary collections, listing archives and writing bibliographies and research guides – essential but unfashionable work which is undervalued in American universities. A generous but judicious reviewer, he has often drawn important works in foreign languages to the attention of English-speaking scholars, and has himself published in French, German, Swedish and Spanish in addition to English. Amongst a long list of honours and awards he has been given the Alfred Thayer Mahan Award by the US Navy League, a Superior Civilian Service Award by the Secretary of the Navy, the Admiral of the Navy George Dewey Award by the Naval Order of the United States, the Dudley W. Knox Award by the Naval Historical Foundation, the Dartmouth Medal of the American Library Association, and the Caird Medal of the National Maritime Museum. In 2011 he achieved a sort of apotheosis by becoming a medal himself, when the Naval War College created the Hattendorf Prize for Maritime History. He serves on numerous editorial and advisory boards – and it is by no means over: he is at present working on at least thirteen books and articles. The conference at which the papers gathered in this volume were originally delivered was held to mark John's announced retirement, but at the time of writing the US Navy has not yet released him. Battleships may be paid off and carriers scrapped, but the navy cannot do without John Hattendorf.

N.A.M. Rodger
All Souls College, Oxford

Introduction

This *Festschrift*, made up of papers given at a conference held at All Souls College, Oxford, in April 2014 to mark Professor John B. Hattendorf's impending retirement from the Naval War College, is meant to reflect the respect and affection in which he is held by a great number of scholars and naval officers from all over the world. It is also meant to reflect the nature and breadth of his studies, which present a challenge to the editors as we attempt to draw out some common themes. It is tempting to side-step the topic and declare 'Strategy and the Sea' to be nothing more than a sufficiently generic label for Professor Hattendorf's career. But as Lawrence Freedman identifies in his recent survey of all things strategic, '[S]trategy remains the best word we have for expressing attempts to think about actions in advance, in the light of our goals and our capacities.'[1] The difficulty in defining and discussing strategy is not, therefore, a hurdle to be overcome but rather a characteristic to be embraced. The contributions to this volume encompass all three elements of Freedman's definition: how to think about actions in advance, how to define goals and how to understand capabilities.

Often the most straightforward decision, at least in the abstract, for leaders on the eve of war is to determine whether their navy's actions will be primarily defensive or offensive. Roger Knight and Agustín Guimerá both question the perceptions of the eighteenth-century British and Spanish navies as being primarily offensive and defensive strategic tools, respectively. When considered together, Knight and Guimerá demonstrate the significance of a strong defensive perimeter as a prerequisite for effective offensive operations. Paul Kennedy picks up on the same theme in discussing naval strategy in terms of contested space. The statesmen responsible for the grand strategy in each of the three wars he discusses defined their goals this way. How could Britain make inroads into Napoleon's continental space? What was the use of a battle fleet in the First World War when faced with new asymmetrical technologies that limited its ability to patrol the enemy's coast? How could the Allies realise the goals of the Casablanca Conference and take control of the vital contested space of the North Atlantic? All three wars were ultimately won on land, and so one of the key questions for strategists both before and during these wars concerned the role of sea power. Thinking about naval actions in advance and defining naval goals therefore required not only an understanding how naval power could form the foundation for a successful campaign, but also an understanding of their navy's capacities.

---

[1] L. Freedman, *Strategy: A History* (Oxford, 2013), p. x.

The most significant argument put forward by the collective effort of the contributors to this volume involves that last part of Freedman's definition: capacities. Freedman emphasises that strategy is often determined more by the starting point than by the end point.[2] In other words, the constraints imposed on a state matter more than leaders' goals. The contributors to this volume have broadened the categories of historical analysis of a state's capacities.

In existing studies of strategy, geography and economic strength are frequently considered fundamental constraints on a state's capacities; nevertheless, a number of contributors have approached these topics in innovative ways. The maritime geography of the Netherlands and Britain is often cited as the impetus for their strong navies. What Knight and Jaap Bruijn show is that their navies were fundamentally defensive tools constructed to prevent invasion. To do so effectively, Britain insisted on dominating the English Channel, which was both the logical path for an invader and the shortest route to the North Atlantic and the Mediterranean for Denmark, the Netherlands and other northern European states. As a result of Britain's insistence on an aggressive defensive strategic stance, the strategic choices available to Britain's rivals were: fight their way through; avoid the Channel by sailing around the British Isles; or lower their flags in honour of the British domination of the Channel. The latter option was, as Jakob Seerup's chapter demonstrates, not palatable; both the Dutch and the Danish moved between the other options instead. Pride, combined with geography, constrained those states' strategic options.

The enormous financial resources necessary to sustain an effective navy required a sustained commitment from the state. Prior to space exploration, a navy was the state's most technologically advanced, financially demanding and logistically complex organisation. The challenge of building a sustainable system to develop and supply naval forces tended to place significant constraints on strategists; Napoleon's failure to understand the unpredictability of naval operations and the logistical complexity of building and supplying a fleet are often cited as significant reasons his naval war was generally unsuccessful.[3] Louis XIV's problem was related but slightly different, as Benjamin Darnell shows. When a state's resources were strained, the decline in a navy's capacities could be steep. France's attempts to co-opt private industry failed to produce a coherent and manageable fiscal foundation for the navy's huge expenses. It was not just early modern states that depended on private industry to meet the challenge of naval operations. Similar constraints can be found in George Peden's analysis of the British Navy on the eve of the Second World War, when shipbuilding firms struggled to meet ministers' demands. When the interests of the private sector and the state are mismatched, strategists face difficult choices.

---

[2] Ibid., p. xi.
[3] N.A.M. Rodger, *The Command of the Ocean: A Naval History of Britain, 1649–1815* (London, 2004), pp. 536, 562.

Social issues can also influence strategy, a conclusion reached by a surprising number of contributors. Whereas it is common to find studies exploring how statesmen grappled with geographic and economic constraints, it is far less common to find studies exploring how they managed their human resources. Carla Rahn Phillips and Evan Wilson argue that keeping officers happy, well paid and employed in the necessary areas of naval life presented difficulties to both British and Spanish statesmen in the early modern period. Throwing money at the problem was one solution, but more astute administrators realised that officers valued intangible status symbols even more highly. Without willing captains or experienced navigators or competent surgeons, navies struggle to meet the goals laid out by strategists. These two chapters are useful reminders that strategy can be shaped by factors usually ignored or seen as irrelevant by both statesmen and historians.

J. Ross Dancy's chapter also addresses social issues. He asks the most fundamental question for any navy, particularly in the age of sail: how do you find enough experienced sailors to deploy an effective naval force? Sufficient manpower is an essential precondition for projecting sea power. Britain's manpower recruitment system balanced positive incentives and coercion; it was never simple or easy to man the fleet, and manning issues became fraught political topics not only for contemporaries, but also in the historiography. Naval administrators' options for manning the fleet were constrained by practical concerns, such as the pool of available experienced deep-sea sailors, and also by cultural factors, such as the traditional idea of the liberty of Englishmen. Duncan Redford's chapter picks up on a similar theme, noting that non-material and political issues such as national identity can be drivers of strategy. No statesmen operate in a sterile environment, free from cultural and social biases. Peter John Brobst notes that a fundamental question for British, American and Soviet strategists concerned their nations' identities as land or maritime powers. Projecting power into the Indian Ocean presented not only financial and logistical challenges, but also hit directly at the heart of questions such as: was Britain still a world-spanning imperial maritime power? Should projecting naval power be a priority for an Asiatic land power like the Soviet Union?

Other contributors explore whether states were able to keep their internal affairs in order, beyond the foundational concerns of fiscal and logistical health. Service rivalries feature in a number of contributions. One explanation for the collapse of French naval finances during the Nine Years' War is that Louis XIV, when faced with difficult budget choices, tended to fund the army before the navy. No state was immune from these concerns, particularly when, as Bruijn notes, there were compelling reasons to argue that both the army and the navy were essential for national defence. The advent of air power added a third dimension to the long-running funding feuds between armies and navies. Redford narrates the challenge that the RAF posed to the Royal Navy: Britain's status as a 'maritime nation' no longer seemed so essential to national identity, and, as a consequence, to strategy. Peden's description of the RAF's dominant funding position on the eve of the Second World War was one result of that cultural shift.

After the war, as Tim Benbow highlights, both military leaders and historians debated the lessons to be drawn and the implications for funding and strategy. Their views were, and continue to be, heavily influenced by institutional and cultural pressures and biases.

The factors that can shape a state's capacity to realise its strategic goals are wide-ranging and often surprising. Geography, economic strength and the significance of leaders' world-views are familiar topics for strategists. The dominant theme of this book is that humans devise and execute strategies carried out by other humans; recruiting, managing and deploying human resources are necessarily messy and subject to human concerns. Strategy is difficult to define, but that makes it all the more important for historians to recognise the variety of topics that can shape it.

Professor Hattendorf is of course well aware that historians need to be willing to look beyond the immediate and the concrete: his career exemplifies that approach. His study of the War of the Spanish Succession was, as N.A.M. Rodger says in his tribute, an excellent example of a multinational and wide-ranging approach to strategic studies. Subsequent publications have been similarly ambitious and encyclopedic, from *America and the Sea: A Maritime History* to his lead editorship of *British Naval Documents, 1204–1960*. We hope that this volume is a suitable homage.

The editors were the organisers of the conference, and they are glad to take the opportunity to thank those who helped to make it possible. Foremost among them must be named All Souls College and the Guy Hudson Memorial Trust, which supported the conference financially and practically, and E-Graphics, which designed the conference website. Among the many people in the College who contributed, the organisers especially wish to thank Professor Ian Maclean the Fellow Librarian, Dr Norma Aubertin-Potter the then Librarian Gaye Morgan, Helen Green and Demelza Shaw. Midshipmen Aaron Edwards and Darren Twort of the Oxford University Royal Naval Unit efficiently convoyed the delegates around the College. The volume itself appears in print thanks to the tireless support of Peter Sowden of Boydell & Brewer.

Evan Wilson
National Maritime Museum

Benjamin Darnell
New College, Oxford

J. Ross Dancy
Sam Houston State University

1
Spanish Noblemen as Galley Captains: A Problematical Social History

CARLA RAHN PHILLIPS

Sailing vessels formed the vast majority of the ships in Spanish military service in medieval and early modern times. Nonetheless, Spain also used galley fleets in the Mediterranean in the late Middle Ages,[1] and later expanded their use wherever Spain had a presence in the world, including the coastal waters of the Americas and South-East Asia. Unlike the Republic of Venice in its heyday, Spain used galleys exclusively for military purposes. In the Mediterranean, they formed a crucial element of Spain's defensive and offensive strategy during the confrontation with the Ottoman Empire and its satellite states in North Africa in the sixteenth century.[2]

Because Spanish galleys performed well at the Battle of Lepanto in 1571, King Philip II sought to increase their numbers. However, the government had difficulty finding enough men to pull the oars and enough captains and other wage-earning officers with the necessary skills to organise and command multinational crews. There were a number of reasons for the difficulty, in part because mariners and naval officers had more attractive choices than the galleys. Spain's transatlantic fleets were approaching their peak in the late sixteenth century, with some two hundred vessels involved in the trade each year.[3] Moreover, the military needs of the crown increased in the same period, spurred by English and French incursions into Spanish America in the late 1570s and Philip II's contested claim to the Portuguese throne after 1578. The naval build-up preceding the armada sent against England in 1588 also increased the demand for mariners at all ranks. The recruitment of captains for Spain's Mediterranean galleys required particular care. By the late sixteenth century, most of the galley oarsmen were slaves, prisoners of war or convicted criminals. Keeping order on board, as well as encouraging the best performance from all hands, required more than the usual skills of a

---

[1] L.V. Mott, *Seapower in the Medieval Mediterranean: The Catalan Fleet and the War of the Sicilian Vespers* (Gainesville, FL, 2003).
[2] J.F. Guilmartin, *Gunpowder and Galleys: Changing Technology and Mediterranean Warfare in the Sixteenth Century*, 2nd edn (London, 2003), devotes considerable attention to Spanish galleys.
[3] For tables of ships and tonnages employed in Spain's transatlantic trade, see P. Chaunu and H. Chaunu, *Séville et l'Atlantique, 1504–1650* (8 vols in 12, Paris, 1955–59), vols 3 and 4.

competent naval officer.[4] For noblemen, serving the king as a galley captain challenged not only their abilities as leaders, but also their sense of honour.

Considerable documentation regarding galley service by Spanish noblemen exists in the Archivo General de Simancas (AGS), the Archivo del Museo Naval (AMN) and the Biblioteca Nacional de España (BNE), both in Madrid, and in other depositories. By all accounts, it is clear that some Spanish noblemen served in the galley fleets willingly and with distinction, certainly until Lepanto. Thereafter, it appears that many Spanish noblemen decided that the disadvantages of such service far outweighed the benefits.

One extraordinary summary of those disadvantages is contained in a lengthy letter of advice to an unnamed correspondent who wanted to become a galley captain. The author of the letter argues strongly against serving the crown in the galleys and indirectly criticises Philip II for failing to provide adequate support for such service. The manuscript covers seven double-sided folio pages in a volume of copied documents from the fifteenth and sixteenth centuries. Its title translates as the 'Discourse of García de Toledo Regarding the Disadvantages of High-Ranking Positions in the Galleys'.[5] If the attribution is correct, and internal evidence suggests that it is, the discourse provides a stunning repudiation of one kind of service that the nobility owed to their monarch. The author's full name was García Álvarez de Toledo y Osorio (1514–77). He was the grandson of the II Duke of Alba (Fadrique Álvarez de Toledo y Enríquez de Quiñones), and the nephew and contemporary of the III Duke of Alba (Fernando Álvarez de Toledo), the distinguished general who served the Spanish monarchy in numerous venues.[6] Don García's father (Pedro Álvarez de Toledo y Zúñiga) was Viceroy of Naples for two decades (1532–53), and his mother (Juana Pimentel) held a noble title in her own right as the II Marquise of Villafranca del Bierzo. Don García's sister, Leonor de Toledo, married Cosimo d'Medici, I Grand Duke of Tuscany, bringing prestige and Spanish noble connections to the Medici line.[7] In other words, García de Toledo came from the highest ranks of the Spanish nobility.

At the start of his career, Don García continued a family tradition by owning two galleys and serving with them in the Squadron of Naples under Andrea Doria. By 1535, at the age of twenty-one, Don García commanded (and presumably

---

[4] The qualities desired in military officers featured in European treatises since ancient times. In the sixteenth century, Niccoló Machiavelli, *Discourses on the First Ten Books of Livy*, Book III, dealt at length with those qualities, as did numerous other treatises. Current scholarship has shown a renewed interest in the topic, including the recent edition of N. Elias, *The Genesis of the Naval Profession*, ed. René Moelker and Stephen Mennell (Dublin, 2007).

[5] 'Discurso de García de Toledo sobre los inconvenientes que tienen los cargos de galeras', in Juan Martínez de Burgos, 'Miscelánea literaria de los S. XV–S. XVI', Biblioteca Nacional de España (BNE), Madrid, MS 19164, fols 100r–107v.

[6] For the family's tradition of military service, especially in the Mediterranean, see W.S. Maltby, *Alba: A Biography of Fernando Álvarez de Toledo, Third Duke of Alba, 1507–1582* (Berkeley and Los Angeles, 1983), ch. 1.

[7] The Florentine artist known as Bronzino painted a well-known portrait of Leonor/Eleanor and her first-born son (Florence: Uffizi Gallery).

owned) six galleys and soon distinguished himself in various Mediterranean battles during the reign of Charles I of Spain (otherwise Charles V of the Holy Roman Empire).[8] The king named Don García as General of the Squadron of Naples and in 1544 as Captain General of the Sea, after he had defeated the pirate Barbarossa. During the reign of Charles's successor, Philip II, Don García served as Colonel General of the Infantry of the Kingdom of Naples, Viceroy of Catalonia (1558–64) and Viceroy of Sicily (1564–66). In the latter position, he reconquered the Peñón de Vélez in North Africa in 1564 and the following year sent relief to the island of Malta, which was under siege by the Ottoman Turks. Before the Battle of Lepanto, Philip II dispatched Don García, by then a member of his Council of State, to advise his young half-brother, Don Juan of Austria.[9] Don García's advice presumably contributed to the Christian victory over the Ottomans in that battle, and he carried on a warm correspondence with Don Juan thereafter.[10]

After decades of serving the crown on land and sea, however, Don García wrote his discourse about the negative aspects of galley service. The discourse dates from about 1575, just as Spain's Mediterranean galley fleets reached their peak, with some 150 vessels in service. In part, Don Garcia's disillusionment may have had a financial basis. The Spanish crown preferred to negotiate contracts (*asientos*) to administer one or more galleys for a set fee, rather than running them directly. For example, Don Álvaro de Bazán, the Marquis of Santa Cruz, ran the forty galleys of the Squadron of Naples from 1575 to 1577 for a fee of 1,046.3 Neapolitan *ducatos* per year for each galley.[11] For that fee, Don Álvaro was expected to pay all the costs of the squadron, including food for all ranks, the clothing worn by the unfree oarsmen and the purchase of slaves when the squadron needed to replace oarsmen who died, suffered injuries or had otherwise become unable to serve. With careful management and the booty from captured enemy vessels, contractors such as Don Álvaro could earn profits as well as military glory, presuming the crown paid the contracted fee in a timely fashion.

Like Don Álvaro and other Spanish noblemen, García de Toledo often had to advance his own funds to carry out official duties on land and sea. Given the myriad demands on royal finances, reimbursement sometimes proved difficult. According to one estimate, King Philip owned Don García 130,000 Spanish *ducados* by the late 1560s.[12] Instead of paying the debt, the king created the Italian titles of Duke of Fernandina and Prince of Montalbán for him in 1569. Upon

---

[8] The battles included La Goleta (Tunis), Algiers, Sfax, Calibria and Mebredia.
[9] BNE, MS 20210, 71–1.
[10] See, for example, letters from 1574 in BNE, MS 20212, 36–9, 12, 13, 15.
[11] BNE, MS 10433. According to J.A. Marino, *Pastoral Economics in the Kingdom of Naples* (Baltimore, 1988), p. 69, the Neapolitan *ducato* = 0.833 Spanish *ducado* in the late sixteenth century. Both words are translated as ducat in English which can lead to confusion, so the original words are used here.
[12] From the genealogical website: http://www.fcmedinasidonia.com/archivo/casa_villafranca.html.

the death of his brother that same year, Don García became IV Marquis of Villafranca del Bierzo, a Spanish title that carried grandee status. Curiously, however, he used only his Italian titles until his own death in Naples in 1577.[13] His choice of titles, and his discourse against the galley service in which he had spent most of his career, suggest that towards the end of his life he distanced himself from Spain and from his king.

Directing his discourse to the unnamed correspondent who had asked for his advice, Don García begins by noting his own difficulties in withdrawing from galley ownership and command. To discourage his correspondent from becoming a galley captain, he promises to discuss all the disadvantages of galley service to 'one's person, finances, life, honour and perhaps even one's soul'.[14] Adding to the perils inherent in seafaring, he complains about the poor character of the men serving in the galleys. By this, he does not seem to mean the enslaved or felonious oarsmen, known collectively as the *chusma*,[15] but the free wage-earners. 'Instead of dealing with men who are well-born and virtuous, you have to deal with men characterised by vileness, self-interest and evil, and a large proportion of the king's service depends on these persons'. Don García's disdain may reflect a prejudice against lesser-born naval officers, an attitude common among noblemen who went to sea.[16] Nonetheless, many of his other complaints cut across the boundary between nobles and non-nobles. For example, he notes:

> that a man's honour is more affected by fortune at sea than in any other circumstance. In many instances, neither good judgment nor experience will help you – though you have them – and in infinite other instances, the lack of good judgment and experience will destroy you. It is like holding a wolf by the ears; if it is dangerous to hang on, it is no less dangerous to let go.[17]

He adds that in his experience:

> there were only two galley captains who might be envied, but many more who came to grief in various ways, some by drowning, others by having their ships smashed to pieces on land, others by dying at the hands of their enemies, others ending their labours as slaves of the Turks, others having their ships burned, others being rowed to Barbary by their own crews, and others who, in maintaining their ships, destroyed their limited finances. ... Their names are so familiar that even a 4-year-old child could recite them.[18]

---

[13] Some sources date his death as 1578, but that seems to be an error.
[14] 'Discurso de Garcia de Toledo', fols 100r–100v.
[15] The word *chusma*, from Greek and Genoese, referred to the chant used to synchronise the strokes of the oars and came to denote the oarsmen as a group. By the late sixteenth century, the word could also mean a rabble, mob or riffraff, which indicates the general reputation of the oarsmen by then.
[16] For example, see Elias, *Genesis of the Naval Profession*, pp. 33–40.
[17] 'Discurso de García de Toledo', fols 100v–101r. This well-known saying is usually attributed to the Roman emperor Tiberius.
[18] Ibid., fols 100r–101v.

Don García speculates that the only reason God had spared him from most of the ills afflicting his cohort was that he had left the sea when he did.

The discourse gives considerable attention to financial matters. According to Don García, wage-earning mariners are loyal and competent only if they are paid regularly. 'If you do not have the payments in hand because they have not been consigned to you, the men turn against you, fail to do their jobs at sea, and commit outrages on land that damage your reputation and honour.' Even when money is provided at the start of a voyage, if the payments are later suspended, 'because many times the needs of kings require this', the consequences are even worse.[19]

Don García warns that his correspondent's two principal reasons for wanting to become a galley captain – to gain honour and wealth – will be very difficult to achieve. Spanish galleys in the past were much more secure, he argues, because the paid crew members were all experienced hands, and their ships could easily outdistance 'the Turks and Moors' who opposed them as predators or prey, 'and from this they gained honour and profit'. He states that more recently the Turks had acquired more and better ships, while Spanish forces had become weaker in all categories, 'so that they can neither flee nor overtake an enemy. And if you say that one does not always encounter enemies, I would respond that unless you encounter them, there is no way to achieve the honour and wealth that you wish to gain.'[20]

Don García returns repeatedly to the difficulties of finding good experienced officers to manage the ship and the oarsmen. Even a new ship will not function well without good leadership, he notes, and incompetent officers will make the whole crew dispirited, which is a crucial disadvantage in battle.[21] Moreover, the scarcity of good subordinates can damage a captain's reputation in many ways:

> If you decide not to take inexperienced crews out in bad weather, some will call you a coward. If you stay near port for some months until the sailors and the *chusma* learn to work together efficiently, some will accuse you of being too fond of life in port, wasting the king's wages, and will argue that it would be better for the king not to have galleys at all.[22]

He also complains that dishonour results when the general of a fleet interferes with matters that properly pertain to each captain, for example:

> assigning *patrones*,[23] *cómitres*,[24] or officers to your galleys, which will cause your own men, who hoped to be promoted to such jobs, to grumble and complain against

---

[19] Ibid., fols 102r–102v.
[20] Ibid., fols 103r–103v.
[21] Ibid., fol. 104r.
[22] Ibid., fols 104v–105r.
[23] In the context of Spain's Mediterranean galleys, a *patrón* was second in command to the captain and often more knowledgeable in nautical matters.
[24] A *cómitre* was the officer charged with directing the work of the crew, whether oars or sails propelled the galley at any given time.

you. Even so, in the face of such interference, it is better not to absent yourself to do other tasks, because at least you can defend yourself in person before the general.[25]

Towards the end of his discourse, Don García returns to the career of Andrea Doria, who – his correspondent had argued – became famous only after he shifted from land warfare to the sea. Although acknowledging that Doria was one of the two men whose career one might envy, Don García notes that 'those were other times, … and he was also sustained by a great master (*amo*), despite the perils that assailed him from the sea and from shifts in fortune'.[26] Doria served Charles I, as did Don García at the start of his career, so the remark can be taken as an indirect criticism of Philip II. Don García continues in that same vein, noting the threats to honour and fortune in commanding a large fleet, and the even greater difficulties involved in trying to disengage from a principal command in the galleys.[27] He seems to write from bitter personal experience, arguing that whatever reasons you have for leaving naval service, 'you will be accused of putting your own particular interests above service to the king, and you cannot be freed from blame without shifting the blame to your master'.[28]

In his final paragraph, Don García urges his correspondent to stay at home and manage his estates, which provide a steady and secure source of income and honour, rather than risking everything by seeking a career in the galleys. 'That choice will expose you to financial ruin and an early death, leaving your children not only fatherless, but penniless.'[29] Whether or not Don García's sentiments represented many members of his social class, they help to explain why the crown found it difficult to recruit noblemen into galley service after Lepanto.

From the king's point of view, the most convenient course of action was to continue contracting the administration of the expanded galley fleets in the 1570s to trusted and experienced individuals such as Don Alvaro de Bazán, the Marquis of Santa Cruz. With so many other opportunities, however, there were not enough noblemen willing to serve as galley captains. The Committee on Galleys (*Junta de Galeras*) of the Council of War (*Consejo de Guerra*) was well aware of the problem. During the summer and autumn of 1584, the committee had a series of discussions regarding how to attract more noblemen to galley service. The general context of those discussions was the belief that noblemen could be trusted to govern and administer the galleys well, because of their military training and their honour and loyalty to the crown. The members of the committee agreed that noblemen serving as galley captains would increase the discipline and effectiveness of the crews, as well as ensuring more humane treatment of all the men on board. They noted, however, that the noblemen recruited would have to be knowledgeable about maritime matters. In other words, without

[25] 'Discurso de García de Toledo', fol. 105r.
[26] Ibid., fol. 105v.
[27] Ibid., fols 105v–106r.
[28] Ibid., fols 106v–107r.
[29] Ibid., fol. 107v.

seafaring experience their upbringing as leaders with military skills would not ensure that they could command at sea.[30] To attract men with the necessary qualities and skills, the government would have to provide adequate compensation. An unstated but obvious hope of the committee was that young noblemen who established a career on the galleys would be more likely to take on the management of whole squadrons as they matured.

In short, the members of the committee seem to have decided that the crown could no longer rely as heavily on contractual arrangements to run the galleys, and that financial incentives were the best way to attract a new generation of noblemen to galley service. Financial incentives were central to their 1584 discussions, including concerns that recruiting noblemen might substantially increase the cost of running the galleys. The committee estimated that the total cost would not necessarily rise, because a higher base rate of pay for captains would eliminate the need for the supplements that traditionally accompanied their wages.[31] After preliminary discussions in August 1584, the committee asked the king to request opinions (*pareceres*) from the Marquis of Santa Cruz and other senior officials. The committee noted that there were already many excellent men among the non-noble officers in the galleys, including captains. They requested their opinions as well, presumably to demonstrate that the crown would continue to value their services, even as more noblemen joined the ranks of galley captains. The committee also collected data on the total compensation for officers already serving.

Having gathered this information, the Committee on Galleys resumed discussions in early October 1584.[32] By then, the king had agreed that the government needed a new approach to attract more noblemen to the galleys. Each member of the committee gave his opinion about wages for captains in the meeting held on 6 October 1584. Don Francisco de Álava proposed 35 *escudos* per month and ten daily rations – the extra rations for members of each captain's entourage, including servants.[33] Ordinary captains on the galleys were served by men from the *chusma*; to allow personal servants for the noble captains would mark a major deviation from standard procedures. The Marquis of Aguilar suggested a wage of 30 *escudos* per month and six daily rations. Aguilar thought that the crown should not pay wages for any personal servants, but he urged the king to reward a nobleman who performed well with appointment to one of the military orders. The Commendador of Castile agreed with Aguilar on the monthly wage but preferred an allowance of twelve rations per day for each nobleman's entourage, which would attract 'persons of quality and satisfaction' as galley captains.

---

[30] Their insistence on seafaring competence contradicts Elias, *Genesis of the Naval Profession*, pp. 33–40.
[31] Archivo del Museo Naval (AMN), Madrid, Colección Sanz Barutell, MS 389, fol. 164r.
[32] Ibid., fol. 186r.
[33] The value of an *escudo* varied between 10 and 15 silver *reales*. A *ducado* was officially valued at 11 *reales*.

The non-noble members of the committee held less generous views.[34] The Royal Accountant Francisco de Garnica proposed giving new noble captains 30 *escudos* and six rations, with extra benefits if a man served well but no personal servants permitted. Juan Fernández de Espinosa agreed that the new captains should be 'gentlemen and principal persons', but he argued that they should not receive a wage at all until they had proven worthy; at that point, they should earn between 30 and 35 *escudos* per month, with twelve daily rations. The last to give his opinion was the committee's president, Rodrigo Vázquez. He agreed that it would be suitable to appoint noble gentlemen as captains of the galleys, but 'not excluding from [their ranks non-noble] persons who were apt [for the job] and good mariners'. According to Vázquez, the new recruits should be selected on the basis of reports from the official known as the Governor of Castile (*Adelantado de Castilla*)[35] and the Marquis of Santa Cruz. Vázquez thought that those chosen should earn 40 *escudos* per month and eight to ten rations per day, but with no personal servants permitted.[36]

The basic wage of galley captains in the late sixteenth century was 10 *escudos* per month, though competent galley captains generally received sizeable supplements – sometimes two or three times as much as their basic wage. By comparison, the principal officer on a transatlantic merchant vessel earned the equivalent of 8.8 *escudos* per month from 1567 to 1623.[37] Officers on Spain's Atlantic fleets had the opportunity to supplement their basic wages through trade; officers on the galleys did not. The committee's recommendations would have raised the basic wage for galley captains to a level that could attract noblemen and lessen or eliminate the need for supplementary pay for exemplary service. It was not clear, however, whether higher wages alone would be sufficient to counter the myriad disadvantages of galley service discussed by García de Toledo.

The juxtaposition of Don García's discourse and the Council of War's efforts to attract more noblemen to the galleys raises some interesting questions. Did the king implement the recommendations of the Committee on Galleys? Did they have the desired effect? How many noblemen served on the galleys in the seventeenth century, and how did their numbers change over time? The questions are difficult to answer in the current state of my research, and they are complicated by the decline in the importance of galleys in Spain's Mediterranean strategy during the seventeenth century. Although the galleys continued to use the Mediterranean port of Cartagena as a winter base, their main focus of operation shifted to the Atlantic port of Cádiz to protect Spanish commercial fleets returning from

---

[34] Noble members of the committee were invariably referred to with the honorific 'Don' before their names; non-nobles were not. Although the honorific later came into more generalised use, in the late sixteenth century it was a reliable marker of noble status.
[35] The Adelantado de Castilla was the highest royal official in the galley administration.
[36] AMN, Colección Sanz Barutell, MS 389, fols 186r–187r.
[37] E.J. Hamilton, 'Wages and Subsistence on Spanish Treasure Ships, 1503–1660', *Journal of Political Economy* (1929), pp. 430–50.

America, which reached a peak around 1600.[38] With the decline of those fleets later in the seventeenth century, and encroaching sandbars near Cádiz, the galleys were officially shifted back to Cartagena in 1668. By then, galleys no longer held primacy in Spain's Mediterranean strategy, but they remained important to combat North African piracy, and grandees and titled noblemen held the exclusive right to command galley squadrons.[39]

Some of the best available records for noblemen serving on the galleys come from the late seventeenth century. Compiled in Cartagena, the records include separate double folio books for galley slaves (*esclavos*), condemned criminals (*condenados*) and free wage-earners (*gente de cabo*). Each man is identified by name, parentage, place of birth, age and significant physical characteristics, followed by his service record. Historians in the early twentieth century were still able to consult the books,[40] but the humid climate on the Mediterranean coast caused significant deterioration in the paper over time. In the last several years, conservation teams working with the Naval Museum in Madrid have begun to restore the twenty-five books that remain.[41]

Noblemen represent a significant proportion of the men listed in one book of free wage-earners.[42] Of the 373 men whose records are legible, 142 (or 38 per cent) were noblemen, designated by the honorific 'Don' before their names and other indications of high status. In the individual listings for each man, a few are identified as the son of a titled nobleman. Others are simply identified as a known person (*persona conocida*), rather than by the details of their parentage; their families were sufficiently prominent to make further information unnecessary. Among the 142 noblemen, 47 served as galley captains – 59 per cent of the total captains listed from 1649 to 1681.[43] Judging from the registers, noblemen serving as galley captains received the same compensation as their non-noble counterparts. The starting pay was 44 *escudos* per month, rising to 55, and then 66 *escudos* with experience. Two other noblemen were in charge of the body of craftsmen (*maestranza*) that maintained and repaired the galleys. In those two cases, the post seems to have been largely honorific, bestowed on men who were not fit for sea duty. The other noblemen were soldiers with the military contingents serving on

---

[38] See Eufemio Lorenzo Sanz, *Comercio de España con América en la época de Felipe II* (2 vols, Valladolid, 1980) for a detailed analysis of Spain's Atlantic trade in the late sixteenth century.
[39] *Restaurando el testimonio del pasado. Los libros generales de galeras* [exhibition catalogue], with text by Carmen Torres López, María del Carmen Hidalgo Brinquis and Rebeca Benito Lope (Madrid: Órgano de Historia y Cultura Naval, Subsistema Archivístico de la Armada, 2010), pp. 14–16.
[40] For example, Félix Sevilla y Solanas, *Historia penitenciaria española (la galera). Apuntes de archivo* (Segovia, 1917).
[41] AMN, *Libros Generales*, uncatalogued. Many of the pages have blank spaces where there were holes in the original, so that it is impossible to recover full information for every entry. Moreover, some pages could not be salvaged and are missing from the restored books.
[42] AMN, *Libros Generales – Gente de Cabo, 1654–88*. The book was originally foliated, but many of the folio numbers do not survive on the restored pages. Unless otherwise noted, the following preliminary analysis comes from this source.
[43] Although the official dates for the book are 1654–88, a few records date from the 1640s.

the galleys, including one man identified as the proprietary captain of an entire infantry unit (*tercio*).

The highest ranking noblemen listed – eleven in all – received the highest compensation from the crown, ranging from 100 to 330 *escudos* per month. Four of the eleven received their compensation as wages for unspecified duties, presumably as soldiers during sea battles. One received 100 *escudos* per month in wages and another 100 as a maintenance allowance (*entretenimiento*; lit., entertainment). The other six received a maintenance allowance alone, which was standard practice for members of the entourage of the chief naval officer on a Spanish vessel. Among them was the man who received 330 *escudos* per month, after only four years' service. In fact, he was the son of the captain general – the highest official for all Spanish galleys.[44] Rank had its privileges, but the presence of the captain general's son no doubt encouraged other noblemen to fulfil their duty to the crown in the galleys.

The records for the late seventeenth century suggest that the crown had some success in attracting noblemen to serve in the galleys far beyond the era of Lepanto. Financial incentives played a part in that success. The wages for galley captains in the late seventeenth century were considerably higher than the figures suggested by the Committee on Galleys a century earlier. Monetary deflation made those wages even more appealing, particularly for younger sons who had to find a socially acceptable source of income. The dire analysis of galley service by García de Toledo in 1575 described the disadvantages of that service, but later generations of noblemen evidently continued to see the galleys as a potential venue for their military careers.

---

[44] The captain general was the II Marquis of Bayona, Enrique de Benavides y Bazán. His son was Don Francisco de Benavides y Pimentel.

2
Strategy Seen from the Quarterdeck in the Eighteenth-Century French Navy

OLIVIER CHALINE

It is a truth universally acknowledged that historians are prophets of the past. Reporting on naval campaigns whose results are known, historians enjoy a comprehensive understanding of events that enables them to produce a clear and logical narrative. However, this narrative does not necessarily correspond with the seamen's experiences of the same campaigns. Historians have too often taken for granted that those who served on board, from the quarterdeck to the lower deck, were more or less aware of the strategic issues at hand and that they knew the fleet's destination and its objectives. This can be truly illusory and even misleading. I would like to assess the degree of knowledge that captains had about their missions when they set sail and the extent to which admirals were more informed than everyone else on board.

Not unexpectedly, the term strategy was never used in its modern sense. However, a clear, if not necessarily accurate, definition of objectives and means of action did exist at the level of the *Conseil du Roi*, where operations were decided year after year. What remains to be ascertained is what was communicated or explained to the admirals and captains. What did the officers on the quarterdeck know about what they were expected to do? Had someone at Versailles consulted them prior to ordering naval operations? To answer these questions, we must investigate the instructions given to flag officers or captains, official and individual logbooks, letters and memoirs.

Let us first examine how officers understood the concept of strategy as being something they carried out. However, the lack of being in on the secret did not prevent some officers from expressing their views, and many of them tried to understand the purpose of their missions.

Strategy in Theory and Practice
It should be observed that in France naval officers left behind many treatises on naval tactics or shipbuilding, but not on what we would define today as strategy. This is hardly surprising given that decisions on matters of war and peace – the heart of politics at the time – were made exclusively by the *Conseil du Roi* at Versailles and were consequently shrouded in mystery. Secrecy and surprise were the mainsprings of victory. Thus the quarterdeck was frequently not kept

apprised of the various operations that officers and men had to carry out. There was no reason for them to have a perfect understanding of royal decisions, unless someone at Versailles found it necessary to inform them. Advice was rarely sought from naval officers in the planning stages of campaigns, except perhaps during the American War.

Preparing a naval squadron was not a particularly secretive operation, but it was possible to keep its destination a secret. In many cases, it is quite difficult to establish precisely whether an admiral was aware of his destination when setting sail. Undoubtedly, in 1756 La Galissonnière knew that his objective was Minorca,[1] and in 1778 d'Estaing was conscious of the fact that he had to head for North America,[2] but it is hard to be certain that La Clue-Sabran had a similar understanding when he left Toulon in 1759.[3] The same question can be applied to the naval *intendants*, who were in charge of fitting out ships and overseeing their victualling. They were ordered to supply a certain number of ships at a particular date with however many months of provisions, but this information was insufficient for them to be able to guess the fleet's final destination.

The instructions given to admirals before they set sail were often intentionally silent on strategic issues. These orders were kept in sealed packets, which were to remain unopened until a certain date or when a specific location was reached. In 1746, the duc d'Enville was not allowed to open his instructions before passing the Prime Meridian through Tenerife, 16°34'W of Greenwich.[4] It was only when he crossed this line of longitude after sailing from Brest and putting in at Rochefort that he learnt that his destination was Louisbourg, the French fortress which he had to recapture. In 1755, in the uncertain period between peace and war, two squadrons were fitted out at Brest: one under Du Bois de la Motte, who was to sail for Canada with reinforcements, and another one under Macnemara's command, which was designed as an escort or even as a decoy.[5] Versailles' intentions for Macnemara's squadron after it had left Du Bois de la Motte's naval force had to remain a secret. Macnemara's orders stipulated that he was only allowed to open his instructions when Du Bois de la Motte's vessels had disappeared below the horizon. In 1759, La Clue-Sabran, who had sailed from Toulon, was instructed to wait until he had passed the Straits of Gibraltar before reading his instructions. But as he was subsequently pursued and defeated by Boscawen, we

---

[1] Archives Nationales Marine B⁴ 70, for example fols 59, 73, 89, 10 April 1756, when he set sail from Toulon to Minorca.

[2] Jacques Michel, *La vie aventureuse et mouvementée de Charles-Henri comte d'Estaing* (Paris, 1976), pp. 167–8, 390–1.

[3] It is commonly believed that La Clue-Sabran's destination was Brest in order to reinforce Conflans's fleet which was preparing to sail against the Western Squadron. However, we have no archival evidence of it, especially in Conflans's correspondence. See Lieutenant de Vaisseau Costet, 'Une erreur historique', *La Revue Maritime*, 119 (Nov. 1929), pp. 635–41.

[4] James Pritchard, *Anatomy of a Naval Disaster: The 1746 French Expedition to North America* (Montreal, 1995), p. 90.

[5] Jacques Aman, *Une campagne navale méconnue à la veille de la guerre de Sept Ans: L'escadre de Brest en 1755* (Vincennes, 1986), pp. 1–14.

do not know what was specified in his instructions. For this reason, it has been commonly but incorrectly assumed that he was going to join Conflans at Brest.

Opening instructions did not mean that an admiral was allowed to inform his subordinates about the scope of the mission they had to carry out. In 1746 d'Enville was explicitly forbidden from doing so. But in 1778, after passing the Straits of Gibraltar, d'Estaing disclosed the declaration of war against Britain and the American destination of his squadron.[6] It was quite common for instructions to tie admirals' hands and to forbid them from taking the strategic initiative. This was illustrated in the orders given to Du Bois de La Motte and Macnemara in 1755: 'You should avoid encountering British squadrons, if possible. In the event that you encounter any, you will be on your guard and pay attention to their movements. If you suspect that they mean to attack, I should prefer that you avoid action as far as you can without compromising the honour of my flag.'[7]

For Louis XV and his ministers, the Royal Navy's numerical superiority meant that the French Navy had no other mission than to maintain links with the colonies as long as possible and sometimes to protect a landing in the British Isles. Admirals were simply expected to carry out orders, without deviating from the specific instructions they had received.

However, a decisive change took place during the American War in 1781 when France gave up any projects of landing in Britain and returned to its previous indirect strategy of long-distance strikes against European enemies in the Americas and India. The instructions given to the comte de Grasse and the comte d'Orves, and after his death the bailli de Suffren who took his place, for their respective expeditions to North America and India were entirely different, leaving them with an unusual degree of operational freedom. De Grasse's fleet was sent with the intent of establishing Allied (French and Spanish) supremacy in the Caribbean. With a portion of his fleet, de Grasse was then expected to gain command of North American waters. Operational decisions were left to de Grasse after Spain's consent was obtained since he was explicitly defined as a Spanish auxiliary.[8] He caught the British admirals by surprise when he sailed to Chesapeake Bay with the entirety of his fleet and not simply a part of it. For the operation in the Indian Ocean, d'Orves's instructions were quite unexpected: 'The king, in allowing his admirals to judge which operations are likely to be the most useful and bring the greatest glory to his forces, requires that they [the admirals] attack the British, whether divided or united, everywhere possible, even

---

[6] Michel, *La vie aventureuse*, pp. 168–9.
[7] Archives Nationales Marine B⁴ 68, fol. 97, 10 avril 1755: 'vous devés éviter, s'il est possible, la rencontre des escadres anglaises. Supposé que vous les rencontriés, vous vous tiendrés sur vos gardes relativement aux manœuvres qu'elles feront. Et si elles vous donnent lieu de soupçonner qu'elles en veulent venir à une attaque, je trouverai bon que vous cherchiés à l'éviter autant qu'il sera possible sans compromettre l'honneur de mon pavillon.'
[8] Archives Nationales Marine B⁴ 216, fols 199r–200v, Castries to de Grasse, 17 March 1781 and fols 201r–205v, Castries to Vergennes, 16 March 1781.

without verifying that their forces have been destroyed.'[9] In this instance, strategic decision-making has been relocated to the quarterdeck. The secrecy clause did not separate the admiral from the king's council, but it did create an information divide between the admiral and his main subordinates, including the *major d'escadre*, the senior officer in charge of signals. Nevertheless, this did not prevent subordinates from discussing strategy.

Secrecy is Not an Obstacle for Expression
There are many instances of senior officers expressing their views, without being asked for advice. Once again, it is necessary to distinguish the War of the Austrian Succession (1740–48) and the Seven Years' War (1754–63) from the American War.

During campaign preparations, some rather unexpected initiatives occurred that, in principle, were incompatible with naval hierarchy and the chain of command. In 1759, *capitaine de vaisseau* Bigot de Morogues corresponded directly with the *secrétaire d'État de la Marine* (naval minister), without his superior's awareness, in an attempt to remove the *maréchal* de Conflans from an upcoming operation on the western coast of Scotland. For de Morogues, a squadron of six vessels under his own command was sufficient for escort purposes and, as a result, Conflans, with the main Brest fleet, should be relegated to the inglorious role of creating a diversion.[10]

During the campaign itself, an admiral could face a challenging situation if some of his captains called into question the strategy he had to carry out. This happened in 1746 after d'Enville's death, when his reluctant successor, the *commandeur* d'Estourmel, eventually discovered the true, but by then unrealisable, objective of the campaign: the reconquest of Louisbourg. However, the marquis de la Jonquière, a far more experienced officer who was travelling to Canada as the new governor, and some of the captains sought to convince d'Estourmel to attack Halifax and then set sail for Quebec. Terrified, d'Estourmel tried to kill himself after a contentious war council meeting and he eventually resigned a few days later.[11] In less dramatic circumstances, but in the same area, in 1757, M. de Guichen, flag-captain of Admiral Du Bois de la Motte, called on the admiral, on behalf of several officers, to exploit the French fleet's superiority and launch a surprise attack on Halifax. Despite his confidence in Guichen, Du Bois de la Motte refused, judging such a raid too risky and in contravention to the instructions he had received.[12] Conversely, actions without words could express

---

[9] Archives Nationales Marine B⁴ 196, fol. 325. See Rear Admiral Rémi Monaque, *Suffren: Un destin inachevé* (Paris, 2009), p. 206: 'Le roi, en laissant ses généraux les maîtres de déterminer les opérations qu'ils estimeront les plus utiles et les plus glorieuses à ses armes, leur prescrit d'attaquer les Anglais séparés ou réunis partout où il sera possible de le faire sans l'évidence de la destruction de leurs forces.'
[10] Archives Nationales, Marine B⁴ 87, fol. 55.
[11] Pritchard, *Anatomy of a Naval Disaster*, pp. 135–44.
[12] François Jahan and Claude-Youenn Roussel, *Guichen, l'honneur de la Marine royale* (Paris, 2012), pp. 82–3.

reluctance about impending operations. In 1780, when Guichen set sail to join Don José Solano y Bote's Spanish convoy, de Grasse deliberately ordered his ship to be repaired.[13] Two days later, after Guichen's departure, de Grasse set sail for Saint-Pierre in Martinique on his own and remained there.

No French officer in the eighteenth century went as far as Suffren, who in August 1778, as captain of the *Fantasque*, advised Admiral d'Estaing on strategy and how to turn a poorly waged campaign into a successful one:

> British naval superiority in North American waters, which has been brought about by the arrival of several ships from Admiral Byron's fleet and an enemy army of 25,000 to 30,000 men that can be ferried wherever they [the British] choose, as well as the poor condition of two of our ships and the unpredictable nature of victualling, leaves us with little hope for successful high-profile ventures at sea. It is impossible to obscure this truth. It is nevertheless a source of irritation that the costs of preparing the fleet should be lost and that we should be forced to stay in Boston for the rest of the summer. The only way our naval forces could be put to good use would be to prepare a detachment of ships to attack Newfoundland. There would still be time to destroy their fishing trade, capture several vessels and, especially, take many prisoners.[14]

It is unclear whether d'Estaing would have appreciated receiving strategic advice from a subordinate, but the fact remains that Suffren's recommendations were not taken up. Suffren persisted and four months later, after d'Estaing's abortive attack on Saint Lucia, he did not hesitate to explain to the admiral what he could still undertake and, this time, with greater success. The freedom with which Suffren spoke is worth quoting: 'I am taking the liberty of sending you a report on our current situation. While on the one hand I would not go so far as to give advice to a general, on the other I think it is the duty of a good citizen to impart ideas that one finds useful for the good of the state, especially to a general who has shown me confidence and kindness and whose glory I am interested in perpetuating.'[15]

In these various suggestions, strategic input from the quarterdeck was generally limited to operations which had yet to be undertaken or ones that were being

---

[13] Ibid., p. 241.
[14] Quoted by Monaque, *Suffren*, p. 146 : 'La supériorité des forces navales anglaises dans les mers de l'Amérique septentrionale, bien décidée par l'arrivée de plusieurs vaisseaux de l'escadre de l'amiral Byron, une armée ennemie de 25 à 30 000 h. qui peuvent être transportés où l'on voudra, l'état où se trouvent deux de nos vaisseaux, l'incertitude même des subsistances ne nous laissent aucun espoir de faire des entreprises d'éclat. C'est une vérité que l'on ne peut se dissimuler. Il est cependant fâcheux que les frais d'un grand armement soient perdus et que l'on soit obligé de passer dans le port de Boston le peu qui nous reste de la belle saison. Le seul parti qu'on peut tirer de nos forces est de faire un détachement pour agir contre Terre Neuve. L'on serait encore à temps de détruire partie de leur pêche, faire quantité de prises et surtout beaucoup de prisonniers.'
[15] Quoted in ibid., p. 153: 'Je prends la liberté de vous envoyer un mémoire sur notre situation. Autant je serais éloigné de donner des avis sur un général, autant je crois qu'il est du devoir d'un bon citoyen de faire part des idées qu'on croit utiles au bien de l'État et surtout à un général qui m'a témoigné de la confiance et de bonté et de la gloire de qui je m'intéresse.'

attempted again, and it was not given on matters or operations that would have affected the broader strategic outlook. It remained exceptional for a flag officer to give unsolicited strategic advice to a government minister. Only Suffren dared to do so, who wrote to the comte de Vergennes, *secrétaire d'État des affaires étrangères* (foreign minister) in December 1782:

> If the king wants to pursue the planned campaign in India, ships are necessary, particularly good ones. Two options must be considered: either [the king] leave[s] cruisers here to disrupt enemy commerce, or [he] strongly reinforce[s] the naval squadron. In the second case, secrecy must be kept and the captains must remain unaware [of the mission]; otherwise, the British will send a naval force proportionate to ours. In the first case, the Dutch would lose all of their colonies and we would lose any hope of setting foot in India, but our cruisers would inflict great damage on British commerce, which should not be disregarded, especially if problems were to intensify to the point that we were forced to abandon everything.[16]

It is worth noting that, in addition to having direct access to the foreign minister, Suffren sought to keep his own captains ignorant of the operations they would have to carry out.

Understanding What You Are Performing

For the most strategically offensive-minded French flag officer, it was simply unthinkable that subordinates should interfere with strategy or even be informed about it. For flag officers, as with de Grasse, being in on the secret gave them power over their subordinates and provided a means of control through withholding information on the fleet's real objectives. It is little wonder then that, in both fleets, relations between the admiral and many of his officers were poor. Nevertheless, strategy was not as absent from the quarterdeck as one might imagine it to have been. Archival sources are not entirely silent on this matter.

A real desire to understand existed on the quarterdeck, as attested, for example, by young officers. In 1781 the chevalier de Goussencourt in de Grasse's fleet noted when the fleet set sail from Santo Domingo: 'August 5th, all being ready, … our fleet numbered 24 vessels, and the wonder is that everybody, the English included, knew where we were going, while we had not even a conjecture as to the operation that our admiral was about to undertake.'[17] Conversely, one month

---

[16] Quoted in ibid., p. 288: 'Si le roi veut poursuivre l'entreprise de l'Inde, il faut des vaisseaux et surtout des bons. Il faut de deux choses l'une, ou ne laisser ici que des croiseurs pour inquiéter le commerce, ou renforcer puissamment l'escadre. Dans le deuxième cas, il faut qu'on garde le secret, que les capitaines ne le sachent pas eux-mêmes, car sans cela les Anglais enverront des forces à proportion. Dans le premier cas, les Hollandais perdraient toutes leurs colonies et nous tout espoir de remettre les pieds dans l'Inde, mais des croiseurs feraient grand mal au commerce anglais, objet qu'il ne faut pas perdre de vue, si les malheurs multipliés obligeaient à tout abandonner.'

[17] *The Operations of the French Fleet under Count de Grasse in 1781–1782 Described in Two Contemporary Journals* (New York, 1864), p. 61.

later, just before the Battle of the Virginia Capes, Enseigne Lescure was well informed of the various armies' movements from New York to Yorktown.[18] The fleet can be an incredible echo chamber of information, especially at anchor in the Chesapeake Bay.

The following year on board the *Ajax*, one of Suffren's vessels in India, Huet de Froberville, an infantry officer who had become an artilleryman, attempted to understand Suffren's intentions: 'But what was the nature of these plans? We lost ourselves in conjecture.'[19] Froberville's interlocutors, the senior officers and perhaps the captain himself were just as unaware. They would subsequently understand during the course of operations and would attempt to guess what would happen immediately afterwards, but to say the least, the limited information at their disposal precluded their ability to form a broader strategic understanding of the war in Asia.

Four years earlier, at the other end of the naval hierarchy, the comte de Guichen wrote to his daughter on 29 June 1778, just before Admiral d'Orvilliers's fleet left Brest. In his letter, de Guichen provides a highly informative account of what was being said in public and what one of the *chefs d'escadre* thought about and expected from the forthcoming campaign. Moreover, it shows how freely he discussed strategic matters:

> I have every reason to believe that the British fleet has returned to port, with six of our frigates having been sent to keep watch at the entrance of the Channel. [Of these frigates,] four have returned without having seen [the fleet] and the other two are still patrolling. It is commonly held that [Admirals] Keppel and Byron had set sail together with no other motive but to disguise their separation, and that Byron's fleet broke away to attack d'Estaing's fleet in North America, whereas the other one [Keppel's fleet] returned [to port] … The news about my long campaign, which you have heard, my dearest daughter, seems unfounded to me, since it would appear that the three-deckers will not be held in readiness to sail and that if we leave, it will not be for long. The Spaniards will decide on our operations, which depend on the role they will take, but they are taking a long time to come to a decision, which is being

---

[18] Archives Nationales, Marine B⁴ 259, Journal of *Le Zélé*, kept by the Enseigne Lescure, fol. 106v: 'Nous avons appris que les Anglois commandés par le général Cornwallis étoient campés au nombre de 7000 à York et à Glocester, bourgs situés sur les 2 côtés de la rivière d'Yorck, à 3 lieues de l'embouchure de cette rivière, et qu'ils étoient bloqués par M. de La Fayette qui n'avoit qu'un corps de 2000 h. Les troupes de débarquement que nous avons amenées sont au nombre de 3300 se joindront à M. de La Fayette qui est campé à Williamsbourg. Nos troupes doivent débarquer à James Town, bourg désert, situé à 18 lieues de l'embouchure de la rivière de James. Charlestown est bloqué par le général Green, quoi qu'avec des forces inférieures. Le général Washington est avec un corps considérable devant New Yorck. Il se trouve dans la rivière d'Yorck 40 bts marchands, un vaisseau de 50 nommé le Caron, 1 frégate nommée la Guadeloupe et 5 ou 6 corvettes ou bricks.'

[19] Barthélémy Huet de Froberville, *Mémoires pour servir à l'histoire de la guerre de 1780 des Français avec les Anglais dans l'Inde* (Chailles, 1986), p. 160: 28 December 1782 'À la route que le général nous faisait tenir, il était aisé de s'appercevoir qu'il avait quelques projets sur les comptoirs anglais situés dans le Nord de la pointe de Divi. Mais de quelle nature étaient ces projets? C'était sur quoi on se perdait en conjectures.'

attributed to the fact that their galleons have yet to return. However, the season is advancing and we are accruing costs without any benefit to the state.[20]

The level of information and analysis is infinitely superior here and exceeds what officers would have been normally able to understand from the quarterdeck. Guichen read newspapers, but he was probably well informed about the orders that d'Orvilliers received from Versailles. It must be noted too that d'Orvilliers was one of the most affable and valued French admirals of the time.

Such a letter is uncommon, and it is highly exceptional to find an individual criticising, with a discordant voice, not only the government's strategy but also the alliances chosen by the king in the course of war. Scipion de Castries, then an ensign, describes in the memoirs he wrote after the Revolution and his emigration from France how enthusiastic young noble officers were about the opportunity to exact revenge on Britain. Many years later, believing as an old man that the fall of the French Ancien Régime had been a direct consequence of the fateful American War, he reminisced:

> Each and every one gave his opinion and considered the idea of grabbing North America from the King of England as a magnificent endeavour. M. de Ribiès, in all his usual solemnity, told us in a sententious and serious tone: 'I hope that this war brings as much good fortune to France as its motive currently gives you joy and pleasure.' After having uttered these few words, he left us and returned to his room.[21]

This exchange happened three years before the Battle of the Virginia Capes. Criticism of alliances was quite common in the French Army during the Seven Years' War, but evidence of similar criticism is quite scarce in the case of the navy and during the American War.

Seen from the perspective of the quarterdeck, what we now call, with some

---

[20] Guichen Family Archives, quoted by Jahan and Roussel, *Guichen*, pp. 158–60: 'J'ai tout lieu de penser que l'escadre anglaise est rentrée dans leurs ports, six de nos frégates ayant été envoyées pour les observer à l'entrée de la Manche, quatre sont revenues sans en avoir eu connaissance, les deux autres sont restées en croisière. L'on juge que la sortie des escadres anglaises de MM. Keppel et Byron n'a eu d'autre motif que de couvrir leur séparation, et que celle de Byron s'est détachée pour aller s'opposer à celle de M. d'Estaing à l'Amérique, et que l'autre est rentrée … Les nouvelles que l'on t'a débitées, ma très chère petite, de ma longue campagne ne me paraissent pas fondées, car toutes les apparences sont que l'on ne tiendra pas consignés en rade les vaisseaux à trois ponts, et que si nous sortons ce ne sera pas pour longtemps. Les Espagnols décideront de nos opérations, qui seront relatives au parti qu'ils prendront, mais ils sont bien longs à se déterminer, ce que l'on attribue à leurs galions qui ne sont pas encore rentrés. Cependant, la saison s'avance, et nous nous consommons en frais sans qu'il en résulte rien de bien favorable pour l'Etat.'

[21] Scipion de Castries, *Souvenirs maritimes*, ed. Gérard de Colbert-Turgis (Paris, 1997), pp. 225–6: 'Chacun disait son avis et regardait comme sublime politique l'idée d'arracher l'Amérique au roi d'Angleterre. M. de Ribiès, avec sa gravité ordinaire, nous dit d'un air sentencieux mais avec un profond sentiment: "Je désire que le motif de cette guerre procure à la France autant de bonheur qu'il vous cause de joie et de plaisir dans ce moment-ci." Après avoir dit ce peu de paroles, il nous quitta et rentra dans sa chambre.'

anachronism, strategy can be interpreted at two different levels: the first is truly political, involving the formulation of war aims and the selection of alliances, and the second is operational, dealing with missions and objectives. The first one fell outside the competence of naval professionals and it is quite uncommon in archival evidence. The second one, concerning what seamen had to carry out, was in principle more within their comprehension. But the level of strategic awareness on the quarterdeck varied greatly from one campaign to another and from one ship to another. Even if French flag officers were the most likely to be informed by the king and his minister, they were not necessarily ready to bring their subordinates into the loop. It depended on their style of leadership. For the protagonists themselves, the exact nature and details of naval operations could be obscure. More often than we might realise, men did not know where they were sailing, what they were really expected to do, which ships they had fought and the extent of the damage they had inflicted.

3

Danish and Swedish Flag Disputes with the British in the Channel

JAKOB SEERUP

On 11 August 1694 an incident took place which strained Anglo-Danish relations seriously. The Danish ship of the line *Gyldenløve* of fifty guns under the command of Captain Niels Lavritzen Barfoed, peacefully anchored at the Downs, was attacked by the seventy-gun HMS *Stirling Castle* from Sir Cloudesley Shovell's Squadron.[1] The *Gyldenløve* suffered three men dead and eighteen wounded, including Captain Barfoed himself. On the *Stirling Castle*, Captain Deane reported that he had eight men dead and about twenty wounded. The Danish ship was seriously damaged and had to undergo significant repairs. Barfoed and his officers were subsequently arrested, and they were only released after prolonged negotiations between Denmark and England.

Denmark remained neutral during the ongoing Nine Years' War of 1688–97. However, the Danish king did provide auxiliary troops for the English war in Ireland from 1689 to 1691. Politically it would seem very unwise to compromise the good relations between the two countries by attacking a Danish warship, unless there was a very good reason. So what serious offence had the *Gyldenløve* committed to provoke such an attack? Or was it perhaps all a mistake? Surprisingly, the underlying cause was what we today might regard as a trifling matter of courtesy. The battle was the result of a dispute over the right of English warships to demand that foreign warships strike their pennants in the Channel. It was not the only incident of its kind, and in the period around the year 1700 such 'courtesy battles' involving both Danish and Swedish warships strained England's relations with the Scandinavian kingdoms. These conflicts have been noted by researchers before, but the fact that the English insistence on striking of pennants had long term strategic implications for the sailing patterns of the Danish and Swedish navies has not previously been described.[2] This chapter seeks to present the flag disputes in their context as seen from a Danish and Swedish perspective.

---

[1] See R.C. Anderson, 'An Anglo-Danish Incident in 1694', *The Mariner's Mirror*, xiv, no. 2 (1928), pp. 175ff.
[2] See for instance Anderson, 'Anglo-Danish Incident', passim, and F.E. Dyer, 'An Anglo-Danish Incident in 1694', *The Mariner's Mirror* xiv, no. 3 (1928), pp. 278ff. In Danish the incidents are described thoroughly in C. Bastrup, 'Konvojrejser I Slutningen af det 17. Aarhundrede', *Tidsskrift for Søvæsen* (1900), pp. 241ff.

Before we look at the wider perspective of the flag disputes, let us return to the situation in the Downs in August 1694. The wider context of that and other battles needs to be included in order to understand the incident. In 1691 Denmark and Sweden had signed a treaty to bilaterally protect their merchant ships sailing through the Channel from being ransacked by the warring navies.[3] If Danish and Swedish merchant ships were sailing in convoy with warships from either country, the two kings were guarantors that ships under their protection did not sail with contraband goods. The treaty was supplemented by separate treaties between Denmark and Sweden and England, Holland and France outlining the conditions of the neutral trade and specifying which goods were to be considered contraband. The ships had copies of these treaties on board so that they could give proof of their right to trade if approached by ships from the warring states. However, both France and England and their allies were suspicious of this neutral trade. So, disregarding the treaties, convoys were regularly harassed by both British and French warships. This was why the *Gyldenløve* was anchored at the Downs in the first place. The *Gyldenløve*, along with a Swedish warship, the *Wachtmeister*, had been escorting a convoy of some sixty merchantmen going from Norway to France through the Channel. First the convoy was stopped and searched by eight Dutch warships, in contradiction with the treaty. Three ships were confiscated as prizes by the Dutch but saved by the arrival of a French squadron under command of Jean Bart, who fought the Dutch while the confiscated ships were spirited away by the *Wachtmeister*. Then the convoy was stopped by a superior force of twelve English ships that, without any formalities, sent boarding parties on board every ship, arrested the captains and confiscated their papers. At the same time the weather worsened, and the entire convoy chose to follow the English ships to the Downs where they dropped anchor on 30 June. The entire convoy was inspected by the English authorities.[4] The English prize court representative took some time investigating the papers and ladings of the convoy, so Captain Barfoed of the *Gyldenløve* had enough time to go to London to report the incident to the Danish envoy there. It was only after his return to the Downs in August that Barfoed's ship was attacked.

On 10 August, Sir Cloudesley Shovell's squadron had arrived at the Downs. When the admiral observed that the *Gyldenløve* did not strike its colours, he sent the *Stirling Castle* to demand this the next morning. When two officers from the *Stirling Castle* came on board the Danish ship and informed him that he was obliged to strike his colours, Barfoed replied that he would not strike for any man in the world.[5] Shovell noted that the Swedish warship also present at the Downs

---

[3] The full text of the treaty is printed in Bastrup, 'Konvojrejser', pp. 243ff.
[4] Anderson, 'Anglo-Danish Incident', pp. 175ff. He says that the convoy had been obliged to anchor at the Downs because of head winds, but in Barfoed's own report it is stated that he was indeed forced to the Downs by the English.
[5] Dyer, 'Anglo-Danish Incident', p. 279.

did not fly its pennant.[6] The English officers returned to the *Stirling Castle*, which then fired two shots aimed at the *Gyldenløve*'s pennant and one shot at her stern.[7] An English officer, sword in hand, asked again if the Danes would strike, and upon receiving a negative answer the English commenced firing. The Danish ship fired its broadside at the English. A short battle ensued, as summarised by Captain Deane:

> I weighed and ran up under his quartr & fired 2 Gunns over him and he took no notice of itt, then I fired one into him & by that time I was got up along his side, then began ye dispute, we firing our broadside into him and he into us, then struck.[8]

Barfoed decided to strike his pennant when one more English warship with seventy guns approached, and fighting no longer seemed prudent. After the battle, Barfoed and his officers were arrested and escorted to Sheerness. The ship was only released on 18 November. Because of winter storms the *Gyldenløve* only made it back to Norway by March the following year. The Swedish *Wachtmeister* was able to carry on her convoy duties and also made it back to Norway in March – after one more skirmish with a British warship.

The Danish resident in London, Pauly, was outraged over the incident and wrote a note of protest. One of the points he made is especially poignant:

> This outrage is not only a violation of the laws of hospitality, but is the more flagrant because my master [i.e. the Danish king] always allows English men-of-war to carry their pendants in the ports under his jurisdiction, and under the very guns of his castles.

In his report to the Admiralty, Shovell defended his actions. He argued that he was merely enforcing the legitimate claim of His Majesty's ships in the Channel to force foreign warships to strike their pennants. Furthermore, he noted 'that the States Generall's Ships did it notwithstanding our Present Union ... and the better to induce him to a compliance added that if he Strooke he should have liberty to hoyst his Pendant againe'. These two quotes sum up the difference of opinion between the Scandinavians and the English.[9]

The following year, 1695, much the same situation arose.[10] Captain Just Juel on the fifty-gun ship *Lindormen* sailed with a convoy from France to Denmark and encountered the English frigate *Jersey* on 30 May. The *Jersey* fired at the *Lindormen* to force her to stop and strike pennant, but the *Lindormen* escaped. The next day, the *Lindormen* met the *Charles Galley* of thirty-two guns. A pitched battle ensued, and five hours and twenty-two dead sailors later, the *Lindormen*

---

[6] It has not been possible to ascertain the reason for this, but it seems to be confirmed by the Danish sources.
[7] The description of the incident builds on a combined reading of Dyer, 'Anglo-Danish Incident', p. 279 and Bastrup, 'Konvojrejser', p. 241.
[8] Quoted from Dyer, 'Anglo-Danish Incident', p. 279.
[9] Ibid., pp. 279–80.
[10] Bastrup, 'Konvojrejser', pp. 257ff.

was able to escape the scene of the battle. The *Charles Galley* was said to have suffered twenty-nine dead and wounded in the action.

A Dramatic Battle at Orford Ness
The dramatic outcome of Barfoed's and Juel's battles in 1694 and 1695 also had implications for Sweden. A Swedish ship had been present in 1694, and the dispute was intimately connected to the 1691 treaty between Sweden and Denmark. In 1695, the Swedish king Charles XI decreed that foreign warships were to be met 'with friendship' and that violence was to be avoided when Swedish men-of-war sailed in the Channel. If foreign ships demanded to board and inspect the ships, the Swedish were to defend themselves – but only if they determined that they were likely to have success. Otherwise they were to tolerate boarding under protest. And most importantly, the Swedish 1695 regulations required the Swedish men-of-war to sail without their pennants after they had passed the Scaw.

But the warlike young king Charles XII who ascended the Swedish throne in 1697 was not happy with this situation. So even though he kept the pragmatic regulation in place that instructed Swedish ships not to fly the pennant in the Channel, he gave very firm orders to Captain Gustaf Psilander of the forty-eight-gun ship *Öland* in 1703 not to strike his flag or topsails for anyone. If he failed to comply with this he was to suffer the death penalty, and one in every ten of his crew was to be hanged. Charles XII was not very keen on the concept of honourable surrender.

But this meant that Psilander had been dealt a very difficult hand when he eventually did encounter English warships in the Channel on 28 July 1704. The scene was set for a memorable event in Swedish naval history.[11] Psilander was escorting a convoy of ten Swedish merchant vessels when he encountered eight English ships of the line and one frigate off Orford Ness. When the English ships caught up with Psilander's convoy they greeted him with two sharp gunshots from the HMS *Worcester*. An envoy from the *Öland*, Lieutenant Schmidt, was sent on board the English ship to demand an explanation. The captain of the *Worcester*, Thomas Butler, and Schmidt engaged in a heated discussion:[12]

> Butler: Do you not see the flag of the Queen of England?
> Schmidt: Yes, we do, but do you not see the King of Sweden's flag?
> Butler: Yes, but why do you not pay your respect to the Queen of England?
> Schmidt: What respect must the King of Sweden pay the Queen of England?
> Butler: You must strike your topsail.

---

[11] The affair in 1704 is well described in literature. See A. Munthe, *Svenska Sjöhjältar* (Stockholm, 1898), vol. i, s.v. 'Gustaf von Psilander' and Lybeck et al., *Svenska Flottans Historia* (Malmö, 1941), vol. ii, pp. 94f. I owe a great deal of thanks to Bengt Nilsson's website about Psilander, http://members.tripod.com/Bengt_Nilsson/ where much of the source material has been made public and the details of the battle thoroughly analysed.
[12] Here translated from Munthe, *Svenska Sjöhjältar*, p. 16.

Schmidt: My Captain is under orders not to strike.
Butler: Well, I'll teach you to strike!

And that was the beginning of the battle. Even as Lieutenant Schmidt and his men were rowing back to their ship, the guns on both sides commenced firing. The Swedes tried to escape, but they had to stop briefly to wait for Schmidt's return, costing them their chance. The battle was joined on very unequal terms. Even though Psilander was vastly outnumbered and outgunned, the battle lasted four and a half hours. In the end, the *Öland* was entirely ruined: of a complement of two hundred, sixteen men died and thirty-seven were wounded in the battle. On the English side, three ships were so damaged that they later had to be docked and repaired. Some seventy fatalities and a large number of wounded were reported. However, Psilander did not capitulate. He cunningly found a way around his strict orders not to strike. He hoisted his flag with a knot in it (known as a 'wheft' or 'whaft'), thus turning it into a signal of distress (flying the Scandinavian flags upside down for obvious reasons would not work as a signal of distress). This was seen as the signal to stop the fire, and Psilander went to pay his respects to the English commander Whetstone. The *Öland* was captured and escorted to the Nore, and the Swedish merchant vessels were taken as prizes. Psilander and his men were arrested and were only released in the middle of August after Queen Anne had protested to King Charles XII and instructed him to punish Psilander. Charles did no such thing and instead replied in support of Psilander, asking Queen Anne to punish her captains for their unjust actions in the Channel.

The whole affair almost brought the two countries to war. But in the end both countries were too concerned with their other ongoing wars in respectively Spain and Poland, so they let it be. However, the Swedish convoy seemed to be jinxed. When the Öland at long last had been repaired, and the convoy released, the passage back home to Sweden went horribly wrong. Off the Scaw, she ran aground and was wrecked. Psilander managed to get his men ashore, and somehow they got back to Sweden. Psilander went on to have a very fine career, and he was ennobled in 1712 as 'von Psilander'. In 1734 he was president of the Admiralty, the highest position in the Swedish Navy. The battle at Orford Ness acquired an air of mythology in Sweden, and Psilander obviously held the memory of the battle high, as was reflected in his coat of arms featuring a lone Swedish flag surrounded by eight English naval ensigns.

How to Avoid Saluting Battles

The dramatic incidents in the Channel in the years around 1700 were to have far-reaching implications for both the Danish and the Swedish navies. Even though all the captains involved were commended by their sovereigns for honourably having defended their flags, both the Danish and Swedish kings had reasons to modify their policies. The tactical situation in the Channel called for prudence rather than heroics. Upholding the right to fly the Danish and Swedish naval pennants in the Channel simply was not possible given the circumstances. And even if the men-of-war were not flying pennants they would still be forced to strike their flag or their topsails. Charles XI's regulation about not flying the naval pennant in the Channel was kept in place even after Charles XII's ascension to the throne in 1697, and was in effect during the Psilander affair in 1704 – but that obviously did not prevent the conflict.

The simple solution for both the Danish and the Swedish navies was to avoid entering the Channel with warships. A route west of Ireland was preferred for most of the rest of the eighteenth century. Exceptions were made if there was an urgent need to get to the Mediterranean quickly. In such cases the orders were given not to fly the pennant. The Danes and Swedes never accepted or understood the British demand for foreign warships to strike the pennant or flag – and never made the same demand in their territorial waters.

With all probability neither the English nor the Swedish and Danish officers were aware of the exact background for the English claim for sovereignty in the Channel. And it did indeed go a long way back. It began in 1293 when the English King Edward I had his diplomats fabricate a legal justification for the right of his Gascon ships to attack a Norman fleet in the Channel at the Trade in May that year. Edward, as Duke of Aquitaine, was a vassal of the French king and worried he would be summoned to court in Paris for this incident. To avoid this, he claimed that the kings of England 'time out of mind had been in peaceable possession of the sovereign lordship of the English sea and the islands therein'.[13] This provided a legal loophole for Edward to avoid an embarrassing day in a Parisian court of law. But it also provided justification for English naval captains to demand the striking of pennants and other demonstrations of submission from foreign warships in the Channel for the following five hundred years. Time and again the navy's insistence on enforcing this sovereignty of the sea on behalf of the king would undermine the foreign policy of Parliament in Westminster – as exemplified in the 1694–95 and 1704 incidents.

And the problem just would not go away. In 1755 Swedish Captain Rajalihn was instructed that he should fly the Swedish naval ensign when passing the Sound.[14] But during his passage from the Scaw to Cape Finisterre he was to fly the commercial flag; if he came across British men-of-war he was to first salute them, but not to strike sail for them. The order was repeated in 1758 when a new squadron was sent to the Mediterranean. That same decade, the two Danish ships *Slesvig* and *Christiansborg* had similar instructions for their voyages to North Africa. The *Slesvig* was instructed not to go through the Channel, but still abstain from flying the pennant from the North of Jutland to Cape Finisterre in order to avoid trouble with the British. The *Christiansborg* went through the Channel. Captain Johan Christopher Holst was taken ill and died from diarrhoea off the

---

[13] N.A.M. Rodger, *The Safeguard of the Sea: A Naval History of Britain, 660–1649* (London, 1999), p. 78.
[14] C.A. Gyllengranath, *Sveriges Sjökrigshistoria* (1840), p. 85.

Isle of Wight on 11 July 1752, and his body was taken ashore to be buried.[15] This was an embarrassing moment for the Danish ship's officers who now had to identify themselves. But apparently the British authorities did not protest and we have no reports of differences about striking the flag or pennant. Again, in 1761, Danish naval officer Samuel Akeleye reported to the Admiralty that he had ordered his men to battle stations in the Channel when a British frigate had demanded that he strike his pennant and salute. He refused to strike the pennant but offered to give the salute if the Englishman would reply the salute with the equal number of shots. The British captain was satisfied with this arrangement.[16] In 1779 we have reports of an incident between Danish frigate *Møen*, under Captain Ole Budde, and 'British warships' in the Channel.[17]

One must wonder whether the captains of Danish and Swedish warships really thought they could pass for civilian ships if they refrained from flying their pennants. Even though large merchant ships regularly carried guns, warships would have been easily recognisable. The rigging and conspicuous stern ornaments and general shape of the ships would probably indicate that they were indeed warships. Also, different navies and nations had specific traits characteristic to them, and a trained naval officer would be able to tell the difference between, for example, a Danish and a French ship even without visible flags or pennants.[18] The decision not to fly pennants seems to have been motivated purely by legal concerns.

We now know the English position on the matter of demanding salutes in the Channel. We have also seen how this was considered an affront by the Swedes and the Danes. In order to better understand the strong Scandinavian reaction, we need to examine the Scandinavian view on saluting traditions and customs. In our own time navies and civilian sailors still retain the tradition of 'dipping the flag' in certain situations as a sign of reverence. So what was the big problem? First of all, we need to acknowledge that it was not a matter of simply 'dipping the flag', that is, lowering and hoisting the flag again as a polite gesture to the English warship. No, what the English ships tried to do in the above-mentioned cases in 1694 and 1695 was to make the foreign ships strike the pennant. The pennant is the very symbol of a warship being under command. Only when the captain is on board does the pennant fly. So the pennant is the very symbol that his sovereign has commissioned the officer with his ship. Given the significance of this symbolism, the strong reactions make more sense.

But as we have seen, the English went further than just making the foreign ships strike their pennants. They also wanted them to fire the salute while the

---

[15] H.G. Garde, *Efterretninger om den danske og norske Søemagt* (Copenhagen, 1833), vol. iii, p. 377. See also J. Seerup, 'The Royal Danish Naval Academy in the Age of Enlightenment', *The Mariner's Mirror*, xciii, no. 3 (2007), p. 327.
[16] Topsøe-Jensen and Marquard, *Officerer i Den Dansk-Norske Søetat* (1935), vol. i, p. 17.
[17] Ibid., p. 221.
[18] S. Willis, *Fighting at Sea in the Eighteenth Century: The Art of Sailing Warfare* (Woodbridge, 2008), pp. 7ff.

pennant was struck. The significance of this will elude most modern readers. To fully comprehend the symbolism of this gesture we need to consult a Danish manuscript from the middle of the eighteenth century. The Danish naval officer Peter Schiønning wrote an unpublished manual in practical seamanship in the 1760s. In the more than three thousand manuscript pages we find a large number of interesting details that reflect not just what regulations said but also what the practice of the day was. He describes the practice of striking the pennant while giving a gun salute.[19] A man would go aloft and with his hands pull in the pennant. When the pennant was folded in his arms, the ship would fire the grand salute of twenty-seven guns, and when the last shot had rung out, he would release the pennant. This was a salute reserved for one specific situation only: when a Danish warship saluted another Danish warship on which the sovereign was embarked. This explains why the British demand was considered such an affront to the Danish officers. Striking the pennant to a British warship simply was not an option.

But the English expected foreign ships to salute in this way, and they were partially successful in enforcing this claim. Indeed, it seems that the Dutch Navy had completely accepted and adopted this way of saluting. At least, Admiral Shovell in his report about the 1694 incident cited that 'the General States' struck their pennants and saluted. We do not have much in terms of documentation of the practice, but in an older book on Swedish naval history there is an interesting reference to this custom. It mentions how in the summer of 1742 a Swedish squadron met a combined British and Dutch squadron in the North Sea. Much to the surprise of the Swedish officers, the Dutch ships not only fired a salute but also struck their pennants. The exact wording in Swedish is *'palmade in vimplarne'* – literally handed the pennant as described by Schiønning above.[20] The reason why the Swedes would have made a note of this was that it was considered so perfectly strange!

The British insistence on forcing foreign warships to salute and strike their pennants in the Channel was never completely abandoned in the eighteenth century. However, both the immediate tactical situation and general political situation dictated how seriously the Royal Navy insisted. In the 1790s, neutral Danish ships were regularly stopped and searched by the Royal Navy in the Channel as a result of the ongoing war with France. This resulted in the deployment of warships to escort the Danish vessels, and subsequently very similar confrontations as the ones that had happened a hundred years before. The most dramatic of these incidents happened at the Downs on 25 July 1800 when the Danish forty-gun frigate *Freya*, under the command of Captain Peter Greis Krabbe, was forced to stop by four British frigates and a lugger and allow her convoy to be searched by British officers after a half-hour battle with dead and

---

[19] Royal Library, Copenhagen, Manuscript Collection, Schiøn. 44, 4to, Haandbog i Practisk Søe-Mandskab, pp. 2290ff. See also J. Seerup, 'Søetatens Flagføring i 1700-tallet', *Marine-historisk Tidsskrift*, no. 4 (2009).
[20] Gyllengranath, *Sveriges Sjökrigshistoria*, vol. ii, p. 64.

wounded on both sides.[21] As we have seen, the renewed confrontations between Danish and British warships in the Channel during the 1790s did not represent a new practice. They were a continuation of the practice that had been going on since at least the seventeenth century, if not all the way back to 1293.

Following the end of the Ancien Régime and the Great Wars of 1789 to 1815, a number of old traditions, from fashion to culture to politics, finally disappeared. The centuries-old royal prerogative of demanding salutes from foreign warships was not officially abandoned. But the *Regulations and Instructions* for the Royal Navy in 1806 did not include a reference to the practice. It was not officially abolished, but just simply omitted from the text; nor was it mentioned in the 1816 peace treaty.[22] The tradition disappeared almost unnoticed. Both the Danish and Swedish navies encountered much more demanding challenges in those same years, though, so even if this British change of policy might have been seen as a small victory for Denmark and Sweden, it was certainly overshadowed by the British capture of the Danish Navy in 1807. Today the battles and the captains are still to some extent remembered, but the context is all but forgotten. Hopefully this chapter has changed that a little.

---

[21] See O. Feldbæk, *Dansk Søfartshistorie*, vol. iii, p. 126.
[22] W.G. Perrin, 'The Salute in the Narrow Seas and the Vienna Conference of 1815', in W.G. Perrin (ed.), *Naval Miscellany III* (Navy Records Society, 1927), pp. 287–329; N.A.M. Rodger, *The Command of the Ocean: A Naval History of Britain, 1649–1815* (London, 2004), p. 583.

4

Reconsidering the *Guerre de Course* under Louis XIV: Naval Policy and Strategic Downsizing in an Era of Fiscal Overextension[1]

BENJAMIN DARNELL

The Expansion and Contraction of the Colbertian Fleet

Between the late 1660s and early 1690s, the French Navy underwent an unprecedented operational and administrative expansion, the latter of which was reflected in the extensive 1689 *Ordonnance pour les armées navales*. Naval minister and *contrôleur général* Jean-Baptiste Colbert (1663–83) and later his son, the Marquis de Seignelay (1683–90), had presided over a series of naval reforms in an effort to create a strong battle fleet that competed with the English and Dutch fleets by incorporating the latest tactical and technological refinements.[2] Rebuilding the navy had been a comprehensive effort that required not only the acquisition or construction of ships, but also the management of a complex logistical network, extensive investments in ports and arsenals at Toulon, Brest and Rochefort, the formation of a conscription system to supply the navy with approximately 50,000 sailors, and the oversight of an administrative system of maritime *intendants* and *commissaires* with a broad array of responsibilities.[3] While the Colbertian navy was built on a network of 'fisco-financiers' where administrative and subcontracting roles were often conflated,[4] the growth of *La Royale* echoed, it would seem, a wider determination by Louis XIV to reassert monarchical sovereignty and establish firm royal control over the armed forces.

With impressive speed, the navy increased in size and sophistication over the course of three decades, expanding from 18 ships in 1661 to 132 rated warships

---

[1] I would like to thank Dr David Parrott for his comments and advice on an earlier version of this piece. My thanks also go to Dr Guy Rowlands for suggesting this area of research and to Miss Catriona Stephen for copy-editing.
[2] J. Glete, *Navies and Nations: Warships, Navies and State Building in Europe and America, 1500–1860* (2 vols, Stockholm, 1993), vol. i, pp. 187–92, 200–6, 220–2.
[3] For an overview of the navy's development, see B. Lutun, *La marine de Colbert: Études d'organisation* (Paris, 2003), pp. 55–266; M. Vergé-Franceschi, *La marine française au XVIIIe Siècle* (Paris, 1996), pp. 33–73.
[4] D. Dessert, *La Royale: Vaisseaux et marins du Roi-Soleil* (Paris, 1996), pp. 46–59, 74–7.

by January 1692.[5] By 1676, when it gained an important victory over a combined Spanish–Dutch fleet at Palermo during the Franco-Dutch Wars (1672–78), the navy had demonstrated its importance as an instrument of war by enabling the French monarchy to project its military power and influence beyond its immediate reach. The offshore bombardments of Algiers (1682–83), Genoa (1684) and Tripoli (1685) underscored not only the strategic value of a standing fleet, but also the devastating effect with which it could be deployed.[6] On the surface, the results of the Colbertian naval reconstruction programme were decisive, leading to the creation of a fleet capable of challenging the Anglo-Dutch navies for superiority, in warship tonnage terms, and for relative strategic dominance of the Mediterranean between 1676 and 1693.[7]

Yet, as the French Navy reached the apogee of its numerical and operational strength during the Nine Years' War (1689–97), Louis XIV's government made a series of decisions in 1694–95 that would lead to a comprehensive drawdown of the fleet. The decades-long revival of *La Royale* came to a halt as fleet operations were suspended and Louis XIV's large rated warships, emblematic of royal prestige and dynastic might, were laid up in Brest and Toulon. By 1695, the French fleet in the Atlantic had ceased to exist as an operational entity.[8]

Interpreting the Shift from the *Guerre d'Escadre* to *Guerre de Course*

Given the efforts and resources spent by Colbert and Seignelay to rebuild and sustain the French Navy, historians have found the French government's decision to abandon fleet operations deeply problematic.[9] Indeed, the events of c.1694–95 appear even more striking following the French Navy's victory over the Earl of Torrington's fleet off Beachy Head (Bévéziers) in July 1690, which created

---

[5] Archives nationales de France, Fonds de la Marine (ANM), G 10 bis, fols 29 and 97: 'État abrégé de la marine', 1692; O. Chaline, 'La marine de Louis XIV fut-elle adaptée à ses objectifs?', *Revue historique des armées*, 263 (2011), pp. 40–52.

[6] J. Cénat, *Le roi stratège: Louis XIV et la direction de la guerre, 1661–1715* (Rennes, 2010), pp. 121–5, 134–7.

[7] Glete, *Navies*, pp. 220–3; G. Rowlands, 'The King's Two Arms: French Amphibious Warfare in the Mediterranean under Louis XIV, 1664 to 1697', in D.J.B. Trim and M.C. Fissel (eds), *Amphibious Warfare and European Expansion, 1000–1700: Commerce, State Formation and European Expansion* (Leiden, 2005), pp. 263–73.

[8] G. Symcox, *The Crisis of French Sea Power, 1688–1697: From the guerre d'escadre to the guerre de course* (The Hague, 1974), pp. 143–63; ANM, B² 111, fols 165–70: Pontchartrain to Vauvré, 24 August 1695.

[9] E.g. L.L. de Lapeyrouse-Bonfils, *Histoire de la marine française* (3 vols, Paris, 1845), vol. i, pp. 352, 373, 448–50; H. Rivière, *La marine française sous le règne de Louis XV* (Paris, 1859), pp. ix–xv; E. Chevalier, *Histoire de la marine française ...* (Paris, 1902), pp. 166–7; G. Lacour-Gayet, *La marine militaire de la France sous le règne de Louis XV* (Paris, 1902), pp. 7–12; J. Tramond, *Manuel d'histoire maritime de la France* (Paris, 1916), pp. 283–92; S. Goubet, 'Deux ministres de la Marine: Seigneley et Pontchartrain', *Revue des questions historiques*, 114 (1931), pp. 53–92.

great political pressure and unease in London.[10] Traditional accounts of Louis XIV's navy fixate on rationalising the halt to the Colbertian naval expansion and subsequently question the government's decision to encourage an alternative, decentralised form of naval organisation, in the form of the *guerre de course*, just as the fleet was reaching its peak strength. In reconciling the Colbertian project's successful revival of naval power with the fleet's demobilisation by 1695, historians place an overwhelming emphasis on identifying an abrupt strategic shift, if not transformation, from the *guerre d'escadre* to the *guerre de course* in the 1690s.[11]

According to conventional wisdom, the *guerre d'escadre* and *guerre de course* diverged greatly in strategic and operational terms. In the *guerre d'escadre*, the standing fleet's objective was to engage and destroy the enemy's force in order to gain control of the seas or, more feasibly for the early modern state, to temporarily deny the enemy access to vital maritime corridors and chokepoints.[12] As a direct contrast with these large-scale strategic ambitions, the *guerre de course* purposely avoided fleet engagements. In this strategy, the enemy's trade routes and merchant vessels were specifically targeted, destroyed or captured, with the objective being to inflict economic damage on the enemy.[13] Private initiative, enticed by a state-sanctioned opportunity for profit making through the sale of prizes and cargo, played a greater role since the economic barriers to entry into maritime violence, raised by the development of line-of-battle tactics, were lower in a *guerre de course*. As a result, naval operations were not under the strict purview of the state and could be undertaken by privateers armed with state commissions, acting individually or backed by large syndicates.[14] By transferring presumably non-negotiable sovereignty to private individuals and allowing them an explicit role in the conduct of war, the *guerre de course* lacked the centralised state control typically associated with the Colbertian navy. Implicit in this perspective is a traditionalist late nineteenth-century naval doctrine that emphasised the need to gain hegemony at sea through battle fleets and formed the basis of the French Mahanian reaction against the offensive commercial warfare advocated by *jeune école* theorists following France's defeat by the Prussians in 1871.[15] In deviating from a strategy prioritising the maintenance of a standing navy, the *guerre de course* inevitably appeared as a weaker alternative to fleet warfare.[16]

---

[10] N.A.M. Rodger, *The Command of the Ocean: A Naval History of Britain, 1649–1815* (London, 2005), pp. 144–7.
[11] C. de la Roncière, *Histoire de la marine française* (6 vols, Paris, 1899–1932), vol. vi, pp. 160–231; Symcox, *Crisis*, pp. 3–9, 143–220.
[12] Symcox, *Crisis*, pp. 4–7.
[13] Ibid.
[14] J.S. Bromley, 'The Loan of French Naval Vessels to Privateering Enterprises, 1688–1713', in Bromley, *Corsairs and Navies, 1660–1760* (London, 1987), pp. 187–9; Bromley, 'The French Privateering War, 1702–1713', in *Corsairs*, pp. 215–19; Symcox, *Crisis*, pp. 5–7.
[15] A. Røksund, *The Jeune École: The Strategy of the Weak* (Leiden, 2007), pp. ix–xviii, 1–51; M. Motte, *Une éducation géostratégique: La pensée navale française de la Jeune École à 1914* (Paris, 2004), esp. pp. 54–64, 261–96, 660–79, 714–19.
[16] L. Vignols, 'La course maritime, ses conséquences économiques, sociales et internationales', *Revue d'histoire économique et sociale*, 15 (1927), pp. 196–200.

Seeking to explain the decision to adopt the less desirable strategy of commerce raiding, orthodox interpretations of France's naval decline emphasise the twin effects of naval losses and ministerial incompetence.[17] The defeat at the battles of Barfleur and La Hougue in May–June 1692, in which Admiral Russell's fleet destroyed fifteen ships in the ports of Cherbourg and La Hougue, was portrayed as a watershed, marking the fleet's eclipse by the Royal Navy and a resulting acceptance that the fleet was unable to control the Atlantic and Channel seas. In addition to stressing the singular importance of La Hougue, historians contrasted the administrations of Seignelay and the Pontchartrains, extrapolating from the factional change in 1690 a broader move away from the Colbertian principles that guided the fleet's build-up.[18] Louis Phélypeaux, comte de Pontchartrain, was personally blamed for causing the navy's decline, with an emphasis placed on his apparent willingness to abandon the fleet and his mismanagement of naval affairs, including indecisive directives and poor relations with the comte de Tourville, the French commander at La Hougue, and with subordinates who had been loyal to the Colberts such as *intendant général* François d'Usson de Bonrepaus.[19]

The extent to which naval battles and misdirection from the naval ministry prompted the shift to the *course* has been overplayed. Alongside the oft-repeated notion that Louis XIV was disinterested in naval affairs, the idea that the fleet deteriorated as a result of Pontchartrain's ineptitude has seen significant revision.[20] Despite presiding over a reduction of naval strength, Pontchartrain remained committed to the institution, partly out of his need to cultivate the Colbert family's client network after assuming the post of naval minister in November 1690.[21] The defeat at La Hougue may have been disastrous for morale within the officer corps and among the sailors, but the losses suffered, totalling fifteen ships or 30,000 tonnes, were not the debilitating blow to the fleet characterised by historians.[22] After La Hougue, France's shipbuilding programme continued, with

---

[17] A.M. de Boislisle, 'M. de Bonrepaus: La Marine et le désastre de la Hougue', *Annuaire-Bulletin de la Société de l'histoire de France*, 14 (1877), pp. 88, 110–11, 153–9; C. Rousset, *Histoire de Louvois* (4 vols, Paris, 1863), vol. iv, pp. 512–13; Lapeyrouse-Bonfils, *Histoire de la marine française*, vol. i, p. 308.

[18] Goubet, 'Deux ministres', pp. 53–92; Roncière, *Histoire de la marine française*, vol. vi, pp. 81–4.

[19] C. Farrère, *Histoire de la marine française* (Paris, 1962), pp. 187–92; Roncière, *Histoire de la marine française*, vol. vi, pp. 89, 100–2; P. de Villette-Mursay, *Mémoires du marquis de Villette*, ed. M. Monmerqué (Paris, 1844), p. lvii; Boislisle, *Bonrepaus*, pp. 88–91, 105–11, 153–9, 166–75, 181–92, 199. For further information on the difficulties between Pontchartrain and Colbertian naval administrators, as well as with Tourville, see Symcox, *Crisis*, pp. 107–8, 116–17, 126–8; D. Dessert, *Tourville* (Paris, 2002), pp. 250–88.

[20] Dessert, *La Royale*, pp. 33–7; P. Masson, *Histoire de la marine* (2 vols, Paris, 1992), vol. i, pp. 67–70; Vergé-Franceschi, *La marine française*, pp. 61–3; F. Bluche, *Louis XIV* (Oxford, 1990), pp. 432–6; Symcox, *Crisis*, pp. 103–220.

[21] S. Chapman, *Private Ambition and Political Alliances: The Phélypeaux de Pontchartrain Family and Louis XIV's Government, 1650–1715* (Rochester, 2004), pp. 115–44.

[22] This point has been made by Glete, *Navies*, pp. 220–1; Symcox, *Crisis*, pp. 116–28; Masson, *Histoire*, pp. 142–3.

over 100,000 tonnes added to the navy between 1691 and 1693: an expansion equal to the combined size of the Venetian, Swedish and Danish fleets.[23]

Explanations for the shift to the *guerre de course* typically centre on the assertion that La Royale had lost its numerical supremacy after France's rivals outpaced her shipbuilding abilities, but, as Jan Glete has shown, Louis XIV's navy had in fact achieved parity by the 1690s and was leading the naval arms race until efforts stalled in 1694. French naval construction at this time was being driven by not only interstate competition, but also an important technological change in 1690–92, which allowed for the wider introduction of higher calibre bronze cannons followed by the production of less expensive, yet heavier cast-iron guns.[24] Since the existing rated ships, particularly the first rates built before 1677, were incapable of structurally accommodating these new, higher calibre pieces, naval construction was accelerated in 1690.[25] Between 1690 and 1696, a total of sixty large warships, including twenty-five first rates, were launched, with a further twenty-seven second- and third-rated ships built from 1696 to 1707.[26] The pattern of naval shipbuilding clearly establishes that the government remained committed to a *guerre d'escadre* strategy and fleet *mentalité* well after 1694–95.

Downsizing the Colbertian Fleet

Complications to the traditional picture of France's naval strength in the early 1690s suggest the presence of more fundamental and long-term factors driving the shift in maritime strategy and operations. The tangible successes of the Colbertian naval programme – France's relative dominance of the Mediterranean between 1676 and 1693 and its ability to match the combined strength of the Anglo-Dutch fleets – in actuality belied significant, underlying problems associated with a rapid expansion of naval power. With the onset of the Nine Years' War, the demands of large-scale mobilisation exposed latent weaknesses in Colbert's naval reforms. Paralleling similar disruptions during the mobilisation for the Genoa campaign in 1684, the scale of administrative and logistical shortcomings in 1688 was tremendous: dockyards were in disarray across France; munitions stores were undersupplied; manpower demands outstripped the supply of sailors; naval arsenals were short of over 1,600 artillery pieces; subcontractors

---

[23] Glete, *Navies*, p. 222.
[24] J.C. Lemineur, *Les vaisseaux du Roi Soleil* (Nice, 1996), pp. 87–104; Glete, *Navies*, pp. 244–5; P. Villiers, *Marine Royale, Corsaires et Trafic dans L'Atlantique de Louis XIV à Louis XVI* (Dunkirk, 1991), pp. 106–14; ANM, G 10, fols 67–8: 'État abrégé de la marine', 1690; G 10 bis, fols 89–90: 'État abrégé de la marine', 1692; G 11, fol. 41: 'État abrégé de la marine', 1696.
[25] Villiers, *Marine*, pp. 106–14; Lemineur, *Les vaisseaux*, pp. 67–74.
[26] ANM, G 10, fols 1–26: 'État abrégé de la marine', 1690; G 10 bis, fols 1–30: 'État abrégé de la marine', 1692; G 11, fols 1–14: 'État abrégé de la marine', 1696; G 12, fols 1–19: 'État abrégé de la marine', 1701; G 15, fols 1–13: 'État abrégé de la marine', 1707; A. Demerliac, *La marine de Louis XIV: Nomenclature des vaisseaux du Roi-Soleil de 1661 à 1715*, 2nd edn (Nice, 1995).

failed to produce enough gunpowder and supply saltpetre of sufficient quality; and, after a year, only 94 out of 120 warships were prepared for service.[27] These inefficiencies were compounded by an inadequate internal financing mechanism, which proved unable to sustain the mobilisation of the Colbertian fleet across consecutive campaigns. In order to ensure the navy had a steady supply of cash, the officers that collectively constituted the naval treasury were expected to act as a stopgap between expenditure and the receipt of funds. However, since 1677 Louis de Lubert had exercised a monopoly over the naval treasury, having acquired all three venal offices of *trésorier général de la Marine*.[28] Until 1692 and 1696 when reforms brought in two additional officers who alternated on the basis of fiscal years, the navy was limited by one individual's ability and willingness to lend his credit in order to generate the cash liquidity the navy needed.

Underlying these administrative and structural weaknesses was the fact that the Colbertian navy had been created and maintained on unsustainable principles. From Colbert to Pontchartrain, the naval ministry was unable to break away from a strategic ambition that prized line-of-battle tactics: warship designs were increasingly divorced from their practical application, driven by notions of prestige and escalating demands for concentrated firepower.[29] These precepts had led to the creation of a sizeable rated fleet of increasingly cumbersome and powerful ships of the line, which not only swelled operating costs but also contributed to the indecisive nature of naval engagements.[30] Moreover, the state had lost an important element of flexibility in the navy, since the development of broadside gunnery in the 1660s and 1670s precluded the conversion and integration of privately owned merchantmen into the fleet.[31] By the early 1690s Louis XIV's rated fleet had become a highly specialised and inflexible force, fundamentally geared for the line-of-battle, fiscally unsustainable to maintain, and ill-positioned for the piecemeal downsizing required by 1694–95.

As more recent studies identify the underlying, long-term factors that caused the standing fleet's decline, the decision to adopt the *guerre de course* subsequently emerges as a logical response by the state.[32] The strategic shift was, in fact, a

---

[27] D. Pilgrim, 'The Colbert-Seignelay Naval Reforms and the Beginning of the War of the League of Augsburg', *French Historical Studies*, 9.2 (1975), esp. pp. 242–9.

[28] H. Legohérel, *Les Trésoriers généraux de la Marine (1517–1788)* (Paris, 1965), pp. 66–71, 296–7.

[29] Lemineur, *Les vaisseaux*, pp. 186–8.

[30] Glete, *Navies*, pp. 199–203, 244–6. On the development of line-of-battle tactics, see M.A.J. Palmer, 'The "Military Revolution" Afloat: The Era of the Anglo-Dutch Wars and the Transition to Modern Warfare at Sea', *War in History*, 4 (1997), pp. 123–49. On similar trends in late sixteenth-century Mediterranean galley warfare, see J.F. Guilmartin, *Gunpowder and Galleys: Changing Technology and Mediterranean Warfare at Sea in the 16th Century* (London, 2003), pp. 277–88.

[31] Glete, *Navies*, pp. 205–6. On the broader transition from flexible fleets to permanent navies comprised of purpose-built ships in the seventeenth century, see L. Sicking, 'Naval Warfare in Europe, c.1330–c.1680,' in F. Tallett and D.J.B. Trim (eds), *European Warfare, 1350–1750* (Cambridge, 2010), pp. 255–63.

[32] Symcox, *Crisis*, pp. 143–221; J. Meyer, 'La course: Romantisme, exutoire social, réalité économique. Essai de méthodologie', *Annales de Bretagne*, 78.2 (1971), pp. 323–44; Bromley,

pragmatic repositioning by Louis XIV's government, which recognised that new fiscal realities made it difficult to maintain the standing fleet on the scale which the state had previously attempted. Strategically overextended and financially strained in the Nine Years' War, the French monarchy found itself in increasing difficulties trying to sustain its colossal military commitments. An agrarian crisis in 1692–94 and a demographic contraction hit tax revenues – a 16 per cent fall in 1694 alone, according to Symcox – and induced a fiscal crisis, which left the navy and army competing over diminishing resources.[33] Seemingly bearing the brunt of the fall in revenues, the French Navy experienced rapid and severe budget reductions: spending fell from 30.3 million *livres* in 1693 to 20.2 million *livres* in 1694 and then to 16.5 million *livres* in 1695.[34] Since the Colbertian navy was badly placed for an orderly strategic downsizing, the decline in spending had a disproportionate impact: ship construction ground to a halt in 1694, with the moratorium maintained well into 1695, and the number of operational vessels plummeted as the rated fleet was mothballed, particularly in Brest.[35]

However, the singular importance of the crown's revenue shortfall in 1694 has been overstated. Pontchartrain, who was also the finance minister at the time, was able to initiate an aggressive tax reform that targeted the hitherto exempt privileged elite and caused revenues to rebound by 32 per cent in 1695.[36] Moreover, since spending rarely reflected the availability of funds due to the disjointed nature of Louis XIV's appropriation and expenditure systems, the navy would not have been immediately responsive to the decline in revenues in the way that has been described. The crown was unable to maintain the levels of spending seen in 1691–93 because the fleet's unsustainable development and large-scale mobilisations had challenged the limited capacity of the state. Overspending by the naval ministry, particularly in 1693 when the fleet sailed with an unprecedented ninety-three ships, and the corresponding response by the naval treasurers to limit their financial exposure through underpayment led to administrative and operational disruptions: in September 1696, and as late as February 1700 for some years, the government was still sorting through the navy's accounts and gaining an understanding of what its treasurers had spent between 1691 and 1695.[37] It was

---

'French Privateering War', pp. 214–20; A. Lespagnol, *Messieurs de Saint-Malo: Une élite négociante au temps de Louis XIV* (Rennes, 1997), pp. 377–93.

[33] Symcox, *Crisis*, pp. 146–59; M. Lachiver, *Les années de misère: La famine au temps du Grand Roi* (Paris, 1991), pp. 115–18, 203–8.

[34] C. Le Mao, 'Financer la marine en temps de conflit: L'exemple de la Guerre de la Ligue d'Augsbourg (1688–1697)', *Revue d'Histoire Maritime*, 14 (2011), p. 317.

[35] Symcox, *Crisis*, pp. 151–69; ANM, B² 111, fols 165–70: Pontchartrain to Vauvré, 24 August 1695; G 11, fol. 14: 'État abrégé de la marine', 1696.

[36] A.M. de Boislisle, *Correspondance des contrôleurs généraux des finances* (3 vols, Paris 1874–97), vol. i, pp. 592–6.

[37] ANM, E 6, fols 27–8: Pontchartrain to Lubert, 16 February 1694; ibid., E 10, fol. 259: Pontchartrain to Clairambault, 31 May 1695; ibid., fol. 381: 'Circulaire aux intendants de la marine', 15 September 1696; ibid., fols 672–3: Pontchartrain to Lubert, 17 February 1700; Le Mao, 'Financer la marine', pp. 297–300; Roncière, *Histoire de la marine française*, vol. vi, p. 147.

through curtailing naval activity that the crown's administrators tackled fiscal and organisational overextension.

Louis XIV's leading military engineer, Sébastien Le Prestre de Vauban, proposed a more cost-effective strategic outlook in 1693 that balanced the need for efficiency savings with military imperatives.[38] In addition to previously asserting that France could outlast its enemies by abandoning the initiative and repositioning its armed forces towards a more defensive stance, Vauban echoed in his *mémoire sur la course* of November 1695 a wider mercantilist belief that international commerce was providing the economic and monetary lifeline sustaining the Anglo-Dutch war effort.[39] Disrupting sea-lanes and targeting commerce was therefore vital to ending the war, and Vauban proposed a comprehensive strategic reorientation towards the *guerre de course*.[40] The suggestion to maintain a reduced fleet of forty-five to fifty ships and pursue the *course* far more systematically came against the backdrop of a variety of factors: the monarchy could no longer expend the resources necessary for sizeable fleet engagements; large naval armaments were inefficient and ill-suited for commerce destruction; France remained exposed by its extensive coastlines; and the suspension of fleet operations would free sailors and officers to take part in the *course*.[41] A transition to privateering on a greater scale would enable the French monarchy to continue a strategy of attrition at a lower direct cost to the state.

The crown would not adopt the full extent of his proposals, but Vauban's 1695 memorandum on the *course* highlighted an important trend which characterised France's maritime presence following the fleet's drawdown: Versailles's increasing reliance on a devolved form of naval organisation. Privateering – the state-authorised targeting of commerce by private ships and crews – had long been present as a strategy and organisational mechanism, particularly at Dunkirk, but the period after c.1693–94 witnessed an explicit dependence by the state on entrepreneurialism in the navy. This was an attempt, borne out of fiscal necessity, to shift onto wider society some of the organisational, operational and logistical burdens associated with the maintenance of a navy. By 1695, the French monarchy was extending state commissions to *armateurs* (privateering entrepreneurs) with the expectation that the pursuit of their own financial interests, through the targeting of enemy shipping and commerce, would strain the maritime-dependent Anglo-Dutch economies.[42] With official encouragement, naval operations using purpose-built vessels or ships loaned by the crown were organised, supplied and financed by consortiums or individuals, ranging from local merchants and members of court society, to opportunistic *loups de mer* and naval officers. This was, then, a visible devolution of naval power by a sovereign state.[43]

---

[38] S. de Vauban, 'Mémoire des dépenses de la guerre …', in *Les Oisivetés de Monsieur de Vauban*, ed. M. Virol (Seyssel, 2007), pp. 487–535.
[39] Vauban, 'Mémoire concernant la course …', in *Oisivetés*, p. 336.
[40] Ibid., pp. 335–57; Vauban, 'Mémoire des dépenses de la guerre …', in *Oisivetés*, pp. 499–500.
[41] Vauban, 'Mémoire concernant la course …', in *Oisivetés*, pp. 335–57.
[42] J.A. Lynn, *The Wars of Louis XIV, 1667–1714* (London, 1999), p. 101.
[43] Bromley, 'Loan', pp. 187–206; Bromley, 'French Privateering War', pp. 215–43.

Complicating the Strategic 'Shift'

While the decline in spending had immediate consequences for the fleet, the strategic shift from the *guerre d'escadre* to *guerre de course* was not as dramatic and complete as it has been presented in previous accounts. Historians' preoccupation with identifying turning points has created an oversimplified view of Louisquatorzian naval policy, which sees strategy in binary terms and frames the shift in strategy and operations in 1694–95 as a sudden and massive change. Moreover, excessive emphasis on Vauban's memorandum has furthered this polarisation by giving the impression that prior to this memorandum the *course* had been nonexistent. Although presenting a strategic argument for the shift to privateering, it gave a deliberately misleading picture of privateering efforts prior to 1695 in an attempt to lobby government for more lenient regulations and greater support for *armateurs*. Indeed, far from being an uninterested strategist, Vauban stood to gain financially from the acceptance of his proposals given his investments in multiple privateering syndicates.[44]

The notion that the government entirely abandoned the navy and only started encouraging the *course* as an alternative strategy in 1694–95 may fit in with a traditional narrative of naval decline, but it fails to match up to the reality of French naval policy. The French monarchy had shown a willingness to support naval enterprises between state forces and private individuals since the Dutch War (1672–78). Reacting to calls by Dunkirk privateers for support in their attacks on Dutch shipping in the Channel between 1674 and 1678, Colbert permitted in the *règlement* (regulation) of October 1674 the loaning of royal vessels, albeit limited to fifth rates, light frigates and other small ships.[45] The ships would be delivered fully stocked with munitions and gunpowder and the crown would assume officer pay and the risk of loss in exchange for a third of the prize proceeds.[46] As evidenced by fluctuating regulations from 1688 to 1694, the naval ministry manipulated the various incentive structures at its disposal, including altering the crown's share of prize proceeds and the requirement for *armateurs* to pay repair costs, to encourage private initiative.[47] Under Seignelay, the November 1688 ordinances were set firmly in favour of the *armateurs*: the crown's traditional claim to the third was renounced and the *armateurs* were relieved of the need to reimburse the cost of repairs and the replacement of supplies.[48] It is likely that these advantageous terms were accorded in order to stimulate private armaments at a time when the fleet's wartime mobilisation in 1688–89 had uncovered severe logistical failures. Far from presiding over a loosening of privateering regulations,

---

[44] Symcox, *Crisis*, pp. 181–2.
[45] P. Villiers, *Les corsaires du littoral: Dunkerque, Calais, Boulogne, de Philippe II à Louis XIV (1568–1713)* (Villeneuve D'Ascq, 2000), pp. 194–6; J.Y. Nerzic, *La place des armements mixtes dans la mobilisation de l'Arsenal de Brest sous les deux Pontchartrains* (2 vols, Milon-la-Chapelle, 2010), vol. i, pp. 188–9.
[46] S. Lebeau, *Nouveau code des prises …* (3 vols, Paris, 1799–1801), vol. i, pp. 64–6.
[47] Nerzic, *Armements mixtes*, vol. i, pp. 188–207.
[48] Ibid., pp. 192–3, 205–7; Lebeau, *Nouveau code*, vol. i, pp. 112–13.

Pontchartrain sought to balance the navy's increasing dependence on private enterprise with the need to reduce the crown's financial exposure. The regulations of December 1691 revoked prior concessions and reinstated the requirement that the *armateurs* replace or pay for consumed goods and equipment.[49] A further rebalancing was necessary after the crown realised that supplies were not being paid for or replenished due to organisational complexities or outright evasion: new regulations in October 1694 addressed the issue by introducing the crown's claim to a fifth of the net proceeds of prizes in return for relieving the *armateurs* of their obligation to restore or reimburse consumed items.[50]

Beyond the fact that regulations show that the strategic shift was not the simple replacement of a state-run fleet with privateering, the *guerre de course* and *guerre d'escadre* were not mutually exclusive strategies. Late seventeenth-century naval engagements were characterised by tactical indecisiveness, and commanders, particularly Tourville, focused on maintaining numerical superiority and treated naval warfare as part of a long-term struggle of attrition.[51] Within this context the *course*, in terms of its emphasis on economic attrition, did not represent the wholesale departure from the *guerre d'escadre* that has been often implied.[52] The crown had shown an interest in pursuing commercial warfare, as either a primary or a secondary objective, as early as June 1691 when Tourville's fleet targeted the returning Smyrna convoy.[53] In June 1693, Tourville successfully intercepted the Allied merchant convoy off Lagos, causing losses in the region of 20–30 million *livres*.[54] Joint operations were also undertaken prior to 1694–95, with Jean Bart and Claude de Forbin destroying the Dutch fishing fleet at Dogger Bank in August 1691 in an operation using seven loaned vessels and thirteen private ships.[55] Following the resumption of the Dutch whaling trade in Spitsbergen in 1692, privateering proposals by Malouin merchants had caught the attention of Pontchartrain who subsequently commissioned a naval squadron of three loaned royal vessels and a privately built ship. Highly successful, the expedition returned in August 1693 having captured twenty-six Dutch whalers, as well as intercepting on its return, with the aid of additional private armaments, an English merchant convoy returning from the West Indies.[56]

Further complicating the picture of a complete shift, continued naval activity from 1694 to 1696 shows that the monarchy still held pretensions for a state-controlled fleet. In June 1694, the fifty ships under Tourville's command off the

---

[49] Lebeau, *Nouveau code*, vol. i, pp. 143–4.
[50] Bromley, 'Loan', p. 188; Nerzic, *Armements mixtes*, vol. i, pp. 205–6; Lebeau, *Nouveau code*, vol. i, pp. 193–4.
[51] Dessert, *Tourville*, esp. pp. 226–88; Symcox, *Crisis*, pp. 115–16, 228.
[52] Symcox, *Crisis*, pp. 228–9.
[53] Dessert, *Tourville*, pp. 258–69, 302–5.
[54] Villiers, *Marine*, p. 155; Symcox, *Crisis*, p. 135; Roncière, *Histoire de la marine française*, vol. vi, pp. 139–48.
[55] Villiers, *Marine*, p. 155.
[56] P. Henrat, 'French Naval Operations in Spitsbergen during Louis XIV's reign', *Arctic*, 37.4 (Dec. 1984), pp. 544–51.

Catalan coast provided critical amphibious support to the duc de Noailles's army during the capture of Palamós.[57] While the fleet would be inactive throughout 1695, expenditures rebounded from 16.5 million *livres* in 1695 to 19.8 million *livres* in 1696 and 18.2 million *livres* in 1697.[58] The naval ministry's continued desire to put a large fleet to sea was evident when in February 1695 Pontchartrain ordered a major rearmament of the fleet.[59] In these final years of the war, naval policy in the Mediterranean reacted largely to the presence of the English fleet based at Cádiz, with fleet preparations being undertaken and abandoned based on the enemy force's suspected movements. The desire to avoid a potentially disastrous engagement in the Straits of Gibraltar underlines an increasing conservatism in the strategic parameters set by Louis XIV and the *conseil du Roi*, which was subsequently communicated to the flag officers, particularly once royal finances were strained and when the navy's commitments expanded during the War of the Spanish Succession (1701–14). Likely spurred by information that Admiral Russell had departed Cádiz in October 1695 and left behind a reduced naval force,[60] the French dedicated the remainder of 1695 to fleet preparations. In late March 1696, the comte de Château-Renault left Toulon with a fleet of fifty ships.[61] With the crown's instructions referring to an opportunity in the Channel for an '*action d'éclat*', these efforts formed part of a Franco-Jacobite plan to invade England from Dunkirk.[62] However, the scheme collapsed by the summer of 1696 and the entire French fleet remained concentrated at Brest.[63]

The extensive efforts to prepare the fleet between 1695 and 1697 point to the broader strategic or dynastic concerns motivating French naval policy in this period: from the battles of Bévéziers (1690) and La Hougue (1692) to the mobilisation at Toulon in 1695–96, the French monarchy's use of its fleet had been defined by plans to restore the Stuart monarchy. Since Louis XIV's government lacked a comprehensive strategy on how to use the fleet otherwise, the rationale for maintaining the navy on a large scale was only undermined once attempts to restore James II to power failed.[64] Concomitantly, Colbert and Seignelay had created an unsustainable instrument, backed by an underdeveloped internal financing mechanism, which was difficult to maintain on the scale that the crown attempted in the early 1690s. Policy evolved to attract private investment and

---

[57] Rowlands, 'Amphibious', pp. 272, 295–6; K.A.J. McLay, 'Combined Operations and the European Theatre during the Nine Years' War, 1688–1697', *Historical Research*, 78.202 (Nov. 2005), p. 533.
[58] Le Mao, 'Financer la marine', p. 317.
[59] ANM, B² 120, fols 97–101: Pontchartrain to Le Vasseur, 16 February 1695.
[60] Rodger, *Command*, p. 155.
[61] ANM, B² 119, fols 143–7: Pontchartrain to Vauvré, 15 February 1696; ibid., fols 256–61: Pontchartrain to Vauvré, 28 March 1696.
[62] Ibid., fols 207–8: Pontchartrain to Château-Renault, 7 March 1696; Symcox, *Crisis*, p. 165; Rodger, *Command*, p. 156.
[63] Rodger, *Command*, p. 156.
[64] A. James, 'Raising the Profile of Naval History: An International Perspective on Early Modern Navies', *Mariner's Mirror*, 97.1 (2011), pp. 200–1.

to help pare down the costs borne by the state, bringing the navy's management closer to entrepreneurial practices in the army where Louis XIV leveraged private interest for royal service.[65] The wider problem in the 1690s was that Louis XIV had been unable to meet the fiscal and organisational challenge of maintaining the Colbertian navy and the result was a disjointed naval policy: the state's attempt to reduce its liabilities by loaning naval assets to private individuals and syndicates fragmented the crown's broader strategy, yet continued pretensions to maintain the fleet meant that there was a limit to the resources that could be diverted to support private efforts. Even after the Bourbon succession to the Spanish throne in November 1700 changed French geostrategic calculations, Louis XIV's naval policy remained disjointed as it sought to attract private involvement where fiscally necessary and convenient whilst simultaneously pursuing wide-ranging fleet objectives. It was only once the navy began to collapse in 1707–8 after its financially overexposed treasurers failed to acquit its costs that a strategic shift to the *guerre de course* was more fully and systematically embraced.

---

[65] See G. Rowlands, *The Dynastic State and the Army under Louis XIV: Royal Service and Private Interest, 1661–1701* (Cambridge, 2002).

5
British Naval Administration and the Lower Deck Manpower Problem in the Eighteenth Century

J. ROSS DANCY

For the British Navy of the eighteenth century, there was no aspect of naval warfare that caused as much difficulty and anguish as manning the fleet. Finding the necessary skilled seamen to man warships was the alpha and omega of the navy's problems. Over the course of the so-called 'Second Hundred Years' War' between Britain and France, British fleets were forced to grow in order to gain and maintain seaborne superiority, in both home and distant waters. Larger and more numerous warships required increasing numbers of men. The English Navy of 1695 employed around 48,000 men, while the Royal Navy of 1810 employed over 145,000 men to face Napoleonic France.[1] As each progressive conflict superseded its predecessor in size and scope, so too did the matter of manning British warships. Finding enough men, and in particular enough skilled men, to man the navy's ships was a strategic as well as a logistical problem for naval administrators. This chapter argues that successfully manning the fleet was the foundation of British naval strategy in the late eighteenth century. The Impress Service and the controversial system of impressment largely succeeded in providing skilled seamen for the navy and laid the foundation for the navy's remarkable performance in the two decades of war with Revolutionary and Napoleonic France. However, contrary to most of the received historiography, impressment did not provide the majority of naval recruits.

The historiography of British naval manpower, and in particular the extensive literature on impressment, has suffered from a noticeable lack of statistical data. At the heart of this chapter is the first substantial and statistically significant study of naval manpower, which examines the recruitment of over 27,000 sailors during the French Revolutionary Wars.[2] Its analysis suggests that most of the assumptions underpinning the current scholarship on impressment are inaccurate: most members of the lower deck were volunteers; impressment was comparatively rare and targeted a select group of experienced sailors. By examining the archival

---

[1] N.A.M. Rodger, *The Command of the Ocean: A Naval History of Britain, 1649–1815* (London, 2004), pp. 636–9.
[2] For a longer treatment of this data, see J.R. Dancy, *The Myth of the Press Gang: Volunteers, Impressment and the Naval Manpower Problem in the Late Eighteenth Century* (Woodbridge, 2015).

record – rather than relying, as too many historians have done, on Victorian polemics on the evils of impressment[3] – this chapter revises the historiography of British naval manning policy and simultaneously demonstrates its significance for British naval strategy in the eighteenth century.

Manning Practices in the Eighteenth Century

During the second half of the seventeenth century, Charles II's navy relied mainly upon ships' officers to man the fleet. There was little in the way of administrative organisation and a constant shortage of volunteer skilled manpower, so the navy had to rely on impressment, a medieval prerogative of the crown.[4] Often these efforts were not enough, and naval manning had to be supplemented by placing embargos on outward-bound shipping until merchants provided enough sailors.[5] The navy of Charles II and James II was usually only employed seasonally to fight in the local waters of the North Sea against the Dutch. This meant that mariners could be found locally to man the navy, and during the Second and Third Dutch Wars the majority of fighting seamen came from the towns and villages of the Thames and Medway.[6] The seasonal nature of naval warfare resulted in seamen only having to serve for a few months before being paid off as the fleet was laid up in ordinary for the winter.

The accession of William III in 1689 and the beginning of more than a century of wars with France changed the naval manpower equation. War with France was fought throughout the year, in distant waters, with substantial fleets, and over long periods.[7] The War of the Grand Alliance ended the concept of seasonal naval warfare. During the winters of 1691 to 1694, the English government decided to keep the fleet manned in an attempt to avoid having to re-recruit seamen in the spring.[8] Thus, men were not being released after the traditional campaign season, and as the War of the Grand Alliance lasted nearly a decade, volunteering or impressment involved several years of service. There were seldom enough volunteers to man the service, and the navy was forced to rely upon compulsion to man

---

[3] See, for example, S. Gradish, *The Manning of the British Navy During the Seven Years' War* (London, 1980); J.R. Hutchinson, *The Press-Gang Afloat and Ashore* (London, 1913); M. Lewis, *A Social History of the Navy, 1793–1815* (London, 2004); M. Rediker, *Between the Devil and the Deep Blue Sea: Merchant Seamen, Pirates and the Anglo-American Maritime World, 1700–1750* (Cambridge, 1987); N. Rogers, *The Press Gang: Naval Impressment and Its Opponents in Georgian Britain* (London, 2007).

[4] R.G. Usher Jr, 'Royal Navy Impressment During the American Revolution', *The Mississippi Valley Historical Review*, xxxvii, no. 4 (1951), p. 679.

[5] B. Capp, *Cromwell's Navy: The Fleet and the English Revolution, 1648–1660* (Oxford, 1989), p. 263.

[6] J.D. Davies, *Gentlemen and Tarpaulins: The Officers and Men of the Restoration Navy* (Oxford, 1991), p. 68.

[7] D.A. Baugh, *British Naval Administration in the Age of Walpole* (Princeton, 1965), pp. 147–8; Rodger, *Command of the Ocean*, pp. 205–6.

[8] Rodger, *Command of the Ocean*, p. 206.

the fleet.[9] At the same time, the Royal Navy was growing in size and required more seamen. Rather than paying off ships when they came in to be refitted, men were turned over to another ship, which made recruiting new men even more difficult. Manning the navy haphazardly was no longer an option (Figure 5.1).

The manning problem under Queen Anne appeared to be less severe than it had under William III. There were fewer complaints and impressment was better regulated.[10] The burden of recruitment fell less on civil authorities and more on the navy, which found more suitable men. Furthermore, the rapidly growing English and Scottish sea trade provided more seamen to fulfil the navy's needs.[11] A 1706 Proclamation granted constables 20 shillings a head for able-bodied seamen brought to the navy, gave them the right to 'break open the doors of any house where they shall suspect any such seamen to be concealed', and declared a fine of 5 pounds for harbouring seamen from the press.[12] Even though improvements were made relative to the struggles of William III's reign, extreme measures were still occasionally taken to man the navy.

Although the Admiralty made many unsuccessful attempts to change naval manning policy over the first half of the eighteenth century, it was not until they took the manning issue out of the hands of ships' officers and organised it into a dedicated recruiting service that they made any major progress towards supplying their vastly expanding naval force with the necessary manpower. The key administrative development derived from the manning crisis associated with the War of Austrian Succession. As Figure 5.1 demonstrates, the Royal Navy was larger than it had ever been, which forced the Admiralty to revoke the protections it had issued to the trading companies and claim one in six men from merchants to man warships.[13] During this conflict, two Regulating Captains were introduced in London, who inspected men taken by press gangs before they were sent to ships. The introduction of Regulating Captains streamlined impressment in the London area and ensured that men being conscripted were actually seamen and not vagrants or criminals.[14] By simplifying and centralising the process of naval manning, the Admiralty took manning out of the hands of officers aboard warships.

During the Seven Years' War, the Royal Navy was more than 'wooden walls' that defended the British Isles from invasion; it also supported British operations overseas, and this war was increasingly fought in foreign waters. The Royal Navy's success derived in part from the administrative innovations of the previous

---

[9] J. Ehrman, *The Navy in the War of William III, 1689–1697: Its State and Direction* (Cambridge, 1953), p. 113.
[10] 'Admiralty to the Captains Appointed to Regulate the Press on the River Thames', in R.D. Merriman (ed.). *Queen Anne's Navy: Documents Concerning the Administration of the Navy of Queen Anne, 1702–1714* (London, 1961), p. 201.
[11] Rodger, *Command of the Ocean*, p. 211.
[12] NMM, PBB/7521, 'Proclamation for the Encouragement and Increase of Seamen, 1706'.
[13] 'Admiralty Memorial to the Lords Justices, 1 August 1745', in D.A. Baugh (ed.), *Naval Administration, 1715–1750* (London, 1977), pp. 137–8.
[14] C. Lloyd, *The British Seaman, 1200–1860* (London, 1968), p. 128.

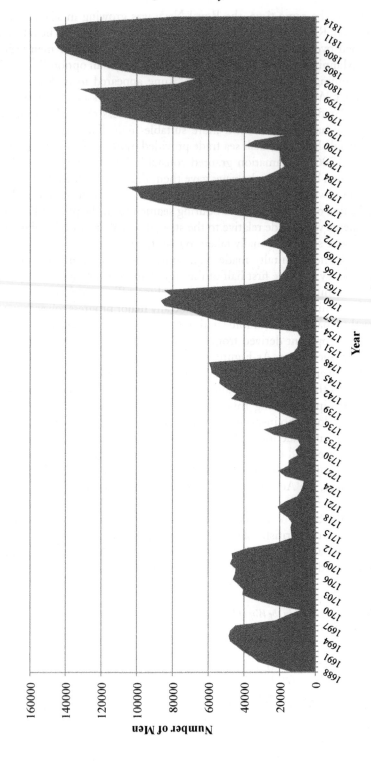

Figure 5.1: Royal navy manpower in the eighteenth century. Figures are reproduced from Dancy, *The Myth of the Press Gang*.

war. The two Regulating Captains of the War of Austrian Succession became an entire administrative branch of the navy: the Impress Service. In 1754, Regulating Captains were posted in several coastal cities, including Bristol, Liverpool, Whitehaven, Newcastle, Yarmouth and Edinburgh. Further expansions in 1756, 1759 and 1762 saw many other cities receive Regulating Captains to supervise press gangs, including Gloucester, Winchester, Reading, Southampton, Aberdeen, Exeter and Cork.[15] Press gangs were generally manned with local 'tough men' and commanded by a lieutenant who held a press warrant that gave him the legal right to take men for service in the navy. Press tenders at sea were also armed with undated warrants and ready to collect men from incoming merchant ships once war broke out. The creation of an administrative branch of the navy specifically dedicated to recruitment made the process of naval manning and mobilisation significantly more efficient.[16]

Accompanying the creation of the Impress Service was the Navy Act of 1758, arguably the single most important piece of legislation that addressed the manning problem during the eighteenth century.[17] The bill addressed one of the major grievances that mariners had with the Royal Navy, namely irregular pay. Seamen often spent years in the navy without receiving their wages. The Act granted regular pay to seamen employed in the navy: they had to be paid either two months' wages every six months or a year's wages every eighteen months.[18] The Act also provided for seamen to have a portion of their wages sent to either their mothers or wives, allowing their families to benefit from their employment. Although the Act addressed the timing of pay, it still did not increase seamen's low wages, which remained unchanged between 1653 and 1797.[19]

In keeping with the pattern of ever-larger conflicts, the War of American Independence once again forced the navy to raise more men than it ever had before.[20] Britain needed a fleet large enough to fight France, Spain and the Dutch Republic simultaneously. The Impress Service proved its value and raised 116,357 of the 230,000 to 235,000 men that served the navy throughout the war.[21] In 1782, at the end of the American War, the Royal Navy employed over 105,000 men. But by 1792, peacetime cuts had reduced naval manpower to 16,000.[22] In other aspects of naval administration and logistics, the navy was in good shape. Two brief mobilisations – one against Spain over Nootka Sound in 1790 and another against Russia over Turkey the following year – had left the navy's ships

---

[15] Gradish, *Manning*, p. 57.
[16] Lewis, *Social History*, p. 103; Dancy, *The Myth of the Press Gang*, p. 186.
[17] S. Gradish, 'Wages and Manning: The Navy Act of 1758', *English Historical Review*, xciii, no. 366 (1978), p. 46.
[18] An Act for the Encouragement of Seamen employed in the Royal Navy …, 31 Geo. II c.10.
[19] Gradish, 'Wages and Manning', pp. 46–7.
[20] Rodger, *Command of the Ocean*, p. 395.
[21] Ibid., p. 396.
[22] TNA, PRO 30/8/248, 'Account of Seamen …', fol. 29.

in relatively good condition.[23] Ships without men were useless, however. There was still no large-scale naval reserve, and the idea of compulsory registration had been dismissed as 'French and tyrannical'.[24] With only a few guard-ships in reserve to call upon, the Royal Navy was forced to expand threefold in 1793 alone,[25] and the French Revolutionary Wars stretched the navy's manning capabilities to their limit.

Impressment

But what percentage of sailors were conscripted? The historiography of impressment has been filled with misconceptions and few attempts to examine the archival record. The database that underpins this chapter explores British naval manpower during the French Revolutionary Wars of 1793 to 1801. It demonstrates that only 16 per cent of seamen in the Royal Navy were actually impressed, while 73 per cent volunteered.[26] This finding undermines the majority of the historiography of impressment, as even the most conservative estimates have placed the number of impressed seamen at one in three. Some historians have even claimed that three in four sailors were pressed.[27] The high percentage of volunteers is also significant because it challenges the existing interpretation of how press gangs functioned. The database's analysis of the rates of pressed and volunteer seamen turns the historiography of impressment on its head (Figure 5.2).

If the majority of sailors volunteered, then the stereotypical picture of the press gang lurking in dark corners to surprise ordinary men by dragging them off to sea needs serious revision. A press gang's base of operations, called a rendezvous, was usually in a local inn or somewhere else where sailors usually congregated.[28] The purpose of the rendezvous was to recruit skilled seamen to volunteer, not to impress men against their will. Thus the rendezvous was highly visible and marked with flags, recruiting posters and patriotic symbols: it was important that these places did not look ominous, as such places had little chance of attracting volunteers. Press gangs conducted recruiting drives, which included speeches glorifying naval life and improvised bands playing patriotic tunes while

---

[23] W.M. James, *The Naval History of Great Britain During the French Revolutionary and Napoleonic Wars, 1793–1796* (London, 2002), vol. i, p. 48; R. Harding, *Seapower and Naval Warfare, 1650–1830* (London, 1999), p. 259.

[24] D. Aldridge, 'The Navy as Handmaid for Commerce and High Policy, 1680–1720', in J. Black and P. Woodfine (eds), *The British Navy and the Use of Naval Power in the Eighteenth Century* (Leicester, 1988), pp. 56–7; J.S. Bromley, 'The British Navy and Its Seamen after 1688: Notes for an Unwritten History', in S. Palmer and D. Williams (eds), *Charted and Uncharted Waters* (London, 1981), p. 150.

[25] Rogers, *The Press Gang*, pp. 5–6.

[26] Dancy, *The Myth of the Press Gang*, p. 38.

[27] Lewis, *Social History*, p. 139; Gradish, *Manning*, p. 62; Rogers, *The Press Gang*, pp. 3–5.

[28] N. Blake and R.B. Lawrence, *The Illustrated Companion to Nelson's Navy* (London, 1999), p. 64; Usher Jr, 'Royal Navy Impressment', pp. 675–7.

British Naval Administration and the Lower Deck

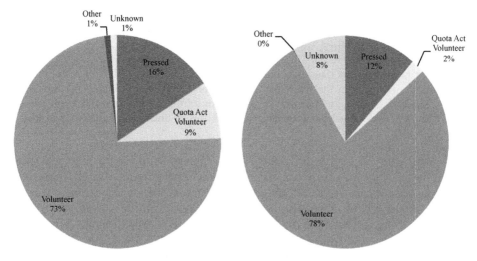

Figure 5.2: Factored seamen and petty officer recruitment

marching up and down the street.[29] The chance to win glory and prize money was a common theme. A good example is a recruiting poster for the frigate *Pallas* under the command of Lord Cochrane from 1804, which is filled with references to prize money.[30] Admittedly, Cochrane had a reputation as a daring and lucky officer, but recent research has shown prize money was much more abundant for all members of the Royal Navy than previously thought.[31] Another example is a 1797 recruiting poster put up in Shoreham by Lt W.J. Stephens, which appealed to the patriotism of seamen and also provided a splash of fear-mongering as motivation:

> Let us, who are Englishmen, protect and defend our good King and Country, against the Attempts of all Republicans and Levellers, and against the Designs of our Natural Enemies, who intend this Year to invade Old England, our happy Country, to murder our gracious King as they have done their own; to make Whores of our Wives and Daughters; to rob us of our Property, and teach us nothing but the damn'd Art of murdering one another ... If you love your Country, and your Liberty, now is the time to shew your Love.[32]

While Lord Cochrane sought to find men through financial motivations and Lt Stephens used patriotism. In both cases, the officers sought volunteers.

---

[29] Lewis, *Social History*, p. 93; Lloyd, *The British Seaman*, p. 130.
[30] NMM, PBH3190, 'Recruitment Poster for the *Pallas*'.
[31] D. Benjamin and C. Thornberg, 'Organization and Incentives in the Age of Sail', *Explorations in Economic History*, 44 (2007), pp. 317–41.
[32] NMM, PBB7084, 'Recruitment Poster for Volunteers'.

When impressment was necessary, lieutenants of both the Impress Service and those sent ashore with press gangs from warships were under unequivocal instructions from the Admiralty:

> not to impress any Landmen, but only such as are Seafaring Men, or such others as are described in the Press-Warrant, and those only as are able and fit for His Majesty's Service, and not to take up Boys or infirm Persons, in order to magnify the Numbers upon your Accounts, and to bring an unnecessary charge upon His Majesty.[33]

Clearly, the Admiralty did not want press gangs to bring in more unskilled landsmen. In such a large operation some mistakes were unavoidable, especially as sailors not wanting to be conscripted commonly claimed not to be seamen.[34] But on the whole, press gangs targeted experienced seamen. Contrary to what some historians have said, the majority of the men on the lower deck of British warships were not strangers to the sea and indeed many were highly skilled. Petty officers made up about 12 per cent of the crew, and able seamen made up a further 36 per cent.[35] Together, they formed nearly half of the lower-deck complement of a ship. These men were the navy's lifeblood, without which it could never function to its fullest ability. A further quarter of the lower deck was comprised of ordinary seamen, who had experience at sea, often in coasters or fishing boats, but likely had little experience in large square-rigged blue-water sailing vessels. That left just over a quarter of the men to be rated as landsmen, meaning they had little experience at sea. Volunteers were more likely to be landsmen or ordinary seamen, while the skill levels of pressed men were often high: nearly half were rated either as able seamen or petty officers. Though pressed men made up a minority of the lower deck of British warships, it was a highly skilled minority (Figure 5.3).

Impressment sought deep-sea sailors for Royal Navy service.[36] Able seamen were difficult to find because it took years to learn the required skills. Most began working at sea in their early teenage years, likely in coasting or fishing vessels which used light sailing rigs capable of being handled by boys.[37] In order to be considered able seamen they needed to have acquired years of skill, they needed to be agile enough to work high in the rigging, and they also needed the strength of a full-grown man to be able to handle the large, heavy sails involved in sailing

---

[33] TNA, ADM 7/967, 'Instructions to Officers Raising Men, 1807'.
[34] Lloyd, *The British Seaman*, pp. 161–2.
[35] Dancy, *The Myth of the Press Gang*, p. 42.
[36] M. Duffy, *Soldiers, Sugar and Seapower: The Expeditions to the West Indies and the War against Revolutionary France* (Oxford, 1987), pp. 20–1; N.A.M. Rodger, '"A Little Navy of Your Own Making": Admiral Boscawen and the Cornish Connection in the Royal Navy', in M. Duffy (ed.), *Parameters of British Naval Power, 1650–1850* (Exeter, 1998), p. 83; D.J. Starkey, 'War and the Market for Seafarers in Britain, 1736–1792', in L.R. Fischer and H.W. Nordvik (eds), *Shipping and Trade, 1750–1950: Essays in International Maritime Economic History* (Pontefract, 1990), p. 37.
[37] Rediker, *Devil and the Deep Blue Sea*, pp. 12–13.

British Naval Administration and the Lower Deck 57

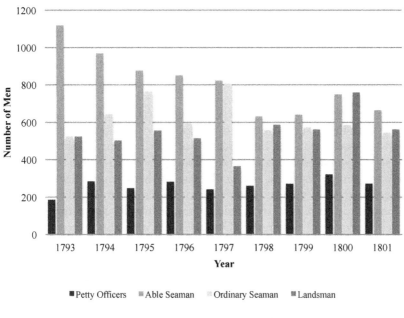

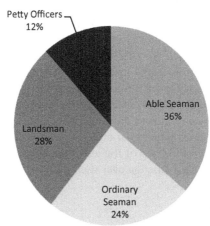

Figure 5.3: Seamen and petty officer ratings (total: 20,213 men)

warships. Therefore, the window in which men could fill this vital position aboard a naval ship was relatively narrow. The average age for pressed able seamen was twenty-two, while the average age of pressed ordinary seamen and landsmen was twenty.[38] The fact that able seamen were on average two years older than ordinary seamen and landsmen demonstrates the time it took for able seamen to gain the knowledge and experience necessary to perform at the necessary level of competence. While both of the figures show the youth of seamen, it is clear that press gangs were not targeting men outside their twenties, and the majority of the recruiting effort brought in men under twenty-five years of age (Figures 5.4 and 5.5).

Impressment was not only a system to target specific men for naval service, but also a system for preserving others from naval service. Many men with seafaring skills were essential to the infrastructure of wartime Britain, and their loss to naval service would have proved catastrophic to the Royal Navy's ability to build, supply and service warships, and would have further been problematic for Britain's economy. Many men had statutory protections by virtue of their positions in merchant ships, such as masters, chief mates, boatswains and carpenters, as well as essential dockyard personnel.[39] Other seamen were also protected, including fishermen, men serving on coasters, colliers and whalers, apprentice boys and foreigners, as long as they had served less than two years in a British ship.[40] In 1757, during the height of the Seven Years' War, 50,000 men held protections from impressment, while at the same time Parliament had voted funds for 55,000 men to serve in the navy.[41] Thirty-nine years later in 1796, double that number was voted for naval service.[42] The increase in naval manpower suggests that greater numbers of protections were needed to keep the British economy and infrastructure running. Press gangs did not simply sweep up everyone who fell into the category of seamen or 'person who used the sea'. Many of these individuals were vital to British infrastructure and consequently the nation's ability to wage war. Impressment did not increase the number of seamen in Britain; rather it ensured that the Royal Navy maintained enough skilled manpower to make certain it could function in top form without draining other essential maritime services of skilled men. Impressment helped guarantee the success of British sea power by ensuring that the overall skill level of the lower deck remained high enough that British warships maintained an edge over their adversaries. The maritime labour

---

[38] Dancy, *The Myth of the Press Gang*, p. 149.
[39] Lewis, *Social History*, p. 106.
[40] D.E. Robinson, 'Secret of British Power in the Age of Sail: Admiralty Records of the Coasting Fleet', *The American Neptune*, xlviii, no. 1 (1988), p. 6; T. Clayton, *Tars: The Men Who Made Britain Rule the Waves* (London, 2007), p. 170; D.A. Brunsman, 'The Evil Necessity: British Naval Impressment in the Eighteenth-Century Atlantic World' (Unpublished PhD Thesis: Princeton University, 2004), p. 11.
[41] P. Earle, *Sailors: English Merchant Seamen, 1650–1775* (London, 1998), p. 190; N. Rogers, 'Impressment and the Law in Eighteenth-Century Britain', in N. Laundau (ed.), *Law, Crime and English Society* (Cambridge, 2002), p. 88.
[42] TNA, PRO 30/8/248, 'Account of Seamen …', fol. 29.

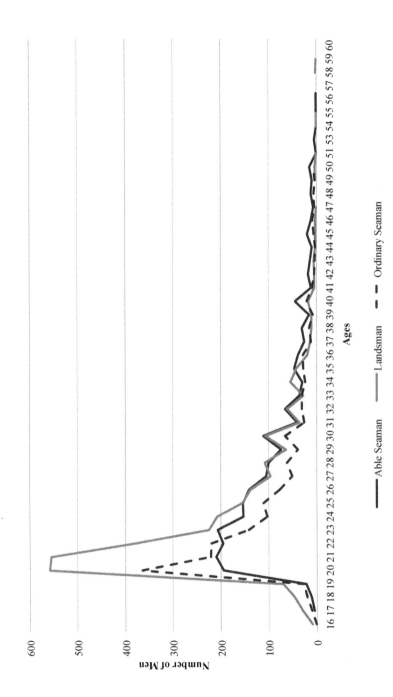

Figure 5.4: Volunteer seamen ages and rating (total: 7,572 men)

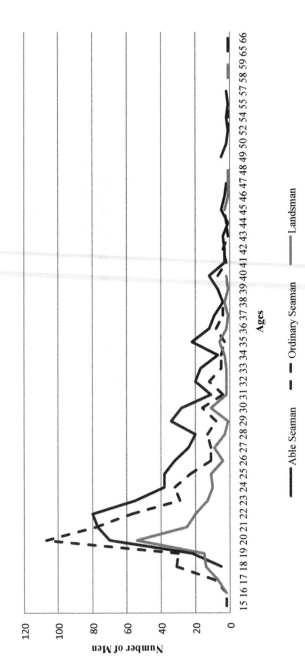

Figure 5.5: Ages of pressed men (total: 1,561 men)

market could not accomplish this without impressment's intervention.[43]

The function of impressment was to provide the Royal Navy with the necessary skilled and experienced men, especially topmen.[44] The shortage of seamen volunteers was constant, and therefore impressment lasted throughout any given conflict.[45] Impressment was always difficult, and few of those involved actually enjoyed the experience. No matter how unpopular it was, it proved a potent tool for adding seamen to Britain's warships, and aided the navy in achieving a high ratio of skilled to unskilled men.[46] Though it has been claimed that landsmen were pressed in large numbers, doing so was illegal. Only anecdotal evidence has been produced to suggest that, as war went on, landsmen were being impressed in great quantity.[47] Further, the database demonstrates that landsmen only formed 16 per cent of pressed men,[48] and landsmen were eligible for impressment if they 'used the sea' and had skills that were valuable to the navy. The reality was that the Royal Navy had no desire to recruit men without seafaring skills.

Strategy and the Lower-Deck Manpower Problem

Between 1660 and 1815, the British Royal Navy grew from a seasonal force of around 20,000 men to a year-round force of over 145,000 men in wartime. During the half-century leading up to the French Revolutionary Wars, the number of seamen employed in the merchant service during peacetime nearly doubled, from fewer than 54,000 in 1738 to over 98,000 in 1791.[49] Though the navy required over seven times more men in 1810 than it had in 1665, the impact on naval administration and the seafaring population of Britain was far greater. Keeping the fleet commissioned throughout the year transformed the manpower problem, as well as many aspects of naval administration. The recruitment of large numbers of men required a streamlined administrative system that raised men more efficiently, yet did not tie down more naval resources than absolutely necessary. This was critically important during the early phases of war, when many ships had to be commissioned quickly.

The introduction of the Impress Service during the Seven Years' War began the most significant step towards a centralised manning process. Officers serving

---

[43] Rogers, *The Press Gang*, p. 31.
[44] Robinson, 'Secret of British Power', p. 6; N.A.M. Rodger, 'Officers and Men', in J.B. Hattendorf (ed.), *Maritime History: The Eighteenth Century and the Classic Age of Sail* (Malabar, 1997), p. 141; Rodger, 'A Little Navy of Your Own Making', p. 84; Usher Jr, 'Royal Navy Impressment', p. 684; Rodger, *Command of the Ocean*, p. 497.
[45] Usher Jr, 'Royal Navy Impressment', p. 682.
[46] Starkey, 'War and the Market for Seafarers in Britain', p. 37; Usher Jr, 'Royal Navy Impressment', p. 681.
[47] N.A.M. Rodger, *The Wooden World: An Anatomy of the Georgian Navy* (New York, 1996), pp. 150–1; Rodger, 'Officers and Men', p. 141; Starkey, 'War and the Market for Seafarers in Britain', p. 37.
[48] Dancy, *The Myth of the Press Gang*, p. 133.
[49] Starkey, 'War and the Market for Seafarers in Britain', p. 29.

aboard warships became less involved in manning their ships, and relied more on naval administration to fulfil this crucial role. The fact that naval manning became more centralised with each successive war during the eighteenth century suggests that this process, at least in the eyes of naval administrators, was more efficient and effective than relying on ships' officers to man their own vessels. The creation of the Impress Service proved essential in streamlining naval recruitment. The Impress Service was responsible for recruiting volunteers as well as pressing skilled seamen, and the importance of volunteers to the eighteenth-century Royal Navy is undeniable. This chapter has demonstrated that the number of volunteers serving in British warships was two or three times higher than had been previously considered, which helps explain why resistance to naval manning during the French Revolutionary Wars was comparatively rare.[50]

However, even though volunteers turned out in large numbers, the fact that labour-intensive sailing vessels demanded large numbers of experienced seamen – combined with the intense competition for the limited supply of men with maritime skill – meant that the Royal Navy could not recruit enough skilled men by relying solely upon volunteers.[51] Therefore, impressment was a necessary evil,[52] and seamen accepted naval conscription as an unavoidable aspect of naval life.[53] In all of the grievances of the mutineers at Spithead and the Nore in 1797, impressment was not mentioned.[54] In his own memoirs, William Spavens, who was pressed multiple times, showed no resentment of the press.[55] The British fleets of the French Revolutionary Wars were not manned by impressed men; rather, pressed men formed a supplement to a mainly volunteer force, and functioned to raise the overall skill level of the lower deck. Seamen were conscripted into the Royal Navy by press gangs because their skills were one of Britain's most prized military assets.[56] The introduction of the Impress Service was an essential element in the Admiralty's manpower strategy, which aimed to mobilise unprecedented numbers of skilled seamen in the century-long struggle against France. The Impress Service ensured that the ever-growing Royal Navy could be manned, not only during the Seven Years' War but through the conflicts that culminated with the Napoleonic Wars that consumed Europe half a century later.

Over the eighteenth century, the Royal Navy became the dominant power of the Atlantic, if not the world. By the French Revolutionary and Napoleonic Wars, Britain's ability to float a naval force that could fight simultaneously against the navies of all of Europe and the United States, throughout the Atlantic world,

---

[50] Dancy, *The Myth of the Press Gang*, pp. 56–119.
[51] Rogers, *The Press Gang*, p. 4.
[52] Baugh, *British Naval Administration in the Age of Walpole*, pp. 149, 159–61; Bromley, 'The British Navy and Its Seamen after 1688', p. 150; Lloyd, *The British Seaman*, pp. 149–51; Rodger, *The Wooden World*, p. 151.
[53] Rodger, *Command of the Ocean*, p. 499.
[54] Ibid., p. 447.
[55] W. Spavens, *Memoirs of a Seafaring Life: The Narrative of William Spavens, Pensioner on the Naval Chest at Chatham*, ed. N.A.M. Rodger (Bath, 2000), p. 12.
[56] Usher Jr, 'Royal Navy Impressment', p. 680.

and across the globe, was a direct result of the navy's ability to effectively man warships. This became especially important as a war of attrition set in and rival nations were effectively crippled by a shortage of seamen. Britain's ability to meet its manpower needs without recourse to significant financial or administrative disruption was a critical factor in its dominance at sea.[57] In the end, the Admiralty demonstrated that they were as concerned about the strategy of manning warships as they were about fighting them.

---

[57] Harding, *Seapower and Naval Warfare, 1650–1830*, p. 140.

6
British Naval Administration and the Quarterdeck Manpower Problem in the Eighteenth Century

EVAN WILSON

This chapter serves as the previous chapter's quarterdeck companion. It approaches the strategic issue of securing adequate manpower in the context of the officers rather than the men of the lower deck. But it does not examine all officers, despite using the term quarterdeck – the 'grand promenade of all the officers of the first class', which could include not only the lieutenants but also the purser, surgeon, master and chaplain.[1] There is not sufficient space to survey the labour market for all sea officers. For this chapter, the quarterdeck stands as a contrast with the lower deck explored in the previous chapter, and it refers only to the officers who were seamen and navigators: the commissioned officers and master.[2] Thus the 'quarterdeck manpower problem' of the title is the imbalance in the labour market for commissioned officers and masters.

Unlike the problem on the lower deck, described in the previous chapter as a persistent shortage of able seamen, the problem for naval administrators on the quarterdeck was a surplus of commissioned officers and a shortage of masters. Officers were not subject to impressment, of course, so naval administrators had to devise strategies to attract masters to the navy, while also coping with a significant waste of manpower resources. Admittedly, the stakes were lower: failing to man the fleet would have had catastrophic consequences, while leaving a few thousand officers ashore on half-pay was unlikely to play a significant role in shaping the outcome of conflicts. For this reason, manning and impressment have received a good deal of scholarly attention, but few historians have attempted to grapple with employment prospects on the quarterdeck.[3] But a shortage of masters was a serious problem. Examining the labour market for commissioned officers and

---

[1] H.G. Thursfield, ed., *Five Naval Journals, 1789–1817* (London, 1951), pp. 57–8.
[2] For a larger study of both warrant officers and commissioned officers, see E. Wilson, 'The Sea Officers: Gentility and Professionalism in the Royal Navy, 1775–1815' (DPhil Thesis, University of Oxford, 2015).
[3] The major exceptions are N.A.M. Rodger, 'Commissioned Officers' Careers in the Royal Navy, 1690–1815', *Journal for Maritime Research*, iii, no. 1 (2001), pp. 85–129, and C. Consolvo, 'The Prospects and Promotion of British Naval Officers, 1793–1815', *The Mariner's Mirror*, xci, no. 2 (2005), pp. 137–59. T. Wareham, *The Star Captains: Frigate Command in the Napoleonic Wars* (London, 2001), looks at employment for post-captains who commanded frigates.

masters demonstrates how naval administrators' strategic choices were constrained by contemporary notions of social status – a concern often overlooked by historians of administration and strategy. After providing some background on the similarities between masters and lieutenants, the chapter discusses the supply of and demand for officers before concluding with the Admiralty's response to the imbalance in the labour market and its strategic consequences.

Background and Rank Structure
The wardroom, or officer's mess, of a Royal Navy ship during the eighteenth century included officers' cabins, usually separated from the mess table by a canvas curtain. Towards the stern were the cabins of the most senior and important officers in the ship, after her captain: the first lieutenant and the master.[4] It is important to understand the administrative background to these two positions, as well as the navy's rank structure, because the imbalance in the labour market described later in this chapter hinges on the social and professional distinctions between these two positions.

Lieutenants are the most familiar position: commissioned by the Lords of the Admiralty on behalf of the sovereign, they supervised the everyday business of the ship. To reach their position, they had served at sea as a captain's servant, midshipman or master's mate for a minimum of six years, usually before they turned twenty. They were then eligible to sit the lieutenants' exam, which required them to demonstrate a good knowledge of seamanship and navigation. Lieutenants hoped one day to be promoted to commander and given command of one of the smaller ships in the navy, such as a sloop or brig. The next step up the ladder was to be promoted to post-captain, at which point they would be eligible to command frigates and ships of the line. The existing historiography has focused on these captains and the admirals above them.[5] But most officers – more than 60 per cent – were only ever lieutenants, not commanders or captains, and so one of the goals of this chapter is to call attention to the thousands of ordinary lieutenants who toiled in relative obscurity but were essential to naval operations.

There are no existing scholarly studies focused exclusively on masters, so they require a lengthier description. In the medieval navy, masters were analogous to commissioned officers: as the title 'master' suggests, they were once in command of ships. Eighteenth-century masters were little different in terms of their skill set and background from their medieval predecessors, but the navy around them had changed. No longer were masters the only experts in seamanship and navigation on board, as they had been until the seventeenth century. In the late sixteenth

---

[4] They claimed those cabins because in large ships they often included windows and the most convenient access to the officer's latrine. B. Lavery, *The 74-gun Ship Bellona*, rev. edn (London, 2003), p. 80.
[5] See, for example, Wareham, *Star Captains*; N. Tracy, *Who's Who in Nelson's Navy: 200 Naval Heroes* (London, 2006); or any of the hundreds of biographies of Nelson and his 'band of brothers'.

century, gentlemen captains began to seize the opportunities offered by trans-oceanic navigation and the administrative and financial support of the state to infringe on the professional territory of masters. By the 1630s, gentlemen captains began to consider the navy as a career. The creation of the rank of lieutenant particularly rankled masters because it created a parallel career structure and path to command. Some masters did manage to become captains – the famous so-called 'tarpaulins' – but more were crowded out by the influx of career-oriented young men of good birth.[6] Though the conflict between gentlemen and tarpaulin captains had been largely resolved by the creation of a professional standard for commissioned officers at the end of the seventeenth century, eighteenth-century masters were leftover casualties of that conflict. If commissioned officers could sail and navigate, then masters, who held warrants from the Navy Board rather than commissions derived ultimately from the sovereign, were redundant. Yet masters endured throughout the period and were considered essential for all ships. Bureaucratic momentum is surely one explanation, but another is that it was not possible to have too many experienced sailors and navigators on board. Michael Lewis has a useful turn of phrase: '[T]he main quality required of a Master was trustworthiness, for no one on board, perhaps, had so many opportunities of drowning the whole Ship's Company.'[7] Captains often relied heavily on their expertise, as Master Thomas Fotheringham remembered from his experience at the Battle of Copenhagen in 1801: 'My Captain, being all anxiety to get up, stated that my honour was at stake as well as his ... and desired to know what was best to be done.'[8]

Masters had such an important place in the shipboard hierarchy because they were the only warrant officers who normally stood watches. A master's daily responsibilities therefore included four or more hours spent as the senior officer on duty. At noon, he joined the commissioned officers and midshipmen on the quarterdeck to measure the distance from the sun to the horizon. He recorded his calculation of the ship's position in his log, as well as the state of the wind and weather. In all matters of navigation, the master was second only to the captain in importance. He was also one of only three men, along with the captain and the first lieutenant, who signed all the important documents of the ship such as the muster and pay books.[9] Robert Wilson described the duty of a master as navigation first, followed by 'to be a check on the purser' by inspecting the ship's books. 'He is on par with the lieutenants,' Wilson wrote.[10] Captain Graham Moore also emphasised the degree to which commissioned officers could rely on masters when he confidently left a ship fitting for sea to go visit a friend ashore because, he wrote, 'the duty would go on equally as well under the eye of the Master'.[11]

---

[6] N.A.M. Rodger, *The Safeguard of the Sea: A Naval History of Britain, 660–1649* (London, 1999), pp. 137–9, 160, 304–6, 409–10.
[7] M. Lewis, *A Social History of the Navy, 1793–1815* (London, 1960), pp. 240–1.
[8] TNA, ADM 11/2 (Admiralty: Officers' Service Records (Series I). Survey of Masters' Services, Nos. 3–249, 1833–35).
[9] Lewis, *Social History*, pp. 240–1.
[10] *Five Naval Journals*, pp. 250, 337–8.
[11] T. Wareham, *Frigate Commander* (Barnsley, 2004), pp. 29, 5. Masters' exams were thorough

Given the similarities in responsibilities, as well as the transformation of commissioned officers into navigators, it is unsurprising to find that masters often had early careers largely indistinguishable from commissioned officers. George Forbes joined the navy as an able seaman in 1787, a rating common to many future commissioned officers even though, as boys, they were not actually capable of performing the duties of an able seaman. Over the next five years, Forbes's captains gave him a wide range of ratings, which was also common for future commissioned officers. He also spent time as a midshipman in 1795 and an acting lieutenant in 1796 before receiving his first warrant as a master.[12] Up until he became a master, his early career mirrored that of a future lieutenant. Frederick Ruckert is another good example. The description of his career enclosed in his application to qualify as master of a fifth rate is worth quoting in full:

> In 1793 he entered on board the *Speedy* at Gibraltar and was immediately moved into the *Vanneau* Brig and continued in her till 1796 when he was moved as midshipman into the *Captain* and from her as Second Master in the *Ville-de-Paris*, when he was appointed by Sir John Jervis Master of the *Mutine*.[13]

Both Ruckert and Forbes may have initially entertained thoughts of passing the lieutenants' exam and earning a commission. Masters and lieutenants shared similar training experiences, and many were even rated the same as each other as young men. Master's mate was a rating common to both groups. Furthermore, even after they separated into those with commissions and those with warrants, their responsibilities on board were similar.

Nevertheless, the two groups remained separate, and Admiralty administrators had to deal with each group differently. There were two key distinctions between lieutenants and masters. First, lieutenants had opportunities for upward mobility. Promotion to commander carried with it an increase in pay and responsibility, in addition to the courtesy title of 'Captain'. Promotion to post-captain ensured that, if the officer lived long enough, he would die an admiral. It also provided vastly increased opportunities for prize money, as a captain's share of a prize was double the share split among all of the ship's lieutenants and the master.[14] Masters could also be promoted, but usually only into a larger ship or to a shore appointment,

---

and challenging, perhaps even more so than the lieutenants' exam. A transcript of a master's examination from 1780 survives in the papers of HMS *Dryad*, which was a navigation school in the early twentieth century. It is impressively exhaustive: the examiners asked more than one hundred questions about every major anchorage in the English Channel, and expected very precise answers. As a result, masters boasted extensive knowledge of Britain's home waters. NMM, DRY/10 (H.M.S. *Dryad*, 1780).

[12] TNA, ADM 36/16549 (Admiralty: Royal Navy Ships' Musters (Series I). Ship: SWIFTSURE, 1805); TNA, ADM 29/1/60 (Admiralty: Royal Navy, Royal Marines, Coastguard and related services: Officers' and Ratings' Service Records (Series II). Navy Pay Office: Entry Books of Certificates of Service, 1802–14).

[13] TNA, ADM 6/161 (Admiralty: Service Records, Registers, Returns and Certificates. Masters' Passing Certificates, statements of service, 1800–50).

[14] D.K. Benjamin, 'Golden Harvest: The British Naval Prize System, 1793–1815', Unpublished paper, 2009.

such as superintending master of a dockyard. The most famous exception proves the rule. James Bowen, master of Lord Howe's flagship at the Glorious First of June in 1794, saved the admiral and his flagship from an embarrassing and dangerous collision at the height of the battle. Howe gave Bowen the opportunity to choose his reward, and he selected a commission as a lieutenant, even though he was to be placed at the bottom of the seniority list. For an ambitious officer, the opportunity to progress up the ranks with a commission was of greater value than the prospect of a shore appointment with a warrant.

Bowen's decision highlights the second distinction between masters and lieutenants: the social value of a commission exceeded the social value of a warrant. As servants of the crown, commissioned officers benefited from the ancient association of aristocracy with military service. In the late eighteenth century, only a tiny percentage were sons of the aristocracy, but it was understood that commissioned officers were gentlemen. Edward Barker, an aspiring lieutenant, addressed the heart of the issue in a letter to his uncle: a commission, he said, was equivalent to 'an independency and the rank of gentleman in every society and in every country'.[15] Barker's letter, cited frequently in the existing literature, has tended to obscure the social value of a warrant, and indeed many warrant officers claimed to be gentlemen. But contemporaries would not have equated a warrant with gentility, nor would they have been as confident in its value as Barker was about a commission. Masters came from backgrounds not dissimilar from many of their colleagues in the wardroom, but a commission carried greater social prestige than a warrant.[16] Thus masters and lieutenants remained distinct groups during the eighteenth century, despite the similarities in their backgrounds, training and professional responsibilities.

Supply and Demand
The prospects of promotion and the social value of a commission meant that the navy was never short of commissioned officers, and by the end of the century it had far too many. For much of the eighteenth century, the number of commissioned officers and the number of positions on ships on active duty had tracked each other fairly closely. In peacetime, unemployment was rampant as the navy demobilised. But in wartime, the market seems to have reached an equilibrium through to the end of the American War in 1783. After that, though, the supply of officers outstripped the navy's demand. Figure 6.1 shows the relationship between successful lieutenants' exam and commissions from 1775 to 1805, as derived from two different samples of more than five hundred officers.[17]

Passing the lieutenants' exam only made the candidate eligible for a commission, so many passed master's mates received their first commissions at the outbreak

---

[15] *British Naval Documents, 1204–1960*, ed. J.B. Hattendorf et al. (Aldershot, 1993), p. 546.
[16] Wilson, 'The Sea Officers', chs 2 and 3.
[17] Personal correspondence between Rodger and the author. Rodger, 'Commissioned Officers' Careers', p. 99 and Wilson, 'The Sea Officers', introduction.

British Naval Administration and the Quarterdeck 69

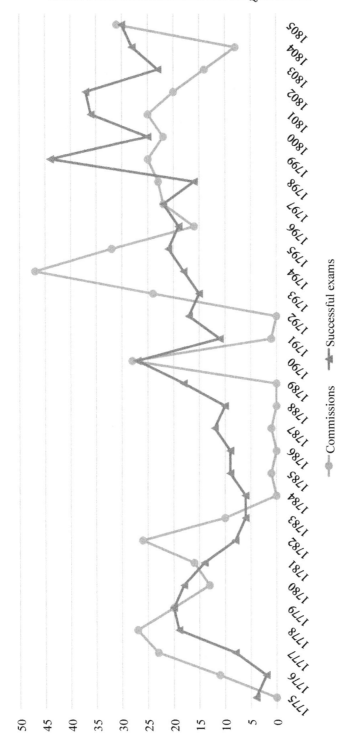

Figure 6.1: Lieutenants' commissions and successful exams, 1775–1805

of major wars. During the American War, the two data sets are closely matched: there are more commissions than successful exams, but that reflects the presence of men who had passed their lieutenants' exam before 1775. When the two data sets diverge, they do so for predictable reasons. During the peace following the American War, for example, more officers passed than were commissioned. This suggests that even though there was little hope of obtaining a commission, aspiring officers nevertheless sat lieutenants' exams so as to be eligible for one when the navy mobilised again. These men received many of the commissions in the spikes of 1790 – the Nootka Sound mobilisation – and 1793.

The problem of the oversupply of commissioned officers appears towards the end of the French Revolutionary War, as Figure 6.1 shows. The navy's popularity was clearly rising. There were three factors, in addition to the attractiveness of a naval commission mentioned earlier, that likely spurred the increase in the supply of available lieutenants. Prince William Henry's presence in the officer corps, the series of great fleet victories from 1794 to 1805, and the emergence of heroic, celebrity officers such as Nelson helped encourage families to send their sons to sea. It is not possible to explore all these topics in depth here. Instead, let us focus on the root of the problem, which was that the Admiralty did not place any restrictions on how many candidates could sit the lieutenants' exam. Captains controlled officer entry, and it was one of their most prized prerogatives. It was a useful way to exercise patronage by bringing the sons of important people on board. The most common entrants were sons of naval officers, as captains tended to look out for the sons of their friends, colleagues and superiors. Because captains could introduce large numbers of young gentlemen into the navy, enter them on their books in a variety of ratings and then encourage them to prepare for the lieutenants' exam, the Admiralty had no reliable way of predicting how many men would sit it.

Administrators approached the problem of decentralised officer entry indirectly by founding the Royal Naval Academy in Portsmouth in 1733. The Admiralty controlled the Academy, and by extension a percentage of the pool of future officers. But it was always too small and too expensive, and only 2 per cent of all commissioned officers were graduates. It provided very little benefit to graduates because it only saved two of the six required years of sea experience. It also had a poor reputation: its students were notorious for drinking and frequenting brothels in Portsmouth. It was eventually reconstituted as the much more successful Royal Naval College in 1806, but it came too late to solve the problem in the Napoleonic Wars. The Admiralty's next attempt to gain control of officer entry was Lord Spencer's introduction of three classes of boys and volunteers in 1794. Third-class boys were to be domestic servants, second-class boys were to be future enlisted men, and only first-class boys, who were required to be sons of gentlemen, could become officers. By limiting the number of first-class volunteer appointments, the Admiralty hoped to gain some measure of control over officer entry. But the beginning of two decades of war, when the navy was fully mobilised and captains exercised a good deal of independence, was the wrong time to introduce this reform. Captains simply ignored the classifications, moving boys from one to the other as spaces became available. Thus the Admiralty's attempts to regulate the labour market for commissioned officers on the supply side largely failed. Hundreds and eventually thousands more young men than could be employed sat and passed the lieutenants exam.

Even though the scale of the French Revolutionary and Napoleonic Wars was greater than that of any previous conflict, it was not enough to keep available appointments on pace with the influx of potential officers. Using data from the Admiralty list books, it is possible to take a systematic approach to analysing officers' employment prospects. Seniority lists were notoriously unreliable and filled with officers unfit for service, but they are the only convenient method of counting commissioned officers. I have combined five-year snapshots of the number of officers at each rank with estimates of the number of positions available, derived from the summaries at the end of the month of January in the Admiralty's list book. The two exceptions were 1790 and 1813. In the former case, I used November's list book to capture the Nootka Sound mobilisation; in the latter, the Admiralty stopped compiling list books after July 1813, so it was not possible to cover 1815 in the same way. Rated ships equated to one position for a post-captain; non-rated vessels categorised as 'sloops' produced one position for a commander. Lieutenants' positions were the most challenging to estimate. The formula used is shown in Table 6.1. Figure 6.2 estimates the ratio of the number of officers to the available active-duty positions in five-year snapshots.

Table 6.1: Estimate of Lieutenants' Positions by Rate

1st Rate	7 Lieutenants
2nd Rate	6 Lieutenants
3rd Rate	5 Lieutenants
4th Rate	4 Lieutenants
5th Rate	3 Lieutenants
6th Rate	2 Lieutenants
Sloops	1 Lieutenant
Other vessels, including store ships, armed vessels, fire ships, schooners, etc.	1 Lieutenant

Briefly summarised, peacetime employment prospects were very poor, with ratios of five or more officers to each available position common across all ranks. During the American War, lieutenants were likely to be employed, and lieutenants perform consistently better than commander and captains throughout the period. However, during the Great Wars, even lieutenants could expect two officers for every available position, indicating an unemployment rate of roughly 50 per cent. Commanders' prospects are generally the poorest, though they get better towards the end of the Wars.[18] Commissioned officers were an

---

18 The likely cause is the expansion of the small-ship navy towards the end of the Napoleonic

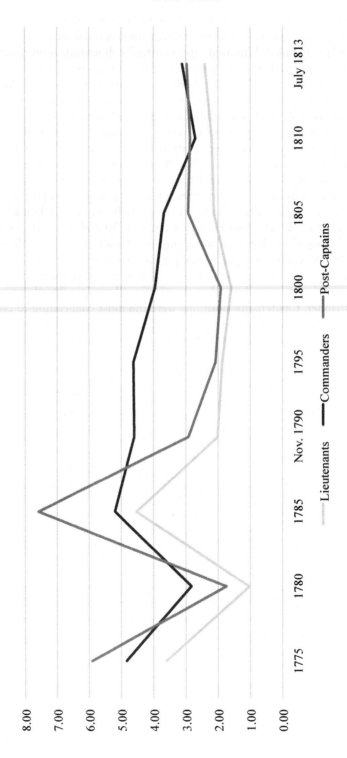

Figure 6.2: Ratio of number of officers to positions available

underutilised resource – not a luxury that Britain could afford in more than two decades of war for her own survival.

The 50 per cent unemployment rate for lieutenants suggested by Figure 6.2 does not take into account shore-based appointments such as signal stations and the bloated nature of the seniority list.[19] Nor were all lieutenants equally likely to be unemployed. Older officers in particular often struggled to remain active.[20] John Smith was thirty-six when he received his commission in 1793, and he only managed to secure employment on two ships. His seagoing career ended in 1795, but he was still ready to answer an Admiralty survey in 1817 and he lived until 1835.[21] He is also a good example of the challenges presented by Admiralty record keeping, since he appeared on the active list throughout the Wars despite twenty years of unemployment. With each passing year, his employment grew less and less likely. Youth did not guarantee employment, though: William Mercer was commissioned when he was twenty-five, and he spent a few weeks as a lieutenant on board the frigate *Polyphemus* in May 1794; the remainder of his active service in the navy was as the commander of first the *Dolphin* and then the *Dover*, both cutters operating in the Channel. After the Peace of Amiens, he was ashore, unemployed, for the duration of the Napoleonic Wars.[22] A lieutenant's first commission usually ensured employment once, and employment tended to be easier to secure in the first five years of a lieutenant's career. But it was never guaranteed: half of the lieutenants in one sample were unemployed in 1810, and those who had been commissioned most recently were most likely to be unemployed.[23] In 1817, the Admiralty surveyed officers' careers by asking them to list the positions they had held. Slightly more than half of the lieutenants from a sample of those surveys spent at least five wartime years unemployed.[24]

In contrast, the navy suffered from a shortage of masters. In particular, as the Navy Board reminded the Admiralty in 1821, the navy needed masters for its smallest ships: 'We request that you acquaint the Lords Commissioners of the Admiralty that the difficulty of procuring suitable Masters for small Vessels, which was so much felt during the War, has not been removed since its termination.'[25] Most masters began their careers in sloops and brigs, but they were paid significantly less than masters of larger ships. Higher pay was a good incentive to pass for a larger ship. The problem was that once a master had passed for a high

---

Wars: in other words, a change in the denominator rather than the numerator. But this topic needs further research.

[19] Consolvo, 'Prospects and Promotion', p. 144.
[20] Rodger, 'Commissioned Officers' Careers', p. 99.
[21] TNA, ADM 107/9/177 (Navy Board: Royal Navy Passing Certificates, Examination Results, and Certificates of Service. Lieutenants' Passing Certificates, 1775–1805); TNA, ADM 9/6/1787 (Admiralty: Survey Returns of Officers' Services, 1817–28); P. Marioné, *The Complete Navy List of the Napoleonic Wars, 1793–1815*, CDROM (Brussels, 2004), s.v. 'Smith, Commander (Rtd) John (04) (d. 1835)'.
[22] TNA, ADM 9/6/1798.
[23] Rodger, 'Commissioned Officers' Careers', p. 99.
[24] TNA, ADM 9/1–17.
[25] TNA, ADM 106/3571 (Navy Board: Records. MISCELLANEOUS, 26 September 1821).

rate, he was not likely to want to return to serving in a small ship. David Blackburn reluctantly accepted a warrant as master of the *Supply*, which was headed to Australia with the First Fleet in 1787. He complained to his sister, 'She is a brigg [*sic*] and I shall be paid only as a sixth rate viz. £5 per month, which of itself is a hardship as I have passed for a third rate which is £7 monthly.'[26] In the peacetime employment market, Blackburn had no choice but to accept the appointment.

In wartime, Blackburn would have had more options. In 1799, there were 716 masters on the Admiralty's seniority list; in 1806, the number had dropped to 559, and then it rose to 615 in 1809.[27] Not all of these men were able and willing to serve, so the number available for active duty was probably lower. But out of a sample of more than one hundred of these masters, only 18 per cent of them spent significant time – more than two months – fit for service but unemployed during wartime. That percentage does not indicate an unemployment rate; rather, it suggests that over 80 per cent of masters were employed whenever they were fit and willing. Furthermore, few of the 18 per cent who did experience unemployment remained unemployed for the rest of their careers, as was the case with Lieutenants Mercer and Smith.

Strategy and the Quarterdeck Manpower Problem

In theory, the imbalance in the quarterdeck labour market was easy to solve. In 1806 the First Lord of the Admiralty was receiving on average twelve to fifteen petitions per day from unemployed officers seeking postings.[28] At the same time, the First Lord desperately needed men to serve as masters. Many of the petitioners had the skills, training and experience necessary to be masters. But the First Lord did not attempt to move unemployed lieutenants into vacant masters' warrants, nor could he consider doing so. Such a move would have been socially unacceptable to the majority of lieutenants. None of the lieutenants in the 1817 survey became masters when they could no longer secure employment at sea. Instead, they joined the Impress Service, became transport agents or commanded signal stations. Those postings, though clearly inferior to sea service, were marginally acceptable to lieutenants; becoming a master was not. The social barrier between commissions and warrants therefore constrained the Admiralty's options when it came to grappling with the supply and demand of officers. Too many officers sought commissions, while too few sought warrants; encouraging downward social mobility was not possible. The result was that many commissioned officers' careers stalled at the rank of lieutenant. They operated under the assumption, which few would have discussed or thought about consciously, that

---

[26] D. Neville, *Blackburn's Isle* (Lavenham, 1975), p. 116.
[27] TNA, ADM 6/132 (Admiralty: Service Records, Registers, Returns and Certificates. Seniority List of Masters, with previous services, 1809); TNA, ADM 118/190 (Admiralty: Officers Seniority Lists. Masters, 1791).
[28] R. Knight, *Britain Against Napoleon: The Organisation of Victory, 1793–1815* (London, 2013), p. 235.

it was better, socially, to be an unemployed lieutenant on half-pay than a gainfully employed master.

The Admiralty, aware of the social constraints, took two uncertain and halting steps to address the problem. First, in the middle of the brief Peace of Amiens, the Admiralty ordered that no person who had served as a master could sit the lieutenants' exam.[29] Recall that masters' and lieutenants' early careers were similar: both were frequently midshipmen and master's mates before earning their warrant or commission. By preventing masters from becoming eligible to be lieutenants, the Admiralty hoped to limit the oversupply of lieutenants and halt the exodus of masters. The regulation lasted only two years, though: in 1805, the Navy Board recommended that it should be suspended, and proposed an alternative step: make a career as a master more attractive.[30] The Admiralty implemented the Navy Board's recommendation and addressed both of the barriers separating lieutenants from masters identified earlier. First, they attempted to elevate the social status of warrant officers by improving their uniforms. Warrant officers had only had uniforms since 1787, but the reforms of 1805 revised the pattern to make it more similar to commissioned officers'. A group of physicians led the campaign that resulted in the new uniforms. They demanded recognition of the rank they held 'in the Service and Society'; masters were beneficiaries of their campaign.[31] The second reform in 1805 addressed the gap between the earning potential of a lieutenant, via promotion, and a warrant officer. Masters received a significant pay rise, such that on average and across all rates they now made 37 per cent more than they had for the entire eighteenth century. The master of a third-rate ship of the line earned about £82 annually before the rise, and £137 after. The master of a first-rate now earned more than the captain of a fifth-rate frigate.[32]

As we saw with the letter from the Navy Board to the Admiralty in 1821, though, these reforms were largely unsuccessful. Masters remained in high demand throughout the Wars, while lieutenants continued to struggle to find employment. The social value of a commission compared to that of a warrant constrained the Admiralty's choices. The imbalance in the labour market had an obvious solution, but it was not available to ministers. Unlike manning the lower deck, which was the first concern at the beginning of every war, quarterdeck labour market concerns were secondary. But ministers could not ignore the problem, as dozens of petitions for employment crossed their desks daily. On the other side of the petition, for the men who hoped to be employed on those quarterdecks, the imbalance in the labour market was fundamental. There was a human cost to the supply and demand dynamic.

---

[29] TNA, ADM 49/131 (Wages Branch: Book of Admiralty Orders, 1802–11), 31 October 1802, to be enforced 1 May 1803.
[30] TNA, ADM 12/117 (Admiralty: Digests and Indexes. Digest (71–104), 1805), 19 June, 8 July and 15 August 1805.
[31] Quoted in D. Jarrett, *British Naval Dress* (London, 1960), pp. 63–4.
[32] N.A.M. Rodger, *The Command of the Ocean: A Naval History of Britain, 1649–1815* (London, 2004), pp. 622–8.

7
The Raison d'Être and the Actual Employment of the Dutch Navy in Early Modern Times*

JAAP R. BRUIJN

Formulating the raison d'être for the Dutch Navy in early modern times is not difficult. The Low Countries and later the Dutch Republic bordered the North Sea, and on the inland side the Zuyder Zee. Salt water offered possibilities for invasion or raids from overseas. The Dutch themselves used the sea for merchant shipping and fisheries. They were eager to open the whole world for their economic activities. Naval forces were the foremost safeguard against invasion. Protection of commercial shipping and fisheries required convoys. Overseas expansion required offensive sea power.

The Sixteenth Century

The Habsburg rulers of the Netherlands, Charles V and Philip II, started the organisation of regular naval forces. The city of Veere in Zeeland became the centre of all their naval activities. At some periods there were even some permanent warships. Differences of interests between the provinces hampered the introduction of fixed convoys on shipping routes to western and southern Europe and also for the fisheries, but some occasional state protection could nevertheless be provided.[1] The incursions of the Protestant rebels called 'Sea Beggars' from 1566 to 1572 proved the vulnerability of the coastal areas along the North Sea and Zuyder Zee. Hereafter, nobody in the rebellious North and in the loyal South had to be convinced that a navy was an absolute necessity.

In the North it was impossible to establish one centralised naval organisation. Provincial and local interests, the accidents of war and simple power politics created five different admiralties, located in the three maritime provinces of Zeeland, Holland and Friesland, and specifically in the cities of Middelburg, Rotterdam, Amsterdam, Hoorn or Enkhuizen, and Dokkum, later Harlingen. The newly born Republic badly needed naval forces in a war that would last for eighty years until 1648. Spain and the Southern Netherlands, and in particular the Dunkirk privateers, represented a constant threat, not only by numerous raids

---

* Much to my comfort, Richard W. Unger (University of British Columbia, Vancouver) has inspected my English text.
[1] L. Sicking, *Neptune and the Netherlands: State, Economy, and the War at Sea in the Renaissance* (Leiden, 2004).

and invasions, but also by their efficient attacks on herring and other fishing boats, and of course on all kinds of merchantmen. The enemy endangered the Dutch economy, which was growing very fast in particular from the 1590s. The Dutch entered into the Mediterranean trades and crossed the equator. Naval protection was required on an increasing number of trading routes. The variety of types and the number of warships were great. In 1596 the navy had 140 vessels; only 14 were bigger than 200 tons. About thirty years later, in 1628, the navy had 124 ships, half of them over 200 tons.[2] Year after year this fleet blockaded the Flemish coast and cruised in the North Sea and the Channel in search of Dunkirk privateers. It also convoyed merchantmen and fishermen, by this time into the Mediterranean as well.

The Dutch Republic was a small country in territory, with not more than 1.5 million inhabitants. The naval forces had to be paid as well as the land forces, which needed twice as much money as the navy.[3] Where did this money come from? Always from the commercial world, that was supposed to profit from the navy's protection. Almost at the start of the rebellion against the king of Spain – in 1573 – the so-called *licenten* were introduced, permitting trade with the enemy in the South.[4] The total yield by the issue of these permissions (*licenten*) was earmarked for naval protection, thus for convoy escorts and their fitting out. This system soon developed into a whole scheme of duties paid by the commercial world, the so-called *convooien en licenten*, functioning as import and export duties, later extended by the so-called *last- en veilgelden*, levies on the tonnage and total value of goods of each vessel. This total yield could be used by the five admiralties straight away. Warfare itself was funded in a totally different way. In time of war this money was made available by the seven provinces, according to a distributive code, and after a unanimous decision by the States General.

In sharp contrast to our present world with its ever-changing logos, names and institutions, the five admiralties and all their peculiarities never changed for more than two centuries until 1795. French revolutionary soldiers then brought about more change than numerous generations of distinguished early modern politicians. The only major change occurred in 1645 when the Frisian Admiralty at Dokkum was moved to Harlingen, because Dokkum's link with the sea had silted up.

The Navy in its Dutch Context
The late Jan Glete from Stockholm University first pointed out the contradiction between the apparent weakness of the decentralised naval and financial organisation of the Dutch Republic, and the size of its seventeenth-century fleet and its

---

[2] P. Groen et al., eds, *Militaire Geschiedenis van Nederland – De tachtigjarige Oorlog (1568–1648). Van Opstand naar geregelde oorlog* (Amsterdam, 2013), p. 330.
[3] Ibid., p. 386.
[4] Ibid., pp. 73, 145 and 211. See also Jaap R. Bruijn, *The Dutch Navy of the Seventeenth and Eighteenth Centuries*, rev. edn (St. John's Newfoundland, 2011), pp. 6–7.

frequent and often successful warfare. He discovered the apparent advantages of having five admiralties in the pre-industrial age, which made a strong navy possible.[5] These advantages lost their impact in the eighteenth century.

Naval forces were absolutely essential during the Eighty Years' War, and thereafter during the different conflicts with England, Sweden, Denmark, Portugal and France. In the seventeenth century the Dutch Republic was one of the great powers in Europe. It could not stand aside from what happened in its neighbourhood. The rulers in the Republic fully recognised the need for a good navy and were willing to pay for it – though not always on time and for the full amount agreed upon in the States General. And by and large, the Dutch economy was flourishing. An influential part of the governing 'regents' of the cities of Holland and Zeeland still had strong connections with trade and shipping. Either they were merchants and shipowners themselves, or they had family relations in that world. Losses of mercantile vessels, taken by the enemy, could be a strain on their own resources.

Despite the decentralised structure of government in the Republic, important decisions could be taken efficiently. Most members of boards knew each other. There was a regular circuit of meetings at local, provincial and national levels. Water divides, but also unites. Transport by inland barges could be fast. Implementation of decisions and orders was often next door. In 1690, upon receipt of the States General's instruction to start building new ships, the Amsterdam Admiralty Board ordered the head of the shipyard to buy a quantity of specified timber. A few hours later he reported the purchase at 7,590 guilders![6] Good leadership was most of the time available. During the strenuous decades of the 1650s and 1660s Grand Pensionary Jan de Witt was the central figure and leader of the state. He understood the importance of naval power in his days. Later Job and his son David de Wildt, successive Secretaries of the Amsterdam Admiralty, succeeded in coordinating the five admiralties' activities. A group of highly qualified flag officers was successful in welding the different squadrons together, Michiel de Ruyter being the most well known.

These great assets of the seventeenth century – the self-interest and sense of responsibility of the regents, the availability of financial means, speed when required and good leadership ashore and at sea – were gone in the eighteenth century. The Republic was completely exhausted at the end of the War of the Spanish Succession.[7] After the Battle of Malaga in 1704 the Dutch did not fight again until the Battle of Dogger Bank in 1781. As a fighting force the Dutch Navy had ceased to exist. How could this occur?

The French pursuit of hegemony in Europe had ended with Louis XIV. After his death a new pattern of power balances between states had been created, later

---

[5] J. Glete, *War and the State in Early Modern Europe: Spain, the Dutch Republic and Sweden as Fiscal-Military States, 1500–1660* (London and New York, 2002), ch. 4.
[6] J.C. de Jonge, *Geschiedenis van het Nederlandsche Zeewezen*, 2nd edn (Haarlem, 1860), vol. iii, note 2 on p. 120.
[7] John B. Hattendorf, *England in the War of the Spanish Succession: A Study of the English View and Conduct of Grand Strategy, 1702–1712* (New York and London, 1987).

formalised in new alliances between states stronger than the Republic, which had lost its value as an ally. The bonds with Great Britain slackened, eventually ending in a war, the Fourth Anglo-Dutch War of 1780.

In the country itself, conflicting ideas about foreign policy took shape, culminating in a deadlock between a pro-British and a pro-French attitude. This choice was connected with a reinforcement of the army or the navy.[8] But a choice was not made. The discussions went on and on, proving that statesmen of any stature were lacking. The ruling class was no longer interested in the economy. The safety of the state itself was not a point of concern. In 1747, French troops crossed the southern border. Old treaties with Britain provided military support, and the brief scare was soon over. The Republic chose neutrality in the Seven Years' War. Britain then dictated at the expense of Dutch shipping what rights neutral mercantile vessels would be entitled to.

Hardly any regent believed in the possibility of war. This is illustrated by a proposal of 1771 for new naval construction. Only ships fit for convoy service, fourth and fifth rates, were mentioned, no bigger ships. It remained only a proposal because of the paralysis of the political system.[9] No urgency was felt to take steps for repairing or improving either army or navy. The sole concern of eighteenth-century members of the admiralty boards was the fitting out on time of convoy escorts and a few special expeditions.

The Navy as a Battle Force
On the eve of the Second Anglo-Dutch War in 1665 the two biggest navies in Europe were going to be at loggerheads. The English Navy had ninety ships bigger than 500 tons; the Dutch had seventy-nine. Their second position behind England was soon taken over by the French Navy. In 1700 the Dutch still had the third strongest navy: 83 ships of the line; France had 108 and England 127. During the seventeenth century no other European state could equip navies of a comparable size.

The eighteenth century shows a completely different picture in which the then British Navy was still leading. Behind the numbers of ships is hidden a spectacular growth in the size and armament of ships of the line as well as of frigates and cruisers. The Republic could not fully follow this enlargement of warships because of declining funds, and the restricted depths of the waterways to and from most of its admiralties. From the end of the War of the Spanish Succession in 1713 the Dutch Republic was rapidly dropping behind the other major sea powers, Great Britain and France, but also behind the newcomers Spain and Russia in the Baltic – not only in sheer numbers of ships, but also in their size and their armament. Table 7.1 gives information about the number of ships.

Did the first-rate navy of the seventeenth century and the second-rate navy of

---

[8] J.S. Bartstra, *Vlootherstel en legeraugmentatie 1770–1780* (Assen, 1952).
[9] Ibid., p. 60.

Table 7.1: The numerical strength of leading navies in the seventeenth and eighteenth centuries

Date	England/Great Britain	France	Dutch Republic	Spain	Russia
1630	38 (24+14)	57 (16+41)	–	–	–
1665	143 (90+53)	47 (32+15)	115 (79+36)	–	–
1700	177 (127+50)	146 (108+38)	113 (83+30)	–	–
1740	154 (101+53)	59 (47+12)	59 (35+24)	59 (43+16)	31 (20+11)
1770	235 (126+109)	127 (68+59)	75 (31+44)	95 (55+40)	39 (27+12)
1790	312 (145+167)	179 (73+106)	100 (48+52)	145 (72+73)	91 (51+40)

Source: J. Glete, Navies and Nations: Warships, Navies and State Building in Europe and America, 1500–1800, (Stockholm 1993), vol. ii: English/British Navy, pp. 550–3, French Navy pp. 575–9, Dutch Navy, pp. 639–41, Spanish Navy, pp. 629–30 and Russian Navy, pp. 654–5. The first number in brackets refers to ships of more than 500 tons, the so-called ships of the line, the second number refers to ships from 100 to 500 tons, often frigates, later called cruisers. The Russian figures only relate to the Baltic fleet. For the open spaces (–) Glete gives no information.

the eighteenth century have a raison d'être for the Republic? Was there a correlation between being first big and becoming later small? One has to consider the Republic's position amongst the other European states. During the seventeenth century there was seldom a long spell of peace. The Republic was almost constantly involved in a long list of wars: with Spain till 1648, with England three times (1652–54, 1665–67 and 1672–74), with France 1672–78 and 1688–97, with Denmark and Sweden between 1645 and 1660 and with Portugal (1657–61). In 1672 the very existence of the Republic was at stake, when England and France jointly attacked the Republic, supported by two German princes. The navy's contribution to the salvation of the country by preventing Anglo-French invasions from the sea was enormous. The wars against England, Denmark/Sweden and Portugal were fought at sea. The later conflicts with France were mainly centred around dynastic issues and the balance of power on the Continent. The Anglo-Dutch Wars called for the highest input of naval forces. There could be no doubt about the navy's raison d'être! For some time England and the Republic were more or less equal to each other in the frequent sea battles. The first war ended in a Dutch defeat, the second with the raid on the Medway, England's humiliation. In the third conflict England only provoked the fall of Grand Pensionary Jan de Witt and the rise of its future king William III from an unemployed nobleman to the rank of Stadtholder. After its principal role during the invasion of England in 1688, the navy only had a supporting role in the Nine Years' War and the War of the Spanish Succession. During those two wars English flag officers were in command in joint operations, though they were in the initial phase often impressed by the superior quality of their Dutch colleagues.

Though only playing second fiddle, huge fleets had nevertheless to be equipped.

Ships, crews and armaments were bigger than ever before, but it became impossible to support the financial burden. The province of Holland, whose proportion of naval expenses amounted to 60 per cent, contributed 40 million guilders in the Nine Years' War and 65 million in the second one, both times less than officially required.

After the Peace of Utrecht in 1713 the navy played only a restricted role in European politics and warfare. For long periods a battle fleet was non-existent, and only during the Fourth Anglo-Dutch War were a solid number of ships of the line built. In 1781 the provinces paid for their construction, for the first time in decades. The war and the problems generated by the closure of the Scheldt made it obvious to the authorities in The Hague that more warships had to be available. Holland paid almost the whole sum asked for (7 million guilders). As mentioned before, ten years earlier (1771) a smaller subsidy had been refused. The history of the Dutch Navy's activities during the eighteenth century is the tale of convoy protection by individual or two or three small ships of the line and frigates. For this the yield of the fiscal duties was just or barely sufficient. Some financial support from the provinces was only given for a number of special squadrons during short conflicts in which the Republic got involved.[10]

The Convoying Task

Providing convoy by the navy was a kind of *silent* service to the world of trade, shipping and fisheries. A world, that in an indirect way financed this service by paying the *convooien en licenten* and *last- en veilgelden*. For its beginnings we again have to go back to the sixteenth century. In the early 1520s convoying began of private ships to protect them against hostile attacks either during the voyage or on the fishing grounds. At the instigation of the central government in Brussels the provinces of Flanders, Zeeland and Holland each organised a number of convoy vessels for the fisheries. The fitting out was funded by the provinces, in practice however soon only by the fishing ports themselves. The money was yielded by those interested in the herring fisheries. Almost every year during Charles V's reign convoying the fishermen was a topic of discussion.[11] What kind of convoy would be most effective, for 'the sea is large and wide', was an often quoted remark. Armament on board herring busses was not an option. Would the high extra expenses be in proportion to the security it offered to the herring vessels? Who would take the initiative and be in command: the central government, the provinces, the fishing ports? All these considerations resulted in only a few incidental convoys. Important for the future was the fact that the authorities ashore – of whatever kind – were concerned about the safety of their citizens' economic activities at sea and felt a certain responsibility to protect these.

---

[10] R. Liesker and W. Fritschy, eds, *Gewestelijke financiën ten tijde van de Republiek der Verenigde Nederlanden, vol. IV Holland (1572–1795)* (The Hague, 2004), pp. 405–6 and 416–17.
[11] Sicking, *Neptune,* pp. 162–204.

In this same period the safety and protection of merchant shipping were first of all the merchants' and shipowners' own business. Only political circumstances and certain patterns of trade determined whether the government was to be involved, and whether exposure to too great dangers at sea ought to be prevented. A step forward were the Ordinances of Navigation of 1550 and 1551. These were sets of regulations prescribing merchant vessels to sail in groups, in 'admiralship' or 'in company'. Minimal sizes for vessels, crews and armament were laid down, always related to the destination. The first two state-organised convoys soon followed: in 1552 and 1553 on the route from the Netherlands for westbound shipping to the Iberian Peninsula. In 1557 the first true convoy to the East (the Baltic) took place, when the States of Holland and the central government fitted out eight warships.[12]

During the first half of the Eighty Years' War the navy had two major tasks: the blockade of the privateering nest of Dunkirk, and the protection of merchant shipping and the fisheries.[13] The States General, the provinces of Holland and Zeeland and the five admiralties cooperated well in this respect. Every year certain numbers of war vessels were allocated for specified convoy services. Safe trade was in everybody's interest and captains of convoy vessels received extensive instructions. In their ships' logs they had to mention the numbers of vessels in their convoy, weather conditions and so on. The logs were to be submitted at the end of the voyage. Convoy vessels were generally small – sixty men and no more than ten guns – no match for an ordinary man-of-war or a group of heavily armed privateers. The effectiveness of the convoy system in the late sixteenth century was barely discussed. It was just there and most believed in it, though heavy losses regularly occurred.

We do not need to follow in detail and in chronological order the navy's further involvement during the Eighty Years' War in protecting shipping and fisheries. Some general impressions may be sufficient. Firstly, the fighting and nationally funded navy had to blockade, fight when required and, when possible, support mercantile vessels and fishermen. Secondly, shipping and fishing had to pay for their protection, as we know. The state imposed rules that made their sailing more safe. Thirdly, due to the increasing activities of the Dunkirk privateers, Barbary corsairs and briefly also English and Irish pirates, the admiralties were bearing heavier responsibilities of an almost permanent nature. Protection of the fisheries, however, differed from that for mercantile shipping.

There were always two parties participating in convoying the fisheries: the admiralties and the representatives of the fisheries in the fishing ports, the so-called Great Fishery (*Grote Visserij*) and the Lesser Fishery (*Kleine Visserij*). Each year the navy allocated a number of smaller warships (mostly eight to ten) for convoy service, primarily from the admiralties of Rotterdam and Hoorn/

---

[12] Ibid., pp. 205–88. For an example of the fitting out of a squadron of ten vessels in 1544 see J.P. Sigmond, *Zeemacht in Holland en Zeeland in de zestiende eeuw* (Hilversum, 2013), pp. 69–84.

[13] Groen et al., eds, *Militaire Geschiedenis*, pp. 147–8.

Enkhuizen. Paid out of a tax on the quantities of herring caught, the *Grote Visserij* could also fit out some armed vessels, so it had its own warships with their own captains and crews. Each of the two groups of convoy ships was answerable to its own principals. Friction was inherent to the system.[14] An ordinance of 1604 was valid for both. In essence the system was not changed during the Eighty Years' War.[15] The convoy vessels remained only small men-of-war and were seldom able to repel a serious attack despite the fact that the annual convoy force was supposed to consist of twenty-four vessels.

The Barbary corsairs in the Mediterranean developed into a new and serious threat for the lucrative South European trade and shipping. Special naval expeditions in 1617 and 1618 to curtail their activities had small effect. Instead of a further policy of sending more patrolling squadrons, it was decided to switch over to a regular convoy service into the Mediterranean. This decision was part of a complete reshuffle of ideas about trade protection, which happened in 1621 at the end of the Twelve Years' Truce, and it included the Baltic trade as well. Ordinances with strict instructions were issued. Ships were parcelled into convoys, sailing dates were fixed. The size of a convoy had to be more than forty or fifty vessels when a naval escort or even a whole battle fleet was available. For the Mediterranean trade a strict discipline was prescribed. Regular convoys were also arranged to French ports, to London and Scotland and even to northern Russia. Vessels returning from the Baltic had to form in groups of certain numbers at the Sound and obey convoy rules.[16] Protection of shipping and fishing had become a serious business. In 1631, for example, seventy-six ships in all were employed: thirteen for the herring fleet, six for the *Kleine Visserij*, four for the Baltic and fifty-three for the other shipping routes.[17] Sailing as part of a convoy entitled a merchantman to a discount in the marine insurance rate.[18]

Despite all these arrangements to safeguard Dutch maritime activities far too many vessels were captured by the Dunkirk and other privateers, which often were too strong and too numerous. The losses could be heavy, very heavy. Blockading Dunkirk did not help sufficiently: blockaders arrived too late or were not diligent. Moreover, shipowners and their skippers disliked sailing in convoy and favoured private initiative. This was demonstrated in 1628 and following years. Nearly all provinces supported the foundation of a General Insurance Company for trade and shipping. A detailed plan implied amongst other things a fixed convoy service organised by the company, but the most influential cities in Holland rejected this plan. Full freedom of conducting business was of greater

---

[14] Sigmond, *Zeemacht*, pp. 235–8.
[15] A.P. van Vliet, *Vissers en Kapers: De zeevisserij vanuit het Maasmondgebied en de Duinkerker kapers (ca. 1580–1648)* (The Hague, 1994), pp. 108–16, 144–5 and 215–18.
[16] J.I. Israel, *The Dutch Republic and the Hispanic World (1606–1661)* (Oxford, 1982), pp. 110–11.
[17] Groen et al., eds, *Militaire Geschiedenis*, p. 385.
[18] S. Go, *Marine Insurance in the Netherlands 1600–1870: A Comparative Institutional Approach* (Amsterdam, 2009), pp. 113 and 152.

value than financial compensation for possible losses at sea. The plan was definitely dropped only in 1636.[19]

When all other protective measures had failed, the States General in 1631 was forced to accept the creation of private local navies by the cities of Amsterdam, Hoorn, Enkhuizen and three others for escorting shipping to and from the Baltic and Norway. The local *directies* (boards of directors) were ruled by burgomasters and merchants and began to fit out annually a number of heavily armed merchantmen. In 1645, for example, there were as many as fifteen such vessels. These *directieschepen* came under the authority of the admiralties with regard to captains' commissions, articles of war and prizes. Expenses were covered by special duties placed on the merchantmen involved. Nevertheless a second navy had come into being, one which lasted longer than was envisioned and which was badly needed. It was abolished in 1656.[20]

The system of regular convoy services on certain routes was continued after the Eighty Years' War. It even lasted till 1795, when the Dutch Republic was dissolved. The system was still based upon the sixteenth-century agreement that the yield of duties upon trade and shipping would be spent on building and fitting out convoy escorts, in general frigates and smaller men-of-war. For this purpose, for instance, sixty-five ships were built in the period 1682–1700.[21] In wartime, ships of the battle fleet regularly reinforced the protection on endangered routes – not always successfully, as the example of the French attack in 1693 on the huge outward-bound Smyrna convoy off the Spanish Atlantic coast illustrates.[22] During the relatively short Anglo-Dutch Wars mercantile shipping, whaling and fisheries were forbidden to sail, or sometimes allowed to only in spring and summer time.

On and off, shipping through the Sound and into the Baltic occupied the attention of the naval authorities and required sending extra naval forces. More constant were the dangers on the route along the Iberian Peninsula and in the Mediterranean. Barbary corsairs as well as English and French enemies could infest these waters. The Dutch often maintained a naval presence there. The ordinary convoys were then heavily escorted.

After the War of the Spanish Succession convoy services became the core business of the financially exhausted admiralties. The admiralty of Amsterdam was often the only one that gave this service. Each December, for instance, three men-of-war left for Portugal, Spain and the Mediterranean, returning in April. Afterwards two of the three ships were used for the East India convoy. Many mercantile skippers did not like sailing in convoy and preferred to sail on their own. Some captains had to report they had had none or only a few vessels with them. This could have been the effect of increased safety at sea in this time, which

---

[19] *Maritieme geschiedenis der Nederlanden*, vol. ii: *1585–ca. 1680* (Bussum, 1977), p. 204; Go, *Marine Insurance*, pp. 137–9.
[20] Bruijn, *The Dutch Navy*, pp. 27 and 79.
[21] De Jonge, GESCHIEDENIS ZEEWEZEN, III, pp. 117–20.
[22] Bruijn, *The Dutch Navy*, p. 95.

was obvious also in very low marine insurance rates.[23] In 1737 and 1747 two new convoy routes were started: to Curaçao and Surinam respectively. On and off, the Barbary states tried to capture Dutch vessels. Small squadrons were then fitted out, paid from a special fund, to give extra protection, fight the corsairs and restore a tribute peace. Nevertheless, marine insurance policies were occasionally sold reading 'excluding Moorish, Algerian or Turkish pirates'.[24]

At regular times huge quantities of bullion had to be transported from Cádiz and Lisbon to Amsterdam. From the First Anglo-Dutch War (1652–54) onwards merchants regularly wanted safe transport of their silver and gold. Men-of-war and convoy escorts were allowed to provide such safe transport, with the admiralties receiving 1 per cent of the transported value. The naval captain was entitled to a quarter of this freight money. Often many hundreds of thousands of guilders were carried by one or more men-of-war, thus providing naval captains with substantial extra earnings.[25]

Naval captains often considered convoy work tedious, uninspiring and uneventful. Assembling the merchant vessels in a roadstead could be time-consuming. Instructions for the sailing order had to be arranged and distributed. The slowest vessel determined the convoy's speed. During one of the last convoys before the fall of the Dutch Republic in 1795, Cornelis van Kerchem, captain of the *Zeepaard*, escorted a motley group of all kinds of smaller and larger vessels to the Baltic. This was in 1793. In poetic mood, Van Kerchem wrote a long verse called 'Memento Convoying', a complaint by a naval captain. It starts:

> Zoo ik een erge vijand had,
> En mijne wraak zou aan hem boeten
> Wensch ik anders niet als dat
> Hij zal convoyeeren moeten.
>
> [If I had a real enemy, and longed to expend my wrath on him, I could desire nothing better than to make him a convoy escort.]

On such a mission the masters were not always willing to obey orders. Fines and round-shot were the captains' sole sources of power. Captain and officers got grey hair and quickly. In such circumstances the naval poet penned:

> Oneindig beter is het ambt
> Oppasser in de gekkehuyzen
> Dan van 't convooy den commandant
> Of ik laat mij den baart uitpluyzen.[26]

---

[23] J. de Vries and A. van der Woude, *The First Modern Economy: Success, Failure, and Perseverance of the Dutch Economy, 1500–1815* (Cambridge, 1997), p. 138.

[24] J.R. Bruijn, *De admiraliteit van Amsterdam in rustige jaren 1713–1751* (Amsterdam and Haarlem, 1970), pp. 20–31; Go, *Marine Insurance*, p. 192.

[25] Go, *Marine Insurance*, p. 114; Israel, *The Dutch Republic*, pp. 421–3.

[26] V.A.J. Klooster and D.H.A. Kolff, eds, *Driftig van spraak, levendig van gang: Herinneringen van marineofficier Dirk Hendrik Kolff (1761–1835)*, Werken Linschoten Vereeniging CX (Zutphen, 2011), pp. 130 and 193–4. See also M. van Alphen, *Het oorlogsschip als varend*

[Better far to be an attendant in a madhouse than to command a convoy and let them pluck out my beard.]

How convoying the herring fleet functioned is described in the ship's log of the commander of six men-of-war from the Rotterdam Admiralty in 1712. The catching season lasted from 24 June until 24 September 24. Only one of the escorts was a frigate, the others were small ships of the line. Each ship had a special advisor on board, appointed by the *Grote Visserij*, a so-called *gleuser*, who explained to the naval officers how the fishermen practised their fishing. The convoy comprised 270 busses. Due to fog and lack of wind the loss of six busses could not be prevented.[27]

A special convoy service was the annual protection of the homeward-bound East Indiamen on the last leg of their long journey from Asia. It depended on the commanders' instructions whether they sailed via the Channel or by the Shetland Islands. This naval protection had been started in the 1620s when even big East Indiamen were not safe from Dunkirk privateers. A number of arrangements between the state and the East India Company were made, finally laid down in 1665. The state would take proper care for the safe arrival of the East Indiamen by annually fitting out four men-of-war. It had to be four fourth-rate ships, two from the admiralty of Amsterdam, one from Zeeland, and one alternately from Rotterdam and Hoorn/Enkhuizen. The return fleet could always be expected late spring or early summer. Hostile attacks were the prime reason for this convoy service, but it became the main task of the naval captains to prevent the smuggling of Asian commodities into British or French ports. Year after year these convoys sailed. After the War of the Spanish Succession the fitting out of such a convoy ship regularly became the sole activity of two admiralties! It was paid out of the lump sum the Company annually contributed covering the fiscal duties for imported goods.[28]

Conclusion

Protection of mercantile shipping and fisheries was a principal task of the authorities in the Dutch Republic, just as during the Habsburg regime. These authorities were always urged to have adequate naval forces available when the safety of their citizens at sea was in danger. During the Eighty Years' War naval protection was a bitter necessity. The commercial and shipping world paid for this protection, in time of war as well as in peace. Admiralty officials collected all kinds of duties on outgoing and incoming cargoes and vessels. The yield of the duties on inland

---

bedrijf: Schrijvers, administratie en logistiek aan boord van Nederlandse marineschepen 1597–1795 (Franeker, 2014).

[27] A. Poldervaart, 'Het konvooi tot bescherming van de haringvloot onder leiding van kapitein Cornelis van Brakel in 1710', in *Netwerk. Jaarboek Visserijmuseum 2003*, pp. 7–18.

[28] A. Bijl, *De Nederlandse convooidienst 1300–1800* (The Hague, 1951), pp. 80–90; Bruijn, *De admiraliteit*, pp. 21–2.

transport also went to the admiralties. Naval protection became insufficient in the latter part of the Eighty Years' War. Private initiative in the main port cities resulted in extra convoy ships (*directieschepen*).

Little changed after 1648. New wars soon followed. Mediterranean waters remained dangerous and convoying was continued. Occasionally shipping, whaling and fisheries were prohibited or their convoys got greater protection. It is interesting to observe that in years of peace convoy services did not stop. Created out of necessity, it was continued when not really required any longer. It became a routine and it provided regularity to the admiralty and shipping world. Departure times were settled; how to sail in convoy was arranged. Merchants and markets could also count on dates of departure and arrival of commodities. The existence of convoy services was reckoned to be an asset of Dutch mercantile shipping.

The eighteenth century, after the Peace of Utrecht in 1713, illustrates how much it had become routine to have fixed convoy services, but the admiralties were then left with no money and insurmountable debts. Only the Amsterdam Admiralty was able to provide convoys, and so it did, as mentioned above. The other admiralties only occasionally fitted out ships. During this century, however, the admiralties gave shipping and fisheries the little protection that was needed in years of peace and in areas of minor conflicts. The growing importance of West Indian shipping resulted in two new convoy routes. In this context it was all-important that the British Navy was not an enemy. The Fourth Anglo-Dutch War of 1780 shows how dangerous that could be. The navy never had any commitments in the East; the East India Company looked after itself and had its own naval forces. When the military position of the Company slowly deteriorated later in the century, a number of naval squadrons for the first time passed the Cape of Good Hope and gave the Company much needed support, but that was only from 1783 onwards.

The second main task had been to safeguard Dutch territory against invasion and to implement the state's foreign policy. This task had been fulfilled. At times it had been scary, particularly in 1631 and 1672. Thanks to British naval support a French invasion in 1747 was halted. The Dutch Republic had the navy which its political structure had made possible and which it deserved.

8
British Defensive Strategy at Sea in the War against Napoleon

ROGER KNIGHT

Geopolitical constants have ensured that Britain, an island off a continental land mass, used similar defence strategies when faced with an overmighty power dominating Europe. In the last five hundred years the same general pattern can be discerned – when Elizabeth I and Lord Burleigh were faced with the Spanish power of Philip II in the sixteenth century, when William III formed his Grand Alliance against Louis XIV in the seventeenth century, when Britain was facing the armies of Revolutionary and Napoleonic France; and if you add the further dimension of air power, when in the twentieth century the danger of Hitler's Germany was from the ports of north-west France.[1] British defence generally took three forms. The navy would send an expedition or mount a blockade of continental ports controlled by the enemy. Secondly, flotillas of small warships would take up defensive positions around the south and east coasts, not only as defence against invasion but as protection for coastal trade. Thirdly, ports and vulnerable beaches would be fortified and manned by the army, supported by militia, to ensure that at the least an invading force would be compelled to make a large-scale military effort, making a surprise attack by a small mobile force unviable. In conjunction with these naval and military measures, Britain would traditionally sign treaties and lesser agreements with other European powers alarmed at the growth of the one great power, and these treaties were often bolstered by subsidies.[2]

It was not possible for Britain just to withdraw behind Channel fortifications and leave the powers of Europe to fight it out, as has recently been argued in discussions about the First World War.[3] At the end of the eighteenth century

---

[1] D.A. Baugh, 'Great Britain's "Blue-Water" Policy, 1689–1815', *International History Review*, x (1988), pp. 47–9.
[2] In the War of Spanish Succession, for instance, there were 131 agreements between England and the many European states (J.B. Hattendorf, *England in the War of Spanish Succession: A Study of the English View and Conduct of Grand Strategy, 1702–1712* (London and New York, 1987), pp. 274–302.
[3] For an informed view of this question see D.A. Baugh, 'British Strategy during the First World War in the Context of Four Centuries: Blue Water versus Continental Commitment', in D.M. Masterson (ed.), *Naval History: The Sixth Symposium of the US Naval Academy* (Wilmington, DE, 1987), pp. 85–110.

ties between Britain and the Continent were even more complicated than they were in the twentieth century. Here there is space only to point to the Austrian Netherlands, as these territories were in 1792, from which a hostile power could launch an invasion, dangerously near the Thames Estuary and the Essex rivers. In addition, Hanover was still tied to the British crown, with no natural frontiers and indefensible, 'a tempting bait permanently dangled before the open jaws of the French army'.[4] In addition, an absolute necessity lay in maintaining trade with north-west Europe, not only because it was by far the largest market for British exports.[5] If the huge supplies of timber, tar, iron and hemp from the Baltic region were not imported then there would be neither a British Navy nor a merchant fleet.

The French Revolutionary and Napoleonic Wars were no exception to the general rules, though the length of the conflict at over twenty years was unique. Offensively, of course, the story at sea in the 1790s was one of British success. Set-piece big fleet victories, from the Battle of the First of June in 1794, St Vincent and Camperdown in 1797 and Aboukir Bay in 1798, knocked out Holland and Spain as big fleet powers, and pretty well neutralised France, a process which was to be completed at Trafalgar in 1805. The war, however, was to last another ten years. Throughout the wars of the eighteenth century, it was the financial exhaustion of the protagonists which brought wars to an end, and the long-established chaos in the French state finances was the dominating factor here. However, after 1792, Revolutionary France came up with a solution to war finance, which Napoleon ruthlessly refined. The costs of his war were met by the imposition of taxes and army requisitioning from conquered countries. It was this fact more than any other which kept the Great Wars with France going for over twenty years.[6]

The big-battle victories guaranteed to the British general sea control in European waters and in the Mediterranean for the two wars, although this significant strategic advantage did not stop the activities of enemy privateers which remained very active until 1814. However, strength at sea was more than outweighed in both wars by the disadvantages of the military situation on the Continent, and the relative lack of resources, especially of manpower, available to Britain. The weak British terms of the Peace of Amiens in 1802 reflected a tired and disadvantaged nation.

Pessimistic feelings dominated the thinking of subsequent British governments which was suffused by a long-term fear of invasion. Historians have been sceptical about the reality of the danger from invasion from Napoleon, and whether or not he really intended to invade: others have emphasised the lack of French preparation, the poor quality of their shipbuilding, lack of seamen and

---

[4] N.A.M. Rodger, 'The Continental Commitment in the Eighteenth Century', in L. Freedman, P. Hayes and R. O'Neill (eds), *War, Strategy, and International Politics: Essays in Honour of Sir Michael Howard* (Oxford, 1992), p. 53.
[5] J. Davey, *The Transformation of British Naval Strategy: Seapower and Supply in Northern Europe, 1808–1812* (Woodbridge, 2012), p. 17.
[6] Baugh, 'Blue-Water Policy', p. 57.

low morale, though allowing for the French strategic advantage from the massed troops in the harbours of northern France and the Low Countries which tied down very large numbers of British warships.[7] But to contemporaries in Britain, the threat was very real, as was fear of the potential for domestic disorder in the event of an attempted landing. Intelligence reports on French intentions from mainland Europe and the watching blockading fleets were assessed very seriously. Quite apart from the threat to the beaches of the south of England, there was Ireland. Irish loyalty was suspect to the end of the wars, and the British government's complete ignorance of the position of the French fleet that left Brest in the winter of 1796, and which reached Bantry Bay before abandoning the attempt, long haunted Whitehall. The very small French expedition which finally reached the west of Ireland in 1798 caused enough trouble, presaging the general uprising which resulted in thousands killed and a permanently sullen population. For instance, in 1804 an intelligence report still reckoned that French troop-carrying vessels from north Holland were destined to sail 'northabout' for the north of Ireland, while those venturing from Brest, if they eluded the British blockade, would head for southern Ireland.[8] This fear lasted until 1811 when finally the invasion threat was downgraded, a decision on intelligence received in London reporting widespread economic, manpower and morale weaknesses in Napoleonic Europe.[9]

The invasion threat was at its highest and most-remembered between 1803 and 1805, but after the lull between 1806 and 1807, when Napoleon and his army turned towards central Europe defeating Austria, Prussia and Russia, this fear continued until 1811. Anti-invasion measures had been put in place from the time of the first French threats in the Revolutionary War. From 1796 the navy built and controlled a fast visual communication system by means of long lines of shutter towers, which linked the roof of the Admiralty in Whitehall with Plymouth, Portsmouth, Sheerness and the Downs. Naval teams, each commanded by a lieutenant, manned these towers, and sent and received signals by adjustable shutters. With messages sent down the lines of towers in minutes from the naval bases, it was unlikely that the country could be taken by surprise. The last line of shutter towers to be built was London to Great Yarmouth, which opened in 1808. Additionally, on the headlands and high points of the coasts of southern England, simpler coastal signal stations were in visual contact with the next one along the coast, as well as with ships at sea, and enemy or suspicious shipping was

---

[7] Recent biographies portray Napoleon as confident of achieving a crossing of the Channel until he heard of Villeneuve leaving Ferrol and turning south for Cádiz on 11 August. See A. Roberts, *Napoleon the Great* (London, 2014), pp. 362–4; P. Dwyer, *Citizen Emperor: Napoleon in Power, 1799–1815* (London, 2013), pp. 192–3; for the later period of invasion threat see Rodger, 'Continental Commitment', p. 52; N.A.M. Rodger, *The Command of the Ocean: A Naval History of Britain, 1649–1815* (London, 2004), p. 562.

[8] C. Lloyd, *The Keith Papers* (London, 1955), vol. iii, Intelligence report, received 9 May 1804.

[9] Knight, *Britain against Napoleon*, pp. 310–11.

reported along the coast to the admirals commanding the bases. The government kept the Ordnance Board building fortifications until late in the war. Martello towers were being built on the east coast and in Ireland until 1811/12, as was the formidable Western Heights fortification at Dover, which could hold a defence force of six thousand troops. Contingency invasion defence planning in the Horse Guards also continued until 1811, projecting the requirement to face a French invading army of 300,000 – approximately the number of troops with which Napoleon invaded Russia. This 1811 report envisaged the recruitment of 400,000 militiamen in 800 battalions. Had this necessity ever come about, it would have required conscription, which, unlike France, Britain narrowly managed to avoid.[10]

As the Napoleonic Wars progressed, the land war spread towards Northern Europe, and naval operations in the north part of the Channel and the southern North Sea increased: the Western Approaches ceased to be the centre of the naval conflict. Although the blockade of Brest and the other French bases continued, they were now watched by much smaller squadrons. At the end of the French Revolutionary War in 1801, seventy-five warships crewed by 38,000 seamen were off the coasts of Brittany and Normandy; by September 1809 thirty much smaller ships, manned by only 7,000 seamen, were on station, a decrease of 80 per cent. From 1807 Napoleon poured resources into the great dockyard at Antwerp and blockading the River Scheldt became the British Navy's major blockading effort. The French fleet was constrained by a year-round watch at the mouth of the river, under Admiral William Young. Because of shallow water and good holding ground in this part of the North Sea, it was much easier to watch than the Normandy and Brittany coasts. On every day of the year, frigates and sloops were off the mouth of the Scheldt. Ships of the line were kept a hundred miles to the west, moored on chain buoys in the sheltered Hollesley Bay on the Suffolk coast. They were ready to sail at a moment's notice. By 1811 the French Admiral Missiessy had fifteen sail of the line and smaller ships ready to elude the vigilance of the British blockading squadron.[11] But the blockade held fast here, though French squadrons of ships of the line did break out of Toulon and Brest in the last years of the war: unsupplied and chased by British ships, they achieved almost nothing.

This northward shift of hostilities in home waters led to a radical change in defensive strategy against Napoleon's often-stated intention to invade Britain.[12] Instead of a big-ship British Navy, many small warships were now needed for the three central interlocking roles for the navy: the close blockade of North Sea ports under French control, inshore invasion defence and for convoy protection. Admiral Lord Keith, commanding the North Sea station, wrote to the First Lord of the

---

[10] Ibid., pp. 281–3, 299–300, 436–7.
[11] W. James, *The Naval History of Great Britain* (6 vols, London, 1878), vol. v, p. 207.
[12] Further emphasis of the move northwards is supplied by the major naval operations in the Baltic between 1808 and 1812, involved at its height sixty-two warships manned by 15,000 seamen (NMM website, 'Sustaining the Empire' Research Project, National Archives, ADM 8, List Books).

Admiralty, Lord St Vincent, just after the war had resumed in 1803: 'That there is a great extent of coast to defend is true, and I feel, like your Lordship, the weight upon my shoulders because the means are small but increasing. In the meantime I am more anxious to protect our trade than to defend the coast, because I know that the enemy have no assemblages of craft or troops at any one point.'[13]

It was fortunate that Britain had the industrial capacity to create a small-ship navy at short notice, enabled by an intense countrywide shipbuilding effort, primarily by private yards contracted with the Navy Board. There was considerable debate in Parliament about the capacity of the country to build these proposed warships to a high enough standard. William Pitt, who had had an interest in the 1780s in the design of small craft designed to defend Gibraltar, brought the subject up in Parliament in the debates that culminated in the end of Addington's government.[14] Horatio Nelson set down his opinion in a memorandum of April 1804, written out in the Mediterranean, and was clear that gunboats and gun vessels were needed in case there were calm conditions in the Channel. He reckoned that one-hundred-gun brigs and fifty-gun and mortar boats were necessary. Having commanded the squadron which blockaded Boulogne in 1801, his opinion was worth having and he discounted the fears that some naval men had of the capacity of the merchant yards to build these ships.[15]

Warship-building output was spectacular. Between 1803 and 1815, 518 warships measuring 323,000 tons were built, trebling the tonnage built in the French Revolutionary War. The British fleet reached its maximum in 1809: 709 ships in commission, measuring 469,000 tons. To achieve this remarkable output, the Navy Board had to change its ways, which it did under protest, pleading that it would be difficult to ensure quality control when warships were being built in distant parts of the country. For the first time, the Board contracted with all those private shipyards which could prove that they had the capacity to build a warship. Often the Board started off the shipyard with a small ship, progressing to larger if the first results were satisfactory. This is what happened with the merchant yards in Devon and Cornwall which had never built a warship before, but between 1804 and 1815 they built sixty-eight warships measuring 27,000 tons.[16] This was a pattern that was repeated around the country. Increasingly sophisticated contracts went a long way to maintain building quality, though they did not eliminate professional jealousies between shipwrights in the royal dockyards and those in the private sector. This new pattern of industrial relationship between government and contractor was just as radical as the Admiralty's new small-ship fleet.

The new warships initially replaced the large number of merchant ships which

---

[13] Lloyd, *Keith Papers*, vol. iii, 22 June 1803.
[14] J. Ehrman, *The Younger Pitt* (3 vols, London, 1969, 1983, 1996), vol. iii, p. 632; Knight, *Britain against Napoleon*, pp. 7–8.
[15] A. Aspinall, ed., *The Correspondence of George, Prince of Wales, 1770–1812* (5 vols, London, 1963–71), vol. iv, no. 1845, pp. 535–7.
[16] Knight, *Britain against Napoleon*, pp. 361–8.

the navy had hitherto hired: in 1803 and 1804 there were 92 and 102 vessels under contract, but by 1805 that number had fallen dramatically to 6.[17] It was clear that the navy had had difficulty with hired ships, whose owners tried to push up chartering rates as the need for the ships became greater. Difficulties with the lack of cooperation from revenue cutters, which had been ordered to assist, constituted another problem.[18] In early 1804, Keith wrote to Rear Admiral John Markham, on St Vincent's Admiralty Board, urging the Board to order more building: 'You will be obliged to build some, and 20-gun ships like the *Perseus* and 12 gun brigs, perhaps of fir, to be out of the mercy of the Dover men.'[19] Nor was it in Keith's nature to hold back when giving advice, writing again to Markham two years later, once again returned to the Admiralty Board under the Talents Ministry: 'I hope you are not building any more of the small sloop brigs, they do not answer, all complain they are wet, do not sail and draw 12 feet, the large brigs are excellent.'[20] These adaptable ships became the navy's 'maids of all work'. Eighteen- and ten-gun brig sloops were dramatically increased: in 1804 there were 33 in commission; by 1810 there were 169, making them the largest single class in the *Navy List*: in spite of losses at the end of hostilities in 1814 there were 155 still in commission.[21] Through these continual demands, the navy was 'transformed from a big ship, blue water navy into a small ship, brown water navy'.[22]

Keith, therefore, had an increasing number of brig sloops, gun brigs and gun vessels under his command which provided the first line of invasion defence. Some ships of the line were usually anchored in the Downs, but most of the hard work was done by smaller vessels which could get close to those French ports which were collecting invasion barges. In May 1804, at a maximum point of danger from Napoleon, Keith commanded 179 ships and gun vessels, spread out along the French and Dutch coasts, smothering this large area with British eyes and with the signalling capacity to move information around very quickly and back on shore to England if necessary. Lord Melville, First Lord of the Admiralty, made his defensive tactics clear to Keith, wanting 'a threefold protection: I mean that the enemy should be met first at the mouth of their own harbours and on their own coasts; secondly they should be annoyed every inch of their passage in crossing the sea, and lastly that they should be again met by every resistance that can be opposed to them on our own coast when they approach it'.[23]

---

[17] R. Winfield, *British Warships in the Age of Sail, 1793–1817: Design, Construction, Careers and Fates*, (London, 2005), pp. 390–5.
[18] C. Markham, *Selections from the Correspondence of Admiral John Markham during the years 1801–4 and 1806–7* (Navy Records Society, 1904), pp. 144, 164.
[19] NMM, Markham Papers, temporary box 37/1c, 27 January 1804.
[20] NMM, Markham Papers RRK, 37/1c, 6 April 1806.
[21] R. Gardiner, *The Naval War of 1812* (London, 1998), p. 89.
[22] This modern concept was adapted for the early nineteenth century by Michael Duffy in a review in the *International Journal of Maritime History*, 26 (2014), p. 391, of *Nelson, Navy and Nation: The Royal Navy and the British People, 1688–1885*, ed. Q. Colville and J. Davey (London, 2013).
[23] Lloyd, *Keith Papers*, vol. iii, p. 83, Melville to Keith, 6 June 1804.

Keith's fleet was divided into squadrons commanded by four highly competent rear admirals – John Holloway, Sidney Smith, Edward Thornborough and Thomas McNamara Russell – either in defensive positions off the Downs, Dungeness or Yarmouth, and as far north as Leith, or in forward positions off Calais and Boulogne or the Dutch coast. Off the Texel in May 1804, for instance, Rear Admiral Edward Thornborough commanded five 74s, three 64s, three large frigates, four cutters and three gun vessels: two sloops and a cutter stationed off Heligoland were under his order.[24] The shallow water at the mouth of the Scheldt and Flushing were watched by five heavy frigates, four sloops and four cutters, commanded by Sir Sidney Smith in the *Antelope* (fifty) and his squadron provides just one incident in a hard fought and skilful two-year defensive campaign.

On 15 May 1804 an invasion flotilla left Flushing, consisting of fifty-nine praams, schooners and schuyts, heading down the coast towards Ostend. They were immediately and ruthlessly attacked by British small warships. The French vessels tried to turn back to Flushing but the strong wind and tide sweeping down the shallow coastal waters compelled them to carry on, constantly harried by the British ships. Some French vessels were captured, others were left stranded on sandbanks. The French vessels' shallow draft enabled them to stay close to the beach under the coastal batteries, but, although the majority escaped, it was an important moral victory. However, Sidney Smith reported to Keith, 'I have to regret that, from the depth of water in which these vessels move, gunboats alone can act against them with effect.'[25] Shallow water affected much of the hostilities for the rest of the war, in particular the waters around Denmark in the Sound and the Great and Little Belts. Similar tactics were used by the Danes against Britain after hostilities had started in 1807, when they in turn concentrated on building gunboats to attack British trade convoys. By April 1808 Thomas Byam Martin reported in a letter to his brother from the Sound that the Danes had thirty-five gunboats, 'and from the quantity of timber I see about, it would be no difficult matter to have as many as a hundred by midsummer'.[26]

These small warships divided opinion in the Royal Navy for many years and perhaps too much was demanded of them. In June 1805, for instance, an eighteen-gun brig and two sixteen-gun brigs were lost in the Channel without trace, with the loss of 350 seamen.[27] Casualties were high. There were 205 losses from all causes of eighteen-gun brigs and smaller vessels between 1803 and 1815, an average of over eighteen a year.[28] The smallest, the four-gun schooners, were palpably too small: William James referred to their 'flimsy and diminutive frames'

---

[24] NMM, Markham Collection, temporary box 12.
[25] Lloyd, *Keith Papers*, vol. iii, pp. 79–81, 16 May 1804.
[26] R.V. Hamilton, *Journals and Letters of Admiral of the Fleet Sir Thomas Byam Martin, 1773–1854* (Navy Records Society, 1896), vol. ii, p. 9, 23 April 1808.
[27] T. Grocott, *Shipwrecks of the Revolutionary and Napoleonic Eras* (London, 1997), p. 196: for further examples of the loss of the small warships, all over the world, see pp. 237, 285–7.
[28] James, *Naval History*, appendices to vols ii–vi.

and called them 'tom-tit cruisers'.[29] Graham Moore, a distinguished frigate captain, deplored the fact that his crew had been split up to man some of the gunboats: they had been 'obliged to play the part of advanced Picquets until the end of December, very much exposed to the weather, not a little to the enemy's shot, and cooped up in a vessel not much bigger than a sentry box. It has ruined my ship's crew.'[30] Yet writing twenty years later, another officer defended ten-gun brigs. They were 'nice little sea boats when well managed, and sail remarkably well; if we put an officer who has always been accustomed to a line of battleship into one of them, and he proves headstrong and self-sufficient, ten to one he upsets her; but in the hands of a good brig sailor, they are as safe as any other vessel'.[31]

However, it was the role of these small warships in convoy protection which was to last longest in these wars, after the threat from invasion fell away. From the start to the finish of the Napoleonic Wars, a vital weak link which had to be protected by convoy was the coastal shipping along the east coast of England. These merchant ships were carrying most of the heavy goods required in London, and upon which the supply of the army and navy depended: the supply chain of coal, wheat, industrial goods, including armaments, was extremely vulnerable to privateers, although canal building was beginning to increase the amount of goods which could be carried internally.[32] These convoys had to be continued between English ports throughout the war, but hostile privateers never slackened their efforts to capture British cargoes and ships all over the world. Although it is a lesser known facet of warfare in the Napoleonic Wars, none was more important. Between 1809 and 1814, 1,674 convoys sailed to and from England, protecting 57,448 voyages of merchant ships and government-hired transports. More convoys and ships sailed within the years 1809 and 1813 than any other: respectively, 298 convoys escorting 10,217 convoyed ships and 366 convoys protected 16,228 voyages. By far the most ships in both years were convoyed to and from the Baltic, which had between two and three times the number of ships as the next destination, the West Indies; and after that, in descending order, the Mediterranean, the Continent to Portugal and North America trebled between these two years, as the Peninsular War and the conflict with America had its effect in 1813.[33]

---

[29] Ibid., vol. iv, p. 335.
[30] J. Gore, *Creevey's Life and Times* (London, 1934), pp. 45–6, Moore to Thomas Creevey, 9 January 1810.
[31] 'Commander', *The State of the Navy* (London, 1831), p. 41.
[32] To give an idea of the numbers involved, it is worth mentioning an entry in the log of a coastal signal ship moored off the Blackwater when the captain counted ninety-six merchant ships in sight at one time in the Swin (TNA, ADM 51/2974, 13 June 1811).
[33] TNA, ADM 7/64, Admiralty Notifications of Convoys to Lloyds, 1808–14. Figures by destination for 1809 and 1813 were: Baltic (4,997/7,243), West Indies (2,031/2,907), Mediterranean (1,101/1,722), Continent (674/281), Portugal/Peninsula (905/2,308), North America (402/1,114). South American figures (208/391) included East Indiamen which watered at Rio on the way from England to India.

This was an unsung effort which, proportionally to population, matched the number of convoys and ships (if not, of course, the tonnage) of the Second World War. As with the later conflict, the amount of losses per ships convoyed was a very small percentage.[34] It was no less vital to British trade as it was in the twentieth century, keeping the credit of the government and the City of London healthy, and enabling taxes to be raised at a high level, which, in turn, was sufficient for Britain to outlast and outperform the finances of the French Empire. None of this could have been achieved without the frigates, sloops, gunboats and gun vessels built during the war. Even so, the very large numbers of convoys resulted sometimes in very thin naval cover. One example taken at random from hundreds was a convoy from Gothenburg to English ports at the beginning of August 1809. Four brig sloops, under the command of the *Diligence*, fourteen gun, ninety-nine-foot long and 361 tons, gathered up 270 merchant ships at the Wingo Beacon, with three similar but smaller vessels, all of them built or acquired since 1800. They weighed anchor on 4 August and made slow progress across the North Sea. The log records that strange sails were investigated, signals were exchanged with two westbound convoys from Britain. and when the English coast was near, the ships dispersed by previous arrangement. Progress was painfully slow, for the *Diligence* did not reach Yarmouth Roads until 18 August.[35] No losses were incurred, and as a result, as with hundreds of others, it has been lost to history. But these were the convoys which counted.

The weather was an even greater enemy than the enemy privateers. While convoy patterns were dictated by the monsoons in the Indian Ocean or the hurricane season in the West Indies, convoys to supply Wellington's army in the Peninsula left England in all seasons. The Bay of Biscay took its toll of a number of convoys through violent winter weather. One example is the *Garland*, a twenty-two-gun sloop, launched in Bideford in 1807, which weighed anchor from Spithead on 26 November 1813. By 2 December only eighteen of her convoyed ships could be seen. Her log continues

> Strong gales & heavy squalls at 1.30 shipped a heavy sea, stove the yawl, carried away part of the bulwark & washed one of the long 12 lbers overboard, at 2 the storm staysail blew in pieces ... at daylight 7 sail of the convoy in sight, washed overboard by the sea both the waist hammock cloths. At 8 strong Gales, & heavy squalls, shipped a heavy Sea which washed the spanker boom overboard & was lost.[36]

Nevertheless, the *Garland* reached Santander three days later, and by early January was in the Tagus waiting to collect the homebound convoy.

More should be known about these convoys and their escorts, their organisation and their losses. The safe transporting of goods and raw materials for trade,

---

[34] Cp. with the Allied convoy statistics in M. Murfett, *Naval Warfare, 1919–1945: An Operational History of the Volatile War at Sea* (London, 2009), Appendix 1, pp. 530–3.
[35] TNA, ADM 51/1933, log of the *Diligence*.
[36] TNA, ADM 51/2433, log of the *Garland*.

and provisions, stores and reinforcements for the war in the Peninsula and the naval operations in the Baltic, were critical to British defensive strategy in the war against Napoleon. Overall Britain was at its most disadvantaged after 1807, when the emperor had consolidated his power in central Europe, having in turn brought Austria, Prussia and Russia to heel. Then he imposed his continental blockade. British helplessness and lack of an offensive strategy were demonstrated by ferocious arguments in Parliament on how the war should be fought. This dangerous vacuum could so easily have led to the breakdown of political will, and seeking of what would have been draconian peace terms from Napoleon – as, indeed, Charles James Fox tried to do when briefly Foreign Secretary in the Talents ministry in 1806: after months of fruitless negotiation, even that muddled-headed optimist saw that there was no making peace with the emperor who was never prepared to compromise.

Fortunately for the prosecution of the war, the weaknesses of the Tory governments under Portland, Perceval and Liverpool were exceeded only by the Whig opposition's ineffectiveness, caused by deep personal divisions amongst them. From 1809 the Whigs opposed the maintenance of Wellington's army and the defence of Portugal on the grounds that it was unaffordable, but, as often with Parliamentary oppositions, failed to come up with an alternative. Not surprisingly, for there was no alternative. Only in 1812, when it became clear that Wellington was not only winning but advancing up through Spain and towards France, and after tens of thousands of Napoleon's veteran troops had died in the Russian winter, was political peace and consensus achieved in Whitehall. Britain had at last stumbled upon a grand strategy, of which the unsung part was control and use of the sea, made possible by the British Navy, which had adapted to the new conditions of warfare in the seas of the north of Europe. With their allies, Britain had been the means of wresting control of the extremes of the north and south of Europe from Napoleon, who had only the land on which to march his armies. The ability to move trade, money, stores, troops and cavalry, efficiently and cheaply, was made possible by sea control to support fighting the dominant land power. By the end, Napoleon was outmatched for resources, and the armies of Russia, Prussia and Austria from the north and of Britain, Spain and Portugal from the south, closed in on the emperor.

9

The Offensive Strategy of the Spanish Navy, 1763–1808

AGUSTÍN GUIMERÁ

[N]aval warfare alone [with Great Britain] is entirely manageable for Spain ... But it is necessary to do it well: not to be side-tracked by expeditions, attempting to seize or recapture [territory]. This is the main point: to aim carefully and to fire only at the target that is the foundation of her pride ... her navy and her commerce, which are one and the same.

Vice Admiral José de Mazarredo, 1795[1]

In this tribute to Professor Hattendorf, a renowned expert in naval strategy, it seems fitting to offer an analysis of a little-known aspect in the history of the Spanish Navy in the eighteenth century: its offensive strategy. The common perception of the Bourbon dynasty in Spain and her colonial empire during this period is that it was always on the defensive, pressured by the double leviathan of the French Army and the British Navy. According to this conventional perception, Spain focused its energies on a traditional active defence of the status quo, aimed at securing communications and protecting its trade monopoly with Spanish America, in addition to sustaining its far-flung possessions overseas. This strategy forced its enemies – the French, Dutch and British – into expending a great deal of effort to turn the tide. Moreover, throughout the eighteenth century, the superiority of the British – Spain's principal rival at the time – in naval warfare and seamanship, and in commerce, manufacturing, technology and finance, had forced Spanish political and naval leaders to emphasise a defensive strategy. It truly was suicide to go looking for battle in the absence of superiority, or at least parity, of force. It was playing into the hands of the enemy. Spain's defensive stance, moreover, benefited from the line of battle, which meant that both opponents could not overpower each other, and was especially detrimental to the interests of Great Britain.[2]

But this is only part of the picture. As is well known, strategy is the art of the dialectics of force, of opposing interests. It is also the art of creating, maintaining and regaining power. It pursues political objectives by means of different

---

[1] Vice Admiral José de Mazarredo to the Secretary of Marine Antonio Valdés, 27 August 1795; *Archivo Histórico Nacional-Madrid*, Estado, 4039/1.

[2] It is not possible to describe in full the extensive Spanish bibliography on naval strategy in the second half of the eighteenth century, due to the limited length of this chapter.

instruments, including armed force. But, like politics, it is an art of the possible. Strategy is governed by its beginning, not its end. The strategist delves into the realm of uncertainty and risk, where there are no silver bullets. He or she therefore needs to develop a capacity for flexibility, resourcefulness and improvisation, all of which rely on imagination. In confronting Great Britain, Spain's strategic creativity was put to the test by the naval superiority of its rival.

When facing this kind of challenge, the strategist can devise a direct and forceful confrontation with the enemy – the function of Achilles, to allude once more to a felicitous metaphor of Freedman's – or an indirect approach, making use of deceit and deterrence – the function of Odysseus. This chapter is an attempt to demonstrate that, at certain points during the eighteenth century, the Spanish Navy followed Achilles' strategy: an offensive war in which strength and audacity played a part and unequivocal victory or defeat was at stake. When favourable circumstances presented themselves, the Spanish Navy did seek out the enemy to engage them in battle in multiple theatres of operations.[3] This study comprises the period between the end of the Seven Years' War (1763) and the beginning of the Peninsular War (1808).

Strategic Background

The Spanish Empire faced numerous challenges following the signing of the Treaty of Paris of 1763. It had recovered the coastal strongholds of Havana and Manila, while Gibraltar and Minorca – sticking points in its thorny relations with Britain – remained in British hands. It had also lost both East and West Florida. Generally speaking, it was very difficult for Spain to remain neutral in the numerous conflicts besetting eighteenth-century Europe, among other things because of the vastness of its American empire, which by 1783 covered sixteen million square kilometres. Spain was obliged to forge alliances sometimes with one power and at other times with another, depending on the circumstances. A case in point is its relations with France, an ally throughout most of the period, except for the years during which it fought against Revolutionary France (1793–95).

The empire's maritime space, extending from Europe to the Americas and the Philippines, constituted a maritime true frontier, in the political and spatial senses of the word. The theatres of operations where the Spanish Navy was active corresponded moreover to the strategic axes of European navigation and trade during the period.

The Spanish Empire's most important trade routes – to the Americas, the Philippines and Northern Europe – converged in the Strait of Gibraltar and surrounding areas. The strategic value of the Strait was vital for the routes that

---

[3] The history of strategy has been studied by H. Coutau-Bégarie, B. Heuser, J.H. Hattendorf, M.I. Handel, W. Murray, L. Freedman, H. Strachan and others. The Achilles and Odysseus metaphors are in L. Freedman, *Strategy: A History* (Oxford, 2013), p. xii.

united the Gulf of Cádiz to the Caribbean via the Canary Islands, returning via the Azores, where the route forked, with branches continuing to Galicia via Cape Finisterre or to Cádiz via Cape St Vincent. It is not surprising that the major naval battles against Great Britain took place in this theatre of operations. Recapturing Gibraltar or neutralising it through the presence of a dockyard and a naval base in Cádiz was a strategic priority. The Bay of Algeciras and the dockyard at Cartagena also constituted a deterrent, if not a threat, as was also the case with British-held Gibraltar and Minorca with respect to Spain.

The Western Mediterranean was also an area of primary strategic importance, since it connected the coast of Spain and the Balearic Islands with North Africa, the south of France, the Italian states and their neighbouring islands – Corsica, Sardinia, Sicily and Malta. The grain trade – critical for Spain, which was not self-sufficient in this category of basic foodstuffs – as well as the trade in wax, fish, colonial products, luxury goods from the Orient and other commodities required the active defence of shipping in these waters.

North African privateering was therefore a matter of concern for the Spanish monarchy, because of its impact on shipping, trade, daily life in Mediterranean coastal communities and training in seamanship. Maritime security involved maintaining Ceuta, Melilla and other smaller military enclaves, as well as holding Oran and Mers El Kébir (1732–91). These strongholds had a clear role as deterrents against the threat of privateering. The naval base at Cartagena – with its division of ships of the line, frigates, galleys and xebecs – also put pressure on North Africa.

But to protect shipping required diplomacy to supplement the use of force. Though Spain negotiated a peace treaty with the sultan of Morocco in 1767, the inconsistency of Moroccan foreign policy obliged the Spanish government to exert itself militarily and diplomatically with the possibility of occupying or neutralising Tangier or Tetuán in case war broke out. The Spanish monarchy also signed treaties with the Ottoman Empire in 1782 and Tripoli in 1784, with the aim of facilitating trade and shipping in the Western Mediterranean. Algiers was always Spain's most problematic neighbour, since foreign aid supported its privateering activity. It was a source of irritation to Spain to see the ambivalent attitude of its ally France, which continued to provide ground and naval assistance to the Algerian Regency for strictly commercial motives. For its part, Great Britain always openly sided with Algerian corsairs against the Spanish. The Spanish monarchy took vigorous measures through both its army and its navy against this Algerian threat, as we will see.

Portugal, an ally of Great Britain since the seventeenth century, represented an additional problem for Spain, since the Portuguese ports of Lisbon and Porto, and to a lesser extent Lagos, had become anchorages and logistical bases for British fleets. These Portuguese ports had a more decisive role than Gibraltar and Minorca did in the operations of the Royal Navy in this theatre of war. This had repercussions for diplomatic relations between Spain and Portugal and gave rise to border skirmishes and the well-known plans for a land invasion on the part of France, the Spanish ally.

The maritime route to the North Sea and the Baltic through the English Channel had always been of great strategic importance, not least because it was a source of essential materials for the navy, such as timber for making spars, hemp, tar, etc. Spain was at a disadvantage vis-à-vis Great Britain in these waters. Accordingly, on numerous occasions it joined forces with France to open up shipping in this part of the Atlantic, including some attempts to invade the British Isles. Spain also tried to build alliances with other Northern European maritime powers. Lastly, the naval base and dockyard at Ferrol, in Galicia, were intended to monitor the sea routes that united Spanish America with Europe and Spain with Northern Europe.

The Americas were the key to this imperial strategy, especially the Caribbean and the Gulf of Mexico. Their plantations and raw materials provided a store of riches for Europe's nascent industrialisation, but they also constituted a defensive glacis for the focal points of the empire: Mexico and Peru. It is no coincidence that of the eleven Spanish naval bases, yards and stations defending the empire in 1774, five were located in this critical region. The Caribbean and the Gulf of Mexico were thus a privileged theatre of operations, especially in light of circumstances such as the British occupation of parts of Honduras – for logwood exploitation – or the brisk direct trade between Britain's Caribbean possessions and the Spanish colonies. The proliferation of contraband and the illegal occupation of Caribbean territories, considered by Spain to be the property of the crown, led to an outright trade war between the two powers.

The Spanish government always hoped to recover the Caribbean territories that the empire had lost in the seventeenth century, mainly Jamaica, the richest British colony in the region and a constant threat due to its central location. Spain also would have liked to recapture Florida, which menaced traffic and trade between Veracruz, Havana and Spain. Likewise, taking the British-held Bahamas was an ongoing political objective, since these islands were a natural point of departure from the Caribbean and the Gulf of Mexico in the age of sail.

In the second half of the century, the 'frontier islands' of the Caribbean and the Gulf of Mexico were re-evaluated in terms of their strategic importance. Cuba and its ports stand out first and foremost. Havana – located on the Straits of Florida, which provide the best passage from the Gulf of Mexico to the Atlantic – had been a gathering point for silver fleets for centuries. In the eighteenth century, Havana would be endowed with a powerful naval yard which together with multiple reforms from 1763 onwards launched the economic development of the island in the 1790s. Santiago de Cuba had always been considered a base for intimidating Jamaica. The island of Puerto Rico and its well-fortified capital, San Juan, was another key to the Caribbean. Santo Domingo and its natural port at Samaná also attracted the attention of Spanish politicians. The strategic value of Trinidad was likewise reconsidered. This island, which is to windward of the Caribbean and at the end of the Lesser Antilles – occupied by other European powers – was one of the first points of arrival for ships from Europe. From Trinidad, the trade winds made it easy for ships to come to the aid of Spanish ports in the southern part of the Caribbean. After centuries of neglect, the island was finally developed in the 1780s, although the measures taken were too late.

In South America, continual pressure from the Portuguese in Brazil lent greater strategic importance to the Río de la Plata region. The Pacific coast of America and the Philippines acquired greater strategic value as a result of the active presence of other European powers, principally the British, who took Manila in 1762. The Philippines were always crucial in the exchanges between China and the Viceroyalty of New Spain by the Manila Galleon. This also explains the building of a new port at San Blas on the Pacific coast of Mexico, used as a base for expeditions to the American Northwest. In order to improve the navy's effectiveness, the Spanish monarchy replaced its old surveillance fleets in the Americas – the *Armada de Barlovento* (Windward Fleet) in the Caribbean and the *Armada del Mar del Sur* (South Sea Fleet) in the Pacific – with coastguard vessels and other warships. When diplomatic relations became strained or if war was imminent, military reinforcements – both fleets and troops – were sent from the metropolis to overseas.

Grounds for an Offensive Strategy

The Spanish Navy never dismissed the possibility of the destruction of enemy forces as a counterweight to its policy of active defence. During most of the period from 1764 to 1808, the Spanish–French alliance favoured an offensive strategy. Spanish and French fleets often outnumbered British fleets, even if the results of battles often favoured the British. When Vice Admiral José de Mazarredo analysed the 1782 battle in the English Channel between a Spanish–French fleet, with forty ships of the line, and that of Admiral Howe, with only twenty-three, in which the numerical superiority of the allies was offset by the speed and manoeuvrability of the British, he complained:

> What do we have to say now to the general negative perception of the navy, that naval battles don't determine the outcome of war? ... What a bitter day is this 12th of July – because of the slowness of the Allied Armada, the Spanish flag lost the glory of destroying twenty-three enemy ships and forcing them as a result to beg for peace on their knees![4]

Following Spain's successes in the War of American Independence, the prime minister, Count Floridablanca, backed a similar strategy: 'In short, we must consider going on the offensive and assess the means for doing so with some degree of success, since defensive war is impossible with the number of remote areas that we have to protect.'[5] As for Great Britain, as British historians themselves have

---

[4] Mazarredo/Secretary of Marina, 30 July 1782, *Archivo Museo Naval-Madrid*, 2381, fols 8 y 10.

[5] Strategic plan of the Secretary of the State, Count Floridablanca, in case of war with Britain, 1790; C. Fernández Duro, *Armada española desde la unión de los reinos de Castilla y de Aragón*, facsimile edition of 1900 (Madrid, 1972), vol. viii, pp. 21–4. See the 'Reserved Instruction that the *Junta de Estado*, created by My Royal Decree of this day, 8 July 1787, should observe in all the points and subjects of its commitment', written by Floridablanca, *Obras originales*

made clear, the Royal Navy had too many tasks and areas to attend to. In 1800, Vice Admiral Mazarredo, who was conscious of the limitations of the Spanish naval forces vis-à-vis the Royal Navy and the great disadvantages of a battle between equal forces, advocated an allied attack far from the Spanish naval bases in Cádiz, the Mediterranean and the Caribbean, using the element of surprise:

> 5th The Spanish and French navies should not be regarded as inactive relative to their possibilities, as long as their forces are equal or superior to those of England: the further these forces are from England, the greater the loss and embarrassment they could impose.
> 6th The navies of France and Spain, because of their inferiority, cannot attempt any operation that does not involve an element of surprise, by getting a head start so that the operation is over by the time the enemy arrives with superior forces.[6]

The Spanish Navy should find favourable circumstances for carrying out strategic manoeuvres; that is, when it had superior means in a given theatre of operations, in a single operation and at a particular moment. The space-time factor was essential.

In the plans for allied operations in the Mediterranean that he presented to First Consul Bonaparte in 1800, Vice Admiral Mazarredo provides us with a clear illustration of this strategic flexibility. He reminded Bonaparte that the Franco-Spanish alliance had expelled the British from their Mediterranean bases for almost two years, between 1796 and 1798. Now he was advocating a remote, coordinated strategy – a well-managed campaign that could turn the Mediterranean into a 'dry sea' for the Royal Navy. He criticised the French Navy for having acted alone in 1799. If the allied fleets in Cádiz had been marshalled on time, their numerical superiority would have been substantial and they even would have been able to come to the aid of the army in Egypt:

> Thus was squandered a year full of glory and advantage such as 1799 might have been if the Directory had communicated its designs to my lord the King in January or February, so that a wise allied plan could have been agreed upon for surprising the enemy. If the twenty-five ships of the line at Brest had been joined by the six at Ferrol and later the seventeen that I had at Cádiz, nothing would have been able to resist such a torrent of force; and by the time the enemy perceived what they were up against and deployed [further] divisions, those [divisions of the enemy] that were off Cádiz as well as their cruising divisions at the Balearic Islands and off the coast of Spain could already have been destroyed, and Malta could have been given aid, and even further, with the consequence of retaking Minorca and the successive destruction of newly arriving enemy divisions.[7]

---

del conde de Floridablanca y escritos referentes a su persona (Madrid, 1952), pp. 226–72.
6 Mazarredo to First Consul Bonaparte, Paris, 9 March 1800; E. Barbudo Duarte, *Don José de Mazarredo, Teniente General de la Real Armada* (Madrid, 1945), pp. 209–10.
7 Mazarredo/Bonaparte, 11 January 1800; Barbudo Duarte, *Don José de Mazarredo*, pp. 197–209.

Spain's offensive strategy was not limited to major fleet actions. In addition to battles between squadrons or unattached ships, there were also many missions of an offensive nature that the navy undertook in the wars that were being fought during the period under study: logistical support for the army, blockades, privateering and amphibious operations, including seizing enemy territory or ports, shore bombardments and *coups de main*. The Spanish monarchy made evident its extensive experience in amphibious warfare, though its prowess declined at the end of the eighteenth century for multiple reasons. In these operations, the navy achieved important strategic victories. The best way to confirm these arguments for an offensive strategy is to enumerate the naval operations that Spain carried out in the different theatres of war.[8]

The Western Mediterranean and the Strait of Gibraltar

Spain dealt with North African corsair activity through a variety of actions: cruising, stronghold blockades and amphibious operations. First of all, the monarchy supported privateering by private individuals. The privateers of the Balearic Islands were particularly noteworthy in this regard and wrought significant damage on the Algerian fleet. The most outstanding example was Antonio Barceló, who would go on to be appointed vice-admiral and whose career has been amply studied.

The Spanish government also organised cruising operations with its own warships. Clashes between Spanish and Algerian xebecs – the preferred vessel in this kind of confrontation – constituted the best naval and military training for naval cadets and young officers. Many of them would go on to demonstrate their skills in naval warfare in more momentous battles. There were the heroes of Trafalgar among them: Federico Gravina, Antonio de Escaño, Dioniso Alcalá Galiano, Cosme Churruca, José Alcedo y Bustamante, etc. The Spanish Navy was even able to blockade the roadstead of Algiers for short periods of time.

But the 'guerrilla warfare' between corsairs was an advantage for the Algerians, making it difficult for Spain to maintain control of these waters. So the Spanish monarchy initiated a series of amphibious operations: *coups de main* against enemy ports, the attempted occupation and bombardment of Algiers.

In 1765, Barceló himself destroyed three xebecs that were under construction in the River Martin of Tetuán in a well-planned amphibious operation. This exploit was a decisive factor in the peace treaty signed with Morocco in 1766. However, the sultan wanted to occupy the Spanish strongholds on the Moroccan coast, which led to the siege of Ceuta in 1770 and 1790–92 and the sieges of Melilla and the Peñón de Vélez de La Gomera during the period 1774–75. On those occasions, a coordinated defence by the Spanish Army and Navy forced the Moroccans to abandon the siege. Spain even bombarded Tangiers in 1792 with

---

[8] See the studies of the Spanish naval operations during the period 1764–1808: Fernández Duro, *Armada Española*, vols vii–viii; and J.M. Blanco Núñez, *La Armada española en la segunda mitad del siglo XVIII* (Barcelona, 2004).

a small naval force, and as a result the sultan signed a definitive treaty in 1799. Moroccan privateering would no longer be a threat to Spain in the seas off the Strait and North Africa.

As for Algiers, the Spanish government took even more drastic steps. In 1775, an expedition was organised to capture the city. The campaign required an immense military effort. Although it failed, the expedition is an extraordinary example of Spain's offensive capabilities.[9] The final operation against Algerian privateering was the attack on its capital, as Venice and Denmark had done in 1767 and 1770, respectively. In August 1783, a large naval force bombarded the city for seven days, inflicting heavy damage on the city's buildings and some ships at anchor.[10] In July of the following year, this punishing operation was repeated with a much larger naval force, including some units from the Kingdom of Naples and the Order of Malta. However, the second bombardment was not as effective, despite having more resources than the first.[11] Nonetheless, the offensive strategy yielded results. Spain compelled Algiers to sign a suspension of hostilities in 1785 and a peace treaty the following year.

Meanwhile, the conflict with Great Britain over Gibraltar and Minorca continued. During the War of American Independence (1779–83), the Spanish monarchy took advantage of British naval forces being scattered throughout European and American waters to carry out various offensives. Most noteworthy among them is the 'Great Siege' of Gibraltar, which took place between 1779 and 1782. The Spanish Navy subjected the stronghold to an almost impenetrable land and sea blockade. For the sea blockade, smaller vessels were used, prominent among them gunboats.[12] These naval forces, based in Algeciras, took a heavy toll on trade and threatened the very survival of the garrison in Gibraltar. Squadrons made up of French and Spanish forces attempted to close the area off to possible relief convoys. However, this strategy turned out to be unsuccessful due to the enemy ships' technological improvements and to the superior seafaring skills of their crews. The British were able to get three consecutive convoys through to Gibraltar. One example is the Battle of Cape Spartel in 1782, between the allied Spanish–French fleet, with forty-six ships of the line, and the fleet commanded by Howe, with thirty-four ships of the line.[13] Despite these failures, the offensive strategy served its purpose: the British forces were sidetracked in Gibraltar, to

---

[9] The fleet had 6 ships of the line, 12 frigates, 26 minor vessels and 334 transports. The land forces amounted to 21,000 men – infantry, artillery and cavalry. There were 142 guns of every sort, 32 mortars and 8 howitzers.

[10] The expedition had eighty-five sail: four ships of the line, four frigates and forty-eight minor vessels. During the attack, Algiers lost one quarter of its bigger warships and one-third of the city was destroyed.

[11] The fleet had 133 sail of all sorts.

[12] The technical innovation in the Gibraltar blockade was the transformation of the launches belonging to the ships of the line and frigates into mobile divisions, armed with twenty-four-pound guns. They had sails and oars. These gunboats were good at manoeuvring and conducting night attacks.

[13] The dramatic failure of the new floating batteries during the night attack on Gibraltar, in September 1782, is well known.

the detriment of other, more decisive theatres of operations, where their presence was sorely needed.

There were other gains. Spain scored a strategic coup in 1781, gaining temporary numerical superiority in the Strait of Gibraltar with the help of France. While an allied squadron of fifty ships of the line drew British attention during their incursion into the English Channel, a Spanish division attacked Minorca, forcing the garrison there to surrender within a few months.[14]

During the war against Revolutionary France (1793–95), the Spanish Navy was able to arm and maintain, with much sacrifice, large forces in different theatres of operation. In the Mediterranean, in August 1793, the naval forces that were detached off the coasts of Catalonia and the South of France totalled twenty-nine ships of the line, eleven frigates, and thirty-five lesser vessels. Throughout the conflict, the Catalonian Army and the Spanish contingent that invaded the Rousillon were assisted by the navy, which transported troops, ammunition and supplies. In May 1793, a Spanish fleet captured the islands of San Pietro and Sant'Antioco, which were returned to Spain's ally Sardinia. During the occupation of Toulon by Spanish and British forces (August–December 1793), the Spanish were able to defend the stronghold against a numerically superior French force. The Spanish squadron also acted with courage during the evacuation, saving the lives of many French royalists.[15]

The Atlantic

The Spanish Navy also fought in this theatre of operations, when conditions were right. As we have seen before, during the War of American Independence, allied squadrons made multiple incursions into the English Channel and directly threatened Great Britain. The British squadrons did not give battle, given the numerical superiority of the enemy.[16]

The Spanish Navy conducted an offensive in 1780 that was a strategic success: an allied fleet captured a large British convoy near the Azores on its way to the Caribbean. This capture decisively influenced the operations of the British fleet already stationed in the Caribbean. It is an example of strategic symbiosis between different theatres of operation, even remote ones.[17]

---

[14] The Minorca expedition had two ships of the line, ten frigates and nine minor vessels. The transports amounted to seventy-five sail, with 7,909 men on board. Later on, 4,000 French soldiers joined the land forces.
[15] Following Spanish sources, each fleet – British and Spanish – had seventeen ships of the line, several frigates and minor vessels. The total land forces favoured Spain's enemies: there were 4,435 Spaniards, 1,435 British, 4,332 Neapolitans, 1,594 Sardinians and 1,542 French royalists.
[16] In the 1779 campaign the Combined Fleet had sixty-six ships of the line confronting thirty-six ships of the line of Hardy's fleet. In the 1782 campaign the former had forty ships and Howe's fleet only twenty-four ships.
[17] The Combined Fleet had twenty-four Spanish ships of the line and six French ships of the line. The British convoy amounted to fifty sail.

The Spanish Navy deployed an offensive strategy in the Caribbean, the Gulf of Mexico and the Bahamas during this war, making particular use of amphibious warfare. According to Richard Harding, after France and Spain entered the war on the side of the Americans, the war's centre of gravity shifted from North America to the Caribbean and the Gulf of Mexico, with the threat to British possessions there forcing Britain to take a defensive stance.[18] When the allied fleets united in July 1780 in the Caribbean, the allies gained temporary control of the Straits of Florida and the Gulf of Mexico, wresting it from Rodney's fleet. This allowed Spain to support the siege of Pensacola in 1781. The loss of Mobile and Pensacola in 1779–81; the British evacuation of some enclaves in Campeche, Guatemala and Nicaragua in 1779 and Honduras in 1781; and the capture of the Bahamas in 1782 constituted a great setback for Great Britain. De Grasse's defeat at the Battle of the Saints in 1782 kept Spain – who participated in this amphibious operation – from realising her earlier goal of recovering Jamaica. But the offensive strategy still bore fruit. In the Treaty of Versailles (1783), Great Britain returned Florida and Minorca, in exchange for recovering the Bahamas and some Central American enclaves.

It is also important to note the large expedition sent to the Río de la Plata region in 1776, which brought about the definitive defeat of the Portuguese colony of Sacramento, which was ceded to Spain in the Spanish–Portuguese treaty of 1778.[19] The offensive capability of the Spanish Navy was also demonstrated in the Nootka Crisis of 1790. Britain and Spain nearly went to war. The Spanish monarchy ordered a naval armament. In only four months a large fleet was armed in Cádiz and sent to Cape Finisterre as a deterrent to British naval forces. The British themselves recognised the speed and efficiency with which the Spanish Navy was able to accomplish this feat.[20] Lastly, during the war against Revolutionary France, a Spanish fleet took Fuerte Delfín (St Domingue; now Fort Liberté, Haiti) in a skilfully executed surprise attack.[21]

Epilogue: The Trafalgar Campaign
In 1795, the Spanish war fleet was bigger than ever: 75 ships of the line – 14 of which were three-deckers – 51 frigates and 182 lesser vessels. But during the period 1796–1808, the political and financial crises besetting the Spanish monarchy triggered the rapid decline of the navy and its operational capability.

---

[18] R. Harding, 'Operaciones anfibias británicas, 1700–1815', *Guerra naval en la Revolución y el Imperio*, pp. 39–58. In 1780, the Spanish monarchy sent to Havana fourteen ships of the line, five frigates and three minor vessels. This fleet was reinforced by the Havana division.

[19] The expedition amounted to eight ships of the line, seven frigates and five minor vessels. The convoy had eighty sails transporting 10,000 men. In February 1777 the Island of Santa Catalina was conquered and the colony of Sacramento was occupied in May.

[20] The fleet was large: it had twenty-six ships of the line, twelve frigates and three minor vessels.

[21] The fleet amounted to fourteen ships of the line and seven frigates and other minor vessels.

The situation was exacerbated by poor harvests and the outbreak of severe epidemics. Outfitting the fleet became more and more difficult, due to the chronic shortage of sailors and the lack of resources. In 1797, Spain's Ocean Fleet was only able to marshal nineteen ships of the line to face Jervis's blockading squadron. In 1805 the Spanish Navy could offer Napoleon only fifteen ships. However, its offensive resolve did not diminish during the campaign that led to the Battle of Trafalgar, a topic that is impossible to enlarge upon here due to space constraints.[22] In summary, the Spanish monarchy used a combination of offensive and defensive naval strategy to help maintain its American empire up until the beginning of the independence movements in 1810.

---

[22] This Spanish offensive behaviour was evident during Calder's action – the Battle of Finisterre in Spanish sources – on 22 July 1805, and the sortie from Cádiz of the remains of the Combined Fleet in order to continue the fighting, on 23 October 1805. See A. Guimerá, 'Trafalgar: Myth and History', in R. Harding (ed.), *A Great and Glorious Victory: New Perspectives on the Battle of Trafalgar* (Barnsley, 2008), pp. 41–57.

10

The Influence of Sea Power upon Three Great Global Wars, 1793–1815, 1914–1918, 1939–1945: A Comparative Analysis

PAUL KENNEDY

While many great and extended conflicts involving the use of the sea have been fought over the past two thousand years, the three most notable in modern times were undoubtedly those struggles for global mastery in the years 1793–1815, 1914–18 and 1939–45. Each of these conflicts has produced a plethora of detailed works upon aspects of the war in question, but the profession has avoided making a comparative study of them to draw broader conclusions about the influence of sea power in the modern world.[1] This chapter makes an attempt to do that, and with a particular interest in examining why the exercise of naval force during the second of the three conflicts is generally regarded as having had much less effectiveness than in the other two. Examining why naval power in 1914–18 had much less 'influence' than its pre-war advocates hoped might then help us to a better understanding of the limitations of naval force as well as of its positive capabilities. Above all, the essay is interested in the changing contexts in which sea power had to operate over these one hundred and fifty years of what one scholar nicely termed 'the influence of History upon Sea Power'.[2]

This is a lengthy argument, and so the structure of the essay below has been divided, rather obviously, into wartime and peacetime sections. Since the great naval struggle for mastery between 1793 and 1815 is generally regarded as the apotheosis of sea power in action, no detailed account is offered below of the many great battles that took place within those years, or of where British diplomacy and naval influence successfully marched hand in hand, as in the Baltic, or of the campaigns in the Eastern Seas.[3] What seemed more important was to produce a reasonably brief structural analysis of why it was that sea power played such a prominent role in a struggle for the mastery of Europe that in the final

---

[1] There are, however, important observations in two much earlier classic works: B. Brodie, *Sea Power in the Machine Age* (Princeton, 1941) and H.W. Richmond, *Sea Power in the Modern World* (London, 1934).
[2] K. Moll, *The Influence of History upon Seapower, 1865–1914* (Menlo Park, 1968).
[3] G.J. Marcus, *A Naval History of England, Volume 2: The Age of Nelson* (London, 1971); T. Voelcker, *Admiral Saumarez Versus Napoleon: The Baltic, 1807–1812* (Woodbridge, 2008); C. Parkinson, *War in the Eastern Seas, 1793–1815* (London, 1954); N.A.M. Rodger, *The Command of the Ocean: A Naval History of Britain, 1649–1815* (London, 2004).

analysis obviously had to be settled by military victory over Napoleon on land. Not all European great wars saw naval power play a significant part; indeed, the greatest in recent memory – the Thirty Years' War between 1618 and 1648 – had little to do with the sea, or the sea with it. Why it was different in the titanic French Revolutionary and Napoleonic Wars therefore obviously requires explanation before the rest of this essay can unfold.

From time to time this text engages with the arguments and presumptions of Captain Mahan regarding how sea power exactly did influence the wars in question. This is not done in any intellectually hostile way; it simply seeks to offer a reality check upon whether it was sea power itself that caused the outcomes claimed, and if completely or to a lesser degree. It also attempts to test the story of these wars against the strategic theories of the two greatest of Mahan's 'foils': Sir Julian Corbett, with his claim that it was command of control of the ocean routes (not the decisive battle) that counted; and Sir Halford Mackinder, with his claim that it was land power, or who gained control of the great West European land mass, that would count most in the outcome of modern wars.[4]

To undertake a comparative analysis of the influence of sea power upon certain earlier wars – say, between the War of the Spanish Succession, the Seven Years' War and the American Revolutionary War – is not so difficult, simply because so very much about navies and warships stayed the same, and because the battles largely took place within the very similar constraints of time and tide, during the high point of the age of fighting sail. This was no longer the case after the early nineteenth century, because of two enormous, and separate, changes in historical conditions. While the 1793–1815 campaigns took place in the pre-Industrial Revolution era, the circumstances under which the admirals of 1914 had to fight were dramatically different. Further and very large changes in the condition and circumstance of navies were also to occur in the much briefer period between the second and third of the great global wars analysed here. The British Navy (say) of 1940 may have seemed very similar to that of a quarter-century earlier, yet so much had changed, especially in regard to the rise of air power, both carrier-based and land-based. Further, the global naval balances, especially in the Far East, were now quite altered from those of 1914. Captain Mahan, in summarising the 'elements of sea power' in his first, great work, felt that they belonged to the 'unchanging order of things, remaining the same, in cause and effect, from age to age'.[5] It is the intention of this essay to test if that was really so, given the stupendous impact of the Industrial Revolution upon warfare, and the special influence of air power upon fighting in the years after 1919.

It follows that a very large part of this chapter has had to focus on the two periods between the wars. While not originally foreseen by the author, it became

---

[4] J. Corbett, *Some Principles of Maritime Strategy* (London, 1911); H. Mackinder, 'The Geographical Pivot of History', *The Geographical Journal*, xxiii, no. 4 (April 1904), pp. 421–37.

[5] A.T. Mahan, *The Influence of Sea Power upon History, 1660–1783* (London, 1965; first pub. 1890), p. 88.

increasingly clear that no analysis of the influence of sea power upon history could be made unless maritime affairs were tested against change over time, between the great conflicts, especially change driven by the onset of newer technologies. It is not unreasonable to claim that Nelson himself would have been very familiar on board Blake's flagship of 150 years earlier; but Jellicoe and Nimitz would have been quite lost on a century-older warship. 'Sea power in an age of change' is thus the core, and implicit title, theme of the present investigation.

1793–1815

Since this war ended with Napoleon's surrender after being defeated by a great land coalition force at Waterloo in 1815, it seemed incumbent upon Mahan to make his well-known claim that 'those far distant, storm-beaten ships, upon which the Grand Army never looked, stood between it and the dominion of the world'.[6] Writing then as a Professor at the Naval War College, and as the advocate of a much larger American Navy, his position was an understandable one. He had to convince readers, including perhaps congressional sceptics, that sea power counted in world affairs, and the British struggle against Napoleon offered him much evidence for that claim. Later scholars have not contested this. After all, the 1793–1815 conflict in Western Europe was mainly a struggle between three naval nations, Britain, France and Spain, such that if any one side gained at sea the other was very adversely weakened; each intruded upon the other, and therefore navies very much counted.[7]

The geography of these wars at sea was thus of overwhelming significance; it intruded at every stage, and to a degree unimaginable in the modern jet age. Nothing here was new, for geography had played the same critical role in the five previous Anglo-Spanish-French conflicts between 1689 and 1783. Britain benefited, of course, from its insularity and freedom from invasion by land; and after 1603 and 1707, by its union with Scotland. In the age of sail, it benefited from the prevailing currents and winds that so often pinned the French fleets into their harbours, and from an array of good naval bases from Devon to the Thames. It benefited to an incalculable degree by the possession of Gibraltar (as it would again in 1940–43), and also from its possession of Halifax, Kingston and, very soon, Malta and the Cape. But in a struggle against France and Spain geography did not favour Britain to the extent it did in its wars against the Dutch, the Danes or Wilhelmine Germany. Franco-Spanish raiders and larger squadrons could get out to the Atlantic and beyond, and did so repeatedly; and they also of course possessed good harbours in the Mediterranean itself. All these waters were contested space, therefore, which is why the naval battles themselves (the Glorious First of June, Cape St Vincent, Trafalgar and, further north, Camperdown and

---

[6] A.T. Mahan, *The Influence of Sea Power upon the French Revolution and Empire* (Boston, 1894), vol. ii, p. 380.
[7] It is rather like saying that the influence of land power upon the fate of the Kingdom of Poland was incontrovertible.

Copenhagen) were invested with such importance and fought so keenly by each side. Little wonder that Mahan was so impressed at the idea of a main battle force that would sweep all before it, and thus ensure command of the oceans.

Since these were wars of endurance – twenty-three years of struggle – victory would go to the Power with the deepest purse and the greatest economic capacity. Ostensibly, this would have been France, with more than twice the population of Britain and a rich agricultural and commercial base, and a commensurate taxation capacity; but after Colbert's earlier efforts, this potential was never realised, and from the 1720s the advantage swung to a Walpolian Britain which gave the country an adamantine political strength and an astounding creditworthiness. The hard figures told the story; halfway through every great conflict, the UK Treasury could continue to float loans (at much lower interest rates) when its rivals could not. As Osterhammel explains, between 1688 and 1815 UK gross national product rose threefold and taxation revenue fifteen fold; Britain could raise more than twice as much in taxes as France.[8] By the later stages of the war against Napoleon, the island-nation had become a gigantic export-producing machine. If France had been able to shut it down, through the Continental System and other embargoes, London's war strategy would have shuddered to a halt. That never happened; Britain faltered (in 1797, when the Bank of England suspended specie payments), but its insularity, ever-growing economy, political resilience, access to newer global markets and strong naval edge kept it going. And it still had money to subsidise major and minor European allies to take up the fight against Napoleon, by funding their armies, and providing their weapons. Again and again, French victories in the field blew apart these coalitions; and every time they were reassembled and refunded, France's manpower bled a little more and its capacity to interrupt Britain's space grew less. Finally, Napoleon's twin bouts of imperial overstretch, into Spain and into Russia in 1812–14, gave London the chance to play all its cards – naval pressure, massive subsidies, a Wellingtonian army – to assist in toppling France's gigantic bid for mastery.

The later historian is tempted to say: given the many above factors in Britain's favour, all that was needed was for it to maintain a strong and unchallengeable navy, under steady and intelligent leadership. Such leadership for pursuing the war was there, even with a stricken king and when Cabinet coalitions were shaky. From the very onset of the French Revolution, governments in London committed enough funds to build a huge fleet of line-of-battle ships and cruisers, with supporting dockyards, munitions and manpower. While the system groaned frequently under the immense strains of combatting the joint Franco-Spanish fleets and their massive resources, it never snapped. The final advantages, of Nelson's unique charismatic leadership in battle and the remarkably high quality of so many other admirals and captains (Collingwood, Saumarez, Hood,

---

[8] J.H. Plumb, *The Growth of Political Stability, 1675–1725* (London, 1967); P. Kennedy, *The Rise and Fall of the Great Powers* (New York, 1987), p. 149; J. Osterhammel, *The Transformation of the World: A Global History of the Nineteenth Century* (Princeton, 2014), p. 452.

Cochrane, where does the list stop?), can be added in here, but how exactly one weighs each of the above elements of strength that made up Britain's war machine is impossible.

What is clear is that one has here a rare historical example of national and naval strength that was partly foreshadowed (in 1714, and 1763) but now came to full fruition. The conflict had been so lengthy, and drained so many resources, that it left all the other participants exhausted, winded and in need of years of recovery. Little wonder that the Prussian general Gneisenau afterwards inveighed against that 'blackguard' Napoleon whose ambitions had plunged the Continent into war, leaving Britain free to exploit the fruits of the world.[9] In all of this effort, the role of the Royal Navy had counted so much – wherever I go, Napoleon complained, I find it in the way – but it was as one strand, one part of the whole. Mahan was therefore entirely justified in enthusing about the influence of sea power upon history here, but it was an influence that had worked because all of the other strands were in place as well.

1815–1914

No period in the maritime history of the previous two thousand years came close to the special strategic and political circumstances of the century after the surrender of Napoleon. When Rome dominated at sea, it was merely over Mediterranean waters; Admiral Cheng Ho's great expeditionary fleets came and went across the Indian Ocean, without lasting impact; and Philip II's navies were repeatedly challenged in the Atlantic, the Caribbean and the Mediterranean. But here, for the first time, was a global maritime empire. To some degree, the post-1815 'Pax Britannica' can be explained on negative grounds – it happened, and was allowed to happen, because the other major Powers did not contest British naval predominance outside Europe during these many decades. Certain European countries (Prussia, Portugal, Greece, the Italian states) usually found the Royal Navy's protection abroad a distinct benefit to their shipping and seamen in those mid-century decades of growing free trade. The French and Russian navies posed sporadic threats, but on certain other occasions were to be found in cooperating with British naval forces, as in their joint crushing of Mehemet Ali's fleet at Navarino in 1827; or, at least in regard to the French Navy, in shared large-scale operations in the Black Sea against Russia during the Crimean War. For a while after 1815 the fast, very heavy American frigates gave the British Admiralty cause for concern, but American attention to sea power, and to building a substantial national naval force, was never very sustained during the nineteenth century.[10]

But the Pax Britannica also existed because a long line of British governments and parliaments was determined to pay for command of the sea. There was no

---

[9] Rodger, *Command of the Ocean*, p. 574.
[10] Osterhammel, *Transformation of the World*, pp. 452–5; P. Kennedy, *The Rise and Fall of British Naval Mastery* (London, 1976), pp. 149–76.

lack of pressure by MPs to keep naval budgets low, yet spending on the fleets never fell to hopeless levels, and ironically it was the Liberal side of the House that most insisted upon maintaining a decent navy – the more so to keep Britain from being so weak internationally as to rely upon continental alliances. But of course that political prejudice against entanglements rested conveniently upon an economy which by the 1850s, in Hobsbawm's calculation, produced two-thirds of the world's coal, half of its iron and five-sevenths of its steel.[11] Maritime pre-eminence, imperial advantage, technological strength and isolationist preference all nicely reinforced each other at this time, and no foreign competitor came close, or seriously attempted to be a competitor.

Moreover, the naval predominance that was the Pax Britannica was not significantly affected, at least for quite a long while to come, by the advent of steam power and the Industrial Revolution. That may seem remarkable given that fossil fuels could be found in many parts of the world, so competitors had at least the raw potential for imitation and catch-up. But in the first instance what the Industrial Revolution did was to enhance vastly the already great economic and productive power of Britain itself, both vis-à-vis its traditional rivals (some of whom like France were not so blessed in resources of coal and iron), and vis-à-vis non-European societies in Africa and India which had not even the elemental capacities for Western-type modernisation. As British manufactured goods streamed out across the globe in the 1840s and 1850s, the world seemed to be ever more the 'oyster' for the victors of Trafalgar and Waterloo. Thus, the rising exports of steam locomotives and railway equipment to the Rhineland and Pennsylvania seemed only to tie such markets to British manufacturing centres and bring large profits, and not to be enabling future world rivals. And it would be some time before the extensions of foreign railway networks began to create new centres of geopolitical power in the American Midwest and across the Ukraine, far from the workings of any future blockade. And since it was in south Wales that there occurred the very best steaming coals for all types of ships, it seemed that industrialisation merely gave one further advantage in world power indices to a nation already almost unfairly endowed by geographic and other advantages. The longer-term consequences of the Industrial Revolution upon sea power were only to be appreciated, and then just partly, in the final quarter of the century, when other powers began to close the gap.[12]

One can gain a better understanding of all this if the 'long nineteenth century' in its naval dimensions is divided into three chronological subcategories: that between 1815 and c.1885, described above; between 1885 and 1906; and between 1906 and the First World War. This at least was how it was in regard to the Royal Navy's all-important global fleet distributions, as they were amended in each of these times. Geography of course could not change, but the relationship of the

---

[11] B. Semmel, *Liberalism and Naval Strategy: Ideology, Interest and Sea Power During the Pax Britannica* (Boston, 1986); E. Hobsbawm, *Industry and Empire: An Economic History of Britain since 1750* (London, 1968), p. 110.

[12] Kennedy, *Rise and Fall of the Great Powers*, ch. 4.

leading naval powers to each other did change as admiralties adjusted their naval programmes, vessel types and fleet dispositions, and the world's leading naval power then sought to respond. These three chronological cut-off points also reflected some big changes in warship design, the increasingly stepped-up size of naval budgets, as well as the arrangements of the active fleets. There were some exceptions to this general three-part schema, but on the whole this breakdown can help readers of the period understand and locate such well-known events as the coming of the Two-Power Standard, the *Dreadnought* 'leap' and Tirpitz's naval laws.

Mention of these later and very rapid eruptions in naval matters again allows the reader to see better why the maritime and geopolitical contours of the 1815–85 years appear so relatively placid by comparison. Though there were significant changes in naval architecture, there was little standardisation as warships sprouted a rich variety of profiles, funnels, masts (including sails) and gun calibres with little or no standardisation of type compared to, say, the post-1919 era. The greatest war of the mid-century, the US Civil War, had been overwhelmingly a land-based struggle, with sea power operating along its fringes. Bismarck's three successful wars of unification in the 1860s were achieved without sea power being evoked at all. The Anglo-French naval operations against Russia during the Crimean War showed the difficulties of applying maritime pressure against such a land-locked, agrarian nation. For long decades after 1815 not much of naval significance happened in the waters outside Europe apart from anti-slavery patrols and the Opium Wars; later admirals' memoirs could happily recall their frequent times as young lieutenants visiting Valparaiso and Brisbane. The many doings described in Osterhammel's recent *Transformation of the World* rested, lightly and easily, upon an almost invisible and softly applied British naval pre-eminence.[13] An integrated world of commerce and mainly peace was underpinned by the iron frames of the Royal Navy.

The significance of sea power within the Great Power system increased significantly after the mid-1880s, when both the French and Russian governments, already colonial rivals to Britain in the Mediterranean, Africa, the Far East and South-East Asia, embarked upon sustained and very expensive programmes of capital-ship building. This so shook the British press[14] and Parliament out of its complacency that successive London governments could never again be free of the charge that they were underspending upon the Royal Navy, even when the 'Two-Power Act' (the Naval Defence Act of 1889) and various expensive successor bills were announced. Naval spending ballooned, but so too did public agitations about a foreign invasion of England, the loss of control of the Mediterranean and the end of the Pax Britannica.

If the British Admiralty and its planners were shaken by the sudden rise of the

---

[13] Osterhammel, *Transformation of the World*, passim, especially chs VIII and IX.
[14] Beginning with W.T. Stead's sensationalist 'The Truth about the Navy' article in the *Pall Mall Gazette* of September 1884. Scaremongering journalism in Britain never looked back after this.

French and Russian new navies, they had every reason to be so. Geographically, those fleets would be very hard to handle. The fear was that fast and heavily gunned French armoured cruisers, speedier than any Royal Navy battleship and more powerful than any British cruiser, could operate out of such well-situated harbours as Brest, Cherbourg, Toulon, Algiers, Dakar, Madagascar, Reunion (Indian Ocean), Saigon, even French West Indian ports. Russian raiders could operate out of Vladivostock, and later Port Arthur. A combined Russian Black Sea fleet and a French-based Mediterranean force might possibly threaten Constantinople and the Eastern Mediterranean. In that case, the critical British Empire trade routes through the Mediterranean would have to be suspended (as they were, of course, between 1940 and 1943).

All this offered a geostrategical nightmare, and one that seemed to have no obvious solution. Build and build as the Royal Navy did, could it really place strong blockading squadrons off all the above ports all of the time, if French and Russian squadrons were to be based there? It would be an operational and logistical nightmare. How also could an offshore blockade work without grave danger if the French chose to construct dozens of fast-attacking torpedo-vessels (as they did), experiment with minefields and longer-range torpedoes, and design submarines of an ever-longer range? The close blockade was over, and the medium-distance offshore blockade was already at severe risk.[15]

This was the critical naval dimension to the 'crisis of Empire' situation that faced British planners around the year 1900. Military disasters in South Africa led to huge increases in British military spending, at once far larger than anything spent upon the fleet. Russian military advances seemed to threaten across Asia. The Great Powers were snapping up Chinese ports – and thus newer naval bases. A war with France over the Nile Valley had just narrowly been avoided in 1898. Great new navies were being laid down by the United States and Japan, rising extra-European nations that would be impossible to blockade in any future war. The Pax Britannica was at an end, even before a great modern German battle fleet began to be laid down in the North Sea. Had the German Navy remained modest and second-class in size, and Germany stayed friendly throughout the Edwardian years, the British global and imperial crisis would have remained. But the German Navy did not remain modest in size, nor did Germany stay friendly.

Viewed from this larger gloomy perspective, it is now easier to understand that immense flurry of defence measures and newer naval policies that the British engaged in between about 1895 and 1906 – measures that have drawn the attention of a whole host of recent naval historians of these years.[16] The Two-Power Standard was asserted again, and again. Battleships became larger and larger, to

---

[15] The Admiralty's worries about all this are covered in great detail in A.J. Marder, *The Anatomy of British Sea Power: A History of British Naval Policy in the Pre-Dreadnought Era, 1880–1905* (New York, 1940), chs 7, 10, 13 and 17.

[16] Among the most prominent being J. Sumida, *In Defense of Naval Supremacy: Financial Limitation, Technological Innovation and British Naval Policy, 1889–1914* (Winchester, 1989) and N. Lambert, *Sir John Fisher's Naval Revolution* (Columbia, SC, 1999).

accommodate ever-bigger gun calibres, and at the same time became more and more heavily armoured, and faster and faster – and much more expensive in consequence. Giant fast armoured cruisers, even more pricey than battleships, were laid down. Flotillas of torpedo-boat destroyers were constructed, to protect those battleships from attack. Advances were made in various new forms of fire-control, each with their impassioned claimants. Plans were also advanced for super-fast, heavily gunned though lightly protected types of battlecruisers that could scout in advance of the main battle fleet, or range along imperial trade routes. Fresh undersea cables were laid along those same imperial maritime routes. Harbour defences from Dover to Gibraltar, and from Toulon to Dakar, were expensively renewed. Qualitatively and quantitatively, navies were altering fast in this period, but none felt the pressure more than the Number One naval power.

The revolution in naval affairs that so threatened Britain, its imperial possessions and maritime routes, and Royal Navy, in the two decades between around 1885 and around 1905 was eventually handled, and greatly eased, not by some phenomenal new technological *deus ex machina* as Admiral Fisher and other reformers sought, but through diplomacy – that is, by important changes in Great Power relationships which took place between Britain and the other nations precisely in these years. In the Mediterranean, Turkey, Spain and Austria-Hungary remained overall friendly, and Italy very much so. In the Far East, Japan signed an alliance with Britain, crushed Russian land forces and smashed the Russian battle fleet (1905). In the Western Hemisphere, the rising American power was accommodated through territorial concessions and a political rapprochement. Most important of all, Britain entered into a series of colonial agreements between 1904 and 1907 with its two greatest overseas rivals, France and Russia, which (provided they were kept) took away their threats to the empire, and of course to the imperial sea-lanes. The nightmares of the 1890s were receding, although it was understandable that most admirals did not at first understand what was happening, and many feared that the new French and Russian rapprochements might not last. By any objective strategical measurement, however, Britain's global position was far more secure by 1906 than it had been, say, in 1890. And, to repeat an earlier point, all of these diplomatic realignments could and most probably would have taken place even had the German fleet remained small and friendly.

Seen in this light, the final phase of the long nineteenth century (1906–14) is easier to comprehend and requires only a few broad strokes here. The new German Navy was being built, by Tirpitz's intent, to affect British policy and to make London more amenable to Berlin. It was to be a very large, but short-range battle-fleet navy, and thus to have its greatest influence between Wilhelmshaven and the Thames. German public opinion was now virulently hostile, and German diplomacy under the Kaiser unpredictable. As pressures eased upon Britain's world position, a new danger seemed to have arisen much closer to home. British warship numbers were trimmed in the Far East, in the Mediterranean, the West Indies and lesser stations. Land for a new battleship base was prudently purchased at Rosyth as early as 1903. The new *Dreadnought* battleship and *Invincible*-class battlecruiser appeared after 1906; they had not been designed deliberately against

Germany, of course, but now they were there – and the swift German intention to follow suit showed that the new High Seas Fleet would stay as the chief threat to Britain's maritime security, and the more frightening because so close. The Anglo-German 'naval race' consumed all the headlines, agitated the British Parliament, and gripped successive British governments.[17]

But Britain's security position was made much easier by the military-strategical decisions of two men: General Alfred von Schlieffen and Grand Admiral Alfred von Tirpitz. Schlieffen and the Prussian Army planners who followed him played such a vital, albeit negative role because they completely ruled out the diversion of their armies for an invasion of England. It would have been very difficult to carry out such an invasion in any case, but it simply was not going to happen because the Prussian General Staff's obsession throughout this time was the swift invasion of France, via Belgium (possibly also via the Netherlands as well), as well as gigantic campaigns in the east. This prospect meant that, like it or not, British governments now had to consider a threat to the European land balance of power for the first time in a century, a contingency for which the Royal Navy, not liking this at all, would also have to adjust. And Tirpitz eased Britain's strategical dilemmas, ironically, by his unwavering insistence upon constructing a German Navy solely, or overwhelmingly, for deployment in the North Sea – the pre-1914 naval archives show him firmly resisting all schemes to have a larger German naval presence in the Mediterranean and outside Europe, as reducing the effect of his 'lever point' against Britain in home waters.[18] So it was with reluctance that he viewed the existence of Souchon's small force in the Mediterranean, and of von Spee's squadron in the Far East. By the same token, Tirpitz opposed allocating large monies for enhancing naval harbours in the German colonies. So long as he held office, British imperial trade routes were not, despite any apprehensions, going to be in much danger in the years before 1914.

The historian is left only to speculate how the naval strategical situation would have looked had pre-1914 German governments decided instead to construct and then deploy squadrons of fast, powerful cruisers and battlecruisers, and even lesser squadrons, in ports in West Africa, South-West Africa, East Africa, New Guinea, Samoa, the Carolines, Tsingtao, instead of laying down yet another expensive battleship flotilla for the High Seas Fleet. Would this have seemed like a new version of that scarcely faded nightmare of powerful French squadrons at Dakar and Madagascar? Probably not, because Germany could offer a far weaker logistical support system to an overseas base network than could France. Yet because Tirpitz prevailed in his fight against the German Admiralty Staff, that alternative strategy did not happen. Instead, and ironically, the natural geographical advantages which the Royal Navy had had against the Dutch challenge in

---

[17] See especially A.J. Marder, *From the Dreadnought to Scapa Flow: The Royal Navy in the Fisher Era, Vol. 1: The Road to War, 1904–1914* (Oxford, 1961) and P. Kennedy, *The Rise of the Anglo-German Antagonism, 1860–1914* (London, 1980).

[18] P. Kennedy, 'The Development of German Naval Operations Plans Against Britain, 1896–1914', *English Historical Review*, lxxxix (January 1974), pp. 48–76.

the seventeenth century now returned, almost as an act of strategic good fortune, to hem in the newer naval challenge of the Kaiser's improperly named High Seas Fleet. Sea power had not diminished in importance, of course; it simply was returning to manifest itself in an older, familiar locale.

1914–18

The pre-war constellation of prior diplomatic arrangements, military preparations and the overall 'correlation of forces', and the unalterable geographical situation, thus set limits and opportunities for the workings of sea power after 1914, affecting both the Allies and the Central Powers alike. The existing military plans and contractual arrangements of Russia, Austria-Hungary and Germany meant that a vast land struggle, far from the sea, would take place once decision-makers in those capitals decided upon war rather than further negotiation. One of those contracts, namely, France's commitment to its ally Russia, triggered Berlin's declaration of war upon Paris and brought the conflict to Western Europe as well. While a fight against Russia and France seemed deeply satisfying to many among Berlin's leadership during the July Crisis of 1914, the rigidity of their Schlieffen Plan actually meant that Germany first attacked neutral Belgium, thus triggering the intervention of Britain and its empire against the Central Powers, and turning the struggle into a true 'world' war. Wilhelmine Germany was now simultaneously engaged in a massive land conflict, and a premature maritime struggle against a far larger naval power – all this, unsurprisingly, to Tirpitz's dismay and frustration. In his view, Berlin had unwisely and prematurely pushed for a conflict in 1914; there was no sleepwalking into war here.[19] And Tirpitz had fair cause for dismay, for while there were good prospects for a militarily efficient Germany to overcome its next-door neighbours, at sea the odds were badly tilted against the High Seas Fleet.

Several early actions in the war confirmed Germany's weaknesses overseas, but, coincidentally, other events in the southern North Sea and at the Dardanelles suggested that sea power's effectiveness along the littoral waters of a huge continent had been greatly changed and reduced since the age of fighting sail. On the declaration of war, Germany's two relatively small overseas squadrons were left exposed, like foxes in an open field. Because Britain's Far East ally, Japan, came immediately into the war in order to seize Germany's possessions in north China and the Central Pacific islands, Admiral Graf von Spee's squadron had no alternative but to flee across the entire Pacific to the tip of South America, where it smashed a very weak Royal Navy cruiser group at Coronel (November 1914) before in turn being eliminated at the Battle of the Falkland Islands (December 1914) by a force of fast battlecruisers sent out by Admiral Fisher

---

[19] A. von Tirpitz, *My Memoirs* (London, 1919). There is more evidence of Tirpitz's strong disapproval of how the German leadership acted in 1914 in his private papers in the Military Archive in Freiburg. Cf. C. Clark, *The Sleepwalkers: How Europe Went to War in 1914* (New York, 2012).

from home waters. One could say that imperial flotilla defence was working here, then, but afterwards there was nothing for HMSs *Inflexible* and *Invincible* to do but to come home, to risk more dangerous close-water threats (HMS *Inflexible* was heavily damaged by Turkish shore batteries and a mine at the Dardanelles, beached, and then recovered) or face Germany's powerful squadrons in the North Sea (HMS *Invincible* was sunk by plunging fire at Jutland).

Secondly, and even earlier, von Souchon's *Goeben* and *Breslau* had fled through the Mediterranean and forced themselves for refuge at Constantinople, thus partly helping to bring Turkey into the war on the side of the Central Powers (also in November 1914), which in turn led to Anglo-French counteractions and expansion across the Middle East. With an Allied naval blockade in operation in the Atlantic and Channel and Gibraltar, and with all Germany's overseas cable communications cut off, there would be no great naval campaigning in overseas waters in this particular war. And Italy's entry into the conflict (May 1915) kept Austria-Hungary's fleet bottled up as well. Naval clashes in the Baltic and Black Sea were interesting, but local affairs. Only America remained as a major neutral force, albeit tied by finance, trade and communications much more to the Allied side. So the greater part of this war was, in essence, a giant Mackinder-ite land struggle, with surface navies operating at the margins; it could not help being so.[20]

The destruction of Germany's prospects overseas suggested that the workings of sea power were running in Britain's direction, but further encounters pointed to another, unsettling fact; the coming of certain nineteenth-century technologies, when converted into weapons-systems, was going to curb the application of maritime force along well-defended hostile shores, and even a bit further out. In October 1914 a single enemy mine sank the new battleship HMS *Audacious* off northern Ireland, a stunning example of what one would later call 'asymmetrical warfare' and a precedent that deeply worried Jellicoe. Even before then, in September 1914, three large cruisers (HMSs *Aboukir*, *Hogue* and *Crecy*) patrolling off the Dutch coast were sunk by a small, elderly U-boat, causing the loss of a staggering 1,400 British sailors. As Corbett put it in his official history, 'nothing that had yet occurred had so emphatically proclaimed the change that had come over naval warfare'.[21] Close blockade was supposed to have been given up as Admiralty practice years before the war; now it decidedly was.

This left the far easier practice of the distant blockade of Germany's maritime commerce, taking advantage of Britain's favourable position over the entrances to the North Sea. Yet the hoped-for 'squeeze' upon the German economy did not work as decisively as in pre-war planning, partly because the Central Powers (with their extensive grain-fields of the east) were to be largely self-sustaining in food supplies for much of the war, and partly because angry American protests about the interruption of neutral shipping slowed down the operation of the

---

[20] It is worth noting that the massive media coverage of the First World War just recently, at the centenary of 1914, had hardly any reference to the war at sea; and that the comprehensive three-volume *Cambridge History of the First World War*, ed. J. Winter (Cambridge, 2014) contains only one chapter out of seventy-three on 'The War at Sea'.
[21] J. Corbett, *Naval Operations* (London, 1921), vol. i, p. 182.

seaborne blockade of German commerce.[22] Economic warfare against the Central Powers took many forms – the cutting of cable communications, the suspension of German credits, the simple fact that the huge Anglo-German mutual trade spluttered to a halt (as did of course all German–Russian and German–French economic exchanges), the closing-down of the access to British shipping for German goods, the purchase of supplies overseas that might otherwise have gone to Germany and the now cautious inspection of neutral shipping on the high seas – but the effects of this could not be swift, and the whole process was obviously much less visible to the public and their governments than the battles of the Marne and Tannenberg. Ironically, of course, land warfare was also to show itself less decisive and promising by the time of Ypres (1915), causing the generals on both sides to call for an ever greater share of resources and manpower they now needed for carrying out vast industrialised warfare. All pre-war planning assumptions, for land and sea, seemed confounded.

While it was patently clear that in this war the Royal Navy could not operate in the Baltic[23] as it had done in the Napoleonic and Crimean Wars, Admiralty planners and their pugnacious First Lord, Churchill, did still think that they could strike at Constantinople and alter the outcome of the war in the Black Sea and across Eastern Europe itself. However, the disaster that hit the first naval operations again the Dardanelles – the loss and crippling of so many British and French battleships upon the Turkish-lain minefields on the single day of 18 March 1915 – was not only spectacular and devastating in itself. It finally confirmed that the older application of naval force against enemy shores was now impossible in a new age of small 'killer' weapons like the mine, torpedoes, entrenched coastal gunnery, fast torpedo boats and submarines (the bombing of warships by aircraft had not yet arrived). Then the second stage of the Dardanelles campaign, the failure of ever-larger Allied armies to break through at Gallipoli and advance upon Constantinople, showed that the classic weapon of amphibious warfare was also crimped unless the invading forces were to be far better equipped and trained than they were at this time. Future militaries like the US Marine Corps at Okinawa[24] learned much from studying the failures of the Allies at the Dardanelles. At the time, of course, that meant nothing. What seemed to be happening was that while the Central Powers were quite unable to shake the Allied command of the oceans, the Allies could do little or nothing to hurt their foes from the sea. Worst of all, of course, France and Britain also could do nothing

---

[22] N. Lambert, *Planning Armageddon* (Boston, 2012). Lambert shows in great detail the difficulties which the British had in implementing strict economic warfare against Germany in the light of all of the American protests against the interruption of trade. Even if the blockade were to have been much tighter, it is not clear (see p. 501) what difference that would have made upon Germany's overall economic capacities during the war.

[23] Except later, through the rather audacious operations of Britain's own submarine forces in Baltic waters.

[24] J.A. Isley and P.A. Crowl, *The U.S. Marines and Amphibious War: Its Theory, and Its Practice in the Pacific* (Princeton, 1951), pp. 581–4.

to help their beleaguered Russian ally except, so their High Commands argued, by massively increasing land pressures along the Western Front.

But the greatest confounding of the hopes of Allied sea power advocates lay where they had expected a decisive blow against the German Navy to occur – in the North Sea itself. Geography was not a friend to Jellicoe here. Enemy vessels operating from Wilhelmshaven could get to England's east coast more swiftly than could the Grand Fleet coming out of Scapa Flow, and even when the two navies met the actions were fast, furious, confused, and attended by mists, poor communications, and the failure of command and control. What therefore took place between 1914 and 1916 in these North Sea encounters was much more of a cat-and-mouse game than a decisive battle-fleet action like Trafalgar. Early German bombardments of the towns of Scarborough and Whitby shocked the British nation, so the Admiralty had to conjure up a credible response in these new and trying circumstances. The Grand Fleet could not be relocated south with individual battleship squadrons based in the Tyne, Humber, Harwich and the Thames, for bringing them together again off, say, Scarborough Head would be a signals nightmare (signals turned out to be a great Royal Navy weakness), and the possibility of one of them getting into a running fight with Hipper's dangerous battlecruisers or even Scheer's entire fleet was too daunting to contemplate. The best that could be done, and this was sensible enough, was to base Beatty's battlecruisers at Rosyth, and to fill southern ports such as Harwich with cruiser and destroyer flotillas – and rely upon the Germans' loose wireless chatter to indicate when the High Seas Fleet might be emerging. Thus the Grand Fleet would stay far up north, leaving Jellicoe however with another operational problem: should it, upon alert, steam south as fast as possible, shrugging off the risk of newly strewn enemy mines, or proceed instead at around eight knots behind a screen of minesweepers, making things easier for U-boat attack, and being also possibly too late to help an outnumbered Beatty? Clearly, Rodney and Nelson had had no such problems.

All these reminders of space and weather puts the Anglo-German North Sea surface fleet encounters – off the Yorkshire coast, the Dogger Bank, even Jutland – in their context. The historian of an exact century later should be wary of being smart after these events. Jellicoe, Beatty and Tyrwhitt were nervous, excited and worried about a battle scenario that could emerge from the mists in less than fifteen minutes, and so, surely even more so, were Hipper and his bleary-eyed lookouts on the German side. Yet it is impossible to accept Churchill's hyperbolic claim that Jellicoe was the only man who could have lost the war in an afternoon. While the Dogger Bank clash delivered to the Germans a salutary spanking and a warning, Jutland in turn gave the thinly protected British battlecruisers a hammering and the nation a blow to its pride, gave both historians and participants the stuff for endless post-mortems, claims and counterclaims, and also gave rise to a large literature, much predictable and of relatively low value.[25]

---

[25] It is nice to name an exception in A. Gordon's *The Rules of the Game: Jutland and British Naval Command* (London, 1996).

It has never been shown – for how could it be? – that even if the Grand Fleet had lost, say, six capital ships and not three, the overall maritime balance the day after Jutland would have been much different. Nor does a British claim much matter that, had its deficient shells been replaced before the war, the hits that occurred on six further German battleships would have been fatal ones. Improved fire-control here, or improved shells there, were simply not the point. Strategically, Jutland changed nothing. The British nation was understandably shocked at the loss of 6,094 seamen. But on 1 July 1916, on the first day of the Somme, the British Army lost 19,240 men out of a total of 57,500 casualties, and the British press moved on. The German High Command didn't care about Jutland, nor about an invasion of England. So what was Jellicoe to have lost?

The historian can be brief about what was left.[26] If the German Admiralty wished to bring the British nation to its knees after 1916, it seemed it had no practical alternative but to initiate full-scale and unrestricted U-boat warfare against mercantile commerce in the Atlantic, whether Allied or neutral. It thus traded off a high political risk against its increasing post-Jutland naval ineffectiveness, and by April 1917 that risk-playing had led to the entry of the United States into the conflict. That was simply too much. Provoking the British Empire into this struggle ensured that Germany would not win the First World War. Provoking the Americans also to enter meant that Germany would lose; the odds, as A.J.P. Taylor pointed out sixty years ago, were simply too great.[27]

This did not mean that the naval situation for the Allies immediately became any easier, but it did become very different. Success in the maritime conflict was now counted by the tonnage of merchantmen sunk, versus the number of U-boats destroyed and, above all, by the successful flow of New World foodstuffs, munitions and fighting men to British and French ports during 1917 and 1918. And the losses of merchant ships were huge and frightening – 3.6 million tons in six months – yet they were never enough to achieve the German Admiralty Staff's purpose, and the British return to the older practice of convoy gave the operational and tactical advantage to the Allied escorting fleets; if the U-boats wanted to score, they would have to attack the convoys and thus provoke counter-attack. Obviously, in this great struggle, neither the Grand Fleet nor the High Seas Fleet counted very much, except as a manpower drain, and as neutralising each other. To return to a consideration of the three grand theories about sea power mentioned above, one might conclude that the eventual Allied victory in late 1918 chiefly came, not from a big battle-fleet struggle in the North Sea (Mahan), but from the linked strategies of keeping open the North Atlantic lines of communication (Corbett) while beating off Ludendorff's bid for land supremacy (Mackinder). This was difficult for fleet admirals and their later historians to swallow.

This did not of course mean that sea power had not worked at all, but that it

---

[26] See P.G. Halpern, *Naval History of World War I* (Annapolis, 1994) for the best single-volume coverage of the naval conflict.
[27] A.J.P. Taylor, *The Struggle for Mastery in Europe, 1848–1918* (Oxford, 1954), pp. xxv–xxxi.

had operated, and worked, in a very different context from that anticipated by most pre-war planners and policy-makers. When the conflict opened, the signal was sent out that 'The King's Ships Were At Sea'[28] and so they were, or at least the smaller patrolling vessels and the submarines were. But the heavier surface warships came out infrequently, not only because the waters were dangerous but also, importantly, because their actual presence at sea was ever less necessary. The preponderance of naval force, plus geography, had ensured Allied naval supremacy in any case. It just was harder to explain that when the war ended and the leaders of the victor powers assembled at Versailles. The advocates of the influence of sea power had a far easier time of it after 1815 and 1945.

1919–39

There was to be no long century of relative naval peace following 1919, but in the mere twenty-year interlude a remarkable amount did occur that would affect the workings of navies. History speeded things up, as it were. One hundred years afterwards, one can see rather better than did contemporaries why the very special international and domestic circumstances after the First World War wrought havoc upon any traditional attempts to develop a naval policy; indeed, wrought havoc upon the usual ways of thinking about sea power itself. The new features to this altered strategical landscape[29] were daunting, and admirals everywhere, and the policy-makers who controlled them, were at first understandably daunted, distracted and confused by all this. By the second half of the 1920s, however, the landscape of world affairs had settled down a bit and seemed altogether more reassuring.

With a suspicious US Senate and American public forcing Woodrow Wilson and his successors to pull back from leading the efforts to create a post-1919 world order, it was left to policy-makers in London, Paris, Rome and other capitals to shape the contours within which navies would operate and naval planners would work. What is clear is that the challenges uppermost in the minds of Lloyd George and his political contemporaries were very definitely not those of, say, admirals Jellicoe and Beatty – how could they be?

Germany and Austria-Hungary had collapsed, and there was the threat of international mayhem across Eastern Europe as new nationalist forces strove to establish boundaries and governments. Most of the regular armies of the First World War had dissolved and gone home, leaving those of France, Belgium and Italy intact if vastly reduced. Polish, White Russian and Bolshevik forces fought on, with Lenin eventually gaining a breathing space for his new, puzzling regime. All this of course took place on land, indeed on Mackinder's very 'heartland' of

---

[28] J. Goldrick, *The King's Ships Were at Sea: The War in the North Sea, August 1914 to February 1915* (Annapolis, 1984), passim, a fine narrative and analysis of the opening period of the war.

[29] On this, see W. Hitchcock and P. Kennedy (eds), *From War to Peace: Altered Strategic Landscapes in the 20th Century* (New Haven, 2000), chapters in Part 1.

the Ukraine, and therefore had little to do with the Western admiralties' efforts to create their post-war international order. Urgent European issues, on boundaries, war debts, reparations, plebiscites, working out League of Nations practices and carrying out old-fashioned-type Great Power diplomacy at places like Lausanne and Locarno took most of the headlines of the day – to France especially, all this was crucial. In parallel to negotiations over the Saarland and upper Silesia were those over the future boundaries of the entire Middle East, but even here naval considerations played no role because there was no challenge to British and French imperial dominance, and nor was there in Africa. Commonwealth navies were shrinking, and Commonwealth armies dissolving, following the American lead. All the civilised (*sic*) Western world seemed to want was for its armies to come home, allowing governments instead to focus upon reconstruction and social priorities, in which context all defence expenditures had to be brutally cut. Generals were now despised, and navies told to find their place and think themselves lucky that their budgets were not further slashed.

Despite the navalists' dismay, this was not the end of sea power, and in fact the setting of reduced, economy-based priorities by the governments in Washington, London and Paris gave navies a rather good if limited circumstance in which to 'find their place'. All the admirals – including the Japanese, French and Italian – kicked, screamed and protested as they were forced into the straitjacket of the powerful clauses of the Washington Treaties of 1921–22, but when their navies emerged from this harrowing experience into the placid years of the later 1920s, things did not seem so bad after all. Even the very fact that warship sizes were standardised by displacement and gun calibre grew to be reassuring to planners and designers: a heavy cruiser had eight-inch guns, a light cruiser less than six-inch guns. Each class – carriers, battleships, cruisers – was neatly described and circumscribed.

The German Navy was no more, chiefly sunk at its own hands. The French Navy was under firm political control, the Italian Navy small and inward-looking, and no other European navies counted. Sea power as manifested by large fleets was held by the three great navies of Britain, the United States and Japan, and all were being compelled to find their diminished position within their nation's current list of priorities. Treaties established the maritime status quo regarding territories and naval bases across the Far East and Pacific; and in the Atlantic and Mediterranean the Royal Navy enjoyed an uncontested superiority, with the French and Italian navies well behind. The American and British admiralties were still going to quarrel over cruiser sizes and numbers right through until the London Naval Treaty of 1930, but this was a mild affair compared with pre-war passions. A better expression of what was going on might be captured in photographs of the great harbour of Hong Kong in these years, with the 5th RN Cruiser Squadron at anchor, under their awnings, while in the distance a few American warships peacefully took in fuel and other supplies. In the Mediterranean, French, British and Italian vessels paid port visits. Not much else was going on. The age of frantic navalism was over.

The most interesting aspect to the story of evolving sea power in these years was not, therefore, navies, and certainly not traditional battle fleets, but the emerging newer technologies of warfare, especially in the air. Both the Royal Navy and the US Navy experimented keenly with 'flat-tops' after 1919, and although those very early vessels like HMS *Argus* and USS *Langley* were small and primitive it is really remarkable how swiftly the speed, displacement size and striking power of subsequent carriers became. HMS *Ark Royal*, for example, was laid down less than twenty years after the *Argus* had put to sea. And the later carriers had to be so much bigger because aircraft in general were so much more powerful – the ships had to have a longer space for both take-off and landing. The new dive-bombers, torpedo bombers and high-level aircraft flew more swiftly, carried greater armaments and came in so fast. The admirals may have pooh-poohed Billy Mitchell's claims in 1920; but by the late 1930s it is noticeable that all heavy warships, battleships, cruisers and carriers were having ever more anti-aircraft guns fitted. More importantly, at least as far as the Royal Navy was concerned, since it operated chiefly in European waters, the threat might come more from land-based air power than from enemy carrier aircraft. Early in the First World War, mines and torpedoes had made a close-in naval blockade a thing of the past. But what if the threat of land-based aircraft pushed the more powerful navy into operating further and further from the shore? How limited was sea power's 'influence' then?

The years after 1936 saw changes come thick and fast for all the major navies. The historically distorting naval 'holiday' in capital-ship building was at an end, as were the total caps on fleet tonnages. Naval construction surged forward, in the British case, in the form of the new King George V-class battleships, Illustrious-class fleet carriers, Town-class cruisers and flotillas of fleet destroyers.[30] The American Navy also grew rapidly in the late 1930s, although it was not until the 3rd Vinson-Tramell Act of June 1940 and the Two-Ocean Navy Act of the following month that legislation went through which would make it the largest naval force in the world by 1944. The three revisionist fascist states were also investing heavily in new fleets. Italy was laying down powerful, fast battleships and heavy cruisers (although no aircraft carriers). Hitler's huge rearmament schemes also encompassed the German Navy, and if its initial laying-downs were not large, they were enough to have London seek the controversial Anglo-German Naval Agreement (1936), a desperate effort to achieve a one-power standard in home waters while also being able to send a fleet to the Far East as large as Japan's. But the Japanese were also rebuilding, way beyond that calculus. Everyone was building, running faster to keep up, just as the shapes of the wartime coalitions of power took shadowy form. The Axis trio was moving: Italy in Ethiopia (1935), in Spain (1937), in the Balkans (1939), Japan in China (1937), Hitler across central Europe (1938–39). Britain and France stood once more together, diplomatically and navally, by 1939. The USSR desperately bought time, as did a neutralist, geographically favoured USA.

---

[30] J. Maiolo, 'Did the Royal Navy Decline Between the Two World Wars?' *RUSI Journal*, clix, no. 4 (July 2014), pp. 18–24.

In sum, by the eve of the Second World War sea power – always a different thing from navies, or from naval policies, or from naval technologies – possessed a form both familiar and yet unfamiliar. Command over the surface waters of the Atlantic Ocean, and of the Mediterranean, was being asserted, by the battle fleets of the prevailing Western navies (Mahan); and plans were simultaneously being made to protect the enormous yet scattered flocks of individual merchant ships making their way to port (Corbett). One giant commercial map of November 1937 shows the streams of little dots headed to British ports from la Plata, from the West Indies, around the Cape, past Freetown, through the Mediterranean.[31] And even two years later those Elder Dempster, Blue Funnel, P&O and Compagnie de Suez merchant vessels must have all seemed reasonably safe. The Axis navies were locked into the North Sea and Mediterranean, and in the absence of a High Seas Fleet the surface balance of power was even more favourably tilted towards London and Paris than it had been in 1914.

But those vast numbers of Allied merchantmen were also more vulnerable because the greatest threat to their security now came not from hostile surface raiders but from an undersea menace that challenged the power of regular fleets to claim command of the oceans, and threatened merchant fleets, grain carriers, oil tankers and ocean liners alike. This was not completely new, of course; as described above, the early submarines had already shown their threatening capacities, in the North Sea by 1916, in the Atlantic by 1917. But many a traditional admiral, in Japan no less than in the West, had tried to brush away that fact, and the cosy international scene and naval holidays of the 1920s helped to perpetuate the illusion. And illusion it was. Four centuries of surface sea power, from *Hawkins Revenge* to the new *Ark Royal* itself (sunk by a German submarine on 13 November 1941), had been an impressive historical 'long phase' in the larger story of the advance of the West. But a new age had commenced, lasting to the present, whereby surface sea power, when under way upon the high seas, would always be vulnerable to an attack out of the deep.

In those same few years, from roughly 1930 to 1940, the engine-power, speed, carrying capacity and range of the modern bomber aircraft greatly increased in size. This became a mixed bonus to navies. The striking power and reach of the newer Japanese, American and British carriers rose greatly, but so did the danger from their foes' carrier fleets, and the nascent threat from land-based aircraft (from Stuka dive-bombers to the later high-level B-17s) was a completely new factor. While the Anglo-French surface fleets stood in great numerical superiority over those of their foes at the end of the 1930s, what did that mean if hostile air power could threaten their security, and thus their operating maritime effectiveness, up to one hundred or more miles off a theatre of war? What did it mean in the Pacific and South-East Asia if a newer Japanese carrier-based air power threatened the Allied hold over the Philippines, Hong Kong, Singapore?

---

[31] The map is reproduced in P. Kennedy, *Engineers of Victory: The Problem Solvers Who Turned the Tide in the Second World War* (New York, 2013), pp. 8–9.

What did it mean, closer to home, when Italian land-based air power threatened to drive its foes' fleets out of the Central Mediterranean?

When war broke out again in 1939, therefore, the Royal Navy may have been still the leading navy by count of the numbers; and to this could be added the considerable French fleets, plus the preponderance in naval bases possessed by the Anglo-French powers. Yet number-counting alone clearly was not a true measure of the strategical balances here. In September 1939, as Churchill resumed his position as First Lord, the British Admiralty proudly announced 'Winston is Back!', suggesting that things were much the same as in 1914. They were not, on at least two significant counts. While Italy and Japan remained initially neutral, they were obviously potential foes and had to be regarded as such, giving the Royal Navy a much more serious fleet distributional problem than it had had in 1914. And, secondly, there was now the question of how much air power's potential would be of greater advantage to Britain's foes than to the Number One maritime nation itself. Finally, looming in the background although a concern of only a few thoughtful observers of geopolitics, there was the even larger question of how West European maritime power would fare in a new era structured by the emergence of giant nations, real Superpowers.

1939–45

The Second World War was so immense that it is better understood as five great (and interrelated) conflicts rather than as a single struggle for supremacy. From 1937 until 1945 a gigantic land war raged throughout much of China, as the Imperial Japanese Army committed over one million men to crush the Nationalists, who were in turn trying to crush the Communists. From 1941 onwards an even greater land struggle took place along the entire western front of the USSR in a fight to the death between the Wehrmacht and the Red Army (with approximately three million German and five million Soviet men in the initial fighting alone). Across the vast distances of the Pacific Ocean, with outlier campaigns that ranged westwards to the Indian border, a third great struggle, mainly maritime-amphibious, was waged between Japan's forces and those of the American–Australian–British commands and forces. Eight thousand miles away, and starting over two years earlier, another geographically widespread war was fought between Britain and its allies and the German–Italian coalition; its scope was small in 1939–40, though it soon ranged from Archangel to Abyssinia, and from Newfoundland to Egypt, and all the waters in between. And from 1942 onwards a great Anglo-American double strategic bombing campaign was unleashed against the Third Reich from hundreds of British (and later Sicilian–Italian) air bases, as another, and independent, form of winning the war.

All five grand campaigns were interconnected, to a greater or lesser extent, with the Chinese–Japanese War having the fewest links to the other fighting. All five campaigns have each attracted a vast historiography, with the majority of the writings focusing solely on their own zones of battle, often laying claim to its significance for the final victory, sometimes even querying the size of the importance of another campaign.³² This is not necessary in any proper assessment of the influence of sea power upon the Second World War, for the significance of the great battles of the Pacific, Atlantic and Mediterranean are incontestable; and it is clear that the Anglo-American leadership saw those theatres as interlinked, as they shifted warships, air squadrons and landing-craft from one to the other as they judged necessary. And there are other linkages: neither the giant Anglo-American strategic bombing campaign nor the Normandy landings were possible without the Allied naval escorts getting the invaluable convoys safely across the North Atlantic;³³ the bombing of German railways and submarine pens hurt U-boat production, and crippled overall Wehrmacht communications; and seaborne/landborne supplies from the Western Allies gave far greater help to the Red Army than is usually acknowledged, while the same strategic bombing also significantly diverted large resources of German manpower and material to home defence that could have been used on the Eastern Front. As the war went on, certain Luftflotte Fliegerkorps were juggled by Goering's staff between the Mediterranean, Eastern and French/Atlantic fronts, just as many British warships went from Mediterranean operations to Arctic convoy duties to Atlantic campaigning. Few if any leaders and their advisors viewed the war with complete balance, and holistically; though the meetings of the Anglo-American Combined Chiefs of Staff did their best in this regard.

Viewing sea power within this larger, grand-strategical framework best lets historians see where and how it worked, as well as where it played little or no role. In the hard-fought campaigning of 1939 to 1942 in the Western theatres of war – where Britain fought to maintain itself as the major military Power – sea power's importance was undoubted, and was virtually everywhere. The Battle of the Atlantic, where hostilities began on the first day, was after all the longest campaign of the war, and convoys were already under attack and Royal Navy warships being sunk even during the so-called Phoney War period. The diplomacy of the late 1930s had set up the battlefield: Hitler's attack upon Poland drew France and Britain into the fighting, which then escalated greatly with the explosive German assaults upon the Low Countries, Denmark and Norway. Those losses to the Western alliance would have been great enough, but in May–June 1940 the largest strategical change since Napoleonic times occurred when France itself was toppled.

In less than two months, therefore, Britain had forfeited all of its usual geographical advantages, save that incomparable one of being an island-state, protected by its moat. Its control of the two exits from the North Sea was no more. Back in the late 1920s an obscure strategic writer called Rear Admiral Wolfgang Wegener had argued that in a future war the only way that Germany

---

[32] P. Payson O'Brien, *How the War Was Won: Air-Sea Power and Allied Victory in World War II* (Cambridge, 2015), pp. 1–13.
[33] J. Rohwer's invaluable book *The Critical Convoy Battles of 1943* (Annapolis, 1977) does the invaluable task of recording what the contents were of each merchant ship sunk, such as fifty boxed crates of fighter-aircraft, 1,000 sheets of corrugated iron, 2,000 tons of grain, etc.

could escape the geographical 'trap' that it had occupied in 1914–18 would be to have naval bases in Norway or in western France;[34] now it had both. This huge transformation of the balances made the fighting at sea ever more important, and fierce. The Royal Navy lost many ships itself as it mauled its German foe badly in the Norwegian campaign. As it pulled the British and French armies out of Dunkirk, it encountered more losses from Luftwaffe attacks. German bombers hammered away at British shipbuilding yards. German submarines, from their new advanced bases, punished the convoys severely.

Italy's entry into the war, just after the fall of France, made an awful strategic situation for Britain now close to catastrophic. The loss of the French ally, and the entry of the Italian fleet, involved a 'swing' of literally hundreds of warships; and even when the French fleet was brutally neutralised, the plain fact was that Britain had no longer control of the Mediterranean. For the next two and a half years that sea became the most contested naval theatre in all of history, and warships and merchantmen littered the sea-beds, from off Crete to the approaches to Malta. In these years, without a doubt, the Royal Navy had its own 'finest hour'. In these years, as Churchill and his cabinet realised, keeping command of the sea was elemental, vital, urgent … and so very precarious. The reader of the narrative of a Malta convoy – say, the epic 'Operation Pedestal' convoy battle of 11–13 August 1942 – comes away awed at the intensity of the fighting by the British, Italian and German units thrown into the struggle.[35]

The Battle of the Atlantic was even larger, more widespread, more costly: in 1940 the Allies lost 3.9 million tons of merchant shipping, chiefly to surface attacks and U-boats but some also to German aircraft, and to mines; in 1941 that total jumped to 4.3 million tons, including seven merchant ships in the foray by the cruiser *Hipper*;[36] and in 1942 the total was a terrifying 7.8 million tons. Then the fourth year of the campaign started badly for the convoys. It was shortly after March 1943, when no fewer than four convoys had been torn into by U-boat wolf-pack attacks and some 627,000 further tons lost, that the official Admiralty record read, 'The Germans never came so near to disrupting communications between the New World and the Old as in the first twenty days of March, 1943.'[37] Here, clearly, was Corbett's claim that sea power equalled command of the maritime routes most clearly evidenced. Here also was made clear the stark fact: unless control of the sea routes to Britain was maintained, there would be little or no strategic bombing (the fuel for the air squadrons could only come by tanker), and no Allied landings in France (for the equipment for two million US soldiers could not cross the Atlantic unless it was protected).

It is true that certain other Atlantic convoys were being successfully routed

---

[34] W. Wegener, *Die Seestrategie des Weltkrieges* (Berlin, 1929), passim.
[35] S.W. Roskill, *The War at Sea, 1939–1945, Volume II: The Period of Balance* (London, 1954), pp. 302–8.
[36] E. Grove, 'The West and the War at Sea' in R. Overy (ed.), *The Oxford Illustrated History of World War II* (Oxford, 2015), pp. 135–67.
[37] Roskill, *The War at Sea, Volume II*, p. 367.

to avoid the U-boats altogether and thus successfully make it to the Clyde and Liverpool. And it is also true that the enormous American shipbuilding effort was by this stage producing millions of tons of additional merchant shipping (11.5 million tons in 1943).[38] Yet it is not at all certain that, had the U-boat packs not been driven out of the North Atlantic by the extraordinary Allied counteroffensives of April to June 1943, those additional stocks of shipping would have had much of a difference – if undefeated at sea, Doenitz's increasingly larger wolf-packs surely would have sunk more and more ships, and the dreadful losses of merchant-ship crews clearly was not sustainable. So the amazingly swift change of fortune that followed, with the German Navy losing forty-one U-boats in May 1943 alone, actually mean that a strategic watershed had been crossed. With the Allied control of the Atlantic convoy routes never again in such dire danger, the first of the Casablanca military directives had been achieved. Naval specialists will energetically debate which of the newer weapons of war made the greatest contributions to this sharp defeat of the U-boats (the list would include the coming of long-range patrol aircraft, the arrival of the escort carriers, the astounding miniature-radar (cavity magnetron) sets, plus Hi-Fi signals detection, improved depth charges, homing torpedoes, hunter-killer groups and ULTRA signals intelligence decrypts).[39] But the chief point is that the greatest struggle ever for command of the sea had been fought, and with the defending navies triumphing after a long, bloody contest.

That vital maritime campaign won, the Anglo-American alliance could move to the next stages of the Casablanca military agenda, and commence the amphibian counteroffensive against the Third Reich's vulnerable, overextended southernmost holdings. Geography again favoured the Allies, for it was a lot easier to move invasion armies from the Clyde and Virginia to the shores of Morocco and Algeria than it was for the German High Command to send divisions from the Balkans to North Africa – especially at a time when the Wehrmacht was involved in the grinding maw that was Stalingrad. The Anglo-American forces were also lucky in that their large-scale landings were on undefended beaches – there was opposition neither to the large-scale Sicily landings in July 1943, nor to crossing the Straits of Messina into Italy proper the next month. Still, the Admiralty took no chances to ensure that these invasions went undisturbed; for example, not only did it provide enormous naval and aerial close support for the actions to take the Algerian ports, but it sent a heavily augmented Force H from Gibraltar into the Central Mediterranean to deter any sorties by the Italian or Vichy French navies – altogether four fleet carriers, five smaller carriers and six battleships were involved.[40]

All this experience proved immensely useful in the following year, when the Allies at last launched the largest amphibious operation of all time, against the

---

[38] Grove, 'The West and the War at Sea', p. 151.
[39] See Kennedy, *Engineers of Victory*, pp. 50–64.
[40] S.W. Roskill, *The War at Sea, 1939–1945, Volume III, Part I: The Offensive* (London, 1960), pp. 118–25.

Normandy beaches. All the Mediterranean commanders had been brought home (Eisenhower, Ramsay, Montgomery, Patton and so on), as were the most experienced army divisions, and of course the navies and the amphibious units. In a very real degree the Allied invasion of June 1944 was the apotheosis of Western sea power – the Admiralty insisted upon calling this 'Operation Neptune' – but the historian has also to note how integrated the naval side was with the forces of air power and land power. Five armies marched ashore on 6 June, whilst no less than 11,400 (!) aircraft were aloft that day over western France and the Channel. German torpedo boats and U-boats were ordered to interrupt the invasion but they all understood this was a suicide mission and called it so.[41] In other words, the entire littoral of Western Europe was under Allied aerial dominance. (One can again notice the difference with the situation around 1917, when Jellicoe's fleets kept carefully to the other side of the North Sea.) The D-Day operation was indeed stupendous, and yet in the very same month of June 1944 the Red Army launched its most enormous land advance against the Third Reich yet, Operation Bagration, involving 1,700,000 troops.

By contrast, the Battle of the Pacific was a war concerning sea power through and through. Japan's first six months of expansion, using its fleets, air forces and a relatively small military force to seize an astonishing amount of territory ranging from the Philippines to the Burma–India border, was spear-headed by an extremely well-equipped and well-trained carrier force accompanied by supporting cruiser and destroyer flotillas and expeditionary armies. The Royal Navy especially was ill-prepared for this, and suffered defeat after defeat, with the loss of the *Prince of Wales* and *Repulse*, the stunning surrender of Singapore, and the further losses in the Indian Ocean. America's losses, of the Philippines and the battle fleet at Pearl Harbor, were even greater; but the critically strategic position of Hawaii was not taken, nor was the US carrier fleet at all damaged, and both were to be of immense value when the counteroffensive came.

Tokyo's aim was to establish a secure perimeter ring around its recently acquired possessions and then, nourished by the oilfields of Sumatra and Borneo that had been the real object of its southern drive, to resume its massive landward campaigns into mainland China. America's aim was to recover all the territories lost, to smash the Japanese forces in the Pacific and to inflict an overwhelming defeat upon the Japanese nation itself. There would be no great land mass over which this war would be fought, but instead vast distances at sea, with the advantage going to the side that readjusted best to the novel logistical and operational requirements. And there would also be no great Battle-of-the-Atlantic fight over convoys. The reinforcement route from America's west coast to Australia was not contested, and in any case the Japanese submarine force did not focus upon a war against merchantmen but acted in support of its own battle fleets. And the American submarine attacks upon Japanese merchant shipping, while

---

[41] See Kennedy, *Engineers of Victory*, pp. 250–79.

murderously effective after the torpedo defects had been remedied, came late in the day, in 1944 and 1945.

By that stage the main contours of the war in the Pacific had become evident, with sea power playing the central role, albeit in a new hybrid form that merged it with air power and amphibian power. This was most clearly manifested in the massive forces that were assembled under Admiral Nimitz's Central Pacific Command, and in the operations they carried out in an irreversible drive across the Pacific, island group by island group: from Hawaii to the Gilbert Islands, then the Marshalls, Carolines and Marianas, then on to Iwo Jima and Okinawa and the approaches to Japan. Although every one of these operations had their own separate features,[42] there was a common operational pattern: the arrival of a large number of carrier task forces to gain control of the air and punish any Japanese warships and bases (including major ones, like Rabaul) in the region; the offshore pounding by heavy cruisers and battleships – in their new, non-Mahanian role – of the island's land defences; and then the amphibious assault itself. The land fighting was always ferocious, but the garrisons were isolated, and no American assault was thrown back. The last great Japanese counter-attack was in their multi-part operation at Leyte Gulf (October 1944), finally involving their Main Fleet. In retrospect one can see that even this operation, with its various subplots to trap some of the American squadrons, would not have stayed the offensive tide for long; the US economy, eight or possibly ten times greater than that of Japan's, had now geared up to full production.

Around the middle of 1943 that great shift in the global power balances that had been building up, tectonically, since the 1890s and more obviously after the huge American defence spending near the end of the First World War showed itself in full display. In June 1943 the first of the new, fast Essex-class fleet carriers, the USS *Essex* itself, slipped into Pearl Harbor. By August it was joined by another, the new USS *Yorktown*; and afterwards by the USS *Intrepid* and twenty-one more. A new class of light fleet carriers was also streaming into the Pacific, accompanied by fast new destroyers, heavy and light cruisers. The mighty sixteen-inch-gunned Iowa-class battleships were not far behind. A galvanised American shipbuilding industry was also completing fast oilers to accompany the future long-range operations of the carrier groups, and hundreds and hundreds of landing-craft for future amphibian landings on the scattered Japanese-held islands. And, from Seattle (Boeing) to Long Island (Grumman), the US aircraft industry poured out 85,898 aircraft in 1943 alone, and a staggering 96,318 in 1944.[43] Nothing compared.

All this now dated those older disputes between sea power and land power advocates, as Leo Amery had so presciently guessed it would when he made his amazingly insightful commentary upon Mackinder's 'Geographical Pivot of

---

[42] These operations are covered in S. Morison, *History of United States Naval Operations in World War II* (Boston, 1947–62), vols vii, viii and xiv.
[43] Kennedy, *Rise and Fall of the Great Powers*, p. 354.

History' paper of April 1904.[44] The chief thing to understand now was neither the display of great warship fleets occupying the high seas, nor the successful control of the routes of trade, nor even the fight to defeat the giant Nazi land empire – all of them vital, epic, remarkable in their different ways – but the coming of continent-wide Superpowers of 'vast munitioning potential' that brought the winning of wars to a new level of force projection. In this narrative, one can certainly see how sea power influenced the outcome of the Second World War, not as the determinant but as the many-sided instrument of Allied force projection, in specific theatres, to a specific degree.

Concluding Thoughts

Sea power had played an enormously important part in the outcome of the French Revolutionary and Napoleonic Wars. One hundred years later, however, during the second 'Great War' of 1914–18, it seemed both to participants and historians to play a far less significant role in influencing the result of that conflict. Yet twenty-five years after that, in the epic global struggle of the Second World War, sea power once again claimed an indisputable 'influence'. This curious and remarkable discrepancy has never really been explained by naval historians. Nor is the reader helped very much in understanding the difference by drawing from the writings of any one of the three great theorists of modern geopolitical thought concerning sea power and land power, Mahan, Corbett and Mackinder, because each argued and composed, understandably, within the limits of his time and his perspective. Each had magnificent insight, yet saw but a part of the struggle for world power. Still, what they saw, and what they argued, helps us greatly to understand the puzzle.

The best way of helping us comprehend the puzzle is to think about contested space, that is, the struggle by every large and small power to defend its own spheres of influence and to invade and grasp the enemy's. In the French Revolutionary and Napoleonic Wars the emperor not only sought to dominate his immediate continental land space, but to move into Britain's, in the Mediterranean, the Caribbean, Egypt, the Near East; and also in the Atlantic, through the assembling and deployment of large, threatening Franco-Spanish fleets. So, from the beginning of the conflict until 1805, the struggle was indeed determined by vast overpowering force upon the sea, that is, by large consolidated battle fleets that could drive the enemy's forces away and gain control of the central commons. Great fleet fights, prefigured by those in the Anglo-Dutch Wars, the War of the Spanish Succession and the Seven Years' War, occupied the centre of the stage, and from this Mahan drew his theory about what constituted the essence of sea power: the superior battle fleet.

---

[44] Amery's comments are discussed in P. Kennedy, 'Mahan Versus Mackinder: Two Interpretations of British Sea Power', in *Strategy and Diplomacy 1870–1945: Eight Studies* (London, 1983), passim.

Yet strategic space was also being fought over in two other ways during the struggle against Napoleon, and particularly after 1805. Here of course naval warfare was far less glamorous – Trafalgar had been won, but Nelson was dead – yet other battles for strategic 'space' were being fought. There were the really interesting fights in the Eastern Seas, the struggle for the Baltic, the frigate encounters in the Mediterranean and the French privateer wars against British commerce on the seas. The latter, being so much more of concern to Corbett, was just a part of the economic warfare waged during these years between Britain and Napoleonic France that encompassed mutual blockades, the Continental System, the use of credit, and the British subsidies to the land armies of its European allies.[45] Just because an epic, single-day naval battle had not taken place did not mean that sea power after 1806 was not being exerted – and felt.

Finally, fearing a Napoleonic domination of Western and central Europe, the British leadership felt it had no choice but to contest the emperor's own continental space, seeking to defeat him in many ways, from encouraging and funding coalitions of friendly land powers to pull him down from power, to the actual deployments of the British Army, in the Peninsula, in southern France, eventually in Belgium. From Helsinki to Flanders and Dover, down to Lisbon and Gibraltar and on via Naples to the Bosphorus, Britain sought to put a wrap around the emperor's efforts to break out, holding onto the rimland (sic) until there was sufficient coalition force to win at the heartland. This was a long and frequently unsuccessful grand strategy which only saw its successful realisation in the battles of Borodino (1812), Leipzig (1813) and Waterloo (1815), many leagues from Mahan's far-off fleets even if sea power had decidedly affected the outcome of this long struggle. During the mid-eighteenth century, it is sometimes argued,[46] Britain had been torn between a 'maritime' and a 'continental' strategy. In bringing Napoleon down, there was no question but that both were needed.

One hundred years later, ideas about the importance of sea power never stood higher in the public realm. All the Great Powers before 1914 (including land-based ones like Russia) strove to have as large a navy as possible, naval 'races' occurred between so many of these nations, and Mahan's theories about the role of the battle fleet in deciding victory were dominant. What followed in 1914–18, as described in the section above, was therefore all the more disappointing, and yet this is understandable if one thinks again about contested 'space'. During the war sea power was seen by contemporaries to play a lesser role because the German-led Central Powers had no real opportunity to enter the British Empire's maritime space, at least not in the form of surface warfare in the Atlantic and beyond. Grand Mahanian battle fleets there were all right, but they were confined by circumstance to remain chiefly in their North Sea harbours. In the Baltic, North Sea and Adriatic waters there were some small, desultory surface actions,

---

[45] F. Crouzet, 'Wars, Blockade and Economic Change in Europe, 1792–1815', *Journal of Economic History*, xxiv, no. 4 (1964).

[46] R. Pares, 'American versus Continental Warfare, 1739–63', *English Historical Review*, li, no. 103 (July 1936).

but really after 1916 the struggle for mastery at sea became much more a battle for the Atlantic sea-lanes, for Corbett's vital maritime routes.

Since extra-European spheres could not be invaded by Berlin except by this challenge by the U-boat after 1916, and there already existed a gigantic struggle between the Austro-German and Franco-Russian empires for control of the land space of Europe, what took place, to the dismay of the navalists, was the dispatch of huge British Empire and later American armies to swing the land balances on the Western and Italian fronts; the maritime nations were invading continental space, and not the reverse. Significant military operations also took place in Palestine, Mesopotamia and the Caucasus during 1915–19, but those were contested only by Germany's lesser ally, Turkey, and thus the chief battlefronts remained in Europe, in France, Italy and Poland–Ukraine. In none of those areas did sea power play a direct role. When the year 1918 saw each side committing all their respective military resources for the hoped-for victory, the Grand Fleet, to Jellicoe's frustration, swung at anchor in Scapa Flow. Allied naval power had fairly easily preserved Britain's own physical security, and then maintained command of the Atlantic sea-lanes, but those were negative achievements, and ones out of sight, which is why the role of navies was much less celebrated that it had been in the triumphant years following 1815.

Even so, the swift collapse of the League of Nations' system, the rise of the three revisionist nations of Germany, Italy and Japan, and the reoccurrence of another furious worldwide naval arms race in the late 1930s meant that sea power's role was not doubted when the Second World War broke out. The British Admiralty had no other choice but to rely upon a Mahanian battle posture, off Norway, in sinking the *Bismarck* and the *Scharnhorst*, in protecting the Mediterranean convoys, and in shepherding the North African and Sicilian landings. At the same time, it had no other choice but to commit to a massive, unrelenting Corbettian strategy of securing the Atlantic sea-lanes. In the European-Atlantic naval battles, therefore, each theorist had his vindication.

Further east, the navalists' case could be much more easily made. The Pacific War had been from beginning to end about winning or losing maritime mastery. And if one substituted carrier groups for battleship squadrons, it turned out to be much more of a Mahanian struggle for command of the central oceans than a Corbettian fight over convoy routes and sea-lanes. It didn't really matter, though. The point was that, in this war, naval power had proved to be vital for the Allied victory.

In sum, to every navalist author's delight, the Pacific War had joined with the prolonged Atlantic and Mediterranean campaigns in being fought for command of the sea. And even if Stalinist propaganda was to attempt to ignore the fact, the war of the Eastern Front was also affected, in some part, by seaborne supplies to the USSR and the choking-off of such supplies to Germany. Why not then agree that navies, and naval power, had once again counted for such a lot in world affairs? That seemed so obvious, when a vast Allied fleet rested in Tokyo Bay, while hundreds of German U-boats were being scuttled or surrendered to their victorious naval opponents. The end of the First World War was signed in a railway carriage at Compiègne; but now, the end of the Second World War was signed on the afterdeck of the battleship USS *Missouri*. What place of signature, on each occasion, could be more symbolic? As was the case in 1815, but had not been the case in 1918, Neptune in 1945 could again hold his trident high.

But to what end? Even then, as those victorious Allied navies rested in that bay, sea power's role had not really been settled, or, rather, it was about to be unsettled. Over the post-1945 age there hung the immediate shadow, and the conundrum, of the coming of atomic weaponry. The claims of all armed services, navies included, were now thrown into question. This was an odd fate, and an odd ending to a naval historical narrative that otherwise seemed so teleological; but the fact was that the story of sea power's place in the three great global wars of these 150 years simply did end with such a paradox. The Anglo-American navies that had fought so well, so impressively, so successfully, came out of this war with their futures more uncertain than ever before in history.

11
The Evolution of a Warship Type: The Role and Function of the Battlecruiser in Admiralty Plans on the Eve of the First World War

MATTHEW S. SELIGMANN

The battlecruiser, brainchild of colourful First Sea Lord Sir Jackie Fisher, has long been a matter of controversy. Contemporaries argued over the use and value of these warships; the loss by catastrophic magazine explosion of three of these vessels at the Battle of Jutland on 31 May 1916 further polarised this debate; and modern-day historians have, for various reasons, spilt a great deal of ink over their genesis and purpose. In the current historiography there are two rival explanations for their origins. On the one hand there are revisionist historians such as Jon Sumida, who argue that the battlecruiser was conceived as an imperial power-projection vessel, whose roots lay in the need to find an antidote to Franco-Russian plans to wage a *guerre de course* against British shipping with a fleet of commerce-raiding armoured cruisers.[1] On the other side of the debate are historians, such as the present author, who argue that the origins of the battlecruiser are grounded in the Anglo-German antagonism of the early twentieth century. In this formulation, this warship type was specifically devised as a counter to German plans to convert fast transatlantic liners into auxiliary cruisers and deploy them as raiders on the Atlantic trade routes. An exceptionally fast surface warship able to cut through the heavy Atlantic swells that could swallow smaller vessels and so overtake the fast German liners that ploughed this route with ease led first to subsidised British liners and then to the battlecruiser.[2] This essay will contribute to this debate by demonstrating that the former argument is based upon an inaccurate depiction of relative naval strength and illustrate the limitations inherent on focusing purely upon the *origins* of the battlecruiser, without paying sufficient attention to how the craft were actually employed.

---

[1] J.T. Sumida, 'British Preparation for Global Naval War, 1904–14: Directed Revolution or Critical Problem Solving?', in T.C. Imlay and M.D. Toft (eds), *The Fog of Peace and War Planning: Military and Strategic Planning under Uncertainty* (London and New York, 2006), pp. 126–38.

[2] M.S. Seligmann, *The Royal Navy and the German Threat, 1901–1914: Admiralty Plans to Protect British Trade in a War against Germany* (Oxford, 2012).

I

The first of these interpretations assumes that a global Franco-Russian armoured cruiser threat was foremost in the Admiralty's thinking when the battlecruiser was conceived. However, a careful examination of the available documentary evidence reveals this premise to be unsustainable. The first battlecruiser to be laid down was HMS *Inflexible*, the keel plate of which was placed in position on the slipway on 5 February 1906. This was nine months after the bulk of the Russian Navy had been annihilated in the Russo-Japanese War and a year after the First Moroccan Crisis had transformed the Anglo-French *Entente Cordiale* of 1904 from a mere settlement of colonial differences into the beginnings of a fully fledged *de facto* diplomatic partnership. As a result, the first battlecruiser was commenced at a time when the French Navy was friendly and the Russian Navy non-existent. Of course, one might argue that a ship begun in 1906 would have been conceived a year earlier when circumstances were different. It is certainly true that the Committee on Designs, the body which drew up the plans for these vessels, first met at the end of 1904, at a moment when the bulk of the Russian Navy had yet to meet its date with destiny at the hands of the Japanese. However, even at that time it is more than doubtful if the Royal Navy believed that French and Russian armoured cruisers posed any kind of menace. For one thing it was obvious by 1903, if not earlier, that the arms race in armoured cruisers was one that the Royal Navy had comprehensively won. So great was the British preponderance in these vessels that the Naval Intelligence Department believed that any danger was already well and truly neutralised.[3] Moreover, as Russian and French vessels of this type took so long to build and underperformed when completed, there appeared little prospect of this threat being fully realised.[4] Certainly, war with France held few terrors for the Admiralty.[5] In this context, building battlecruisers to fight French and Russian armoured cruisers would have been a way to spend large amounts of money on a problem that had already been solved and for which no additional solution was required.

It is perhaps not surprising given the want of French and Russian armoured cruisers for the new British battlecruisers to face that there are a dearth of statements – either explicit or implied – from the British Admiralty linking the building of these vessels to this particular threat. By contrast, it is notable that the only clear and unambiguous explanation of the function the battlecruiser was supposed to perform expressed prior to their construction by their progenitor, Jackie Fisher, directly links them to the German auxiliary cruiser threat. At a meeting convened on 2 December 1905 that included all the Sea Lords and many of the key officials at the Admiralty, he explained that battlecruisers were

---

[3] Admiralty, 'Memorandum on the Protection of Ocean Trade in Time of War', October 1903, p. 10. TNA, CAB 17/3.
[4] See, for example, the NID's assessment of the *Jeanne D'Arc*. TNA, ADM 231/39, fol. 425.
[5] Matthew. S. Seligmann, 'Britain's Great Security Mirage: The Royal Navy and the Franco-Russian Naval Threat, 1898–1906', *Journal of Strategic Studies*, 35 (2012), pp. 861–86.

necessary to replace the express steamers *Lusitania* and *Mauretania* as Britain's means of defeating Germany's armed liners:

> Originally the two great Cunard ships now completing were subsidised by the Government with the object of enabling the armed merchant ships of this country to be a match for the Great German vessels which were then the fastest on the sea. But such vessels when armed will only be equal to the German vessels, and in war equality only would not suffice – as Nelson said, 'You ought to be 100 per cent stronger than the enemy if you can!' If two ships of that type met, the result of the fight would be a 'toss up', and the British Navy must not be placed in such a position … Therefore foreign vessels of that description must be sought out and dealt with by fast big armoured cruisers of the *Invincible* class, when there can be no doubt of the result. A cruiser like the *Invincible* would 'mop' up such vessels one after the other with the greatest ease, and therefore, if necessary, more *Invincibles* must be built for that purpose.[6]

As this is the only clear statement on this topic from this time that has been discovered to date, ignoring it in favour of a phantom Franco-Russian cruiser threat appears methodologically suspect. The fact that its audience consisted of key Admiralty officials reinforces this notion.

II

It is something of an irony, given the effort I have devoted both here and elsewhere to showing that it was in response to the German menace rather than the Franco-Russian threat that the battlecruiser was brought into existence, that in regard to the battlecruiser's subsequent development this debate about its origins hardly matters. For whatever might have been the initial motive for building these vessels, the fact remains that, on their completion, the Royal Navy's first battlecruisers were used for completely different ends: an important fact all too often ignored. Following sea trials all three battlecruisers commissioned for service in the North Sea as part of the 1st Cruiser Squadron attached to the Home Fleet.

This deployment had a very specific purpose – one that had nothing whatsoever to do with either trade protection or imperial power projection. Instead, the ships of the 1st Cruiser Squadron were there to enforce the blockade of the German coasts that the Royal Navy planned to implement in the event of war with Germany. The timing of their deployment makes this especially straightforward to illustrate. The three newly completed battlecruisers all joined the 1st Cruiser Squadron in March 1909. At the end of the very same month the Admiralty issued to its various senior commanders the latest iteration of its main war plan, known in 1909 as Plan GU.[7]

---

[6] Admiralty Library, Portsmouth: Naval Necessities, vol. iv, paper B, 'Sunday 2nd December 1905'.
[7] 'War Plan G.U. War Orders for the Commander-in-Chief of the Home Fleet', March

The principal goal of the 1909 war plan, as the document made very clear from the outset, was to bring the German fleet to battle and defeat it. To achieve this it was essential to ensure that, if the German fleet put to sea, the British Admiralty should quickly become aware of this fact and be ready to respond. Accordingly, the plan called for the deployment of several flotillas of destroyers directly off the German North Sea littoral, where they would watch for any signs that the German fleet intended to sortie. Should such a move take place, there would be two British fleets, one based in Scotland and one based between the Channel and the Wash, ready to intercept the emerging German forces and give battle. Of course, the fact that the British destroyers were there to gather operational intelligence and thus remove the possibility of the German Navy mounting any kind of operation in the North Sea that enjoyed the element of surprise, naturally gave the German fleet every reason to seek their removal. The obvious means of doing this was for the Germans to dispatch destroyers of their own or even cruisers to drive the British destroyers away. To ensure this could not happen the British destroyers were backed by a line of light cruisers. Supporting these, at a slightly greater distance, were the Royal Navy's armoured cruisers, ready to provide heavy cover should a concerted German effort be made to disperse the watching forces. At the heart of this heavy support force was the 1st Cruiser Squadron with its three brand new battlecruisers.

III

This deployment, as the heavy cover behind the British observational blockade effort, remained in place for a further three years, during which time the original trio of battlecruisers of the Invincible class were joined by the *Indefatigable*, the name ship of the next class of battlecruiser. This lengthy stint in the North Sea, which makes very clear how both Fisher and his immediate successor, Sir Arthur Wilson, viewed the role of these vessels, was only brought to an end in May 1912.[8] The reason for this was not a reconceptualisation of the role of the battlecruiser, but a change in the war plan. In May 1912, observational blockade, which had been central to the strategy for a war against Germany since at least 1904, was written out of the plans. In many respects this is quite surprising. The idea of blockading the German coast had been tested and validated in manoeuvres that had been undertaken as recently as June 1911. Furthermore, the concept had been presented to the Committee of Imperial Defence on 23 August 1911 by First Sea Lord Sir Arthur Wilson, where, contrary to many historical accounts, it had not

---

1909. NMRN, Crease Papers, MSS 253/84/3. On this plan see David Morgan-Owen, "History is a Record of Exploded Ideas": Sir John Fisher and Home Defence, 1904–1910', *The International History Review*, xxxvi (2014), pp. 550–72.

[8] On Wilson's operational ideas see D. Morgan-Owen, 'Cooked Up in the Dinner Hour? A Reconsideration of The Strategic Views of Sir Arthur Wilson', *English Historical Review*, cxxx, no. 545 (2015), pp. 865–906.

been rejected. However, the new naval leadership that was put in place after Sir Arthur Wilson's retirement in December 1911 were troubled by it. They feared that the belated expansion of the German submarine service in combination with the enhanced potential of mine warfare and the upgrading of Germany's fixed coastal defences made the use of inshore destroyer flotillas extremely hazardous. Hence it was decided to pull the forces watching for a German sortie further back into the North Sea.

This decision had significant implications for Britain's battlecruisers. On the one hand it had the positive effect of freeing them up for other roles. Advantage was quickly taken of this. In early 1912 a controversy had arisen over the future strength of the British fleet in the Mediterranean. The new First Lord of the Admiralty, Winston Churchill, wanted to concentrate all of Britain's major surface warships in the North Sea, the region he considered to be of decisive importance, and was willing to reduce the force structure in peripheral areas, such as the Mediterranean, to achieve this. However, many of his Cabinet colleagues, worried about the implications of such a move for British prestige, particularly in the Mediterranean, opposed this. The story of the complex negotiations that resulted has been ably told by Christopher Bell.[9] Thus, all that need worry us here is that the upshot was a compromise whereby the Royal Navy removed its battleships from the Mediterranean and replaced them by the newly formed 2nd Battle Cruiser Squadron, consisting of the four oldest battlecruisers just released from blockade duties. This force was a credible statement of British power, but at the same time possessed sufficient speed to be able to return, if needed, with rapidity to the primary theatre in the North Sea.

If the decision to pull back the watching forces in the North Sea had some positive consequences, it was also not without its drawbacks. The most obvious of these was that it produced enormous tactical difficulties. Summer manoeuvres undertaken both in 1912 and in 1913 to evaluate the new dispositions conclusively revealed what generally became known as 'the North Sea Problem', namely that watching forces in the middle of the North Sea frequently failed to observe, let alone intercept, enemy forces that advanced into the North Sea.[10] Moreover, even when they did spot them, this was often the prelude to the destruction of the watching vessel as the greatly increased distances needed for an observational cordon in the middle of the North Sea meant that the necessarily widely dispersed watching forces generally encountered concentrated enemy ones, with catastrophic consequences for the watchers.[11] The outcome of this was that, under the new dispositions, bringing the German fleet to battle, let alone defeating it,

---

[9] C.M. Bell, 'Sir John Fisher's Naval Revolution Reconsidered: Winston Churchill at the Admiralty, 1911–1914', *War in History*, xviii (2011), pp. 333–56; Bell, 'Sentiment *vs* Strategy: British Naval Policy, Imperial Defence, and the Development of Dominion Navies, 1911–14', *International History Review*, xxxvii, no. 2 (2015), pp. 262–81.

[10] See TNA, ADM 116/1214, 'Naval Manoeuvres 1913: North Sea Problem'.

[11] D. Morgan-Owen, 'An "Intermediate" Blockade? British North Sea Strategy 1912–1914', *War in History*, xxii, no. 4 (2015), pp. 478–502.

was going to be seriously problematic. Worse still, with the enemy easily able to evade or break the new cordon, it was difficult for the Royal Navy to maintain its long-standing guarantee that it could protect the British Isles from raid or invasion.[12]

This was no trivial problem and, quite naturally, the Admiralty urgently sought a solution. But what might it be? The ideal answer would have been to re-establish some form of observational blockade that would once again provide the Royal Navy with reliable advanced warning of German fleet activity. However, despite considerable discussion during this period about seizing a German island as an advanced base, undertaking mass destroyer operations in the German Bight or using submarines as blockade craft, nothing definitive arose out of these ideas before August 1914, although the hope was always there that at least one of these options might be made viable in the near future. Meanwhile, of course, that still left a capability gap in the present.

The existence of this gap focused attention on ways to stiffen the mid-North Sea cruiser cordon so that it was both more effective as an observational system and less susceptible to being broken up by superior force. As a means of addressing this particular requirement the battlecruiser appeared to many senior figures within the Royal Navy to have a great deal to offer.

One such figure was Rear Admiral Doveton Sturdee, the commander of the 5th (later redesignated 2nd) Cruiser Squadron. During the course of 1912 and 1913 Sturdee participated in and subsequently analysed a series of major manoeuvres and exercises that had as their focus understanding the nature of and providing possible solutions to the North Sea Problem. These exercises were too numerous to list here, but the lessons they provided and the conclusions Sturdee drew from them are worth summarising in detail.[13]

First, the tests conclusively confirmed what was already known, namely 'the weakness of a long cruiser line', especially 'when its position becomes known to an enterprising enemy'.[14] Several factors contributed to this. To begin with, there was the limited visibility of the North Sea. In conditions of poor visibility, Sturdee wrote, 'the cruiser patrol … has failed each time it has really been tested'. Added to this was the further problem that the majority of the vessels deployed in the observational patrol were armoured cruisers and this vessel type, Sturdee concluded, was an asset of decidedly limited and declining value. As he explained, armoured cruisers lacked both the speed to evade modern heavy units and also the firepower to engage them. Thus, when the enemy struck, armoured cruisers on patrol were unable either to flee to make their report or to fight their way out of their situation, becoming 'easy prey' for the enemy's forces. Accordingly,

---

[12] The best study of the invasion question to date is D. Morgan-Owen, 'The Invasion Question: Admiralty Plans to Defend the British Isles, 1888–1918' (PhD Thesis, Exeter University, 2013).
[13] TNA, ADM 1/8388/227, Sturdee, 'Report on the Principal Cruiser Work carried on by the Home Fleets during 1913' (O.D.14, July 1914).
[14] Ibid., p. 9.

Sturdee could only conclude that they had been 'declassed' as fighting ships to the point that 'long cruiser lines composed of the present type of (armoured) cruisers are not desirable in home waters'.[15] If they were to remain – and the lack of alternative replacement units probably dictated they would have to – then he recommended that they operate in squadrons, where numbers might make up for lack of fighting power, even though such a concentration of units previously dispersed would create gaps in the cordon. This being the case, the question arose as to which vessels were suitable to act in the place of armoured cruisers in the observational force.

The answer to this led to the second key conclusion, namely that there were two vessel types that the exercises demonstrated to be suitable for observational work in the North Sea. The first of these was the light cruiser. Possessing high speed, at least in good weather, they had the ability to evade most vessels more powerful than themselves and so could, in Sturdee's words, 'be spread ... to watch a broad front'.[16] The one vessel that light cruisers could not evade was the other type to distinguish itself in the manoeuvres and that was the battlecruiser. As fast as the light cruiser, but unlike the light cruiser also able to maintain their high speed in a rough sea or against a headwind, they were extremely powerful fighting ships. As a result, the exercises consistently showed that enemy battlecruisers could make 'easy prey' of armoured cruiser lines and could also be used 'to break an advancing patrol line' even if that line were made up of light cruisers.[17] The only obvious antidote to this was to deploy battlecruisers in support of Britain's armoured cruisers, if such vessels had to be used, and to operate the light cruisers in conjunction with battlecruisers, the latter providing cover to the former. This was a key finding.

The belief that the best way to maintain the mid-North Sea observation system against the anticipated German efforts to break it up was by the use of battlecruisers, preferably alongside light cruisers, was not confined just to Sturdee. Other key members of the naval leadership reached similar conclusions at more or less the same time. The most important of these was the Commander-in-Chief of the Home Fleets, Sir George Callaghan, whose view on this matter, like Sturdee's, derived from witnessing the various tests and manoeuvres. The first indication of his feelings on this matter came in a letter that he dispatched to the War Staff in March 1913. In it Callaghan argued on the basis of 'the recent Cruiser exercises' that it was now 'evident that a couple of Battle Cruisers can completely break up a patrol (or observation line) composed of even our best Armoured Cruisers'. As a result, he concluded that in wartime Britain's battlecruisers would be needed 'to support the Patrolling Squadrons on observation duties in the North Sea' and that they 'cannot be spared for any purpose other than supporting the Patrols'.[18]

---

[15] Ibid., pp. 13 and 17.
[16] Ibid., p. 13.
[17] Ibid., p. 17.
[18] IWM, Battenberg Papers, DS/MISC/20, reel III, file 184, Callaghan to War Staff, 8 March 1913.

Having once reached this conclusion, Callaghan repeated it to the Admiralty on numerous other occasions. In August 1913, for example, when assessing the results of the summer manoeuvres, he echoed Sturdee's belief that the armoured cruiser was 'rapidly becoming an obsolete class of ship' and asserted in consequence that '[a]ll indications point to the fact that the battle cruiser type, in conjunction with the fast light cruiser, now completely dominates the cruiser situation'.[19] Similarly, in March 1914, he informed the Admiralty that armoured cruisers could 'no longer be reckoned' as an effective type and that in his view 'battle cruisers completely dominate the cruiser situation in the North Sea'. Accordingly, he regarded a clear superiority in this type as essential for Britain and went on to comment on the necessity of battlecruisers operating in conjunction with light cruisers.[20] As he put it in a separate letter sent out the very same day, for North Sea operations 'the association of battle cruisers with light cruisers ... is of the first importance'.[21]

Callaghan's views were echoed in large measure by Rear Admiral David Beatty. Appointed to the command of the 1st Battle Cruiser Squadron on 1 March 1913, Beatty quickly made it plain in a memorandum on the 'Functions of a Battle Cruiser Squadron' that he regarded the primary role of battlecruisers as support for either a fast reconnaissance force of light cruisers or a blockading force of armoured cruisers.[22] Like Callaghan, he reiterated this point on numerous occasions. Writing on 8 September 1913, he recorded that 'one of the principal functions of the Battle Cruiser Squadron is to provide supports for the Cruiser Squadrons'.[23] Likewise, on 3 March 1914, he placed at the very top of the list of battlecruiser functions: 'To provide a fast and powerful force for supporting the operations of advanced cruisers or armoured cruisers, whether employed for Patroling, Watching, Searching, making a Reconnaissance, or for other duties.'[24] The point was clear.

If, as seems evident, there was a general concurrence among senior flag officers at sea that the battlecruiser was the key to stiffening the mid-North Sea cruiser cordon, the question that remained outstanding was how best to utilise them for this purpose. At least two different models for how to do this had been suggested on the basis of the various exercises. First, if armoured cruisers continued to provide the bulk of the patrolling forces, notwithstanding any doubts about their suitability for this role, then battlecruisers could be used to provide them with heavy support in order to make up for the deficiencies in speed and fighting power of the armoured cruiser type. Alternatively, battlecruisers could operate in association with light cruisers in some as yet unspecified manner.

[19] TNA, ADM 116/3130, Callaghan, 28 August 1913.
[20] TNA, ADM 1/8372/76, Callaghan to Admiralty, 25 March 1914.
[21] Ibid., Callaghan to Beatty, 25 March 1914.
[22] *The Beatty Papers, Volume I*, ed. B. Ranft (Aldershot, 1989), p. 59.
[23] TNA, ADM 1/8372/76, Beatty to Callaghan, 8 September 1913.
[24] Ibid., Beatty to Commanding Officers, First Battle Cruiser Squadron.

IV

How to resolve this was a question for the Admiralty, a fact that leads inexorably to the question of how it responded to the views from the fleet. While gaps in the documentary record make it difficult to piece together some parts of the story, it seems clear courtesy of a surviving minute by Churchill that the naval leadership in London was looking into the question of North Sea cruiser organisation at least as early as October 1912. At this stage it is evident that someone in the Admiralty had proposed creating mixed cruiser squadrons consisting of two armoured cruisers and two light cruisers, a proposal that Churchill opposed.[25] However, while the First Lord would continue to deprecate associating armoured cruisers and light cruisers, his views on mixed squadrons, if differently composed, would undergo considerable modification.[26] In particular, he could see considerable merit in operating battlecruisers in conjunction with light cruisers. A paper from 3 April 1913 spelt out the merits of this formation:

> Battle cruisers by reason of their great strength ... are particularly suited to reinforce a light cruiser observation line ... The 30-knot light cruiser has nothing to fear from any vessel afloat except the enemy's battle cruiser ... The natural support of the light cruiser against the enemy's battle cruiser is our own battle cruiser. When the Arethusas are ready, it will be desirable to exercise them in groups with battle cruisers ... 4 light cruisers and a battle cruiser in line at 15 miles apart ... will watch with ease in clear weather a front of 90 miles ... There will be no light cruiser in the longest of these lines which the protecting battle cruiser ... could not reach before the attack of an overtaking hostile battle cruiser can be delivered.[27]

This minute did not have any immediate results, but the principle it articulated was clearly discussed further because when in January 1914 the question of the navy's future force structure came under discussion, mixed squadrons were on the agenda. As the War Staff proposal duly recorded, one aim of the new organisation was:

> To give effect, as far as possible, to the principle of mixed squadrons for those units which are detailed for North Sea observation duties, this system having given the best results in the late manoeuvres, and having been recommended by Admiral Sturdee for trial.[28]

The First Sea Lord, Prince Louis of Battenberg, who saw the proposal added the further minute that he was especially eager to see 'how best to combine the battle cruisers for work with the Arethusas'. This idea was not without its opponents. Captain George Ballard, the head of the Operations Division of the War Staff, did not think there would be much direct cooperation between the

---

[25] TNA, ADM 116/3088, Minute by Churchill, 5 October 1912.
[26] Ibid., Minute by Churchill, 15 April 1914.
[27] TNA, ADM 1/8329, Minute by Churchill, 3 April 1913.
[28] IWM, Battenberg Papers, 278, War Staff, 'Proposed Revision of Cruiser and Light Cruiser Organisation to meet anticipated Requirements', 28 January 1914.

two classes of ship. Another opponent was Charles Madden, commander of the 2nd Cruiser Squadron. However, as we have seen, a strong advocate existed in Admiral Callaghan. This was well known in the Admiralty, with Battenberg for one writing that 'C-in-C Home Fleets favours combing Arethusas with Battle Cruiser.'[29] It is quite possible that Callaghan's support may have been decisive in swinging the argument.

Irrespective of whose was the decisive voice, when in early July 1914 the Admiralty finalised their plan for the force structure of its various fleets and squadrons for the period up to April 1917, the decision had been made to institutionalise the cooperation of battlecruisers and light cruisers in the North Sea. The first step was scheduled to be taken in March 1915, when Beatty's period as Rear Admiral commanding the 1st Battle Cruiser Squadron came to an end. As soon as he struck his flag, his squadron was to be 'split up and, with 8 light cruisers, two Mixed Cruiser Squadrons [were] to be formed'. Then, in December 1915 it was intended to bring home the 2nd Battle Cruiser Squadron from the Mediterranean, which would likewise be broken up to form two additional mixed squadrons. As a result, come the start of 1916, the main British cruiser force in the North Sea would consist of four mixed squadrons, each of which was composed of two battlecruisers operating in conjunction with four light cruisers.[30]

Thus, the role envisaged for battlecruisers by the British naval leadership on the eve of the First World War was very much a North Sea one. Operating in conjunction with light cruisers, they would provide the effective cruiser cordon that the abandonment of observational blockade in May 1912 made necessary, but which exercises had consistently shown was not provided by the existing dispersed armoured cruiser formations. This has two important implications. First, in terms of strategy, it demonstrates that imposing a so-called 'distant blockade' was not the Admiralty's objective; rather the aim was to reconstitute an effective observational system. Second, it is hugely revealing about how the Admiralty viewed the battlecruiser type. Originally conceived as a means of ensuring Britain's security on the high seas against German raiders, they were deployed, from the start of their entry into service, with a North Sea theatre of conflict firmly in mind. This was a major evolutionary shift, if not in terms of the intended enemy, then at least in terms of the intended role.

[29] TNA, ADM 116/3088, Battenberg to Churchill, 20 April 1914.
[30] TNA, ADM 1/8383/179, Operations Division, 'Cruiser Squadron and Battle Squadron Programme', 8 July 1914.

12

The Royal Navy and Grand Strategy, 1937–1941[1]

GEORGE C. PEDEN

This chapter is based on John Hattendorf's observation that British sea power was undermined in the 1930s by the strategic need to prioritise first the air force and then the army.[2] The rise of the Luftwaffe posed a direct threat to London, and ministers were more willing to increase expenditure on the Royal Air Force (RAF) than on the other services. A change in the European balance of power after the Munich conference, and the consequent need to support France on land, forced a reluctant Chamberlain government to expand the army in 1939. Professor Hattendorf's point can be illustrated graphically by measuring the navy's declining share of defence expenditure after Britain began to rearm in the mid-1930s (Figure 12.1).

The navy's leading share down to 1937 reflected its role in protecting trade routes and a worldwide empire. The army was engaged primarily in imperial defence, and would require heavy expenditure on munitions if it were committed to fight on the European continent. In the absence of a credible air threat before Hitler came to power the RAF had had the smallest share of defence expenditure, but in 1934 Stanley Baldwin, the leader of the Conservative party, gave a pledge that the National Government would 'see to it that in air strength and air power this country shall no longer be in a position inferior to any country within striking distance of our shores'.[3] The Air Staff claimed that fighter, army cooperation and coastal reconnaissance squadrons had no place in measurement of relative air strength, and that what mattered was parity in bombers, which it wished to order in large numbers.[4] The Admiralty was well aware that it was in competition with the army and RAF for funding. It therefore sought to influence grand strategy in ways that would minimise the other services' demands. In particular, it questioned both the necessity for the army to be ready to fight in Europe and the effectiveness of the RAF's Bomber Command.

---

[1] I am grateful to Gill Bennett for comments on an earlier draft. Responsibility for remaining errors is mine alone.

[2] John B. Hattendorf, 'The Past as Prologue: The Changing Roles of Sea Power during the Twentieth Century', in Hattendorf, *Talking about Naval History* (Newport, RI, 2011), pp. 276–7.

[3] Hansard (Commons), 8 March 1934, col. 2078.

[4] TNA, Ministerial Committee on Defence Requirements, 30 April 1935, Cabinet Office papers, series 27, vol. 508 (CAB 27/508), p. 135. For discussion of Air Staff doctrine see Malcolm Smith, *British Air Strategy between the Wars* (Oxford, 1984), pp. 44–80, 103–5, 169–70, 174–5, 179–80, 184–90, 320.

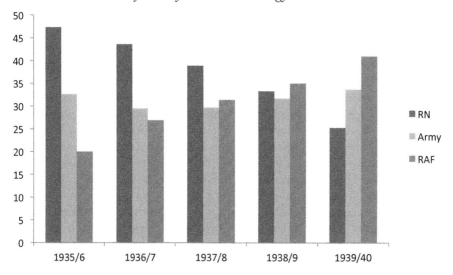

Figure 12.1: Percentage shares of total defence expenditure in financial years

Source: *Statistical Abstract for the United Kingdom (Cmd. 6232)*, Parliamentary Papers 1939–40, and (for 1939/40) Robert Paul Shay, *British Rearmament in the Thirties: Politics and Profits* (Princeton, NJ, 1977), p. 297.

Since the 1920s Admiralty planning had been on the basis that, if Japan threatened British interests, the main fleet would be sent to Singapore. Under the Washington and London naval treaties the Japanese Navy was restricted to 60 per cent of the Royal Navy's strength in capital ships. Consequently when, in 1935, the Germans offered to limit their surface fleet to 35 per cent of the Royal Navy, the Admiralty gave its support to what became the Anglo-German naval treaty, in the vain hope that the Japanese would renew the London treaty in 1936. Italy became a potentially hostile power later in 1935, as a result of the Abyssinian crisis, but the Admiralty continued to define adequate strength as a navy capable of fighting Japan and Germany simultaneously, with no account being taken of the naval strength of either Italy or France.[5]

In 1936 the Cabinet approved rearmament programmes for the navy, army and air force. By 1937, however, it was clear to the Treasury that the programmes were being exceeded. Consequently, the Cabinet agreed to a defence review to set new cash limits for each of the services over the five-year period that rearmament was expected to last. There was no Ministry of Defence in the 1930s. Defence policy was discussed in committee by ministers, the professional heads of the

---

[5] See Christopher M. Bell, *The Royal Navy, Seapower and Strategy between the Wars* (Basingstoke, 2000); Andrew Field, *Royal Navy Strategy in the Far East 1919–1939: Planning for War against Japan* (London, 2004); Joseph A. Maiolo, *The Royal Navy and Nazi Germany, 1933–39* (Basingstoke, 1998).

armed forces, and the official heads of the Treasury and Foreign Office, and then decided by the Cabinet. The defence review was conducted by Sir Thomas Inskip, who had been appointed in 1936 to the new post of minister for co-ordination of defence. Inskip, a lawyer by training, had no department of his own to advise him. Each of the chiefs of staff had radically different strategic views, according to the interests of his service. Consequently Inskip relied heavily on the Cabinet Secretary, Sir Maurice Hankey, for advice. Hankey, an ex-Royal Marine, placed a high priority on the defence of the trade routes and empire; indeed, the Admiralty could not have hoped for a more sympathetic ear.[6] The Admiralty was also helped by the fact that the Chief of Naval Staff, Sir Ernle Chatfield, was also chairman of the Chiefs of Staff Committee and well respected in Whitehall.

Within the Admiralty a key role was played by the Director of Plans from 1935 to 1938, Captain Tom Phillips, who advised Chatfield on strategy. Phillips's starting point in June 1937 regarding the defence review was that it had always been accepted that 'the price of naval supremacy must be the acceptance of inferiority on land, and that a policy of maintaining an army on the Continental scale would spell ruin'. He went on: 'financially the argument is equally valid with regard to air strength … the achievement of aerial "parity" [with Germany] is probably incompatible with the maintenance of naval supremacy'. He pointed out that the Air Ministry was spending large sums of money on a bomber force that was designed specifically for war against Germany, whereas the navy was being prepared for war anywhere. The Air Staff believed that bombers operating independently could deliver a 'knock-out blow', and that counter-bombing German aerodromes and factories was the best form of defence. Phillips denied there was any evidence to support the Air Staff's theory, either as to the potency of air attack or the effectiveness of counter-bombing. Instead, he argued for a less ambitious air strategy of adequate support for the navy and army, and a fighter force for the defence of the United Kingdom.[7] A little later Hankey drew Inskip's attention to intelligence reports on the Spanish Civil War suggesting that the combination of fighters, anti-aircraft guns and searchlights 'might prove much more effective' than hitherto assumed.[8] There was also the prospect that radar would make interception of bombers easier, but Inskip was advised by the Air Staff in October 1937 that radar was still at the experimental stage.[9] Although not wholly convinced by the Air Staff's arguments in favour of counter-bombing, Inskip felt unable in his report to the Cabinet in December to do more than

---

[6] See *History of the Second World War*: N.H. Gibbs, *Grand Strategy*, vol. I: *Rearmament Policy* (London, 1976), pp. 279–95; Sean Greenwood, 'Sir Thomas Inskip as Minister for the Co-ordination of Defence, 1936–39', in Paul Smith (ed.), *Government and Armed Forces in Britain 1856–1990* (London, 1996), pp. 155–89; G.C. Peden, *British Rearmament and the Treasury, 1932–1939* (Edinburgh, 1979), pp. 38–43, 79–92.

[7] TNA, 'Defence Expenditure', note by T.S.V. Phillips, 29 June 1937, Admiralty papers (ADM) 205/80.

[8] Note covering three reports by the Sub-Committee on Air Warfare in Spain, 27 Sept. 1937, CAB 64/3.

[9] Air Ministry note, 22 Oct. 1937, CAB 64/9.

suggest a reduction in the Air Ministry's recent request for additional bombers, while accepting in full the increase in asked-for fighters to defend the United Kingdom.[10] Phillips commented that Inskip's conclusions were 'similar to those which the Admiralty has put forward ... i.e. that fighter squadrons are of great importance for home defence and that absolute parity between counter-bombing forces is not essential'.[11]

Phillips also attacked the War Office's plans to prepare an expeditionary force (then known as the Field Force) capable of fighting in Western Europe at the outbreak of war. 'Can we,' he asked rhetorically in November 1937, 'faced with the maintenance of a Navy and Air Force essential to our security as a Nation and as an Empire, afford to maintain a Field Force for service overseas? It is submitted that we cannot honestly maintain that such a force is vital to our security.' Instead, he thought, the army's role should be limited to providing garrisons at home and in the empire.[12] In the event Inskip recommended that the Field Force should no longer be prepared to fight in Western Europe at the outbreak of war. Instead it should be equipped for imperial defence, with lower reserves of munitions than those required for continental warfare. Inskip admitted that if France were again to be in danger of being overrun, and Britain had to improvise an army to assist her, the government would certainly be criticised for neglecting so obvious a contingency. Nevertheless, he felt that economies had to be made somewhere. He recommended, and the Cabinet agreed, that policy should be guided by the following priorities:

> The first and main effort should be directed to two principal objectives – protecting the United Kingdom against attack and preserving the trade routes;
> A third objective should be maintenance of forces for the defence of British territories overseas against attack by sea, land or air;
> A fourth objective, which could be provided for only after the other objectives had been met, should be co-operation in the defence of the territories of any allies Britain might have in war.[13]

Military historians have been very critical of Inskip's report. Sir Michael Howard, in his book *The Continental Commitment*, remarked that home defence and imperial defence now appeared such overriding priorities that no forces could be spared for the third traditional aim of British defence policy: the maintenance of the balance of power in Europe. How long, he asked, would home defence be possible if that balance were overthrown, and if home defence was not possible,

---

[10] 'Defence Expenditure in Future Years', interim report by the Minister for Co-ordination of Defence, CP 316 (37), 15 December 1937, paras. 80–100, CAB 24/273/41, http://www.nationalarchives.gov.uk/.
[11] Notes on CP 316 (37), 21 Dec. 1937, ADM 116/3631.
[12] Notes by Phillips, 10 Nov. 1937, ADM 116/3631.
[13] CP 316 (37), paras 42–4, 68 and 75.

what would happen to the empire?[14] These are good questions, but in the event Britain's air defences were adequate after the fall of France in 1940, and the navy both successfully defended the trade routes and subjected Germany and occupied Europe to a debilitating blockade.[15] Howard makes no mention of the navy in his critique of the change in the Field Force's role. Yet Inskip's report referred explicitly to priority for protection of the trade routes, on which the United Kingdom depended for essential imports of food and raw materials.[16]

Defence of the empire was given a distinctly lower priority. Inskip recommended, and the Cabinet agreed, that all increases in the RAF should be concentrated in the United Kingdom and that there should be no further increases in overseas squadrons, even at the cost of insecurity vis-à-vis Japan and Italy.[17] Phillips commented: 'It is sad to see that the increase of overseas air forces must be put off, but it seems clear that this cannot be avoided in view of the overwhelming importance of protecting this country.'[18] In the event neglect of the overseas air defence was to have fatal consequences for Phillips in 1941.

In December 1937 it seemed Inskip had begun to reshape grand strategy in ways that would prevent the RAF and the army taking a higher share of resources than the navy. In February 1938 the Cabinet agreed he should divide a fixed sum of money between the services, each of which should then draw up a programme that could be completed by March 1942. However, in March 1938 the Air Ministry presented the Cabinet with an expansion scheme which, Inskip noted, would require the allocation of so much of the available money to the RAF as to reduce the amounts for the navy and army very seriously. The First Lord of the Admiralty, Alfred Duff Cooper, argued that Germany had too great a lead in air rearmament for the RAF to be a deterrent; that war would not be won in the air, but by blockade; and that the Admiralty's contractors were better placed than the Air Ministry's to fulfil orders. The Cabinet, however, responded to pressure in the House of Commons for greater aircraft production, and in April authorised the Air Ministry to place orders for the maximum that industry was believed to be capable of making over the next two years. In contrast, there was no equivalent Parliamentary pressure for ship construction, and in July the Cabinet rejected an Admiralty request for authority to plan on the basis of a New Standard of naval strength.[19]

---

[14] Michael Howard, *The Continental Commitment: The Dilemma of British Defence Policy in the Era of the Two World Wars* (London, 1972), p. 120. See also Brian Bond, *British Military Policy between the Two World Wars* (Oxford, 1980).

[15] For effects of blockade even after Germany had occupied much of Europe see Adam Tooze, *The Wages of Destruction: The Making and Breaking of the Nazi War Economy* (London, 2006), pp. 401, 411–20, 422–3.

[16] CP 316 (37), para. 42.

[17] Ibid., paras 98–9.

[18] Notes on CP 316 (37), 21 Dec. 1937, ADM 116/3631.

[19] Cabinet conclusions (CC) 5 (38), 16 Feb. 1938, CAB 23/92/5; CC 13 (38), 14 March 1938, CAB 23/92/13; CC 18 (38), 6 Apr. 1938, CAB 23/93/5; CC 33 (38), 20 July 1938, CAB 23/94/7, http://www.nationalarchives.gov.uk/.

Phillips, in a paper on the relationship between the bomber force and future naval strength, argued that the Admiralty should press for a more explicit decision than Inskip had given regarding the balance between bombers and fighters. Phillips noted that the development of radar had now reached a stage where the difficulty of intercepting bombers would be greatly reduced. The Air Ministry was spending five times as much on bombers as fighters. He advised that 'strategically ... it is clearly to our advantage to rely more on fighters and less on bombers'.[20] When, in the wake of the Munich crisis, the Air Ministry made a bid for a bigger expansion scheme, the Cabinet accepted the fighter proposals but decided that the Air Ministry should place only sufficient orders for bombers to ensure aircraft factories were not idle.[21]

It is not possible to know how influential the Admiralty was in the curbing of the Air Ministry's ambitions in relation to Bomber Command or the War Office's in relation to the Field Force. The Treasury also pressed for more fighters and fewer bombers, and the Prime Minister, Neville Chamberlain, had long questioned the wisdom of committing the Field Force to support France and Belgium.[22] Whatever the explanation, the Admiralty's successes, such as they were, did not preserve its position as the biggest spender among the defence departments (see Figure 12.2).

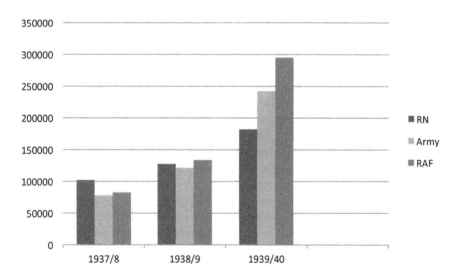

Figure 12.2: Expenditure (£ 000s) in financial years. Sources as for Figure 12.1.

[20] 'Relation between the Bomber Force and Our Future Naval Strength', 6 July 1938, ADM 205/80.
[21] CC 53 (38), 7 Nov. 1938, CAB 23/96/5, http://www.nationalarchives.gov.uk/.
[22] Peden, *British Rearmament*, pp. 122–34; Peden, 'Chamberlain, the British Army and the "Continental Commitment"', in Malcom Murfett (ed.), *Shaping British Foreign and Defence Policy in the Twentieth Century* (Basingstoke, 2014), pp. 86–110.

Air Ministry expenditure surged ahead, and it was not until 1940 that more fighters than bombers were built.[23] There was an inevitable lag between the Cabinet's instruction to the Air Ministry on 7 November 1938 to give priority to fighters and what happened in factories, given the balance between bombers and fighters in contracts placed before that date. In the case of the War Office, the Munich settlement meant the loss of the Czech Army, and France pressed for a British contribution on land. In February 1939 the Cabinet agreed that the Field Force should be made ready to fight on the Continent at the outbreak of war, and in the following month Chamberlain agreed to an expansion of the army, from six to thirty-two divisions.[24] The priorities of the Inskip Report had been overtaken by events.

The biggest event, of course, was the outbreak of war. Initially Britain and France enjoyed overwhelming naval superiority over Germany, but June 1940 saw the fall of France and the entry of Italy into the war. The temptation to Japan to exploit Britain's difficulties was obvious. However, British intelligence assessments reflected racial stereotypes of the Japanese as a cautious, Asiatic race, and defence planning for the Far East was characterised by complacency regarding Japanese intentions and capabilities.[25] Moreover, the exigencies of war required the Royal Navy to concentrate its strength in the Atlantic and Mediterranean. An Admiralty attempt in spring 1941 to persuade the still neutral United States to send a fleet to Singapore failed. Instead the Americans gradually moved major fleet units from the Pacific to the Atlantic, enabling the Royal Navy to redeploy ships to the Far East. The Admiralty planned to build up a fleet in the Indian Ocean, to be based in Ceylon, with a view to moving it to Singapore in March 1942. Churchill insisted in October 1941 on the new capital ship, the *Prince of Wales*, and the old battlecruiser, *Repulse*, being dispatched to Singapore to deter the Japanese. The ships were commanded by the quondam Director of Plans, now Admiral Sir Tom Phillips. Overestimating the effectiveness of his ships' anti-aircraft guns and underestimating Japanese naval air efficiency, Phillips moved to attack the Japanese invasion force while it was disembarking on the coast of Malaya. Japanese aircraft based in Vietnam sank the *Prince of Wales* and the *Repulse* in an action lasting just over two hours. Phillips went down with his flagship. No fighter cover had been provided in time, and what was available would in any case have been inadequate.[26] Churchill described the RAF presence in Malaya as 'meagre'.[27] The low priority given to overseas squadrons in 1937 still

---

[23] *History of the Second World War*: M.M. Postan, *British War Production* (London, 1952), p. 484.
[24] Gibbs, *Grand Strategy*, pp. 491–518.
[25] Anthony Best, *British Intelligence and the Japanese Challenge in Asia, 1914–1941* (Basingstoke, 2002), pp. 158–60, 164–70, 181–7.
[26] Christopher M. Bell, *Churchill and Sea Power* (Oxford, 2013), pp. 236–53; Arthur J. Marder, *Old Friends, New Enemies: The Royal Navy and the Imperial Japanese Navy; Strategic Illusions 1936–1941* (Oxford, 1981), pp. 403–40, 460–521.
[27] W.S. Churchill, *The Second World War*, vol. III: *The Grand Alliance* (London, 1950), p. 548.

prevailed. There were only 158 first-line aircraft in Malaya, many of them obsolescent, compared with the 550 modern aircraft that would have been required to match the Japanese.[28]

With the loss of the *Prince of Wales* and the *Repulse* Britain's sea power in the Far East was, at least for the time being, shattered. The fleet assembled in the Indian Ocean under Admiral Sir James Somerville comprised three aircraft carriers; five old battleships, of which four were too slow to keep up with the carriers; seven cruisers and sixteen destroyers. It was no match for a powerful Japanese fleet, including five aircraft carriers and four battleships, which appeared off Colombo in April 1942, and the British were fortunate to lose only the small aircraft carrier *Hermes*, two cruisers and a destroyer over two days of action. Once more the RAF's air support was inadequate.[29] The Japanese did not appear in force again in the Indian Ocean, a circumstance that may be attributed to losses inflicted on them by the US Navy in the battles of the Coral Sea and Midway. The Royal Navy was able to protect the trade routes in the Indian Ocean, but the creation in December 1944 of a British Pacific fleet was essentially a political gesture, with the US Navy by then having achieved decisive superiority over the Japanese.[30]

What conclusions can be drawn from this story? Professor Hattendorf's point about sea power being lost because of the overriding strategic imperatives of home defence and support for France is historically correct. However, home defence need not have been at the expense of sea power. The RAF could have secured British air space at much less cost than it did, given that bombers cost four times as much as fighters.[31] Britain had the world's most advanced air defence system in 1939 and, while some bombers were required for a balanced air force, counter-bombing played no part in reducing the scale of German air attacks in 1940.[32]

Phillips was correct in seeing bomber parity with Germany as incompatible with maintenance of naval supremacy. The navy's rearmament programme was based on what the Defence Requirements Sub-Committee of the Imperial Defence (DRC) had considered in 1935 would be necessary to maintain a 'one-power' standard, that is naval strength sufficient to enable the main fleet to equal any other fleet wherever situated, and to have local forces capable of preventing vital damage pending the arrival of the main fleet. The New Standard proposed by the Admiralty in 1938, however, aimed to make it possible to send

---

[28] James Neidpath, *The Singapore Naval Base and the Defence of Britain's Eastern Empire, 1919–1941* (Oxford, 1981), pp. 200–2.

[29] *History of the Second World War:* S.W. Roskill, *The War at Sea 1939–1945*, vol. II: *The Period of Balance* (London, 1956), pp. 23–9.

[30] Jon Robb-Webb, '"Light Two Lanterns, the British Are Coming by Sea": Royal Navy Participation in the Pacific 1944–45', in Greg Kennedy (ed.), *British Naval Strategy East of Suez, 1900–2000* (London, 2005), pp. 128–53.

[31] G.C. Peden, *Arms, Economics and British Strategy: From Dreadnoughts to Hydrogen Bombs* (Cambridge, 2007), p. 117

[32] Derek Wood and Derek Dempster, *The Narrow Margin: The Battle of Britain and the Rise of Air Power 1930–1940* (London, 1961).

to the Far East a fleet adequate to act on the defensive and be a strong deterrent to Japan, while maintaining in all circumstances in home waters a force able to meet the requirements of a war with Germany at the same time.[33] The differences between these two conceptions of sea power are set out in Tables 12.1 and 12.2.

Table 12.1: DRC and New Standard fleets compared

	DRC fleet	New Standard fleet
Capital ships	15	20
Aircraft carriers	10	15
Cruisers	70	100
Destroyers	16 flotillas	22 flotillas
Submarines	55	82

Source: Joseph A. Maiolo, *The Royal Navy and Nazi Germany, 1933–39* (Basingstoke, 1998), p. 135.

Table 12.2: New construction programme for New Standard fleet (changes from DRC programme in brackets)

	1937/38	1938/39	1939/40	1940/41	1941/42
Capital ships	3	2	3 (+1)	2 (+1)	2 (+1)
Aircraft carriers	2	1	3 (+2)	1 (+1)	1 (+1)
Cruisers 8,000 tons	5	4	4 (+2)	4 (+4)	4 (+4)
Cruisers 5,300 tons	2	2 (−1)	2 (+2)	2 (+2)	1 (+1)
Destroyer flotillas	2	0	2 (+2)	1 (+1)	1 (+1)
Submarines	7	7 (+4)	11 (+5)	7 (+7)	5 (+5)

Source: as for Table 12.1.

The Admiralty was asking for an additional three capital ships, four aircraft carriers, ten large cruisers, four small cruisers, four destroyer flotillas and twenty-one submarines over and above those included in the DRC programme. Comparison of the costs of warships and bombers is difficult since the latter became obsolete more quickly and had to be replaced more frequently. However, it was calculated in 1936 that forty-three medium bombers would cost as much over a given period as one capital ship.[34] Given that from 1937 the RAF was replacing medium bombers with more expensive heavy bombers, it can be assumed that capital ships did not become relatively more expensive during the period of the

[33] Gibbs, *Grand Strategy*, pp. 23, 332–57.
[34] Peden, *Arms*, p. 119.

rearmament programme. If the cost of building and maintaining a capital ship is taken as roughly the same as that of an aircraft carrier, and slightly more than that of two large cruisers,[35] the rule of thumb of forty-three bombers to one capital ship suggests that the New Standard's additional capital ships, aircraft carriers and large cruisers alone would cost about the same as five hundred bombers. These figures are not, of course, precise and are intended only to indicate orders of magnitude. The Air Ministry was authorised by the Cabinet in April 1938 to build enough bombers to provide Bomber Command with a front-line strength of 1,352, with reserves.[36] British sea power, as defined by the Admiralty, could have been maintained only if the RAF had restricted its ambitions, as Phillips suggested, to air defence and cooperation with the navy and army.

As things were, the navy found that the pace of its rearmament programme was set by the ability of industry to fulfil contracts rather than by the money made available by the Treasury. Years of retrenchment in naval orders and the depression of the early 1930s had reduced the capacity of the shipbuilding industry. By 1935 the labour force was about half of what it had been in the early 1920s, and a housing boom provided alternative employment for skilled workers. By 1938 all the capacity in the yards that could be employed on new construction was fully in use. Existing capacity for making gun mountings was estimated in 1936 to be less than half of what would be required by 1939. Fire-control gear was a bottleneck that could be eased only by drawing in new suppliers, but the most suitable engineering firms were fully engaged on commercial work, and the government's policy down to 1938 was that rearmament should not interfere with normal trade. New armour-making plant was required to meet demand, estimated in 1936 to rise from 22,000 tons to 42,000 tons by 1939, and the position with the supply of guns was similar.[37] Admiralty subsidies were made to private firms to create new industrial capacity, but on a more modest scale than subsidies for the Air Ministry's suppliers (£4.4 million compared with £40 million in 1936–39).[38] Shipbuilding firms might have done more to help themselves, but they feared having redundant plant once the rearmament programme was complete, and they appear to have used their new prosperity to improve their financial position rather than to invest in fixed assets.[39] In the absence of greater investment in new plant by the state or firms, it is not surprising that output per man in shipbuilding in the late 1930s was very little if at all greater than it had been on the eve of the First World War.[40] A major effort to create new plant and

---

[35] The relative cost of capital ships and large cruisers as reported to the Imperial Conference in 1937, see S. R. Ashton and S.E. Stockwell (eds), *British Documents on the End of Empire*: series A, vol. I, part 1 (London, 1996), p. 118.
[36] Smith, *British Air Strategy*, p. 334.
[37] Postan, *British War Production*, pp. 4, 48–51.
[38] *History of the Second World War*: William Hornby, *Factories and Plant* (London, 1958), pp. 61, 202–3.
[39] Hugh Peebles, *Warshipbuilding on the Clyde* (Edinburgh, 1987), pp. 142–53.
[40] J.R. Parkinson, 'Shipbuilding', in Neil K. Buxton and Derek H. Aldcroft (eds), *British Industry between the Wars* (London, 1979), p. 87.

recruit labour, on the same scale as the aircraft industry, would have been required to enable the Admiralty to achieve its New Standard in time to maintain British sea power. However, as Lord Weir, the industrialist and former Secretary of State for Air, who was advising ministers, noted in January 1936, the limiting factor on the rearmament programme as a whole was the supply of skilled labour. Weir believed that numerical parity with the German air force would scarcely be sufficient to give security, given Britain's greater vulnerability to air attack.[41] Ministers agreed. Priority for the RAF in the creation of new industrial capacity meant a lower priority for the navy.

In the light of Bomber Command's indifferent performance in the early years of the war it could be argued that labour would have been better employed on warships than on bombers.[42] Events in the Far East also suggest that Phillips was right to stress the importance of adequate air support for the navy and army. Had some of the resources devoted to Bomber Command been used to create a proper air defence system for Malaya, the loss of the *Prince of Wales* and the *Repulse* might have been prevented. The conduct of the land campaign in Malaya is beyond the scope of this chapter, but the inability of the RAF to inflict heavy casualties on the Japanese invasion force or to provide adequate tactical support for the defenders were significant factors in the British defeat.[43] Had the RAF and army been successful in their roles in the defence of Malaya, the Admiralty's plan for a fleet to use Singapore as a base for offensive action under cover of land-based aircraft could have been implemented. Perhaps the sudden collapse of British sea power in the Far East was not inevitable.

---

[41] Defence Requirements Enquiry: DPR (DR) 4, 9 Jan., and DPR (DR) 1st meeting, 13 Jan., 1936, CAB 16/123.

[42] For Bomber Command's deficiencies see *History of the Second World War*: Sir Charles Webster and Noble Frankland, *The Strategic Air Offensive against Germany 1939–1945*, vol. I: *Preparation* (London, 1961), pp. 125, 129–30, 178–83.

[43] *History of the Second World War*: J.M.A. Gwyer and J.R.M. Butler, *Grand Strategy*, vol. III, part 2 (London, 1964), pp. 419–20; S. Woodburn Kirby, *The War against Japan*, vol. I: *The Loss of Singapore* (London, 1957), pp. 461–4.

13

The Atlantic in the Strategic Perspective of Hitler and his Admirals, 1939–1944[1]

WERNER RAHN

The declaration of war by the Western powers on 3 September 1939 surprised Hitler. Thus, he found himself in a war with Britain and France that he had not wanted in 1939. In his 'Directive No. 9' of 29 November 1939, 'Principles of warfare against the economy of the enemy', he considered interference with the British economy as the 'most effective means' to defeat Britain.[2] Hitler was prepared to adopt this strategic concept for the navy, hitting Britain where she was most vulnerable by disrupting her sea lines of communication.

However, Hitler and his Naval War Staff[3] operated on different planes of strategic thinking: Hitler expected a short war limited to Europe and did not want to jeopardise the hope of better relations with Great Britain. The Naval War Staff, on the other hand, was convinced that the conflict with Britain would be long. It would have to be won in the Atlantic, even if that meant the entry of the United States into the war.

Because of the inaction of the Western Allies, Hitler even believed that they had only declared war to save face. After the end of the fighting in Poland, Hitler therefore made a 'peace offer'. However, for Paris and London there could no longer be any question of negotiating with Hitler. The strategy of the Allies was

---

[1] This chapter is based on my articles: 'The Atlantic in the Strategic Perspective of Hitler and Roosevelt, 1940–1941', in T.J. Runyan and J.M. Copes (eds), *To Die Gallantly: The Battle of the Atlantic*, (Boulder, CO, 1994), pp. 3–21; 'Japan and Germany, 1941–1943: No Common Objective, No Common Plans, No Basis of Trust', *Naval War College Review*, xlvi (Summer 1993), pp. 47–68; and 'The War at Sea in the Atlantic and in the Arctic Ocean', in H. Boog, W. Rahn, R. Stumpf and B. Wegner (eds), *Germany and the Second World War, Vol. 6: The Global War: Widening of the Conflict into a World War and the Shift of the Initiative 1941–1943* (Oxford, 2001), pp. 301–466. See also W. Rahn, 'The German U-boat Campaign in World War II', in B.A. Elleman and S.C.M. Paine (eds), *Commerce Raiding: Historical Case Studies, 1755–2009* (Newport, RI, 2013), pp. 187–207.

[2] Walther Hubatsch (ed.), *Hitlers Weisungen für die Kriegführung*, 2nd edn (Koblenz, 1983), pp. 40–2.

[3] The Naval War Staff (*Seekriegsleitung*) was the key element in the German Naval Command (*Oberkommando der Kriegsmarine*), responsible for strategic and operational planning. From the beginning of the Second World War, Grand Admiral Erich Raeder held two positions: C-in-C of the Navy and Chief of Naval War Staff. See M. Salewski, *Die deutsche Seekriegsleitung 1935–1945* (3 vols, Frankfurt/M. 1970), vol. i, p. 102.

guided by the wish to disrupt the concentration of German forces on the border of France. In the spring of 1940, the spread of the war to Scandinavia gave the Allies the desired secondary theatre, but no opportunity to thwart Hitler's plans for a campaign in the west.

After France had been defeated, Britain was the only nation able to fight Germany and was not prepared to deny Germany's dominance of the Continent: 'Germany had a military position and sufficient freedom of action to make Britain's defeat inevitable, if not quick and easy. Considering the greater resources of German controlled Europe, Britain's position without outside help, was hopeless.'[4] However, as soon as the existence of Britain came under threat, Germany would have to reckon with the United States.

In view of the US Navy's armament programme, time became the most important factor for German strategy. There were three factors concerning this argument:

(1) In an economic war waged against a country that depended on supplies by sea, success could only be achieved in the long run. It was therefore a question of continuously weakening the enemy's maritime transport capacity to the point at which new merchant ships could not be built fast enough.
(2) From summer 1940 onwards, it became apparent that the British war effort was being increasingly supported by the resources of the US. Therefore, the Naval War Staff was intent on 'putting Britain out of action soon, before the effects of even greater American aid make themselves felt'.
(3) The German Navy concentrated on U-boats. Since it took around two years to build U-boats and to make them operational in the quantities envisaged by the navy, plans had to be made at a very early stage.

The German Navy, however, foresaw that there were limits to Germany's production capacities and resources. As early as December 1940 it viewed America's growing support of Britain as a dangerous development 'towards a marked prolongation of the war'. This would have a 'very negative effect on the German ... strategy'.[5] This statement obviously expressed the fact that Germany would not be able to win a long war of attrition against the two Atlantic naval powers.

For this reason, in December 1940, at a time when Hitler was still firmly determined to attack Russia, Grand Admiral Raeder requested that Hitler 'recognise that the greatest task of the hour is concentration of all our power against Britain'. The admiral was 'firmly convinced that German submarines ... are the decisive weapon against Britain'. Although Hitler did not explicitly reject Raeder's view, he did refer to it when he spoke of the need 'to eliminate at all cost the last

---

[4] Alan J. Levine, 'Was World War II a Near-run Thing?', *The Journal of Strategic Studies*, 8:1 (March 1985), p. 41.
[5] Naval War Staff/War Diary, part A, 20 December 1940, published as Facsimile-Edition: *Kriegstagebuch der Seekriegsleitung 1939–1945, Teil A*, ed. W. Rahn and G. Schreiber, vol. xvi [December 1940] (Herford and Bonn, 1990), pp. 233 and 238 (20 December 1940). (In future abbreviated: *KTB/Skl*, part A, vol.)

enemy remaining on the continent, before he can collaborate with Britain. For this purpose the Army must be made sufficiently strong. After that everything can be concentrated on the needs of the Air Force and the Navy.'[6] In saying this, Hitler used an argument, which has a long tradition in navies: the argument that a naval power can only be defeated after its last continental bulwark has fallen.

At the end of 1940, Washington came to the conclusion that, compared to Japan, Germany was not only the stronger enemy, but also, due to its position of power in Europe and its offensive conduct of war in the Atlantic, a much more dangerous enemy – one which threatened not only Britain, but also the United States. With this attitude, Washington was in agreement with the basis of British strategy, which considered the security of the Atlantic sea-lanes as fundamental to all further offensive operations in Europe.

In January 1941, Hitler expressed his firm conviction 'that the situation in Europe can no longer develop unfavourable for Germany even if we should lose the whole of North Africa. Our position in Europe is so firmly established that the outcome cannot possibly be to our disadvantage ... The British can hope to win the war only by beating us on the Continent.'[7] Hitler was convinced 'that this is impossible'. At around the same time, Hitler apparently toyed with the idea of a surprise attack against the United States, instructing the Naval Staff to investigate the prospects of success for a massive U-boat attack on the American Atlantic Fleet. However, the result of this investigation was negative.[8]

On 22 June 1941 neither Hitler nor his military leaders doubted that they had enough time and sufficient means to destroy the Russian forces. After only two weeks, Hitler regarded the campaign as having been won. Yet only a few days later it became apparent that the first operational objectives had been achieved only geographically, not militarily: the 'mass of the Russian army' had not been destroyed.

In July 1941, Admiral Raeder tried to influence Hitler into making a clear decision on cooperation with France and Japan in order to bring about a decision in the Atlantic. However, Hitler was not prepared to do this in view of the unresolved situation in Russia. When Raeder hinted at the hazards arising from a possible occupation of North-West Africa by British and American forces, he touched on the great strategic weakness of the Axis Powers in Europe. Raeder demanded 'a clearing up of the relations between Germany and France' in order to create a basis for wider political and military cooperation. In arguing that this issue could not be resolved until the campaign in the East was brought to an end, Raeder expressed the dilemma that lay at the heart of the German strategy in summer 1941. Hitler took the cue from Raeder and assured the C-in-C of the navy that he still had the same strategy in mind and that he was only trying

---

[6] *Fuehrer Conferences on Naval Affairs* (Annapolis, 1990), p. 162 (27 December 1940). For the original German version see *Lagevorträge des Oberbefehlshabers der Kriegsmarine vor Hitler 1939–1945*, ed. G. Wagner, (Munich, 1972), pp. 173–4.
[7] [7] *Fuehrer Conferences on Naval Affairs*, p. 172 (8–9 January 1941).
[8] See *KTB/Skl*, part A, vol. ixx (March 1941), p. 309 (22 March 1941).

'to avoid having the U.S.A. declare war while the Eastern Campaign is still in progress', and that afterwards he would 'take severe action against the U.S.A. as well'.[9] The German strategy thus did not and could not change. The Naval War Staff's largescale plans could not be realised due not only to a lack of forces to carry them out, but also because there was no 'afterwards' to the campaign in the East. Meanwhile, it became clear that the United States was firmly determined to intensify its support for Britain, short of declaring war, and, in doing so, it would increasingly become the dominant partner.

In order to maintain the position in North Africa, Hitler had seen not only the necessity of continuing the campaign in the East, but also the need to solve the crisis in the Mediterranean. Since there were no other forces available, U-boats had to be withdrawn from the Atlantic to stabilise the situation. The transfer of U-boats into the Mediterranean seriously weakened the concept of sea denial in the Atlantic. It became clear at this point that the Axis Powers had overreached their war potential and that they were only able to maintain their positions by alternating the concentration of their forces. However, an analysis of the overall war situation from Hitler's point of view shows that he still had the illusion that he had achieved his great goal of defeating Russia.

Following Japan's entry into the war in December 1941 and the German declaration of war against the United States, the European-Atlantic war widened into a global conflict. Strictly speaking, bearing in mind the resources and military potential of the powers involved, its outcome was predictable from the start.

Hitler's attitude to the United States was marked by helplessness.[10] He did not know yet how to defeat the United States, as he frankly confessed to the Japanese ambassador in January 1942. This was an understatement: he simply did not know how he would be able to stand up to the country. Hitler tried to conceal his helplessness from his entourage by levelling a series of insults against Roosevelt and the United States itself. But this was an attempt to put on a brave front because Hitler was really afraid of the United States and he had an uneasy suspicion that 'if this war is won by anyone, it will only be America'. Hitler's conviction that America's rise would come at the cost of the British Empire ('if it is lost by anyone, it will be lost by England'[11]) had led him to expect that London would soon abandon the Allied coalition and that Britain would fight shoulder to shoulder with Germany against the United States.[12]

The German declaration of war against the United States took the German Navy by surprise. As a consequence, no operational action had been prepared that

---

[9] Conference Raeder with Hitler, 25 July 1941, *Lagevorträge des Oberbefehlshabers der Kriegsmarine vor Hitler 1939–1945*, ed. G. Wagner (Munich, 1972), pp. 271–3. See *Fuehrer Conferences*, pp. 222–3.

[10] The following passage is based mainly on: *Germany and the Second World War, Vol. 6*, p. 127 (B. Wegner) and Adolf Hitler, *Monologe im Führerhauptquartier 1941–1944: Die Aufzeichnungen Heinrich Heims*, ed. W. Jochmann (Munich, 1982).

[11] Hitler, *Monologe*, p. 199 (15 Jan. 1942).

[12] 'A German-British army will throw the Americans out of Iceland': Hitler, *Monologe*, p. 184 (7 Jan. 1942).

would have enabled the U-boats to advance deep into North American coastal waters within a matter of days. With the extension of operations to the whole of the Atlantic, Admiral Dönitz saw the chance to concentrate his weapon in areas where a significant rise in the number of enemy ships sunk could be achieved, especially along the east coast of North America. As long as merchant shipping continued to sail uncontrolled and largely unprotected and the US Navy lacked experience in anti-submarine warfare, these sea routes promised to be a successful area of operations.

Despite all the efforts of the preceding years, the number of U-boats in operation had not been successfully brought to the level that Germany would have needed to exploit more fully its favourable position in the Atlantic. With a total of 249 boats in service, the German Navy had by that time reached a considerable strength; but this figure was misleading, as only 91 boats were actually in front-line operational service. Of these U-boats, 26 were already committed to the Mediterranean, 6 to Gibraltar and 4 to the Norwegian region. For what was seen as the decisive struggle against the Allies in the North Atlantic, there remained therefore only 55 boats, of which only 22 were at sea in the Atlantic, about half on patrol and half on passage. If only 10 or 12 U-boats were engaged in operations against allied shipping, that is 4.8 per cent of the total potential of the German U-boats, one can hardly speak of a strategic concentration, let alone a 'war winning' fresh start. With their successes so far, the U-boats had shown considerable capability. As in the First World War, this led to an overestimation of the submarine force. Hitler and his high command saw, above all, in the U-boats an instrument which could provide a quick and effective short-term remedy for critical situations.

The landing of Allied forces in North-West Africa and the breakthrough against the German–Italian forces at El Alamein were important offensives. However, these offensives were no substitute for the second front that the Allies needed since Germany's heartland remained unaffected by them. From the global perspective of the Atlantic naval powers, the strongly fortified coast of the European continent could be directly attacked only from a position of strength. Until the Allies' military potential was sufficient for a direct attack on Europe, their only option was a series of offensives along the periphery, combined with massive air raids on the German armament industry and, increasingly, population centres in order to weaken and shatter Germany's material strength and morale prior to the start of an invasion.

In 1942, German strategy progressively shrank to pure survival warfare. In Hitler's opinion, the 'German living-space' had to be secured by a strong west wall in France, a strong north wall in Norway and an equivalent east wall. 'Then Germany would be unassailable. What relations we wanted to have with the rest of the world from this space could be considered later.'[13] If Germany was to win a

---

[13] *Lagevorträge*, pp. 351–2 (6/7 Feb. 1942) [not in translation]. For translation see *Germany and the Second World War, Vol. 4*, p. 1244.

prolonged war it was essential that the second campaign against the Soviet Union should succeed. It was no longer primarily a case of achieving a total defeat of the enemy, but whether the necessary raw-material resources could be seized to continue the German war effort. From Hitler's viewpoint, it was vital to achieve the objectives in the East before the potential of the United States was fully developed and Anglo-American preparations for a second front in Europe were completed.

As early as August 1942, Hitler became sceptical about the prospect of a decisive victory against Russia. Even if Germany defeated Russia, he believed that the 'most formidable forces' would have to be maintained in the East. Since Hitler believed that the German military was capable of fighting on only one front at a time, he concluded that a second front had to be prevented at all costs. Therefore, he planned to fortify the coastal areas. He deployed a rather small number of mobile divisions in the West, hoping that they would be able to ward off possible Allied landings. Yet, the fortification plans had not taken into account a third dimension, leaving a weak spot which Hitler himself had to admit: as the Luftwaffe could not be withdrawn from the East, Allied air superiority had to be expected.

The obvious discrepancy between what was desired and what was feasible emerged most clearly in the Atlantic, where the U-boats were considered to be the main pillar in the supply war. Naval warfare in the Atlantic and coastal waters had effectively opened up a second front at sea by spring 1942. Sufficient maritime transport was vital for Britain's survival, but it was also the most important prerequisite for any offensive against the Axis in Europe.

Regarding the decisive question of the 'race' between the enemy's construction of new ships and Germany's sinking of these ships, Section 3 of Naval War Staff gave a pessimistic prognosis:

> If, however, considering the enemy's rising production output, Germany wishes to diminish the enemy's tonnage from the end of 1942 onwards to the same extent as is currently being achieved, ship sinkings per month will have to be increased to approximately 1,300,000 GRT. Given the current situation, it is doubtful whether such a high rate of ship sinkings will be feasible for a sustained period of time.[14]

By falling back on the historical argument that 'no war in history ... has yet been won by the use of one method of warfare',[15] the Naval War Staff was moving to an understanding that reflected actual conditions. By the end of 1942, the German U-boats had succumbed to the immense industrial capacity of the United States.

In the spring of 1943, the new Commander in Chief of the Navy, Grand

---

[14] See Rahn, 'The War at Sea in the Atlantic and in the Arctic Ocean', in *Germany and the Second World War*, Vol. 6, p. 331.
[15] Annex 1 of Naval War Staff memorandum of 20 October 1942: 'Stand und Aussichten des U-Bootkrieges', in Salewski, *Seekriegsleitung*, iii, pp. 293–303, quotation p. 303. See Rahn, 'The War at Sea' p. 337.

Admiral Dönitz, was faced with heavy monthly losses of U-boats.[16] In April 1943, he told Hitler that he had serious doubts over whether the U-boat war would be successful in the long run.[17] In May 1943, with monthly losses of forty-one U-boats, Dönitz was forced to break off convoy attacks in the North Atlantic. This decision meant the ruin of an offensive naval strategy, in which Germany gave up on the struggle for sea control and was now solely seeking to deny the superior Atlantic naval powers from using the sea freely.

After the defeat of the U-boats, the strategic bridge across the North Atlantic became so effective that the Allies were able to turn the British Isles into both a launch pad for the bomber offensive against Germany and an arsenal for the planned invasion of Normandy. From the summer of 1943 onwards, U-boat operations could only make a contribution to the defence of 'Fortress Europe', attacking Allied shipping in a war of attrition. Therefore, Dönitz was convinced that the U-boat war 'must be carried on, even if great successes are no longer possible'. Hitler at once took the cue from Dönitz and strongly emphasised this assessment:

> There can be no talk of a let up in submarine warfare. The Atlantic is my first line of defense in the West, and even if I have to fight a defensive battle there, that is preferable to waiting to defend myself on the coast of Europe. The enemy forces tied up by our submarine warfare are tremendous, even though the actual losses inflicted by us are no longer great.[18]

However, Allied anti-submarine warfare showed that Germany's previous concept of submarine operations – submersibles which operated on the surface whilst mainly remaining stationary underwater – was doomed to failure. But, as early as July 1943, Dönitz reported to Hitler on the successful design of the fast so-called electro-submarine, explaining the tactical advantages that resulted from its high underwater speed and long underwater cruising range made possible by its snorkelling capabilities.[19] As a naval weapon, the U-boat underwent radical changes and it was now a real submarine.[20] However, when this was achieved at the beginning of 1945, Germany was on the verge of defeat.

The so-called 'Fortress Europe' would have provided a substantial means of defence in the medium run had German forces not been overstretched by

---

[16] Grand Admiral Raeder resigned in January 1943 after a dispute with Hitler about the failure of a cruiser operation against an Allied Convoy in the Arctic Ocean. Admiral Dönitz succeeded him on 30 January 1943 and was simultaneously promoted to Grand Admiral. For more details see Rahn, 'The War at Sea', pp. 461–6.
[17] See *Fuehrer Conferences*, pp. 316–18 (11 April 1943).
[18] *Fuehrer Conferences* [1990], pp. 334–5 (31 May 1943).
[19] Cf. ibid., pp. 338f. (8 July 1943).
[20] Type XXI: 1,621 tons; maximum speed underwater: 17.2 knots (for one hour); range 11,500 nautical miles (nm) at twelve knots or, underwater, 340 nm at five knots. For details see W. Rahn, "The Development of New Types of U-boats in Germany during World War II: Construction, Trials and First Operational Experience of the Type XXI, XXIII and Walter U-boats', in *Les marines de guerre du dreadnought au nucléaire* (Paris, 1990), pp. 357–72.

extensive front lines, but a clear decision in favour of a strategic defence was never taken. After the last offensives in the East had failed in 1943, the bulk of German manpower and equipment remained concentrated in the East. At the same time, the threat in the West was growing quickly, increasing the dilemma for the German high command.

Therefore, in November 1943 Hitler issued a directive concerning the strategic defence of 'Fortress Europe' which led to a redeployment of Germany's dwindling resources. In comparison to the danger in the East, he saw an even greater danger now appearing in the West: 'an Anglo-Saxon landing'.[21] His directive was an attempt to create the conditions in which an invasion could be repelled, thereby securing Germany's rear in the fight against the enemy in the East.

In the spring of 1944, German military leaders believed that the army formations at their disposal would be sufficient enough to fight a second battle for France. They neglected their own experience of 1940, in which the joint efforts of air and ground forces had been successful. By the spring of 1944, there was no Luftwaffe left which deserved the name. It was only a matter of time before the fate of 'Fortress Europe' was decided: after the Allies captured North Africa, their superiority was felt very quickly.

The Axis Powers could only counter with short-term and mostly ineffectual measures. They had their backs to the wall in virtually every area of warfare, and no alternative to ultimate defeat was in sight. In January 1944, Hitler surprised an audience of generals and admirals when he spoke for the first time, in serious terms, about the possibility of an unfavourable outcome of the war. It was Captain Heinz Assmann (1904–54), the naval representative at Hitler's daily military conferences, who witnessed the assembly in which Hitler addressed several hundred generals and admirals on the ideological basis of the war. Assmann published his recollections in 1953 and quoted Hitler's speech as follows:

> My generals and admirals. If Providence should actually deny us victory in this battle of life and death, and if it is the will of the Almighty that this war should end with a catastrophe for the German people, then it should really be so that you, my generals and admirals, would gather around me with upraised swords to fight to the last drop of blood for the honor of Germany – I say, gentlemen, that is the way it should really be.

Then Assmann described the reaction of the assembly:

> A deadly silence pervaded the room. One could have heard a pin fall to the floor. Everyone literally held his breath and awaited any kind of relief from the extreme tenseness which gripped everyone. A voice, carrying no inspiration or conviction, broke the silence: 'My Fuehrer, that is the way it will be!' A fearful silence again prevailed in the room ... One might have expected that now indeed something would happen – that perhaps the generals and admirals would rise from their seats

---

[21] War Directive No. 51, 3 November 1943, *Hitler's War Directives 1939–1945*, ed. H.R. Trevor-Roper, (London 1964), p. 149.

and demonstrate by acclamation that they stood behind these words and that they were really prepared to give their all in fighting for Adolf Hitler, the German people, and National Socialism. But nothing of the kind took place ... Hitler turned pale as he stood on the rostrum and glanced around the room. His gaze stopped on one of the men in the front row and he broke the silence with a serious voice: 'Field Marshal, I have just heard your answer. Would that you were right, yet I have good reason to doubt the faith which your response implies.' ... Hitler finally continued and explained how he had arrived at this adverse opinion and what had warranted such terrible doubt on his part. He then mentioned ..., that he had knowledge of a considerable opposition movement in the Army and of the strongly negative attitude of numerous officers.[22]

During the following months in 1944, Germany's strategic situation was seriously affected, not just by Operation Overlord and the Battle of Normandy. The supreme German military gave in to wishful thinking, despite the dismal war experience so far and often against their better judgment. The weakest point in the German decision-making process was Hitler himself. After the winter of 1941–42, the influence of Army Command over the conduct of the war gradually eroded. The overall strategic responsibility resided in Hitler alone. He was convinced of his military genius and was unable to delegate authority, which would have reduced the workload of decisions at the top level. Concentrating command decisions, from the strategic level down to operational or even tactical matters, in a single person could only result in permanently overburdening the dictator. At critical moments, the decision-making process was often blocked. In the summer of 1944, the only solution to the problem was to remove Hitler physically. The attempt to do so failed on 20 July 1944.

Nine years later, Captain Assmann, who was wounded in the assassination attempt, described Hitler's reaction:

> One might have supposed that the growing resistance movement and the resulting assassination attempts would have induced Hitler to moderate his course; actually it had the opposite effect. The failure of his foes to eliminate him served to increase Hitler's belief in his calling, in his self-confidence, and his overweening opinion of self. He responded with further hardness, inflexibility, much greater obstinacy, and ruthlessness. Thus he rose to demoniac heights.

A few days after 20 July, Hitler visited Assmann in the hospital and made some remarks about the failure of the assassination and the future of the Germany:

> There you are with serious injuries, and yet you are not the one that was to be assassinated. These gentlemen had me, only me, in mind. But I escaped entirely. This is the fourth time in this war that my opponents have sought after my life in order to eliminate me for good. However, they did not succeed a single time despite most favorable conditions; on the contrary they suffered a renewed reverse each time, and

---

[22] H. Assmann, 'Some Personal Recollections of Adolf Hitler', *U.S. Naval Institute Proceedings*, 79:12 (Dec. 1953), p. 1294.

now the Almighty has stayed their hands once again. Don't you agree that I should consider it as a nod of fate that it intends to preserve me for my assigned task? ... Fate has given me the strength to lead the German people in an incomparable ascent to a height which is unique in their history. And the Lord has blessed our arms in the war to date in such manifold ways ... Consequently, the 20th of July can only confirm my recognition that Almighty God has called me to lead the German people – not to the final defeat, but to victory.[23]

Conclusion

As early as December 1941, Hitler recognised that his strategy had failed: Russia had not been defeated; the British will to resist had been strengthened; and American intervention in the war was to be expected in 1942. Over the course of the twentieth century, Germany had tried twice to force a strategic decision in direct confrontation with the Atlantic naval powers, Great Britain and the United States, by cutting the Atlantic shipping routes. Both attempts ended in failure, with the second defeat bringing with it the end of the German Reich and the dissolution of all German armed forces. During a table talk on 27 January 1942, Hitler prophesied to his guests a dark future for the German people: 'If the German people proved insufficiently strong to come through its life-and-death struggle, it deserved to go under.'[24] However, in May 1945, the final defeat brought severe consequences for the German people, but it was not the end of German history ...

---

[23] Ibid., p. 1290.
[24] Original: 'Da bin ich auch hier eiskalt: Wenn das deutsche Volk nicht bereit ist, für seine Selbsterhaltung sich einzusetzen, gut: dann soll es verschwinden.' Quoted from: Adolf Hitler, *Monologe im Führerhauptquartier 1941–1944*, p. 239. For another translation see: *Hitler's Table Talk, 1941–1944*, ed. H.R. Trevor-Roper (Oxford, 1988) in an introductory essay by H.R. Trevor-Roper on Adolf Hitler's mindset, p. 257: 'In that respect, I see things with the coldest objectivity. If the German people lost its faith, if the German people were no longer inclined to give itself body and soul in order to survive – then the German people would have nothing to do but disappear!'

14

The Capital Ship, the Royal Navy and British Strategy from the Second World War to the 1950s

TIM BENBOW

The 1940s and early 1950s were a stormy period for the Royal Navy's capital ships. They were the target of a great deal of criticism from sources at a high level in government, both political and military. These attacks were far more than the usual scrutiny of service programmes and amounted to fundamental questioning of whether the capital ship still had a role in naval strategy or in national strategy more broadly. Its role was debated during the war but was fought over even more intensely afterwards, when the evidence of the wartime years was deployed on both sides of a bitter and high-stakes debate over current and future policy.

This chapter explores the controversy over the role of the capital ship – defined simply as the most important unit of the fleet and specifically in this period meaning battleships, battlecruisers and, increasingly, aircraft carriers.[1] It looks briefly at how the experience of the First World War foreshadowed the challenges that were to come, before examining the role of the capital ship during the Second World War, when the challenge truly manifested. Finally, it surveys the debate through the first post-war decade when the dispute not only intensified but also broadened to call into question the very need for naval power.

The battleship retained a central albeit evolving place in naval strategy during the war and afterwards until (as the Admiralty foresaw on the horizon) its role could be better performed by other means. As the battleship declined – a process far slower than its critics suggested – its role as capital ship was taken on by the carrier. The latter could perform the classic role of neutralising enemy capital ships but also offered other capabilities, countering new threats and adding a whole new dimension to power projection. However, the ambitions of the air

---

[1] Herbert Richmond defined a capital ship as 'merely the most powerful ship'; the largest ships 'are the "capital", principal, or most important ships'; *Sea Power in the Modern World* (London, 1934), p. 59. Geoffrey Till defines them as 'most important ships of their time', and notes that the Pacific War confirmed the aircraft carrier as the new capital ship; *Seapower: A Guide for the Twenty-First Century* (London, 2004), pp. 121, 125. The *Oxford English Dictionary*, 3rd edn (Oxford, 2012) defines a capital ship as a warship 'suitable for use in the line of battle ... first-rate; of the largest size'. It notes uses of the term as early as 1665 in the Netherlands and 1688 in England. Helpfully, it specifies that, 'Since the early 20th century, capital ship refers especially to a battleship or battlecruiser, and since World War II also to an aircraft carrier.'

enthusiasts, both uniformed and civilian, complicated this transition and ensured that for long after the period covered in this chapter, the place in British strategy of the new capital ship, and of the navy in general, would be anything but plain sailing.

The First World War: Foreshadowing the Challenge

Before the twentieth century the role of the capital ship was relatively uncontroversial. It was the fighting heart of the navy and existed to destroy or neutralise its enemy counterpart by a combination of battle and blockade. Countering the enemy fleet in this way was necessary to secure the ability to use the sea while also preventing the enemy from using it. This use would be exercised primarily by smaller vessels, attacking and defending trade, conducting or preventing combined operations. Yet these activities depended on the conditions secured by the capital ships. There were debates over the degree of emphasis that should be placed on seeking battle to enhance command versus exercising command, or over the desirable balance between the assets for these respective roles. Yet the role of the capital ship in naval strategy was clear, as was its contribution to the national strategy of a power that envisaged using the sea in wartime. During the twentieth century, however, things became more complicated.

In one significant respect, the First World War was business as usual for the Royal Navy. Germany planned a fairly traditional strategy, based on a battle fleet which was to contest the command of the sea with Britain. The latter's response was equally traditional – naval blockade (albeit distant rather than close) while seeking a decisive battle. The geographically disadvantaged German fleet was kept bottled up in the North Sea where, beyond the occasional shelling of east-coast seaside resorts, it was prevented from inflicting serious harm on Britain or her strategy. It could neither threaten British shipping nor break the economic blockade which was slowly but remorselessly choking the life out of Germany's economy and war effort on land. The British public was deeply disappointed at the lack of a second Trafalgar, yet the indecisive tactical result of the Battle of Jutland should not obscure the strategic success of the British battle fleet. The German fleet was contained, neutralised and ended the war, like German society more broadly, in revolutionary collapse. Even without a shattering victory in battle, this should have been enough to quell any doubts about the continuing relevance of the battle fleet but for two important novel factors.

First, the advent of the submarine represented a revolutionary development in naval strategy – not so much its use against warships (where, a few successes apart, it had limited impact) but rather in unrestricted warfare against merchant shipping. Here was a means by which a navy could inflict serious, potentially fatal losses on a maritime opponent without first acquiring command of the sea in conventional terms. This was a threat that Britain had to counter but against which the capital ship could do nothing. This is not to argue, as some did, that the capital ships were therefore unnecessary; they were still essential to meet the threat from the enemy battle fleet, which had not gone away. However, they were no longer sufficient on their own and the question of the balance of resources now had to be addressed in a more pressing form than ever before.

The second complicating factor was another innovation. Air power saw its major debut in the war. Over the sea as over the land it was far from militarily decisive but its impact and its far greater potential promised revolutionary change. On the one hand, navies took air power to sea with them, to help conduct familiar roles and to give them important new capabilities – which eventually transferred the title of capital ship to the carrier. More challenging, though, it gave rise to a new body of strategic thought which insisted that land-based air power cast serious doubt on the continuing place of capital ships in naval strategy and even on the role of naval power in national strategy.[2]

For some advocates of air power, land-based aircraft could better perform the traditional roles of the battle fleet in countering the enemy main fleet, preventing invasion and protecting trade. This vision of the impact of air power held serious implications for the capital ship, whether battleship or aircraft carrier – to which, the air theorists argued, land-based air power would inevitably be far superior. If this argument were correct, there would be no need for capital ships as sea power would increasingly be exercised by air power. There would still, some airmen conceded, be a role far from land for anti-submarine escorts but for nothing larger. This account of the future therefore suggested that the days of the capital ship were numbered.

Yet there was also a more ambitious vision for air power. For some (notably Douhet[3] but also much of the leadership of the Royal Air Force), while air power could easily take over the traditional roles of the battle fleet, this was not actually its best use. Rather it represented a superfluous and dangerous diversion from the true role of air power which was strategic bombing. Unlike the older services, they argued, the air force did not need to sully itself with the vulgar business of fighting its enemy counterpart. Rather, it could from the very outset of a war attack the heart of the enemy's ability and will to fight. Strategic bombing would bring about a swift and low-cost victory; thus, while the battle fleet was no longer needed, there was not even any requirement for air power to take on its role.

The emergence of air power therefore set the stage for a change in what was the capital ship, as the torch was eventually passed from battleship to carrier. Yet it also created a new ideology as well as a hungry new institution that sought its place in the sun. This alliance of radical theorists and ambitious practitioners would challenge the navy throughout the interwar period, the Second World War and beyond – and its echoes can still be heard today.

---

[2] This argument is developed at greater length in T. Benbow, 'Navies and the Challenge of Technological Change', *Defence Studies*, viii, no. 2 (June 2008), pp. 207–26.
[3] G. Douhet, *Command of the Air* (trans. D. Ferrari: London, 1943; original 1921).

The Second World War: Manifesting the Challenge

For the Admiralty, the capital ship had much the same role in the Second World War as in previous conflicts: the battleship remained the central asset of the fleet with the carrier as a vital complement.[4] Their core role was to counter the enemy's heavy warships, thereby ensuring that these could not threaten Britain's use of the sea. There was a pressing need for this, given the powerful Italian and German surface fleets, even though the latter was used for commerce raiding rather than to seek command of the sea as in the previous war. The battleship performed this role alongside the carrier, which provided an additional means of striking at enemy ships in port, or slowing them down at sea, as well as protecting the fleet against the air threat. Despite the low priority the government had over a long period attached to the Fleet Air Arm, its achievements against enemy capital ships were remarkable, not least crippling the Italian battle fleet at Taranto, ensuring the sinking of the *Bismarck* and immobilising the *Tirpitz* in the crucial period around D-Day. Yet the carrier needed the battleship as much as the battleship needed the carrier, given the contemporary limitations of aircraft in bad weather or at night and the stunted development of British naval aviation. It was not simply a matter of the navy using battleships because it had them; rather, they genuinely retained an essential role.

The fleets that contained the German capital units in harbour or chased them off when they emerged, and that provided cover to prevent the Italian battle fleet from interfering with the invasions of North Africa, Sicily and Salerno, saw the battleship and the carrier operate side by side as their respective roles evolved. By the end of the war, it was the carrier that was the senior partner, with the battleship operating largely in support. Battleships took on additional roles, notably providing fire support for amphibious operations, yet the greater versatility of the carrier helped it move to centre stage. This transition involved the evolution of the familiar cover role to include defence against air attack but it centred on the additional ability to strike targets ashore and to support amphibious operations. On many occasions – including Operations Ironclad, Torch, Avalanche and Dragoon – it was carriers that provided the air power necessary to conduct landings.

Just as in the First World War, however, countering the threat from heavy surface units although necessary was not sufficient, due to the return in a more deadly form of the submarine threat. Winning this campaign was fundamental to British strategy, whether to sustain the strategic air campaign or to build for the liberation of north-west Europe. The requirements for defeating the U-boats had to be balanced against the other needs of the war at sea; from the beginning of the war, the Admiralty gave the new construction of battleships a lower priority than

---

[4] There was a difference in degree over the role of the carrier between the Royal Navy on the one hand, and the US and Japanese navies on the other: they had more ambitious plans for their naval aviation, as well as a more capable naval air arm, than the Royal Navy largely because, unlike the latter, they had control over their own air arm and did not need to beg aircraft from an independent air force that was ideologically hostile to naval aviation.

escorts and merchant ships. When more resources became available, it put these into carriers rather than battleships. Indeed, in 1944 the Admiralty opted to lay up four old battleships in order to free personnel for landing craft for Operation Overlord and for naval aviation for the Eastern Fleet,[5] which gives an indication of where its priorities now lay.

There was, however, a more fundamental debate over the allocation of resources within British strategy. This prolonged and often bitter clash focused on the demands of the air power advocates as they strove to demonstrate the ability of strategic bombing to win the war on its own. This dispute had huge implications for the war at sea, not least depriving it of the land-based and carrier-based air power that was needed to complement and support surface warships in carrying out their roles. The Admiralty made repeated efforts to secure additional aircraft for RAF Coastal Command, even more than for the Fleet Air Arm, but Portal as Chief of the Air Staff and the other bomber barons refused to cooperate. Blinded by the illusion of 'victory through air power', they stubbornly resisted any suggestion that they transfer to Coastal Command the number of very-long-range aircraft that would be lost in one moderately bad night over Germany.[6] Equally, they did all that they could to minimise the use of Bomber Command against naval targets despite the Admiralty plaintively asking for land-based air support as effective as that of their opponent. Despite the criticisms later directed at the navy for being insufficiently air minded, the problem was not that they did not get the principle; rather that they could not get the aircraft. The result was a grave distortion of British strategy with disproportionate resources devoted to a strategic air campaign that was known not to be achieving what its advocates had promised. The difficulty for the navy was that the seductive claim of 'offensive action' that offered a quick and easy route to victory proved irresistible to Churchill.

The Second World War saw the carrier replace the battleship as the principal unit of the navy, although the latter retained a significant role. It also saw the challenges to the capital ship that had been hinted at during the First World War come to the fore. First, the campaign against the U-boats demanded assets other than capital ships; yet it was only their activities that made victory in the Battle of the Atlantic possible by providing cover for the escorts, which did not need to fear German capital ships. Both elements of naval power were essential. Second, British naval power was badly weakened by the voracious claims of the strategic bombing campaign, the appetite of which left both the Fleet Air Arm and Coastal Command starved of the resources they needed.

---

[5] S.W. Roskill, *The War at Sea 1939–1945, Volume III: The Offensive, Part II: 1st June 1944–14th August 1944* (London, 1961), p. 10.
[6] See T. Benbow, 'Brothers in Arms: The Admiralty, the Air Ministry and the Battle of the Atlantic, 1940–43', *Global War Studies*, xi, no. 1 (2014), pp. 41–88.

The Post-war Period: Intensifying the Challenge

In the post-war period, the Royal Air Force continued to urge the priority of strategic bombing in British defence policy. Yet in addition it pushed far harder than hitherto the claim that land-based air power could directly replace the capital ship in the war at sea.

Between the end of the war and the series of defence reviews that culminated in early 1955, the role of the Royal Navy came under an attack as bitter and sustained as at any time in its history.[7] This onslaught focused on the new capital ships, the fleet carriers, and their strike aircraft and high-performance fighters. Yet it also targeted the very place of naval power in British strategy. The campaign was led by the Secretary of State for Air and his interwar predecessors, many of whom were still in government, with the active support of some but not all Chiefs of the Air Staff; Slessor was the worst, with his crusade against the navy at times bordering on the deranged. Their explicit aim was to gain an increased share of the defence budget for the bomber force at the expense of the navy in general and naval aviation in particular. They were backed by other ministers and officials who doubted the relevance of naval power in the modern world, and by some who simply sought to reduce defence spending and embraced this approach as a convenient way to achieve it.

For this clique, Britain needed to focus her military efforts narrowly on the short opening period of a future war, which would see an intense nuclear exchange. The top priority should be a strategic bomber force, either to fight this war or, as the emphasis of strategy shifted, to deter it. The defence of sea communications would be barely necessary in such a war and should be in a lower category, which would not receive any funding until the needs of the top priority had been fully met. The navy would therefore comprise nothing more than escorts and minesweepers; there was simply no role for the capital ship because there would be little need or opportunity to wage war at sea.

The Admiralty and others who were unconvinced by this approach doubted that the course of a future war could be so confidently predicted or so narrowly defined. They maintained that there was still a need to defend sea communications – both in war and as part of the deterrent to it – and that this still required capital ships. Some of the navy's critics even denied that the Soviet Union presented a significant naval threat but the evidence to the contrary seemed ever more compelling: in 1947 when the Chancellor of the Exchequer noted that the German, Italian and Japanese fleets no longer existed and 'no one claims that the Russians have, as yet, a fleet as strong as any one of these in 1938', he was corrected by Admiral Sir John Cunningham, First Sea Lord, who informed him that whilst Germany had had 65 submarines on the outbreak of war, the Russians currently had 230 in service, as well as 17 cruisers and 69 destroyers, many of

---

[7] For an account of these disputes, see T. Benbow, 'British Naval Aviation and the "Radical Review", 1953–1955', in Benbow (ed.), *British Naval Aviation: The First 100 Years* (Farnham, 2011).

which were new.⁸ The Soviet Union appeared to expect the conventional war at sea to be important and was building an impressive force to fight it, including heavy surface units in addition to submarines and a naval air force.

In broadening their case for the bomber force as the centrepiece of British strategy, the Air Staff went considerably further than they had during the war in arguing that it could perform the roles of the navy in the war at sea as well as making it barely relevant at the wider strategic level. The bomber force, they insisted, could perform any of the roles assigned to the fleet carriers, both more effectively and more cost effectively; there was therefore no need for the carriers. They offered in support their interpretation of the lessons of the Second World War, making extravagant claims regarding the RAF contribution to the war at sea. There was a degree of bare-faced cheek associated with these assertions, not least because the naval achievements of Bomber Command had been remarkably modest, while the very significant achievements of Coastal Command had been accomplished in the face of indifference or even hostility from the bomber-focused leadership of the air force.

The Admiralty sought to refute their claims about recent history, pointing out the limitations of land-based aircraft, the problems the navy had encountered in getting the RAF to make good on its claims of what it could do at sea, and also the continuing role of the capital ships.

During the war, British land-based air power failed to sink or seriously damage any of the German capital ships at sea, or to sink them during the prolonged periods when they were in port. The main successes of Bomber Command, eagerly cited to improve the statistics, came in the closing stages of the war when the warships concerned had long been marginalised. It was the capital ships of the Royal Navy that had countered them and prevented them playing their intended role, sinking three of them and containing the others.

It is instructive to consider the fate of Germany's seven most powerful capital ships. The *Admiral Graf Spee* was damaged by cruisers and then scuttled in the belief that a battleship and carrier force was awaiting her off Montevideo. *Bismarck* was slowed by carrier strike aircraft and then finished off by gunfire and torpedoes. *Scharnhorst* was chased off her Atlantic commerce raiding by capital ships, survived repeated bombing attacks and the 'Channel Dash' and was then sunk in December 1943 by a surface force led by battleships. So far, the score is two battleships and one pocket battleship to capital ships, none to land-based air power. The advocates of the latter tend to cite the sinking of the *Tirpitz* as their great success but it was nothing of the sort; it ranks alongside the sinking of the *Ostfriesland* in bombing tests in 1921 as being ruthlessly exploited by the air power publicity machine but in fact offering little of substance in terms of the wider debate. By the time she was finally put out of her misery in November 1944, *Tirpitz* was crippled and had effectively been out of the war for some time.

---

[8] TNA, CAB131/4, DO(47)9, Chancellor of the Exchequer, 'Defence Estimates for 1947–48', 13 January 1947; CAB131/5, DO(47) 2nd Conclusions, 14 January 1947.

Repeated attacks by land-based air power had failed to do more than temporary damage – during her construction, while she was based in Kiel, or while she was based in Norway. It was the capital ships of the Home Fleet that contained her in Norway – presenting her as a stationary target for Bomber Command – and, incidentally, carrier air strikes that knocked her out for the crucial period of the Normandy landings. Land-based aircraft belatedly delivered the coup de grâce but *Tirpitz* had been defeated by British capital ships. The same can be said of the *Gneisenau,* and the other two pocket battleships *Deutschland* (renamed *Lützow*) and *Admiral Scheer*; at times they suffered varying degrees of damage from land-based bombers in the extended periods that they spent immobile, in known locations, within range of Britain, but this was only temporary; they were prevented from making a serious contribution to German naval or national strategy by British capital ships. It was their helplessness in the face of the superiority of the British fleet's battleships and carriers that led to their marginalisation. *Gneisenau* ended up scuttled as a blockship in March 1945; *Lützow* and *Admiral Scheer* were both finished off by Bomber Command but only in the closing stages of the war in April 1945, long after they had ceased to pose a real threat.

Looking it this issue from the other side (which is important given the claims made about the vulnerability of surface warships), despite the remediable deficiencies in naval aviation and air defence, only two British capital ships were sunk by land-based aircraft – the *Prince of Wales* and *Repulse*, by Japanese naval aircraft operating from land bases. One light fleet carrier was sunk by Japanese carrier-based aircraft; two battleships, three fleet carriers and two escort carriers were torpedoed by U-boats; one battlecruiser and one carrier (operating as an aircraft ferry) were sunk by gunfire of enemy capital ships.[9]

Just as in the previous war, the capital ships deserved more credit than they tended to receive. They were the 'far distant, storm beaten ships' on which the British press and public opinion rarely looked, and whose contribution was either misunderstood or deliberately ignored by some in Whitehall. The capital ships provided years of effective service in containing the German surface threat; the RAF gained disproportionate credit for delivering a few exquisitely publicised but strategically largely irrelevant coups de grâce.

The poor record of land-based aircraft resulted in part from a denial that attacking naval targets was either an important role or a specialised one, with the argument still appearing after the war that a general bombing force could be switched between roles at will. The Royal Air Force had also clung to the theory that high-level bombing would be effective against ships, and resisted with great determination any suggestion that it acquire dive bombers for cooperation with either of the other services. The airmen underestimated the difficulty of locating and hitting warships – in port and even more at sea – and equally underestimated the continuing effect of range, weather and air defences.

---

[9] Despite the supposed vulnerability of large warships, from the beginning of 1943, the Royal Navy did not lose a single battleship or carrier to any cause; R.J. Overy, *Why the Allies Won* (London, 1996), p. 61.

The Admiralty concluded that wartime experience proved the continuing need for capital ships. First and foremost, this now involved a dedicated Fleet Air Arm, trained for operations at sea. The fleet carrier was needed to fulfil the traditional role of providing cover for lighter naval forces and merchant shipping; this was still needed, against the enemy surface fleet but also against heavy air attack. The cover role would also include attacks at source against enemy forces, to reduce the scale of the threat at sea. For Britain, the focus was strongly on the defence of sea communications, in contrast to the United States Navy which looked more to influencing the battle ashore. Simply put, British strategy still needed to defend sea communications and this still required naval forces; land-based air power could not do this (and, experience suggested, would rarely even try), and fleet carriers were therefore essential.

While the Admiralty was quite clear that the carrier was now the centrepiece of the fleet, it also saw a continued need, for the time being, for its wartime partner. The limitations of aircraft in bad weather and at night meant that there was still a supporting role for the battleship. This argument was not merely reactionary admirals clinging to the past, as their detractors in Cabinet, Parliament and the press were quick to allege. Rather it was based on a thorough analysis of the capabilities and limitations of the old and the new capital ship. Moreover, the Admiralty explicitly stated that the continuing value of the battleship was temporary; its role would remain vital but would soon be carried out by improving naval aviation, and also by the development of guided missiles which would provide smaller vessels with the striking power of a battleship. They sought not to replace the existing battleships but rather to retain them, for a limited time, alongside the carriers.

It is striking just how far the arguments in this period about the role of the navy in general and the fleet carriers in particular focused on total war, first waging it and increasingly deterring it. As the reviews of the early 1950s went on, while the carriers' role in hot war was still seen as significant, their value in warm wars and the cold war came to the fore. The ability of the new capital ship to contribute to limited war became an increasingly central part of their rationale, keeping them in service long after the battleship had been confined to history.

Conclusion

One general conclusion of this chapter is that there is a need to topple the wall that sometimes exists between 'World War II' and 'post-1945'. To a remarkable extent, the issues and debates of the wartime years continued immediately afterwards, often in a more strident and bitter fashion. Moreover, these post-war debates frequently saw wartime experience drawn upon in claims and counter-claims. The controversies of the early 1950s often had more in common with those of the previous decade than with those of the following decade, and the two periods can be usefully considered together.

This whole period was one of transition for naval power and its place in national strategy. The classic function of the capital ship, namely countering the heavy units of the enemy fleet, was still required – and despite the claims of the air enthusiasts, this role still fell primarily to warships. The nature of these warships changed, however, with the carrier taking its place alongside the battleship and eventually easing it out of the fleet, not least due to its broader versatility. The carrier could perform the role of the battleship and more besides, particularly in limited war.

As warfare continued to evolve, the components of the fleet and its roles diversified and increasingly integrated with those of the other services. The need to counter the enemy fleet remained, where such a fleet existed, but other assets (not least nuclear-powered submarines) came to share in this role while the carrier's ability to project force ashore took on still greater importance. The concept of a 'capital ship' became less clear and the term itself fell out of fashion as its function was dispersed. Yet the continuing importance of the capital ship through the Second World War and into the decade afterwards is an important reminder of the need to treat with some caution the more excitable claims made on behalf of new technologies, and of the need to balance an appreciation of change with an awareness of continuity.

15

'No Scope for Arms Control':
Strategy, Geography and Naval Limitations in the Indian Ocean in the 1970s

PETER JOHN BROBST

'From the standpoint of military advantage,' Alfred Thayer Mahan wrote in 1902, 'a Russian naval division in the Persian Gulf, although unquestionably a menace to the trade route from Suez to the East, would be most ex-centrically placed as regards all Russia's greatest interests. It is for these reasons ... that the good of Russia presents no motive for Great Britain to concede a position so extremely injurious to herself and her dependencies.'[1] Comparable reasoning continued to suffuse thinking in Whitehall seventy years later, as the British liquidated the remnants of their empire east of Suez. Britain's residual interests in the Indian Ocean remained considerable, particularly on the economic side.[2] Declaring the waters between Suez and Singapore a 'Zone of Peace' was popular throughout the Commonwealth, and held substantial political attraction. But, as in Mahan's time, geography, or rather geopolitics, continued to hold primacy of place in the shaping of strategy.[3] The persistent asymmetry between the continental position of the Soviet Union, on one side, and Britain's maritime posture, on the other, left 'no scope for an arms control solution to Indian Ocean security'.[4] By the

---

[1] A.T. Mahan, 'The Persian Gulf in International Relations', *Retrospect and Prospect* (reprinted Port Washington, NY, 1968), p. 233.
[2] For Britain's persistent interests, second thoughts and even 'non-withdrawal' in the Indian Ocean in the 1970s, see A. Jackson, 'Imperial Defence in the Post-Imperial Era', in G. Kennedy (ed.), *Imperial Defence: The Old World Order, 1856–1956* (London, 2008); and G. Till, 'The Return to Globalism: The Royal Navy East of Suez, 1975–2003', in G. Kennedy (ed.), *British Naval Strategy East of Suez, 1900–2000* (London, 2005).
[3] See R. Hyam, 'The Primacy of Geopolitics: The Dynamics of Imperial Policy, 1763–1963', in R.D. King and R.W. Kilson (eds), *The Statecraft of British Imperialism: Essays in Honour of Wm. Roger Louis* (London, 1999).
[4] TNA, CAB 130/495, Brief for the Cabinet Secretary, Interdepartmental Study on Defence in the Indian Ocean, GEN 30(71), 18 June 1971, Secret. For the theme of this chapter – the importance of geostrategic vision and orientation over technical factors in arms control – in the context of international relations theory, see E.O. Goldman, *Sunken Treaties: Naval Arms Control between the Wars* (University Park, PA, 1994); and C. Gray, *House of Cards: Why Arms Control Must Fail* (Ithaca, NY, 1994). For the historical antecedents, see K. Neilson, '"The British Empire Floats on the British Navy": British Naval Policy, Belligerent Rights, and Disarmament', in *Arms Limitation and Disarmament: Restraints on War, 1899–1939*

mid-1970s, American authorities had come around to a similar view: 'as a major maritime nation, we have more to lose in an exchange of naval concessions than does the USSR, which is still primarily a land power'.[5]

In 1970, one was more likely to hear such a formulation in Whitehall than in the White House. In 1968, the Labour government led by Harold Wilson announced that Britain would withdraw its last major forces still on station east of Suez by the end of 1971. On assuming office in 1970, the Conservative government led by Edward Heath ordered a detailed review of that decision. In the end, British authorities determined that the process had progressed too far to abort and would thus proceed apace. They looked instead to American sea power as the future basis of security in the Indian Ocean, favouring this so-called 'defence approach' over either regional organisation or naval limitations. The diffuse politics of the Indian Ocean's littoral nations rendered regional organisation impractical, while naval limitations appeared incompatible with enduring requirements for sea control and power projection across the Indian Ocean. One issue was maintaining access to the Indian Ocean as a 'manoeuvre space' – in relation to containment of the Soviet Union, on one hand, and to Britain's continuing Commonwealth commitments and constabulary operations along the Afro-Asian rim, as in the then ongoing 'Beira Blockade' against Rhodesia, on the other.[6] Trade defence was also a vital concern.

Britain's economic stake in the Indian Ocean remained concrete and extensive in the early 1970s. According to the Ministry of Defence (MoD), the region accounted at the time for 22% of Britain's combined visible and invisible trade. Over 45% of Britain's crude and refined oil came from the Gulf, and 29% of its non-ferrous metals came from around the Indian Ocean littoral. Some 40% of Britain's sterling liability was tied up in Indian Ocean countries, particularly in the Gulf States. The region as a whole took approximately 42% of Britain's direct overseas investment, with about 20% of the total in Australasia and another 11% in South Africa. Since the closure of the Suez Canal as a result of the Six Day War in 1967, the 'Cape Route' around South Africa had come to carry 27% of Britain's

---

(Westport, CT, 1992); E. Goldstein and J. Maurer, eds, *The Washington Conference, 1921–1922: Naval Rivalry, East Asian Stability, and the Road to Pearl Harbor* (London, 1994); and J.H. Maurer and C.M. Bell, eds, *At the Crossroads between Peace and War: The London Naval Conference of 1930* (Annapolis, 2014).

[5] 'Arms Limitation in the Indian Ocean: Issues and Options', Report to the Verification Panel, Secret, attached to Action Memorandum, from Boverie to Scowcroft, 26 March 1976, Secret, *Foreign Relations of the United States* (hereafter *FRUS*), 1969–76, v. E-9, Documents on South Asia, 1973–76. For a contemporary and vigorous public statement of the argument, see A.J. Cottrell and W.F. Hahn, *Naval Race or Arms Control in the Indian Ocean?: Some Problems in Negotiating Naval Limitations* (Washington, 1978). E.M. Kennedy, 'The Persian Gulf: Arms Race or Arms Control', *Foreign Affairs*, v. 54, n. 1 (1975), presents the other side with equal force.

[6] For the concept of 'manoeuvre space' in the sense used here, see J. Kraska, *Maritime Power and the Law of the Sea: Expeditionary Operations in World Politics* (Oxford, 2011), pp. 76–94; see also I. Speller, 'The Royal Navy, Expeditionary Operations, and the End of Empire', in Kennedy (ed.), *British Naval Strategy East of Suez*.

seaborne trade by value, representing 'more than any other route, except the short route between the UK and Europe'. The MoD assessors anticipated that even if the percentage of British trade going round South Africa were to decline after the Suez Canal reopened, 'the rapid development of super tankers and of large container ships and ore-carriers means that the Cape route will always be more important to the UK and her trading partners than pre-1967'. And while Britain's trade with countries 'east of the Cape' was admittedly reducing *relative* to Europe and North America, the MoD noted a countervailing trend in the import of critical minerals from Australia. On any day there were some 230 British merchant ships underway in the Indian Ocean, and there was little reason to think the number would drop off anytime soon.[7]

If the statistics offered concrete evidence of vulnerability, the salient factor in terms of threat was the recent appearance of a regular Soviet naval presence in the Indian Ocean. Aside from the occasional transit, mainly from the Atlantic to the Pacific, the Soviet Navy had made no deployments to the Indian Ocean prior to 1965. But since 1968 they had kept ships constantly on station in the Indian Ocean, principally in the north-western quadrant outside the Gulf. The number of combatants was both consistent and relatively small: one light cruiser plus three to four frigate- or destroyer-type vessels, sometimes accompanied by a diesel submarine or two. The purposes were unclear and vigorously debated in the West.[8] Admiral Sergei Gorshkov's expansive vision of Soviet sea power raised particular concern. Gorshkov, who headed the Soviet Navy from the late 1950s through the early 1980s, argued that development of a navy with global reach would confer prestige and obtain influence, not least to check 'Western imperialism'. He underscored the importance of Indian Ocean sea routes to the economic life of the West. In 1970, and again in 1975, the Soviet Navy staged coordinated, multi-ocean exercises. 'Okean 70' and 'Okean 75' seemed to validate worries over an extensive Soviet threat to Western sea lines of communication (SLOCs). Yet neither involved a concerted display in the Indian Ocean.

In fact, few if any officials assumed that the Soviet presence in the Indian Ocean *necessarily* reflected an offensive design. Many recognised a defensive purpose

---

[7] TNA, CAB 130/495, MoD Study, DP 36/70, 'Defence Contribution to the Preservation of the Main UK Interests in the Indian Ocean in the 1970s', Secret – UK Eyes Only, attached as appendix to memorandum by the MoD, Interdepartmental Study on Defence in the Indian Ocean, GEN 30(71), 11 December 1970, Secret. For contemporary academic assessments, see M. Burrell, 'The Cape Route and the Oil Trade: A Problem Not Yet Resolved', *The Round Table*, n. 251 (July 1973); and K. Trace, 'International Trade and Commercial Relations', in A.J. Cottrell and R.M. Burrell (eds), *The Indian Ocean: Its Political, Economic, and Military Importance* (New York, 1973).

[8] On the unclassified side, see especially the four essays on 'Forward Deployment in the Indian Ocean', in M. McGwire (ed.), *Soviet Naval Developments: Capability and Context* (New York, 1973), pp. 389–455. For the influence of these and related studies carried out under the auspices of the Washington-based Center for Naval Analyses (CNA), see J.B. Hattendorf, *The Evolution of the US Navy's Maritime Strategy, 1977–1986*, Naval War College Newport Papers, ixx (Newport, RI, 2004), pp. 24–9.

behind Soviet naval deployments between Suez and Singapore. For starters, the Indian Ocean formed an important link between the Soviet Union's European core and its distant territories on the Pacific – an alternative to the trans-Siberian railway and its exposure to interdiction in the event of a fight with China.[9] The main issue, however, appeared to be countering the threat to the Soviet homeland posed by the potential stationing of Western ballistic missile submarines in the Indian Ocean.[10] At least one American admiral was incredulous on hearing such assessments. The commander of the US Navy's Middle East Force told his British counterparts that the Soviets 'were as aware as the Americans of the logistic problems: in terms of transit times, time on station and costs it was quite impossible to maintain the threat'.[11] On the other hand, the British spent almost four years during the Wilson government of the 1960s planning for the possible deployment of 'Polaris' submarines into the Indian Ocean before finally tabling the scheme due to cost.[12] Even then authorities in Washington as well as London held the option open, at least as a theoretical exercise, while they anticipated both improvements to 'Polaris' and the eventual deployment of the 'Poseidon' and 'Chevaline' follow-on systems in the 1970s.[13] 'The day could come,' Admiral Thomas Moorer, the Chairman of the American Joint Chiefs, reminded senior officials in 1971, 'when we might want to put Polaris submarines into the Indian Ocean.'[14] Moorer advised against agreeing to any ban on ballistic missile submarines in the Indian Ocean because such a step 'would greatly simplify [the Soviet] warning system and ASW system. We want them to look 360 degrees.' In nuclear strategy, he said, 'we can use the Indian Ocean against them better than they can use it against us'.[15] Whatever the reality of Anglo-American plans, the Central Intelligence Agency (CIA) assessed that strategic anti-submarine warfare was the driving issue for the Soviets in the Indian Ocean.[16]

Still, a number of officials warned against being 'rather over-comfortable' about Soviet policy and capacities in the Indian Ocean.[17] While the British Naval

---

[9] W.A.C. Adie, *Oil, Politics, and Sea Power: The Indian Ocean Vortex* (New York, 1975), p. 19. For a detailed discussion, see M. Hauner, 'The Soviet Geostrategic Dilemma', in M. Hauner and R.L. Canfield (eds), *Afghanistan and the Soviet Union* (Boulder, CO, 1989).

[10] For example, see the record of the meeting between Anglo-American officials on the Indian Ocean, TNA, CAB 163/174, Washington, 8 December 1970, Secret.

[11] TNA, FCO 46/878, Note by Orchard, 7 June 1972, Confidential.

[12] See M. Jones and J.W. Young, 'Polaris East of Suez: British Plans for a Nuclear Force in the Indo-Pacific, 1964–1968', *Journal of Strategic Studies*, xxxiii, n. 6 (2010).

[13] TNA, DEFE 24/505, Minute by Abraham, Top Secret, 17 May 1967; and 'What Now for Britain? Wilson's Visit and Britain's Future', 7 February 1968, reproduced in J. Colman, 'The State Department's Intelligence Assessment of the Special Relationship', *Diplomacy and Statecraft*, ixx, n. 2 (2008), p. 357.

[14] Minutes of Senior Review Group Meeting, 22 April 1971, *FRUS*, 1969–76, v. XXIV, Middle East Region and Arabian Peninsula.

[15] Minutes of Senior Review Group Meeting, 6 October 1971, *FRUS*, 1969–76, v. XXIV.

[16] Central Intelligence Agency, FOIA Electronic Reading Room, 'Soviet Naval Writings: A Framework for Antisubmarine Warfare Strategy', Intelligence Report, Secret, July 1971.

[17] TNA, FCO 46/1294, Killick to Thomson, 25 November 1974, Confidential,.

Staff 'did not totally discount the possibility' that Soviet operations in the Indian Ocean aimed 'purely to improve the defence of the homeland against maritime attack', they emphasised that 'all speculation on motive and intentions aside, the maritime capability being acquired by the Soviets is most dangerous to the West by virtue of its ability to sink shipping, in particular ships carrying oil, and that this is the most critical aspect of their Indian Ocean presence'.[18] In the Foreign and Commonwealth Office (FCO), one Russia-hand warned that 'if we should not overlook the restraints on Soviet policy ... neither should we forget the revolutionary, determinist, and conspiratorial streak.' He cautioned that 'to argue about whether [Soviet] motives are "political" or "military" is simply hair-splitting'.[19] In the Cabinet Office, Heath's high-level study group on the Indian Ocean maintained that 'Soviet imperialism, if unchecked, could in time alter the political (and perhaps the economic) character of the area profoundly and to our disadvantage. At the same time, an active and powerful Soviet fleet would be in a position to cut off a significant part of our supply of oil and other raw materials.'[20]

Authorities in Whitehall were in no doubt that Britain's ability to deploy any counterpoise of its own was 'strictly limited' after 1971.[21] But arms control did not offer a viable alternative, at least not the schemes for it that actually lay on the table. These would only exacerbate Britain's predicament in the Indian Ocean. Officials in the Heath government objected to both of the two main lines of proposal for arms control in the waters of east of Suez. The first was to designate the Indian Ocean a 'Zone of Peace'. The government of Sri Lanka had originally mooted this idea in 1970 at the Lusaka conference of non-aligned nations. The proposed zone extended from East Africa on the west to Malaysia on the east, and 'appeared' to include the Gulf. It would exclude the 'great powers' from any permanent or war-fighting stance in the Indian Ocean. British officials noted that 'the category of Great Powers included *us*'.[22] The sarcasm aside, the basic objection to the peace zone was that it represented an example of 'regional' versus 'global' arms control. The same held true for the second line of proposal for arms control in the Indian Ocean, which involved a less totalising effort to limit the number, size and scope of operations by external navies as opposed to attempting to exclude such forces from the area altogether.

What British authorities referred to as 'global arms control' described arrangements similar to the naval treaties of the 1920s and 1930s that restricted the

---

[18] TNA, DEFE 24/664, Note by Easton, 'Soviet Naval Presence in the Indian Ocean', 16 February 1971, Secret.
[19] TNA, FCO 46/1294, Bullard to Thomson, 18 November 1974, Confidential.
[20] TNA, CAB 130/459, Report by GEN 30, GEN 30(70) 4, 'Defence Problems in the Indian Ocean', 30 December 1970, Secret.
[21] TNA, CAB 130/495, MoD Study, DP 36/70, 'Defence Contribution to the Preservation of the Main UK Interests in the Indian Ocean in the 1970s', Secret – UK Eyes Only, attached as appendix to memorandum by the MoD, Interdepartmental Study on Defence in the Indian Ocean, GEN 30(71), 11 December 1970, Secret.
[22] TNA, CAB 130/495, Minutes, 6th meeting, Interdepartmental Study on Defence in the Indian Ocean, GEN 30(71), 29 October 1971, Confidential.

size and structure of navies in total rather than declaring any particular region wholly off limits.[23] This type of approach could arguably have benefited Britain in the Indian Ocean, if pursued through a bilateral arrangement between the United States and the Soviet Union. On such a basis, global arms control stood to increase the strength of the medium-sized Royal Navy in relative terms, while simultaneously limiting the capacity of its Soviet rival to deploy in a far-flung and presumably non-essential theatre where the goal appeared largely – if not simply – to stick pins. In contrast, 'regional arms control' worked more to the advantage of the two superpowers, neither of which had extensive, positive interests of its own in the Indian Ocean, at least not comparable to Britain's. Regional arms control, the FCO warned, would limit Britain's ability to meet ongoing security obligations in Singapore and Malaysia, the Seychelles and Mauritius, Oman, CENTO and Australia; it would limit Britain's 'freedom to collaborate in … exercises and visits with countries who want them … and to this end to retain our arrangements for the use of facilities'.[24] As a practical matter, limiting such activities represented as much a threat in the Indian Ocean as the development of Soviet anti-shipping capabilities for World War III. A prominent suspicion was that the visibility of Soviet deployments into the Indian Ocean was largely meant to spook littoral states, fretting over a possible arms race in their backyard, in order to gin-up local support for regional limits. While these might bind the Soviet Union, they would disproportionately affect Britain. In short, a multilateral, regional approach to arms control in the Indian Ocean was 'quite unacceptable' in Whitehall.[25]

Throughout the early 1970s, British officials pressed these views on their American counterparts 'to encourage the United States Administration to take seriously the potential security dangers in the Indian Ocean'.[26] The Americans came off as 'not very interested'.[27] The United States, the British reasoned, was simply 'less directly dependent on Indian Ocean trade routes than other countries'.[28] As late as 1974, regional experts in the State Department could describe the Indian Ocean to British colleagues as lying 'on the opposite side of the

---

[23] Although, as Colin Gray notes, the regionally focused 'non-fortification' clause in the Washington Treaty of 1922, combined with the 'geostrategic terms of operation' of both the British and American navies, 'translated into Japanese superiority where it mattered'. Gray, *House of Cards*, p. 53.

[24] TNA, FCO 46/747, Note by Tesh, 'Peace in the Indian Ocean', 7 October 1971, Confidential.

[25] Ibid.

[26] TNA, CAB 130/495, Brief for the Secretary of the Cabinet, Interdepartmental Study on Defence in the Indian Ocean, GEN 30(71), 18 June 1971, Secret.

[27] TNA, FCO 46/747, Note by Tesh, 'Peace in the Indian Ocean', 7 October 1971, Confidential,

[28] TNA, CAB 130/495 MoD Study, DP 36/70, 'Defence Contribution to the Preservation of the Main UK Interests in the Indian Ocean in the 1970s', Secret – UK Eyes Only, attached as appendix to memorandum by the MoD, Interdepartmental Study on Defence in the Indian Ocean, GEN 30(70), 11 December 1970, Secret.

world, on the way to nowhere'.[29] The Nixon Administration had actually devoted more study to the Indian Ocean than British officials realised, but the sense in Whitehall that authorities in Washington felt little urgency about the region was understandable. The State Department advised exploring the possibilities for arms control in the Indian Ocean, troubled only to the degree that the Soviets might seize on an agreement as a precedent to make demands for 'global naval parity' and concessions in waters that mattered more directly to the United States.[30] In contrast, the US Navy needed no persuasion about the Indian Ocean and the pitfalls of regional arms control.[31] They had worked from the early 1960s to lay a foundation for the future operation of major forces – meaning carrier battle groups – in the area. They had sought and obtained rights from Britain to construct a communications outpost on Diego Garcia, finalising the deal in 1966 and activating the station in late 1972.[32] Within a year mainline policy in Washington had come around to the navy's view.

To be sure, the Americans had sent the aircraft carrier *Enterprise* into the Bay of Bengal in late 1971 in a show of support for Pakistan during the crisis surrounding the secession of Bangladesh. But the real turnabout in Washington's outlook followed from the Middle East crisis of 1973, the resulting oil embargo by Arab producers, and the attendant realisation that the United States had itself become directly dependent on Gulf oil and consequently on the sea-lanes over which it rode. American planners were also interested, after 1973, in guaranteeing a 'back door' to Israel through the Indian Ocean in case the Mediterranean corridor became impassable. Henry Kissinger, for one, judged such an eventuality an 'increasingly likely contingency'. '*In extremis*,' the Secretary of State wrote, 'our "back door" naval forces would play an essential role in tipping the balance against Soviet and Arab forces in the battle area.'[33] In this regard, strategists in Washington expressed as much concern about the Soviet threat to American

---

[29] TNA, FCO 46/1298, Masefield to Cormack, 29 April 1975, Secret. Similar language was still in use at the highest levels in Washington as late as 1976, although the implication of insignificance was gone: 'The Indian Ocean is geographically remote – being on precisely the other side of the globe from the continental United States.' See 'Arms Limitation in the Indian Ocean: Issues and Options', Report to the Verification Panel, Secret, attached to Action Memorandum, from Boverie to Scowcroft, 26 March 1976, Secret, *FRUS*, 1969–76, v. E-9.

[30] 'Non-Strategic Naval Limitations in the Indian Ocean', 15 February 1972, Secret, *FRUS*, 1969–76, v. E-9.

[31] See E.R. Zumwalt, *On Watch: A Memoir* (New York, 1976), pp. 362–3.

[32] See especially W. Stivers, *America's Confrontation with Revolutionary Change in the Middle East, 1948–83* (New York, 1986), pp. 28–57 and 68–9. Less dispassionate but indispensable is D. Vine, *Island of Shame: The Secret History of the US Military Base on Diego Garcia* (Princeton, 2009), which benefits from extensive interviews with the navy's principals in planning for Diego Garcia in the 1960s. V.B. Bandjunis, *Diego Garcia: Creation of the Indian Ocean Base* (San Jose, CA, 2001) provides a valuable first-hand account.

[33] Texas Tech University, Vietnam Center and Archive, Admiral Elmo R. Zumwalt Collection, Letter from the Secretary of State, attached to memorandum for Zumwalt by Cockell, 19 April 1975, Box 8, Folder 3.

carriers as to merchant shipping. The building of Soviet facilities in Somalia to support shipboard surface-to-surface missiles, in particular the SS-N-3, 7 and 9, seemed especially worrisome in this respect.[34] An arms control arrangement that eliminated the Soviet presence in Somalia would not, however, solve the problem, the Pentagon complained. The proximity of Soviet land power and land-based air power to Israel and the Gulf posed the ultimate threat.[35] The Soviet Navy in the Indian Ocean appeared a pawn to remove the counterpoise, however limited, presented by American carriers. In Washington, the geostrategic asymmetry of the post-1973 situation had finally brought the practical disadvantages of Indian Ocean arms control into as sharp a relief as officials in Whitehall had ever perceived.

The Ford Administration nevertheless continued to explore different options for naval limitations in the Indian Ocean through 1975. Their degree of interest corresponded to their level of anxiety about barriers in Congress to stepped-up activity in the region. The specific worry concerned Senate opposition to upgrading the facilities on Diego Garcia to support the regular deployment of carriers in the waters between Suez and Singapore. In May, Kissinger convened a group of senior officials to assess the options. One was simply to hope for the best in the Senate and remain silent on naval limitations in the Indian Ocean, lest the Soviets introduce bases into negotiations that would otherwise focus on ships and thereby delay improvements on Diego Garcia long enough to render resistance to opposition unsustainable. On the other hand, a promise to approach the Soviets after the Senate had signed-off on the plans for Diego Garcia stood to mollify the big arms control camp on Capitol Hill, led by Edward Kennedy of Massachusetts. A declaration that the United States would unilaterally freeze its force-level in the Indian Ocean following a positive Senate decision on Diego Garcia offered another way to achieve the same effect. Whichever option, the objective was to keep Congress at bay, as suggested by this bit of discussion between Kissinger and John Lehman, then the deputy director at the Arms Control and Disarmament Agency:

> Secretary Kissinger: Okay, let's hear the punch line – Option Four.
>
> Mr. Lehman: This option also has not been fully staffed out as yet. What it amounts to is to throw the ball to the United Nations – let them wrestle with the problem.
>
> Secretary Kissinger: That's insanity!
>
> Mr. Lehman: Well, it has the advantage of not giving us more lumps than we would already receive. It has the advantage of showing Congress that we are trying to get some sort of arms control negotiations going.

---

[34] TNA, FCO 46/1299, 'Anglo-American Consultations on the Indian Ocean, 19 and 20 May 1975', record of the meetings, 12 June 1975, Secret.

[35] 'Indian Ocean Strategy', response to NSSM 199, 14 March 1974, Secret, *FRUS*, 1969–76, v. E-9. The Department of Defense expressed similar views in the earlier Indian Ocean studies carried out in 1971 in response to NSSMs 104 and 110, but in those instances the argument was relegated to the footnotes as dissenting opinion.

Secretary Kissinger: What you are saying is that you would rather have the issue kicked around in the General Assembly rather than in the United States Senate.

Mr. Lehman: Yes. We believe the damage that the U.N. could do, would be minimal – as compared to the damage the Senate could do.[36]

In the event, the White House took the first option – doing nothing other than continuing regular consultations on the Indian Ocean with the British – once the Senate finally assented to the plans for Diego Garcia in early 1976.[37]

Ironically, the British had by this time warmed to arms control in the Indian Ocean. The change in attitude largely reflected the change in government. Worries about Britain's image in the Arab world after the October crisis of 1973 had given rise to second thoughts about tacit support for a beefed-up American presence in the Indian Ocean – let alone active encouragement of it – even before the Conservative departure in March of 1974. But the new thinking accelerated with Labour's return under Harold Wilson, who reaffirmed Britain's turn towards Europe. As a result, one official at the FCO pointed out, it could 'be argued that the Indian Ocean will be of only marginal importance to us in future'.[38] Another emphasised the significance of North Sea oil coming online in the late 1970s: 'every year that we move nearer to self-sufficiency in oil surely the argument about the oil routes must become less valid for the UK'.[39] Commonwealth relations also influenced the Wilson government's outlook. Indian Ocean strategists in Whitehall now worried that the British government would 'not be able to resist' calls from within the Commonwealth for action on arms control in the region, in particular the proposal from Gough Whitlam's left-leaning government in Australia for a modified version of the 'Zone of Peace'.[40] Yet for all this, British officials explained to their counterparts in Washington that British difficulties with American policy in the Indian Ocean were 'mainly political and domestic'.[41] Their political masters required public cover against 'parliamentary questions and other pressures [that] flow from our decision to agree ... to extend [US] facilities on Diego Garcia'.[42] Ultimately, the 'official mind' remained supportive, even desirous, of the strengthened American posture in the Indian Ocean, convinced

---

[36] Minutes, Senior Review Group Meeting, White House Situation Room, 6 May 1975, Secret, *FRUS*, 1969–76, v. E-9.

[37] 'Arms Limitation in the Indian Ocean: Issues and Options', report to the Verification Panel, Secret, attached to Action Memorandum, from Boverie to Scowcroft, 26 March 1976, Secret, *FRUS*, 1969–76, v. E-9.

[38] TNA, FCO 46/1298, 'British Interests and Objectives in the Area after the Defence Review', brief n. 9, Anglo-US Talks on the Indian Ocean, undated [April 1975], Confidential.

[39] TNA, FCO 46/1298, Masefield to Cormack, 29 April 1975, Secret.

[40] TNA, FCO 46/1297, Thomson to Jackson, 25 April 1975, Confidential.

[41] TNA, FCO 46/1299, 'Anglo-US Consultations on the Indian Ocean, 19 and 20 May 1975', record of the meetings, 12 June 1975, Secret.

[42] TNA, FCO 46/1286, 'Arms Limitation in the Indian Ocean and Diego Garcia', brief to the Prime Minister by the FCO, 23 January 1975, Confidential.

as it was of the lasting importance of the region's sea-lanes to the defence of the West as a whole.[43]

Debate over arms control in the Indian Ocean lingered through the late 1970s. The Kremlin called for negotiations on the issue following Washington's decision in 1976 to go ahead with expansion of the facilities on Diego Garcia. And in 1977, the Carter Administration expressed its own interest in talks towards a Naval Arms Limitation Treaty, or NALT, in the Indian Ocean. The context was on the face of it markedly different from that just a few years beforehand. Irrespective of partisan issues, authorities in Washington saw less risk and disadvantage now that the navy's access to Diego Garcia had been assured. Short of a new crisis, the navy had no intention (and little capacity) to increase its force levels further. This tacit arms control, however, rendered formal limitations in the region largely irrelevant.[44] That was one problem with NALT. The more fundamental trouble, according to Britain's incoming First Sea Lord, Admiral Terence Lewin, remained the same trouble as earlier in the decade. 'Any serious attempt at arms control and limitation', Lewin told an audience at the Royal Society for Asian Affairs in 1978, 'very quickly runs into snags over the comparison of capabilities, ranges, roles and back-up facilities, to say nothing of varying definitions of the word "base".' Proponents of NALT suggested using 'ship-days' spent in the Indian Ocean as the underlying metric and basis for negotiation. Lewin objected. He cautioned that such an approach would take 'no account of the class of ship and its capabilities ... as manifestly a US aircraft carrier has a greater and different sort of potential than a Russian cruiser and its attendant supply ship'.[45]

The emphasis on 'ship-days' reflected the perception of emerging 'equilibrium' between the geostrategic postures of the United States and the Soviet Union. Each country, this theory held, was in its roots a great land power that had over time developed substantial presence and capacity for action throughout the world's oceans. Where 'schism' between a seaborne West and a land-bound Russia had led ineluctably to rivalry before the late twentieth century, increasing 'symmetry' now pointed to accommodation and possibilities for concert.[46] In reality, the Kremlin's geostrategic outlook remained stubbornly continental. Even under Gorshkov, the Soviet Admiralty remained in effect 'Army Marshals in

---

[43] In contrast to the minutes cited above, in n. 38 and n. 39, see the departmental brief by the MoD on 'Western Naval Presence for the Anglo-UK Talks on the Indian Ocean, 6 to 7 November 1975', 30 October 1975, Secret – UK Eyes B, TNA, FCO 46/1300. See also General Sir J. Hackett et al., *The Third World War* (London, 1978); Admiral Sir T. Lewin, 'The Indian Ocean and Beyond: British Interests Yesterday and Today', *Asian Affairs*, ix, n. 3 (1978); and Admiral of the Fleet the Lord Hill-Norton, 'World Shipping at Risk: The Looming Threat to the Lifelines', *Conflict Studies*, n. 111 (September 1979).

[44] See R. Haass, 'Naval Limitation in the Indian Ocean', *Survival*, xx, n. 2 (1978).

[45] Lewin, 'Indian Ocean and Beyond', p. 256.

[46] See G. Liska, *Quest for Equilibrium: America and the Balance of Power on Land and Sea* (Baltimore, 1977).

Navy Uniforms'.[47] By the end of the decade, intelligence emerging from both signals and human sources was confirming the picture of a Soviet Navy charged primarily to secure waters close to home rather than hunt on the high seas.[48] In this context, arms control focused on ships offered the Soviets a way to exercise sea control in the Indian Ocean by default. As Admiral Lewin explained, 'while the Russians claim that they are concerned about the ability of American "Poseidon" submarines operating in the Arabian Sea to threaten Russian targets, the United States could legitimately claim that the ability of the Russians to deploy the "Backfire" bomber in Southern Russia would enable them to cover the Indian Ocean down to the equator'.[49]

Perhaps maritime 'equilibrium', had it proved real, would have cleared the way for naval arms control in the Indian Ocean. Instead, the geostrategic 'schism' between Western sea power and Soviet continentalism persisted. After invading Afghanistan in 1979, the Soviets gained the capacity to deploy 'Backfire' bombers and other long-range aircraft for maritime strike and reconnaissance in unprecedented proximity to the Indian Ocean. American carrier battle groups, supported from Diego Garcia, presented the ready counterpoise to the Soviet advance in South-West Asia. From this vantage, naval limitations, had they been secured in the 1970s, might have ceded the field to the landsmen. In the final analysis, the limited scope for arms control in the Indian Ocean in the 1970s reflected the basic mismatch familiar to strategists in Mahan's era: the problem of the whale versus the bear, to use an old, imperial aphorism about defence east of Suez. As one British official put it in 1974, great power activity in the Indian Ocean amounted to '19th-century policy with 20th-century equipment'.[50] Vice Admiral Louis Le Bailly, then Director of Britain's Defence Intelligence Staff, stressed the point in a 1972 meeting with Admiral Thomas Moorer, then the Chairman of the American Joint Chiefs. 'The rules of the Great Game', Le Bailly insisted, 'remained unchanged.'[51]

---

[47] Rear Admiral T. Brooks, USN, quoted in C.A. Ford and D.A. Rosenberg, *The Admirals' Advantage: US Navy Operational Intelligence in World War II and the Cold War* (Annapolis, 2014), p. 82.
[48] Hattendorf, *The Evolution of the US Navy's Maritime Strategy*, pp. 29–36; and Ford and Rosenberg, *The Admirals' Advantage*, pp. 77–87.
[49] Lewin, 'Indian Ocean and Beyond', p. 256.
[50] TNA, FCO 46/1294, Bullard to Thomson, 18 November 1974, Confidential.
[51] TNA, FCO 46/877, Presentation to Moorer by Le Bailly, 6 July 1972, Confidential.

16
Sir Julian Corbett, Naval History and the Development of Sea Power Theory

ANDREW D. LAMBERT

In a book honouring a great naval educator it is only fitting that we reflect on the career of another. In the last decades of the nineteenth century navies grappled with the problem of preparing their officer corps for future wars, while the pace of technological change was accelerating, and there were few conflicts to inform the development of tactical and strategic doctrine. The United States Naval War College, established in 1884, addressed this issue as a vital preparatory stage for the creation of a new navy. In Great Britain the problem was compounded by the unique nature of the Imperial state, a global collection of colonies, dominions, informal economic zones and markets, linked by seaborne and submarine telegraph communications, and wholly dependent on sea control.[1] Sir Julian Corbett developed classical strategic theory, hitherto dominated by continental military concerns to explain the strategic logic of British power. This chapter considers the origins and purpose of Corbett's *Some Principles of Maritime Strategy* of 1911.[2] While Corbett's work has long been recognised as an outstanding intellectual contribution to strategic thought and defence education, it seems the case needs restatement.[3]

A public intellectual, intimately engaged with naval and political circles at the highest levels, most of Corbett's contacts were on the Fisherite and Liberal Imperialist sides of the debate. They were the men in power. He worked for the Royal Navy because he loved the Service, found the work congenial, and retained the intellectual independence secured by private wealth, a global investment portfolio and London property.

Between 1902 and 1914 Corbett systematically analysed English/British

---

[1] A.D. Lambert, 'Wirtschaftliche Macht, technologischer Vorsprung und Imperiale Stärke: GrossBritannien als einzigartige globale Macht: 1860 bis 1890', in M. Epkenhans and G.P. Gross (eds), *Das Militär und der Aufbruch die Moderne 1860 bis 1890* (Munich, 2003), pp. 243–68.

[2] Don Schurman only mentioned *Some Principles* twice in *Julian S. Corbett, 1854–1922: Historian of British Maritime Policy from Drake to Jellicoe* (London, 1981), pp. 56, 62. J. Widen's *Theorist of Maritime Strategy: Sir Julian Corbett and his Contribution to Military and Naval Thought* (Farnham, 2012) is not concerned with the book's origins.

[3] N. Lambert, Review Essay 'False Prophet?: The Maritime Theory of Julian Corbett and Professional Military Education', *The Journal of Military History*, 77 (2013), p. 1076.

strategy from the sixteenth to the twentieth century, suitably updated by examining the Spanish–American and Russo-Japanese Wars of 1898 and 1904–5, in a sophisticated attempt to establish a 'British' strategic model that was consistent with the classic texts of Clausewitz and Jomini, rather than naval thinkers like Mahan and Philip Colomb. He sought to explain the primacy of maritime over continental power to contemporary British statesmen and senior officers. He was not a 'navalist':[4] he stressed army–navy cooperation, and dismissed naval strategy as a 'minor' or operational issue.[5]

In August 1902 Corbett was invited to lecture to the new Royal Naval War Course for mid-ranking and senior officers, established by the Director of Naval Intelligence (DNI).[6] The curriculum quickly dropped training programmes in navigation, meteorology and languages to focus on strategy, tactics, naval history and international law.[7] Course Director Captain Henry May asked Corbett for history lectures that were 'so modern that some lessons applicable to present day warfare should be deductable', and critically that 'expediency and strategy are not always in accord', which Corbett summarised as 'the deflection of strategy by politics'.[8]

In Corbett's October 1903 lecture notes, he stressed:

> Object of course to direct & assist private study.
> Practical Advantage of historical study the chief value a method of studying strategy.
> Difficulties of Strategical Study – no set rules ascertainable – continual conflict of expert opinion – not an exact science.
> Therefore difficult to do more than aim at acquiring strategical habit of thought.
> Here history is of greatest value.

He defined naval strategy as a minor form of national strategy, for the 'protection or destruction of commerce, or the furtherance or hindrance of military operations ashore'. The War of the Spanish Succession, 1702–13, was useful as a study of a 'general European war to curb ambitious military power which had rapidly created a new navy'.[9] The navy had already focused on Germany, which dominated lectures, war games, examination questions and course handouts.

Corbett's relationship with successive DNIs and War Course Directors was

---

[4] Ibid., p. 1055.
[5] Definition from the 1906 'Green Pamphlet': J.S. Corbett, *Some Principles of Maritime Strategy*, ed. E.J. Grove (Annapolis, 1988), pp. 308–9.
[6] A.D. Lambert, 'The Naval War Course, *Some Principles of Maritime Strategy* and the Origins of the 'British Way in Warfare', in K. Neilson and G. Kennedy (eds), *The British Way in Warfare: Power and the International System, 1856–1950: Essays in Honour of David French* (Farnham, 2010), pp. 219–56.
[7] Schurman, *Corbett*, pp. 32–4; Lambert, 'The Naval War Course'.
[8] May to Corbett, 14 and 22 August 1902, cited in Schurman, *Corbett*, p. 33; J.S. Corbett, 'The Teaching of Naval and Military History', *History* (April 1916).
[9] King's College, London, Liddell-Hart Centre for Military Archives (LHCMA), CBT MS: War Course Lecture, Spanish Succession, October 1903.

necessarily close. While Edmond Slade, a fellow intellectual and student of strategy, was the most compatible, Corbett was equally impressed with the incisive, if uneducated Lewis Bayly – who had a significant impact on *Some Principles*.

Like any capable service educator Corbett developed his teaching to address naval agendas. The aim and content of the lectures were set by the DNI, acting for the Board of Admiralty, through the War Course Director. In 1905 DNI Charles Ottley was 'delighted to learn that you will undertake the lectures on naval strategy ... I think it is impossible to exaggerate the importance of sound principles of strategy being studied by the Officers of the Navy.'[10] He deputed new War Course Director Captain Edmond Slade to ensure Corbett's contribution dovetailed with the rest of the programme. Slade was at liberty to dispense with Corbett's services; he had no contract of employment.

Corbett's written output after 1898 served the increasingly integrated needs of the War Course, the Naval Intelligence Division and the Committee of Imperial Defence (CID). His texts were purpose-made for service education, in content, analytical method and literary style. Connections between subject, audience and ambition were clearly established, as befits an experienced barrister working to a brief. This was especially clear in the much revised, oft-delivered Russo-Japanese War programme. The lectures began as instant history, but in 1910 Corbett used the revised lectures to study how 'an island power overthrowing a great military and continental power by just combination of fleet & army'.[11] By the spring of 1913 he was using draft chapters from his 'Confidential' history in a more sophisticated treatment, informed by secret Japanese material.[12] By December 1913 Corbett's focus had shifted to the First Dutch War, a purely naval war, against an enemy north of the Dover Straits, helping officers to grasp the nature of the primary object in 'a war between two commercial states'. While Corbett stressed there was no direct read across from that conflict, the course, like all those that had preceded it, would equip officers to think about the present and future. He posed the question: 'How would the various situations have been dealt with under present circumstances?'[13] There can be little doubt the idea of a purely Anglo-German War, uncomplicated by Ententes or alliances, prompted the exercise.

Corbett's lecture handouts trace the evolution of his thinking and his methodology. They were regularly revised, and often completely rewritten, while new lecture programmes worked through British strategic experience to refine and reinforce his ideas. He received significant input from the Course Directors. Rear Admiral Lewis Bayly requested a series on the Napoleonic Wars at sea after Trafalgar, as an analogue for an Anglo-German war; these formed the basis of Corbett's last historical publication.[14]

---

[10] NMM, RIC/9, Ottley to Corbett, 1 July 1905, 'Secret'.
[11] LHCMA, CBT MS: War Course Lecture, Russo-Japanese War, 1910.
[12] LHCMA, CBT MS: War Course Lecture, Russo-Japanese War, 1913.
[13] LHCMA, CBT MS: War Course Lecture, Dutch War, 1 December 1913.
[14] J.S. Corbett, 'Napoleon and the British Navy after Trafalgar', *The Quarterly Review* (April 1922).

The measure of Corbett's success can be seen in the increased demand for lectures, often repeated at Devonport, Chatham and Sheerness. Paid significantly more than other outside lecturers, his fees accounted for half the external speaker budget. Corbett always knew what his work was worth, and never accepted inadequate fees. He would happily work for nothing, but not for a pittance.

By 1905 the War Course had acquired 'staff and planning' functions, the DNI being overburdened with routine business. First Sea Lord, Admiral Sir John Fisher (1904–10) approved, preferring to run at least two independent strategic planning units. When Corbett told Fisher current strategic teaching on the War Course was 'amateur rubbish', Fisher and DNI Charles Ottley immediately commissioned more lectures.[15] These historical case studies used 'strategical terms', explained in the 'Green Pamphlet'. This was a timely step-change, because a far bigger debate was brewing, one that concerned the cultural and conceptual basis of national strategy, something Corbett had recognised back in 1900. He began lecturing at the Army Staff College, Camberley. Colonel Commandant Henry Rawlinson proposed Corbett examine 'the Function of the Army in relation to gaining command of the sea, and in bringing war with a Continental Power to a successful conclusion'.[16] However, the army had lost interest in maritime strategy by 1907, when Corbett published his *England in the Seven Years' War: A Study in Combined Strategy*. With the army refusing to cooperate, the navy was obliged to develop a naval strategy, which Corbett so strongly deprecated.

Here Corbett was at one with Fisher. The army's rejection of maritime strategy posed a fundamental problem: Fisher had based his policy on subordinating the army to the navy in national strategy so that the economising Liberal government would sharply reduce the army, rather than spread cuts across both services. Already impressed by Corbett's work in support of the officer recruitment and education reforms – the 'Selborne Scheme' – Fisher considered *England in the Seven Years' War* 'unrivalled', deploying reviews of Corbett's books to shape the strategic debate in Britain and the empire, in peace and war.[17] Furthermore it was no accident that Naval War Course graduates were sent to oversee the creation of the Royal Canadian and Royal Australian navies. Doctrinal consistency in the language and application of sea power across the empire was far more important than standardising technology. Dominion navies had to think like the Royal Navy to fight alongside it.

---

[15] Churchill College, Cambridge (CCC), Fisher MS: Corbett note on Fisher to Corbett, 24 May 1905; Schurman, *Corbett*, p. 43. See S. Grimes, *Strategy and War Planning in the British Navy 1887–1918* (Woodbridge, 2012) for the development of plans; see also NMM, RIC/9, Ottley to Corbett, 1 July 1905, for the strategic and diplomatic issues surrounding the First Moroccan Crisis.

[16] LHCMA, CBT MS: Slade to Corbett, 22 August 1905 and Rawlinson to Corbett, 25 and 30 August 1905 and Corbett's notes.

[17] CCC, FISR 3/19/117, Fisher, n.d., 'The Strangest thing in the War', June 1918; NMM, CBT 12/54, Balfour to Fisher, 9 July 1910; A.D. Lambert, '"The Army is a Projectile to be Fired by the Navy": Securing the Empire 1815–1914', in P. Dennis (ed.), *Armies and Maritime Strategy: 2013 Chief of Army History Conference* (Canberra, 2014), p. 29.

By spring 1909 Corbett had become so closely enmeshed in Admiralty strategic thought that Fisher invited him to visit the Admiralty War Plans Committee. Within a week DNI Captain Alexander Bethell offered him an official position on the Committee, which needed his unique insight into 'the ideas and operations of the old Admirals'. While the post would fulfil a long-held ambition, Corbett doubted his power for sustained work, typical of his habitual self-denigration, and was unwilling to keep regular office hours. Bethell ignored his doubts, pressing him to select a title and suggest a salary.[18] Nothing came of the initiative, because Fisher's original idea, using Corbett to rebut Lord Charles Beresford's allegation that there were no war plans, was no longer relevant. When the Beresford Enquiry began, Lord Charles accused Fisher of leaking war plans, by implication to Corbett. Consequently Fisher discouraged Corbett from accepting a post that he himself had been instrumental in offering, because he needed Corbett to remain outside the Admiralty, for political purposes.[19] Fisher's change of mind and Corbett's mental collapse after the birth of his son on 27 May encouraged him to refuse, while the long-drawn-out, profoundly political Beresford Enquiry obliged Fisher to keep him at arm's length. However, he continued to enhance and regularise his position on the War Course, by writing *Some Principles* and editing a textbook series.[20]

Corbett wrote *Some Principles* because the CID wanted a strategic text. In late 1909, in an attempt to avoid a formal Admiralty Staff, Fisher decreed that officers employed in staff roles must qualify on the War Course. This, CID Secretary and former DNI Charles Ottley observed, required a syllabus revision to improve the training function. It should impart 'sound strategical principles' and 'strategy should therefore occupy a prominent place', illustrated by naval history, but 'the sole object of the instruction in strategy should be to throw into high relief the fundamental principles on which all sound strategy must be based'. This required a new compact text. The course should avoid discussions of current diplomatic issues and emphasise the deterrent role of the Royal Navy.[21] Fisher knew what was required: in October 1909 he sent Corbett a finely bound volume of blank leaves, and an amusing letter.[22] Corbett completed the proofs of *The Campaign of Trafalgar* in mid-April 1910, and promptly set off for Italy. In late May he stayed with Fisher at Kilverstone for two days.[23] Three weeks later, having cleared his

---

[18] NMM, CBT 43/10, Diary, 12 February 1909; J.A. Fisher, *Fear God and Dread Nought: The Correspondence of Admiral of the Fleet Lord Fisher of Kilverstone*, ed. A.J. Marder (3 vols, London, 1952–59), vol. ii, pp. 243–4; NMM CBT 12/43, Corbett to Bethell, 21 April 1909 draft and Bethell to Corbett, 22 April 1909.
[19] NMM, CBT 43/10, Diary, 25 April 1909. He was not summoned.
[20] J.S. Corbett, ed., *Naval and Military Essays* (Cambridge, 1914), in the 'Cambridge Naval and Military Series' edited by Corbett and Cambridge classicist rifle volunteer Colonel H.S. Edwards.
[21] CCC, FISR 1/9 456, Ottley typescript Memo of conversation with Fisher, December 1909.
[22] NMM, CBT 43/10, Diary, 27 October 1909.
[23] NMM, CBT 43/11, Diary, Italy 15 April–13 May 1910, Kilverstone 28–30 May 1910, 'strategy' 19 June 1910.

in-tray, Corbett began 'an experiment to see if it is possible to produce a useful book on the subject. It seems possible to develop Clausewitz theory from the point where he left off – so as to make it apply to our case & explain or coordinate many things. Such a book ... seems badly wanted if I can only produce it.'[24]

Within days Corbett was rereading Clausewitz, followed by Jomini, and the French Mahanian strategists Gabriel Darrieus[25] and René Daveluy. He wrote the book quickly, working from start to finish, and without significant modifications. In late August he had agreed to write *Maritime Operations of the Russo-Japanese War*, using early drafts of *Some Principles* to illustrate his proposed treatment. On 10 October War Course Director Bayly told Corbett he was keen, and the Admiralty expressed a desire for such a work. By late October Corbett had the first two-thirds of the book in typescript. Bayly suggested important modifications, fewer technical terms, fewer German authorities and more exposition of the argument about the defensive. This was sage advice, which Corbett adopted. Practical men, like Bayly, had no interest in wading through arcane academic diversions, methodology or the history of strategy. They needed an officially approved strategic text.[26]

Admiralty approval would enable Corbett to refocus the strategic debate, using classical theory to move from Germanic generalities into a specific national form. By the end of 1910 Corbett had completed seventeen of twenty planned chapters. The section on trade defence was recast after reading Rene Daveluy's book, which reinforced Corbett's argument that commerce warfare was a minor threat.[27] The final section on expeditions exploited George Aston's new *Letters on Amphibious Wars*.[28] The only primary research was one day at the Public Record Office working on Lord Howe's campaign in home waters and off Gibraltar in 1782.[29]

Corbett followed Clausewitz in emphasising that the relationship between history and strategy – the dialectic between evidence and analysis – was endless. Both men wrote histories as the basis of and the testing ground for strategic ideas.[30] Clausewitz considered generalised accounts of the past useless. 'Far better', he said, 'to study one campaign in minute detail than to acquire vague knowledge of a dozen wars.'[31] Critically both wrote theoretical works on strategy

---

[24] NMM, CBT 43/11, Diary, 25 June 1910.
[25] Captain Gabriel Darrieus was Professor of Strategy and Naval Tactics at the French Naval War College. His *La guerre sur mer: Stratégie et tactique. La Doctrine* (Paris, 1907), pp. 255–88, advocated Mahanian strategy for a future conflict with Britain. A. Røksund, *The Jeune École: The Strategy of the Weak* (Oslo, 2005), pp. 216–17.
[26] NMM, CBT 43/12, Diary, 10 October 1910 to 26 January 1911.
[27] R. Daveluy, *Études sur la Stratégie navale* (Paris, 1905), pp. 240–76; D.B.G. Heuser, *The Evolution of Strategic Thinking* (Cambridge, 2011), pp. 240–5
[28] G. Aston, *Letters on Amphibious Wars* (London, 1911).
[29] Corbett, *Some Principles* (1988), pp. 144–50.
[30] A.D. Lambert, 'The Principal Source of Understanding: Navies and the Educational Role of the Past', in P. Hore (ed.), *The Hudson Papers*, vol. 1 (London, 2001), pp. 35–71, esp. pp. 43–4.
[31] P. Paret, 'The Genesis of *On War*', in C. Clausewitz, *On War* (Princeton, 1976), p. 24.

after sustained, nationally focused historical enterprises intended for officer education. Clausewitz wrote for Prussians in 1825–30, Corbett for Englishmen before 1914. His ability to develop French and German strategic ideas dominated by military needs into British maritime forms was exceptional, and powerful.[32] His primary targets were not naval officers, who needed no convincing that British national strategy should be maritime, but statesmen, and, if possible, those soldiers who had been seduced by the narrow 'Total War' interpretation of Clausewitz promulgated in German military circles. Corbett took maritime strategy beyond Mahan, and other writers on 'naval' strategy, by anchoring it in the theoretical writings of Clausewitz and Jomini.[33] He developed Clausewitz's limited/unlimted war dichotomy in the context of sea power. *Some Principles* was a single volume résumé of the strategic concepts needed to direct the defence of a global maritime empire – and stressed deterrence above war.

The main argument of *Some Principles* was that the principles of strategy were consistent, and could be drawn from existing works, but their practical application at a national level was necessarily a unique cultural construction. British strategy was distinct from that of continental military nations, especially Imperial Germany. His aim was to counter the Germanic conscriptionist and continentalist agenda adopted by the Army General Staff to overturn the existing maritime strategy. A continental strategy was wholly antithetical to British interests, and to Corbett's Liberal politics, not to mention the more radical thoughts of Jacky Fisher. Corbett created the concept of a national 'Way of Warfare', another major intellectual achievement.

Some Principles was a course textbook, not an academic analysis, and, as Bryan Ranft observed, read like a well-designed lecture course. Ranft, another great naval educator, recognised this was intentional.[34] After setting out the core theoretical argument in Part One and Part Two, Corbett developed the applied methods through examples in Part Three. Most of the examples reflect the fact that he began the book after completing the page proofs of *Trafalgar*, that it was directly followed by the *Russo-Japanese War*, and that he was lecturing on the Crimean War as he wrote.

Corbett stressed doctrinal cohesion was the key to the most effective use of naval power, through a judicious combination of dispersed action and rapid concentration for battle. Here he argued that Mahan's obsession with concentration was unsuited to British needs. The Royal Navy needed a seamless, fluid movement between attack and defence, concentration and dispersal to meet the needs of the occasion, something that was only possible with a powerful, coherent and commonly understood doctrine, of the sort that informed the

---

[32] On Clausewitz's inability to develop the distinctive character of limited war, see J.S. Corbett, *England in the Seven Years War* (London, 1907), vol. i, p. 207n, which is the first statement of a dominant theme in *Some Principles*.

[33] He only mentioned Mahan twice: Corbett, *Some Principles* (1988), pp. 131n and 169.

[34] B. Ranft, 'Foreword', in J.S. Corbett, *Some Principle of Maritime Strategy* (London, 1972), p. x.

cruiser operations of 1805.[35] The frigate captains of 1805 had learnt by example to connect the main fleets, convoys and landfalls of the Atlantic theatre. In 1911 Corbett knew such insight would have to be gained without the hard knocks of war, or the inspirational presence of Nelson.

Some Principles had no conclusion – because none was required. Corbett was not teaching naval officers how to wage war, he was providing them with a condensed, analytical résumé of the best intellectual equipment available for their needs, including the emphasis on definitions and terminology begun in the 'Green Pamphlet' of 1906. *Some Principles* was the first public national strategic doctrine primer, designed to inform decision-making at the highest level, and integrate naval, military and civil action to deter, or if necessary wage, war.

Corbett finished the manuscript in late February 1911, a mere eight months' work amidst other demanding literary and lecturing tasks. He circulated the typescript for comment and in early April discussed it with Bethell, Deputy DNI Captain Thomas Jackson and Captain Ernest Troubridge, Naval Secretary to the First Lord of the Admiralty. Troubridge promised to read the completed typescript. Bayly refused to read the typescript, because he was no longer Director of the War Course. Troubridge decided he should 'get Sir Arthur Wilson's opinion before finally writing to you'.[36] Wilson, the First Sea Lord, read the MS over the first weekend in July, delayed by the demands of the Coronation Fleet Review, and raised no objections.[37]

Having secured Admiralty approval Corbett delivered the typescript to his publisher, Longman, on 21 July, but only signed the contract on 3 August 1911.[38] The initial print run was 1,250 copies. A few days later Corbett definitively changed the title from 'the Principles' to 'Some Principles', an intellectual dilemma that can be traced through the gestation of the book. The changed wording reflected Corbett's anxiety about his credentials to publish on the subject. He hoped for an endorsement from his former colleague as War Course Director and DNI Edmond Slade, but Longman would not wait for the Commander-in-Chief East Indies to read the proofs.[39] Instead Corbett removed his title, 'Lecturer in Naval History to the Royal Naval War College' from the title page, leaving only an LL.M. He read the page proofs on the wet days of a Scottish fishing holiday, completing the process by 27 October. While he complained to close friend Henry Newbolt about having to reread 'a difficult tasteless book on "Maritime Strategy"',[40] this was a joke: the book had been written to satisfy his own intellectual curiosity.

The book appeared in early December, and Troubridge was quick to

---

[35] Corbett, *Some Principles* (1988), pp. 128–52.
[36] NMM, CBT 13/3/64, Troubridge to Corbett, 10 July 1911.
[37] NMM, CBT 13/3/66 and 43/12, Troubridge to Corbett, 11 July 1911, and Diary.
[38] NMM, CBT 2/3/12, Longman to Corbett Agreement for *Some Principles of Maritime Strategy*, 3 August 1911.
[39] NMM, CBT 2/3/11, Longman to Corbett, 8 August 1911.
[40] NMM, CBT 3/75, Corbett to Newbolt, 12 November 1911.

congratulate him, while drawing out useful arguments for the new First Lord, Winston Churchill.[41] Within a month Troubridge became the first Chief of the Admiralty War Staff.[42] There were other intelligent readers, as Corbett observed:

> There was an excellent send off for my book in the *Times* yesterday ... in an article on the late changes ... the writer quoted my book at length to show that the Admiralty policy had been quite right. That is better than the best review for everyone interested in the Navy reads such articles.[43]

Some Principles encapsulated Admiralty thinking, and *The Times* recognised that Corbett had explained the intellectual basis of current naval thinking, lifting the debate about national strategy above the Germanic continentalist obsessions of the Army General Staff. Thinking men recognised that he had gone far beyond mere naval strategists, who had been very deliberately ignored in the text.[44] Former War Course Director Sidney Drury-Lowe wrote:

> You have done us a very great service, & we owe you a deep debt of gratitude. I have long looked for a book that would contain the various theories & principles of *maritime* strategy which you discuss, & have thought the want of it has been the cause of a great deal of loose talk amongst Naval officers, & of extraordinary actions too! Some of us have waded through Clausewitz, Jomini, von Cammerer etc, but there was so much that wanted re-adjustment, & so much that had nothing of interest to us (so far as I could see!), & in my own case you have just supplied the want.[45]

One of the navy's brightest staff officers, Captain Osmond de Brock, thought it 'very good ... a book to study carefully'.[46]

Critically Corbett's book emerged just as the War Course was reconnected with Admiralty war planning. In November 1912 Corbett learnt that Henry Jackson would take the War Course under his direction when he became Chief of the War Staff.[47] This reforged the link between the main strategic planner and the War Course that had been central to Corbett's work in the Fisher–Ottley–Slade era.

Despite the congratulations, and some very good reviews, sales were poor. While Corbett wanted to revise the book, and add Slade's name to the title page to deflect some of the simple-minded criticism, Charles Longman had seven hundred copies in hand, and poor sales. By August 1912 the opportunity had passed.[48] He would never return to the book, although he never stopped thinking

---

[41] NMM, CBT 13/3/67, Troubridge to Corbett, 5 December 1911.
[42] NMM, CBT 13/3/68, Troubridge to Corbett, 9 January 1912.
[43] NMM, CBT 11/2/30, Corbett to his wife, 6 December 1911.
[44] NMM, CBT 11/3/35, Corbett to his wife, 28 May 1912.
[45] NMM, CBT 13/3/48, Sidney Drury-Lowe to Corbett, 27 December 1911.
[46] Brock to Slade, 28 December 1911, cited in S. Cobb, *Preparing for Blockade 1885–1914* (Farnham, 2013), p. 85.
[47] NMM, CBT 11/3/27, Corbett to his wife, 26 November 1912.
[48] NMM, CBT 2/3/16–17, Longman to Corbett, 5 and 9 July and 14 August 1912.

about how it could be improved.[49] In early 1913 Longman, with 548 copies unsold, had the type broken up.[50] The edition finally sold out in 1918. Unable to get paper or press time in England, Longman had one thousand printed in America, to satisfy American demand, notably at the United States Naval War College, with 150 for the home market.[51] Finally Corbett's friend Admiral William S. Sims, Commander-in-Chief of US Naval Forces in Europe, volunteered to find space for the new edition on an American warship.

> I was only too glad to have the opportunity of expediting the sending the [sic] England of the 150 copies of MARITIME STRATEGY … I thank you also for your offer to give us any further help in our naval historical work. We have already benefited greatly by your advice and assistance in bringing to the attention of our Navy Department what ought to be done in this line.[52]

As Sims's comments demonstrate, Corbett had been central to the development and delivery of maritime strategy in two great navies. He remains a major influence on both to this day, not least because outstanding educators in both services made sure senior officers had access to his ideas.

Some Principles explained the distinctive strategic culture of Britain. It was written at the prompting of critically placed naval officers, met the educational needs of the expanded War Course, and ensured doctrinal coherence in the higher direction of war by establishing the strategic doctrine of the British Empire. Corbett did not create this strategy; he recovered it from history, and gave it intellectual coherence, developed from the classic strategy texts of Clausewitz and Jomini, but not Mahan. It was the summation of a long-term engagement with the strategic history of a unique Great Power, the last to depend on sea power for security, prosperity and deterrence. Designed for a non-academic audience, it was written in his customary fluent, economical style. The book was read and approved by the makers of naval strategy before publication. While the book did not achieve significant sales before, during or after the First World War, it was a core strategic text for the Naval War Course and United States Naval War College before 1914.[53]

When Britain went to war in 1914 it did so in a Corbettian manner, conducting limited, maritime global warfare, while supporting continental allies.[54] When Fisher returned to the Admiralty in October 1914 his strategy was sustained by Corbett's texts and memoranda. Furthermore the CID hired Corbett to record

---

[49] A.D. Lambert, 'Sir Julian Corbett and the Naval Review', in P. Hore (ed.), *Dreadnought to Daring: 100 years of Comment, Controversy and Debate in the Naval Review* (London, 2012), pp. 37–52.
[50] NMM, CBT 2/3/18, Longman to Corbett, 12 February 1913.
[51] NMM, CBT 1/2/35, Longman to Corbett, 3 October 1918.
[52] NMM, CBT 1/2/36, Sims to Corbett, 9 October 1918.
[53] J.B. Hattendorf, B.M. Simpson and J.R. Wadleigh, *Sailors and Scholars: The Centennial History of the U.S. Naval War College* (Newport, 1984), p. 79.
[54] Maurice Hankey to Captain Geoffrey Blake, 3 September 1928, cited in S.W. Roskill, *Hankey: Man of Secrets* (London, 1970), vol. i, pp. 134–5.

and analyse the conflict, continuing his core task, the strategic education of naval officers.[55] In the twentieth century many strategists, most with a distinctly khaki hue, critiqued Corbett in order to sustain the continental alternative.[56] From the longer perspective of the second decade of the twenty-first century it is clear that this was an aberration. Small, weak, insular states fundamentally reliant upon global commerce and resource flows must prioritise sea control, or perish. No amount of military force, or land-based aviation, can secure the seas upon which such nations depend – any more than it could in Corbett's day.

---

[55] J.S. Corbett, *Naval Operations: History of the Great War Based on Official Documents, by Direction of the Historical Section of the Committee of Imperial Defence* (3 vols, London, 1920–22).
[56] M. Howard, *The Continental Commitment* (London, 1972) is the basis for most of these arguments.

17

The Influence of Identity on Sea Power[1]

DUNCAN REDFORD

Identity – that imagined community of shared ideas which unite a group[2] – is an important aspect of sea power and the strategies used to maintain or achieve it. This should not be a novel proposition. Clausewitz in his analysis of war as a trinity that encompassed the people, the government and the military clearly includes both the political process and the society that supports it in his theoretical model.[3] With regard to sea power, Mahan alluded to this when he noted that one of the six determinants of sea power was 'the character of the people', or 'national character' as he also refers to it,[4] a concept that has proven most long lasting in Britain where the idea that the British (or at least the English) were an island race, a race of natural sailors, or had a special relationship with the sea as a result of their island home was a common place one up to quite recently. On the other hand, Julian Corbett showed very little interest in the links between society, the political process and sea power in the theoretical model he constructed to underpin his *Principles of Maritime Strategy*, preferring to focus on how sea power can meet political goals.[5] Corbett is not alone in avoiding any deep engagement with the swirling and perhaps immutable forces that shift and mould public opinion, the political interest in sea power, or the will to use armed force in war or in peace to achieve national ends. Professor Colin Gray has noted that several significant contributors to the field of strategic studies acknowledge the importance of societal and political issues, but that these same writers also recognise that mastery of sociology, anthropology and local or regional knowledge are not generally strengths of strategists; the inference being that all too often the strategist draws back from them in favour of the more mutable and quantifiable aspects

---

[1] Much of the research for this chapter was carried out while I was a Leverhulme Early Career Research Fellow at the University of Exeter. I wish to thank the Trustees of the Leverhulme Trust for their most generous support.
[2] B. Anderson, *Imagined Communities*, rev. edn (London, 1991), pp. 24–5, 37–46.
[3] C. Von Clausewitz, *On War*, trans. and ed. M. Howard and P. Paret (Princeton, NJ, 1984), p. 89. See also B. Heuser, *Reading Clausewitz* (London, 2002), pp. 52–6.
[4] A.T. Mahan, *The Influence of Sea Power Upon History 1660–1783* (New York, 1987), pp. 28–9, 50–8.
[5] J. Corbett, *Some Principles of Maritime Strategy* (London, 1972), pp. 21–6. See also J.J. Widen, *Theorist of Maritime Strategy: Sir Julian Corbett and his Contribution to Military and Naval Thought* (Aldershot, 2012), pp. 62–72.

of their discipline.[6] Even Clausewitz and Mahan, having identified societal and political factors as being of considerable importance, concentrate on the perhaps more comfortable and more readily analysed pure military aspects of strategy and sea power.

The two principal means by which British national identity interacted with British perceptions of sea power were first, the security conferred by Britain being an island and second, the role of the navy (and by default wider British sea power) in the perception of British prestige – of Britain being a great power, especially through the link between the navy and the empire. Both of these themes cover a wide range of constituent ideas, concepts and illusions, for when dealing with identity, what is believed, rather than what is true or can be proved is of greater importance. Our understanding of the relationship between sea power and identity is also clouded by two issues. First, there was inability by certain contemporary Victorian and Edwardian commentators to be precise in their use of language – specifically the English habit (unlike their Celtic counterparts) of accidentally or deliberately confusing English with British identities and vice versa.[7] For example, in 1895 the Navy League referred to England's not Britain's naval power.[8] Second, there was the less than helpful habit of conflating the relationship between island, security and sea power, with sea power prestige and empire. In 1923 Admiral Sir Doveton Sturdee (the victor of the Battle of the Falklands in 1914) told the readers of *Brassey's Naval and Shipping Annual* that:

> It was generally recognised that a strong and efficient Navy was essential for the safety of the Empire, due to its far-flung Dominions 'on which the sun never sets'; this conclusion was strengthened by the realisation that the home-country now depends on the import of four-sixths of the necessities of life.[9]

Sturdee has clearly conflated ideas of global position and power through the empire with that of the command of the sea needed to ensure the safety of imports into the home islands, demonstrating the interrelated nature of ideas regarding the sea and the navy, but in doing so has strengthened his view of the centrality of the Royal Navy to Britain's physical and indeed moral well-being. Despite the conflation of different aspects of a maritime identity, from the time of Shakespeare's sceptre'd isle, a 'precious stone set in the silver sea',[10] there has always been

---

[6] C. Gray, *Modern Strategy* (Oxford, 1999), pp. 27–8
[7] K. Kumar, '"Englishness" and English National Identity', in D. Morley and K. Robins (eds), *British Cultural Studies* (Oxford, 2001), p. 41; R. Langlands, 'Britishness or Englishness? The Historical Problem of National Identity in Britain', *Nations and Nationalism*, v (1999), pp. 53–69; P. Mandler, *The English National Character* (London, 2006), p. 134; D. McCrone, 'Unmasking Britannia: The Rise and Fall of British National Identity', *Nations and Nationalism*, iii (1997), p. 586; A.D. Smith, '"Set in the silver sea": English National Identity and European Integration', *Nations and Nationalism*, xxii (2006), p. 433.
[8] *Navy League Journal*, no. 1 (1895).
[9] Sir F.C.D. Sturdee, 'Naval Aspects of the Washington Conference', in Sir A. Richardson and A. Hurd (eds), *Brassey's Naval and Shipping Annual 1923* (London, 1923), p. 69.
[10] *Richard II*, act 2, sc. I, l. 46.

the implication that there was something different about Britain because it was an island and because it relied so much on what the sea gave it – its sea power.

This chapter will examine the relationship between island, security and sea power, to argue that changes in British national identity during the twentieth century have had a profound impact on Britain's ability to understand, support and use sea power. Finally, It will examine the impact air power had on the way security provided by being an island was perceived and the impact this had on naval policy.

I

First, what is national identity? Identity is a difficult concept to get to grips with. It involves dealing with perceptions, allusions and the imagined forces that we think or hope make us (whoever 'us' is) the way we are. Identity issues have entranced historians for many years now and it has been made to mean many different things to many different commentators, without necessarily moving closer to an agreed definition about what it is, how it is formed, how it is communicated or indeed how it is changed. The meaning of the term identity has, as part of its increased use by historians, moved away from the philosophical and sociological roots of the term. As the popularity of the term 'identity' within the history discipline has increased, the precision in which it is used has decreased; this is not a new problem, as Peter Mandler has recently pointed out, Phillip Gleason illustrated the origins of the term 'identity' many years ago.[11]

Identity, even without an agreed definition, opens up a massive area of inquiry. Almost every human activity can generate some sort of identity – the football fan cheering on his or her team, church-goers and their denomination, a voter supporting a political party, or the factory worker and his or her union. The identities that are produced by these activities vary in their extent; they can be local – the village, town or city – or regional, or national. Nor does this mean a purely geographical identity as a political, religious and economic tapestry exists within a geographical framework. Despite the issues over exact definition of identity, one of the most important contributions has been Linda Colley's concept of the 'other' where identity is seen through the difference between groups; her use of this concept was given deservedly widespread attention though her 1992 book *Britons: Forging the Nation 1707–1837*, which as the title suggests looked at Britishness during the long eighteenth century. Many historians have made use of Colley's ideas regarding the 'other' in their examination of aspects of national identity.[12] While Colley's analysis of identity has proved very useful, it has been

---

[11] P. Mandler, 'What is "National Identity"? Definitions and Applications in Modern British Historiography', *Modern Intellectual History*, iii (2006), p. 271; P. Gleason, 'Identifying Identity: A Semantic History', *Journal of American History*, lxxix (1983), pp. 910–31.
[12] Examples include C. Hall, K. McCelland and J. Rendall, *Defining the Victorian Nation: Class, Race, Gender and the British Reform Act of 1867* (Cambridge, 2000); C. Waters, '"Dark

prone to be used in an almost mono-casual format, which can severely oversimplify the nuances and complexities of identity at a national level. This is a particular problem when considering how these identities are shared and communicated between individuals on a scale sufficient to be considered national. Instead we must think of identity as multi-layed, with different aspects of an identity dominating at different times.[13]

This multi-layed approach is very important. Thus national identity should be seen as a highest tier of a multi-level interconnecting network of myths, ideas and perceptions that are shared by an imagined community – the nation, as opposed to the state. What are the perceptions, myths and ideas that make up a British national identity at a given moment in time? Do the components of a British national identity include sense of fair play? Being the subject of a monarch? Free trade? Muscular Christianity? Being part of a secular state? Having a Protestant heritage? A strong navy? Again, there has been much debate between historians.[14]

Just as individuals, institutions or corporate bodies can ask themselves who they are and receive different answers depending on time and context and the depth of consideration, so too can the concepts that make up a national identity. This means national identity is not fixed; if the nation is an imagined community, then as that community changes so too will the areas through which the individual and nation are imagined. Just to make things more interesting for the historian or strategic studies acolyte, there is the difficulty of identifying the traces of identity – they are dealing with perception, ideas and interpretation, it is more subjective than objective.

If, or rather when, the 'character' – to use Mahan's concept, or the identity (to use what is perhaps a more accurate interpretation) – of a people changes then there will be an impact on how that society venerates and sustains its ability to use the sea for its political ends. For many decades (if not centuries) first the English and then the British repeatedly told themselves that the sea, sea power and their navy were important to them. However, this internal conversation underwent significant revisions during the twentieth century, as the British, for various reasons, stopped believing their established views about the importance of sea power, and, above all, stopped telling each other their sea power was important.

Strangers in our Midst": Discourses of Race and Nation in Britain, 1947–1963', *Journal of British Studies*, xxxvi (1997).

[13] A.D. Smith, *National Identity* (London, 1991), pp. 15–18; Anderson, *Imagined Communities*, pp. 24–5, 37–46; T. Edensor, *National Identity, Popular Culture and Everyday Life* (Oxford, 2002), pp. 7–8; P. Ward, *Britishness Since 1870* (London, 2004), pp. 2–13, 73–92; M. Billig, *Banal Nationalism* (London, 1995).

[14] Billig, *Banal Nationalism*; L. Colley, *Britons: Forging the Nation 1707–1837* (London, 1992); Edensor, *National Identity*, pp. 12–16; D. Lowenthal, 'British National Identity and the English Landscape', *Rural History*, ii (1991); A. Murdoch, *British History 1660–1832. National Identity and Local Culture* (Basingstoke, 1998); D. Powell, *Nationhood and Identity: The British State Since 1800* (London, 2002), pp. ix–xii; K. Robbins, *Great Britain. Identities, Institutions and the Idea of Britishness* (Harlow, 1998); R. Weight, *Patriots: National Identity in Britain 1940–2000* (London, 2003), pp. 1–19.

The belief that the sea, sea power and the Royal Navy could act as a means of security from hostile powers was a manifestation of the belief that being an island-state imposed a geographical isolation and security that set Britain apart from other countries.[15] Thus Britain's island identity based on its geographical insularity and separation from its neighbours was different from that of a continental power suffering from shared land borders with a rival. This sense of security could be seen in a belief that invasion was difficult, or in times of naval challenges, a possibility – the sea could at times 'seem less a symbol and guardian of national identity, than the means by which invasion from without might come'[16] with a resulting impact on the importance of the navy and sea power within national identity. The combination of security and island status ensured that, as Admiral Bacon pointed out in an article for the journal *Nineteenth Century and After*, 'The people of Great Britain have had ingrained in them, both by heredity and tradition, an instinctive faith in the Royal Navy as their main safeguard in times of peril.'[17] Fundamentally, British views of their relationship with the sea could either negatively or positively influence their investment in their sea power and indeed wider strategy.

The 1859 invasion scare shows clearly how the island security construct could negatively influence British sea power and the importance of public perception. As a result of this scare there was a massive investment in army-run coastal fortifications to protect naval bases from a perceived threat of attack from the landward side by an invasion force. Yet it is more productive to view the ploughing of large sums of money literally into the ground as a result of the fort-building programmes after 1859, incomprehensible as they may be as a realistic means of defence for an island, as merely over-insurance at a time of acute public anxiety, in the same mould as the fort-building phase – the Martello towers – during the Revolutionary and Napoleonic Wars.[18] Indeed, John Beeler explicitly refutes there being any political strength behind the 'Fortress Britain' school of military strategy.[19] Similarly, the naval scares of the late Victorian period can be seen as a wavering in the public confidence in the Royal Navy's ability to prevent invasion and protect British trade, yet this time the anxiety over the security of the British Isles led to investment in the Royal Navy. With confidence in the navy buttressed and navalism gripping many parts of society by the turn of the century, resurgent invasion fears did not lead to significant changes in anti-invasion policy, or the

---

[15] C. Behrman, *Victorian Myths of the Sea* (Athens, OH, 1977), pp. 38–55, 111–35; Robbins, *Great Britain: Identities*, pp. 4–5, 122–3, 228.

[16] L. Colley, 'The Frontier in British History', in W.R. Louis (ed.), *More Adventures with Britannia: Personalities, Politics and Culture in Britain* (London, 1998), p. 17.

[17] R.H. Bacon, 'The Future Needs of the Navy', *Nineteenth Century and After*, cxi (1922), p. 15.

[18] J. Beeler, *British Naval Policy in the Gladstone–Disraeli Era, 1886–1880* (Stanford, 1998), pp. 23–4.

[19] J. Beeler, 'Steam, Strategy and Schurman: Imperial Defence in the Post-Crimean Era, 1856–1905', in K. Neilson and G. Kennedy (eds), *Far Flung Lines: Studies in Imperial Defence in Honour of Donald Mackenzie Schurman* (London, 1997), pp. 29–30; J. Beeler, *Birth of the Battleship: British Capital Ship Design 1870–1881* (London, 1991), pp. 89–91.

Royal Navy's primacy within it, at the national level despite agitation by the army and its cheerleaders such as the National Service League, who wanted a large continental-style army. As the *Daily Mail* put it in 1909: 'For England [*sic*] "there is nothing between sea supremacy and ruin"';[20] the combination of island insularity and sea power made for some a most reassuring, and binary, arrangement. If Britain was strong at sea she was secure thanks to her island position; if there was weakness at sea, that security dissipated.

The security that the sea provided Britain was, however, a double-edged sword in reality and perception. As well as providing security, being an insular island or archipelagic state could be seen as exposing vital imports of food and raw materials to interdiction by hostile powers should the navy be defeated or drawn away – a more frightening variant of the 'bolt from the blue' invasion fear that caused much ink to be spilt in popular journals after the 1880s. The fear that this threat of starvation caused was very real during the late Victorian and Edwardian periods when the containment of the political status quo and the neutralisation of any chance of the organised labour movement exerting pressure for reform, or worse, revolution, was a shared concern for many liberals and conservatives. Trade defence was an area of acute interest for the Royal Navy, while the impact of hostilities on supplies was examined by a Royal Commission in 1903. The Commission's report noted that price rises in raw materials and food supplies were likely, that this would not only affect the poor, but also the exports on which the British economy rested, exposing the poorest working classes to a double blow if the reduction in economic activity led to the closure of factories,[21] as indeed had happened during the American Civil War when cotton supplies to Lancashire were reduced by the Union blockade of the Confederacy. Some of the Commission's witnesses suggested that the resulting rises in the price of food could cause 'serious riots, or, at least to cause pressure to be brought to bear on the Government to make peace at any price'.[22] In 1910 Colonel Repington pointed out that over ten million people in London and the surrounding areas relied on food transported by sea to the Thames.[23] The capital was dependent almost completely on seaborne transport for its fuel and raw materials; an interruption to such transport, Repington thought, might lead to great suffering and perhaps rioting.[24] By 1914 almost 60 per cent of the calorific value of all food consumed in Britain, about 40 per cent in crude weight and around 50 per cent in value, was from overseas, with the working classes consuming proportionally more in food imports than other social groups.[25]

---

[20] *Daily Mail*, 17 March 1909, p. 6.
[21] Cd. 2643, *Royal Commission on Supply of Food and Raw Material in Time of War* (1905), vol. 1, pp. 35–44.
[22] Ibid., p. 43.
[23] Col. A. Court Repington, 'New Wars For Old.– I. The Submarine Menace', *Blackwood's Edinburgh Magazine*, clxxxvii (1910), p. 898.
[24] Ibid.
[25] A. Offer, *First World War: An Agrarian Interpretation* (Oxford, 1991), pp. 81, 218–19.

The Influence of Identity on Sea Power 207

The fears that Britain's home islands were less a refuge than a liability in wartime was also aired in popular fiction, although starvation was far less popular as a genre than invasion literature. There was however one notable exception. In the summer of 1914, Arthur Conan Doyle published a short story in *The Strand Magazine*: 'Danger! Being the Log of Captain John Sirius'. Throughout the story, Captain Sirius recounts the effects of the sinkings with rising insurance rates, rapidly increasing food prices and higher infant mortality, culminating with the most frightening image for the British establishment – revolution.[26] Conan Doyle conjured up for his readers a picture of riot and murder as starving workers rampaged through the cities. He reported that 'There was serious rioting in the Lanarkshire coalfields and in the Midlands, together with a socialistic upheaval in the East of London, which had assumed the proportions of a civil war.'[27] Furthermore, 'In the great towns starving crowds clamoured for bread before the municipal offices and public officials everywhere were attacked and often murdered by frantic mobs, composed largely of desperate women who had seen their infants perish before their eyes.'[28]

Yet the island and security combination could also present itself in far more positive ways to the late Victorian and Edwardian public. It was a matter of common belief that being an island had historically produced the superiority of the British, or often more specifically the English, as seamen due to their island status or a moral superiority thanks to their relationship with the sea as islanders. In 1878 Robert Louis Stevenson argued that the English national symbol was really the sea as it 'is our approach and bulwark; it has been the scene of our greatest triumphs and dangers, and we are accustomed in lyrical strains to claim it as our own'.[29] Moreover, as islanders, the English or British (the Victorians, and others, were infuriatingly imprecise, often saying English when they meant British and vice versa) were seen as being superior mariners as a result of their island identity. The Victorian historian and writer J.A. Froude thought that 'After their island the sea is the natural home of the English man; the Norse blood is in us, and we rove over the waters, for business or pleasure, as eagerly as our ancestors.'[30] Nor was it enough that the English (or British) were natural sailors, their sailors were morally superior as well, demonstrating virtues of courage, discipline and character.

The moral dimension of this relationship is particularly interesting as it links British view of combat, attitudes to non-combatants and private property in wartime, the sea and sea power. The feelings of security that Britain's island insularity had prompted for decades had, during the course of the nineteenth century, combined with classical free trade liberalism. The result was that when Cobden

---

[26] A. Conan Doyle, 'Danger! Being the Log of Captain John Sirius', *Strand Magazine*, xlviii (1914), pp. 12, 16, 17, 18.
[27] Ibid., p. 17.
[28] Ibid., p. 18.
[29] R.L. Stevenson, 'The English Admirals', *Cornhill Magazine*, xxxviii (1878), p. 36.
[30] J.A. Froude, *Oceania: Or, England and Her Colonies* (London, 1886), p. 14.

proclaimed that war should be 'brought as much as possible to a duel between Governments and their professional fighters, with as little stimulus from the hope of plunder and prize money as possible'[31] he was enunciating an idea that was to become widely accepted in the United Kingdom. Even Cobden's political adversary Palmerston agreed, believing that wars were won by armies and fleets, not by inflicting economic or financial losses on individuals.[32]

Although the philosophies of capture at sea and free trade were mutually exclusive, hence the extensive debate over belligerent rights following the abolition of privateering in the 1856 Declaration of Paris, their combination in civil, political and naval consciousnesses produced the idea that the destruction of property at sea was morally wrong.[33] Furthermore, the acceptance of the view that war was between states and not individuals made the killing of non-combatants most unpalatable as 'civilised warfare strives to avoid unnecessary suffering by making a distinction between combatants and non-combatants'.[34] Thus by 1914, non-combatant status for individuals and their private property was closely related to concepts of what was fair and just in warfare.[35] These views were sufficiently strongly held by a cross-section of the country to be considered a part of British culture; it was how they understood their world. Therefore, when Churchill described his views of unrestricted submarine warfare in his memoirs as 'to sink her [a merchant ship] without providing for the safety of the crew, to leave that crew to perish in open boats or drown amid the waves was in the eyes of all seafaring peoples a grisly act'[36] he was not alone. The strength of this view of maritime warfare can be seen in the highly negative reaction by the British in the First World War to being on the receiving end of a campaign that specifically targeted private property and non-combatants, both directly in that merchant ships were sunk without, and indirectly in that Britain's civilian population was exposed to the possibility of starvation in a Conan Doyle-esque submarine war.[37]

Thanks to British ideas about private property, non-combatants in war, fair play and sportsmanship, themselves a function of island insularity, gentlemanly conduct and classical economic liberalism as components of a national identity, the sinking of merchant vessels by British submarines as part of post-First World War plans for any future conflict was not acceptable. The rejection by the British of unrestricted submarine warfare as an acceptable means of maritime

---

[31] R. Cobden to W. Lindsay, 29 August 1856, quoted in W. Lindsay, *Manning the Royal Navy and Merchant Marine; also Belligerent and Neutral Rights in the Event of War* (London, 1877), p. 116.
[32] B. Semmel, *Liberalism and Naval Strategy* (London, 1986), p. 71.
[33] Cobden to Lindsay, 29 August 1856, quoted in Lindsay, *Manning*, p. 116; Semmel, *Liberalism and Naval Strategy*, p. 71.
[34] A. Offer, 'Morality and the Admiralty: "Jacky" Fisher, Economic Warfare and the Laws of War', *Journal of Contemporary History*, xxiii (1988), p. 102.
[35] W.S. Churchill, *The World Crisis* (London, 1938), vol. ii, pp. 720–1.
[36] Ibid., p. 1111.
[37] D. Redford, *Submarine: A Cultural history from the Great War to Nuclear Combat* (London, 2010), pp. 103–11.

combat produced a problem for the early interwar-period Royal Navy: how to use submarines in an acceptable manner (to the British public) in any future economic warfare. The result was that policy ended up reflecting these fairness/non-combatant rights aspects of the British character.

In short, identity was influencing the British application of its sea power. Indeed the most effective way for British sea power to reconcile the use of submarines in a commerce war with the pressures of national identity was to develop a mode of submarine warfare that promised to be both effective and inoffensive to sensibilities over non-combatant casualties. Unfortunately, the interwar *X1* cruiser submarine concept foundered not on the impracticalities of prize crews for captured vessels, nor necessarily on money (as it was recognised that *X1* was an experiment),[38] but on the fact that perfecting the tactical employment of a cruiser submarine concept would not benefit Britain. As the Director of the Tactical Division pointed out, a successful cruiser submarine would disadvantage Britain more than any other nation because:

> The submarine cruiser is undoubtedly the most effective type of craft that can be produced by our enemies to menace our Seaborne Trade. *[Without using unrestricted submarine warfare.]* For this reason it is a matter of utmost importance that Great Britain should refrain from advertising the utility of such a craft to the world at large.[39]

The *X1* cruiser submarine concept was subsequently abandoned. More significantly, when the British used unrestricted submarine warfare during the Second World War, they went to great pains to avoid such phrasing, preferring 'sink on sight' or 'dangerous' areas, which helped them differentiate – at least in their own minds – between the activities of their own submarines and the German U-boats in a way that reflected British concerns and morals over non-combatant casualties.[40]

II

So what happened with the fundamental relationship between island insularity, security and sea power? Quite simply it seems that the British stopped believing that the security conferred by their sea power and their navy was important to them. When did this start to happen? An exact date is hard to state, but it seems that the role of the Royal Navy within the security aspects of national identity started to change in the years after the First World War and was given added impetus during and after the Second World War era, with the result that while the strategic rationale for British sea power remained valid, the British did not

---

[38] TNA, ADM 1/8703/158, *Functions of a Cruiser Submarine or Submersible.*
[39] Ibid., Minute by Director of the Tactical Division, Naval Staff, 8 April 1925.
[40] Redford, *Submarine*, pp. 142–54, 208–22.

believe this was the case, and political interest and support for the navy slowly atrophied.

The security required by constructs of national identity and provided by the navy weakened in the interwar period and the response by the British to challenges to their sea power changed in the aftermath of the First World War. It was often argued that naval armaments had caused the war, and that Britain's interests were best served by pursuing collective security arrangements rather than relying on sea power. For example, the acceptance of parity with the USA under the Washington Naval Treaty was without the squeals of anguish and agitation that had accompanied any suggestion that Britain was falling behind in the pre-war Anglo-German naval competition, or indeed earlier naval competitions with France. Indeed, the self-appointed protectors of British sea power – the Navy League – had since 1919 abandoned their mantra of British naval supremacy in favour of collective security and disarmament. It is very easy to overlook the Navy League's response, which far from criticising such an abrogation of Britain's traditional naval position, actually applauded it. In autumn 1921 the evident progress towards a naval arms limitation treaty at Washington enthused the Navy League's senior leadership to describe the prospective agreement in such laudatory terms as 'noble aims' and 'the highest ideals of British policy'.[41] The membership of the Navy League, however, took a rather different view to that of their Executive Committee and in early 1922 the League was riven by internal disagreements over policy which prevented any attempts to influence public opinion over the Washington Treaty and even for a short time threatened the dissolution of the League. Yet the League's problems were merely a symptom of wider changes in the perceived importance of sea power.

The reason for this change? Aircraft. As soon as Blériot flew across the Channel, the *Daily Mail* was trumpeting the 'fact' that Britain was no longer an island. Once aerial attack was viable, it demonstrated to the British that their frontier was not the English Channel but possibly as far east as the Rhine. This was a security problem that could not be solved by naval power and fundamentally questioned the importance of being an island in British national identity. However, in the case of identity and sea power it was the very strength of the conceptions of islandhood within national identity that made the illusion of aircraft and air warfare a powerful force in the British psyche. Britain's island status had protected it from invasion for centuries and the insularity and sense of security conferred by being an island was a key concept in national identity,[42] with British sea power being seen as the first and last line of defence. Britain's frontier was the sea; the English Channel had allowed them to absorb the best of European culture over the centuries without succumbing to continental despotism.[43]

---

[41] Lord Somerset, V. Biscoe Tritton, 'The Navy League', *The Times*, 31 December 1921
[42] Behrman, *Victorian Myths*, pp. 38–40, 43, 44, 47–9; R. Colls, *Identity of England* (Oxford, 2004), pp. 239–41; K. Kumar, *The Making of English National Identity* (Cambridge, 2003), p. 8.
[43] Colls, *Identity*, p. 239.

During the First World War, what had been only the figment of writers' imaginations became real for Britain with the raids by German Zeppelins and aircraft; these raids caused a great deal of panic within the civil population, particularly in London.[44] Such attacks brought home that the aircraft meant Britain was no longer an island – an idea that had gained currency before the war, boosted by films emphasising the destructive potential of a future air war and by the pre-war 'air-mindedness' campaign orchestrated by Lord Northcliffe and his *Daily Mail*, which declared in 1906 that 'There will be no more sleeping safely behind the wooden walls of old England with the Channel our safety moat.'[45] Furthermore, it was suggested that Britain's obsession with the sea had blinded them to the danger they faced:

> We have grown up for so many generations to think that there is a special element protecting us which has always been our field, namely, the sea, that we are apt to shut our eyes to the fact that this element no longer protects us, and developments in aircraft have laid us open to attacks through the air which destroy our previous ideas of 'splendid isolation' due to our surrounding sea.[46]

The claims for the bomber continued in the interwar period, with widespread public fears about air warfare, leading to apocalyptic descriptions of bombing in the late interwar period.[47]

By the 1930s the bomber was widely perceived as allowing, for the first time, a direct attack on anyone on the island, irrespective of British sea power and the English Channel that had together defended Britain for centuries. When the Prime Minister, Stanley Baldwin, in 1932 told Parliament that 'the bomber will always get through'[48] it was accepted as a statement of fact, ignoring such minor questions such as whose bombers will get through and to bomb what? After all, at this time, the mainstay of the RAF's bomber force was the 1920s Vickers Virginia, with a combat radius of about 490 miles, which was less than the distance from Lincoln to Essen.[49] Furthermore, in late 1932 the only air force that could effectively strike at Britain was France's – hardly a serious threat. Yet

---

[44] J. Ferris, 'Airbandit: C3I and Strategic Air Defence during the First Battle of Britain', in M. Dockrill and D. French (eds), *Strategy and Intelligence: British Policy during the First World War* (London: 1996); G. Robb, *British Culture and the First World War* (Basingstoke, 2002), p. 200; D. Stevenson, *1914–1918: The History of the First World War* (London, 2004), p. 303; Sir C Webster and N. Frankland, *The Strategic Air Offensive against Germany 1939–1945* (London, 1961), vol. i, pp. 34–5, 38.

[45] *Daily Mail*, 6 November 1906, p. 6.

[46] *Daily Express*, 20 December 1921, p. 1.

[47] W. Murray, 'Strategic Bombing. The British, American, and German experiences', in *Military Innovation in the Interwar Period*, eds. W. Murray and A. R. Millett (Cambridge, 1998), pp. 102–3.

[48] K. Middlemas and J. Barnes, *Baldwin: A Biography* (London, 1969), p. 736; P. Williamson, *Stanley Baldwin* (Cambridge, 1999), pp. 47, 305–306.

[49] http://www.rafmuseum.org.uk/research/archive-exhibitions/not-quite-extinct/vickers-virginia.aspx;http://www.raf.mod.uk/history/bombercommandheavybombersavroaldershot.cfm.

island insularity status was no longer a seen guarantor of security, especially for non-combatants. The experience of the Second World War, with the myths of the Battle of Britain and of the Blitz, all reinforced this triumph of perception over reality with regard to the security that island insularity and sea power gave Britain. Only with the development of nuclear weapons was this relationship broken. Britain stopped believing its insularity and sea power gave it security long before this was actually a reality.

III

The relationship between national identity and sea power is a massive one. Yet a number of conclusions are possible at this stage. First, it is clear that as far as the British are concerned there is a security component to national identity and there is no reason to assume that other national identities will not, on investigation, also display security issues or concerns within their identity matrix. Second, that although neglected, the societal or identity aspects of sea power, notably the perceptions of public and political classes towards the maintenance and use of sea power, are an essential part of our understanding of sea power. Third, in the British case the perception of the security provided by being an island has been a cornerstone in the generation and maintenance of public and political support for their navy and the will to use sea power. Fourth, it is the importance of the island security trope within British identity that has caused such rapid and unfounded concern with air power up to the development of nuclear weapons. For in air power – the bomber – was a weapon that invalidated Britain's island insularity and its sea power, to attack non-combatants in a terrifying view of future war.

18

Professor Spenser Wilkinson, Admiral William Sims and the Teaching of Strategy and Sea Power at the University of Oxford and the United States Naval War College, 1909–1927[1]

PAUL M. RAMSEY

Introduction

In 1918, Admiral William S. Sims, the newly appointed President of the United States Naval War College, wrote to Professor H. Spenser Wilkinson, the first Chichele Professor of Military History at the University of Oxford:

> I have been an interested reader of your reviews in the Press for the past year (and of course I am well acquainted with your books), but I am particularly interested in your article in THE TIMES of Sunday, December 22nd [1918], in regard to educational questions, particularly as it relates to general staff training ... [I would like] to discuss with you the above questions, particularly as relates to Naval War College work in time of peace.[2]

These men shared a correspondence over the next four years concerning 'ideas on education for Officers for the Navy' and 'the principles of the art of warfare'. Their conclusions shaped the teaching of strategy and sea power at the Naval War College throughout the interwar period, creating an intellectual legacy still evident today in the courses and material taught.[3]

---

[1]   I would like to thank several organisations for the following awards that made this research possible: the US Naval War College Foundation's Edward S. Miller Research Fellowship in Naval History, the Director of the Foundation, the expert help of the Naval Historical Collection's archivist, Dr Evelyn Cherpak, and the kind guidance of Professor John B. Hattendorf throughout my research trip in Newport, RI; the University of Calgary, University Research Grants Committee's Thesis Research Grant and Conference Travel Grant; the National Army Museum, UK, Research Bursary. I am grateful to the archives consulted for allowing me to quote from the material in their possession and to the copyright holders. I would also like to thank: Professor Andrew Lambert, for his guidance; the editorial team for their help; and especially, Professor John Ferris for his comments and advice.

[2]   William S. Sims to H. Spenser Wilkinson, 24 December 1918, Spenser Wilkinson Papers, National Army Museum, Ogilby Trust, MS NAM 9011, OPT 13/43/1.

[3]   Sims to Wilkinson, 27 December 1918 and 2 October 1922, Wilkinson Papers, OPT 13/43/2 and 13/43/10: Wilkinson's papers contain nine letters from Admiral Sims and one letter from his aide Commander J.V. Babcock.

Their short exchange of letters and meetings in London and Oxford created a mutual interest and an important exchange of ideas, particularly for the reforms Sims was about to make at the United States Naval War College. Towards the end of Sims's time as president, he told Wilkinson, 'As you doubtless know, many of your books are in constant use at the Naval War College and are widely quoted in naval writings.'[4] Indeed, Sims requested an extra thirty copies of *The Brain of the Navy* (1895) from Wilkinson, because '[the College] consider[ed] this to be so suggestive and valuable to the beginners at the college that [it] wish[ed] to have these copies for their use'.[5] As Sims wrote, 'This little book will never be out of date as far as this college is concerned.'[6] Wilkinson secured one hundred copies for Sims.[7] This transfer of ideas and influence poses a number of key questions about our understanding of the development of the Naval War College not only under Sims's presidency, but also throughout the years before the Second World War.

Students of the intellectual mindset of Sims and the College in this period have largely focused on the legacy of Stephen B. Luce and Alfred Thayer Mahan.[8] Yet, Sims's reforms were at least in part guided by Wilkinson. Almost all the Naval War College students, including luminaries such as Harold R. Stark, Chester W. Nimitz, Ernest J. King and Charles P. Snyder read and regularly quoted in their essays Wilkinson's major works. In the student theses and staff presentations, Wilkinson's intellectual footprint compares favourably with those of Mahan and Luce.[9] Furthermore, in 1923, encouraged by Sims, J. Marius Scammell, the first assistant in the tactics department from 1919, moved from Newport to Oxford to study military history under Wilkinson's supervision, establishing the basis for an informal academic association.[10] The modern study of strategy and sea power at Oxford and the Naval War College owes much to Wilkinson and Sims. Their collaboration is an overlooked aspect in the development of an Anglo-American approach to the study of war.

---

4   Sims to Wilkinson, 18 March 1922, Wilkinson Papers, 13/43/7.
5   Sims to Wilkinson, 19 May 1922, Wilkinson Papers, 13/43/9.
6   Sims to Wilkinson, 2 October 1922, Wilkinson Papers, 13/43/10.
7   Sims to Wilkinson, 19 May 1922, Wilkinson Papers, 13/43/9.
8   J.B. Hattendorf, B. Mitchell Simpson, III and J.R. Wadleigh, *Sailors and Scholars: The Centennial History of the U.S. Naval War College* (Newport, RI, 1984); see also, R. Spector, *Professors of War: The Naval War College and the Development of the Naval Profession* (Newport, RI, 1977); M. Vlahos, *The Blue Sword: The Naval War College and the American Mission, 1919–1941* (Newport, RI, 1980); Branden Little and K.J. Hagan, 'Radical, but Right: William Sowden Sims (1858–1936)', in J.B. Hattendorf and B. Elleman (eds), *Nineteen-Gun Salute: Case Studies of Operational, Strategic, and Diplomatic Naval Leadership during the 20th and Early 21st Centuries* (Newport, RI, 2010); E.E. Morison, *Admiral Sims and the Modern American Navy* (Cambridge, MA, 1942).
9   US Naval War College Archives, Naval Historical Collection, Newport, RI: RG 13 Student Theses and RG 14 Faculty and Staff Presentations.
10 Sims to Joseph M. Scammell, 13 September 1923, Joseph Marius Scammell Papers, Duke University Libraries, Box 1.

Professor Spenser Wilkinson and the Study of War at Oxford

In 1909 Spenser Wilkinson was appointed Oxford's first Chichele Professor of Military History, after a long and distinguished career writing on military affairs. His interest in war began while studying at Oxford between 1873 and 1877. Wilkinson gained some practical military experience when he joined the University Volunteer Corps and afterwards formed the Oxford Kriegspiel (war game) Club. On returning to Manchester in 1878 he joined the Volunteers, and in 1881 he helped found the Manchester Tactical Society, which aimed to study the operations of war and advocate for Volunteer and army reform. In 1883 he secured a position on the staff of the *Manchester Guardian*, writing leaders on military subjects and foreign policy. Despite recognition for his good work, however, he lasted less than a decade at the liberal newspaper. The *Guardian*'s editor, C.P. Scott, disliked Wilkinson's analysis of international relations and he was dismissed in 1892, remaining jobless until 1895 when he secured a position on the *Morning Post* newspaper.[11] Wilkinson used this break to further his studies, by visiting Lord Roberts, Commander-in-Chief in India, on the North-West Frontier, and by reading Carl von Clausewitz's *On War* in full for the first time. By 1889 he was convinced of the need to reorganise the War Office and he wrote his most recognisable works on strategy and military reform between 1890 and 1900.[12]

A major theme in these works was the need to improve education and training for soldiers and sailors through the study of the principles of the art of war.[13] *The Brain of an Army* and *The Brain of the Navy* studied the principles of General Staff work, comparing it to 'a sort of university ... for training and testing admirals and generals'.[14] *Imperial Defence*, written with the Liberal politician Sir Charles Dilke, and *The Command of the Sea* outlined British strategy, arguing for the primacy of the navy in defence planning and of the command of the sea in defence policy. In *War and Policy*, Wilkinson emphasised that the interrelationship between government policy and strategy was vital to success in war. His perceptive understanding of the dynamics of British power stressed the importance of the higher direction of war, the primacy of policy in national defence and the role of sea power in British imperial strategy. In his view, British policy should aim at maintaining the balance of power in Europe and the international status quo. British naval strategy should seek to command the sea and to use the power of the Royal Navy

---

[11] S. Wilkinson, *Thirty-Five Years* (London, 1933), pp. 7–8, 18–21, 135; J. Luvaas, *The Education of an Army: British Military Thought, 1815–1940* (Chicago, 1964), pp. 253–90.

[12] Wilkinson Papers, 13/51, pp. 13–16

[13] Wilkinson's advocacy for professional military education continued throughout his life. After the Boer War, Wilkinson edited *The Nation's Need: Chapters on Education* (London, 1903), and wrote the chapter on officer education. Halford J. Mackinder contributed a chapter on university education. See also, for example, Wilkinson's *The Early Life of Moltke* (Oxford, 1913) and *Learners as Leaders* (Manchester, 1918).

[14] S. Wilkinson, *The Brain of the Navy*, pp. 34–5, in A. Lambert (ed.), S. Wilkinson, *The Brain of an Army, The Command of the Sea, The Brain of the Navy* (Aldershot, 1992).

to turn the scales in a European conflict.[15] When Lord Milner, the former High Commissioner of South Africa during the Boer War, recommended a 'professional advisor on defence' to Herbert Asquith in 1908, when the latter became Prime Minister, he explained that Wilkinson had 'given more <u>continuous and instructive thought</u> to the subject of national defence than any man in England ... studying all the factors, naval, military and <u>civil</u>, bearing on national defence, as a whole'. As Milner wrote, 'He is a natural thinker ... on what I can only call national strategy, something wider than the strategic case of either army or navy by itself.'[16] Oxford soon recognised the expertise Asquith rejected.

Teaching History, Strategy and the Theory of War
As Wilkinson explained in his inaugural address on the 27 November 1909, 'The University and the Study of War', his remit at Oxford was to 'lecture and give instruction in military history, with special reference to the conditions of modern warfare'.[17] 'Military history is the effort to understand war, to get to know what war is and what it means,' Wilkinson argued, and 'There is no method of getting to know war except the study of wars.'[18] Therefore, 'the only basis for a science or for an art of war is Military History'.[19] Wilkinson aimed to 'arrive at an historical understanding of the rise of modern strategy', and to develop and study the theory of war.[20]

In order to 'cultivate, develop, and diffuse the true idea of the nature of war', Wilkinson thought that any theory of war 'ought to explain all phenomena, great and small'.[21] Its first principle was that the art of war is the 'function primarily of the statesman rather than the soldier' and the directing 'art is policy, or politics'.[22] As Wilkinson explained, 'The features common to all wars are that they

---

[15] C. Wentworth Dilke and S. Wilkinson, *Imperial Defence* (London, 1892); Andrew Lambert (ed.), S. Wilkinson, *The Brain of an Army, The Command of the Sea, The Brain of the Navy* (Aldershot, 1992); Spenser Wilkinson, *War and Policy* (London, 1900).

[16] Alfred Milner to Herbert Asquith, 17 April 1908, Herbert Asquith Papers, Bodleian Library, MS. Asquith 11/102–7.

[17] S. Wilkinson, *The University and the Study of War* (Oxford, 1909), p. 21; see John B. Hattendorf, 'War History at Oxford: The Study of War History at Oxford, 1862–1990', in Hattendorf and Malcolm H. Murfett (eds), *Limitations of Military Power: Essays Presented to Professor Norman Gibbs on his Eightieth Birthday* (New York, NY, 1990) and Hew Strachan, 'The Study of War at Oxford 1909–2009', in C. Hood, D. King and G. Peele (eds), *Forging a Discipline: A Critical Assessment of Oxford's Development of the Study of Politics and International Relations in Comparative Perspective* (Oxford, 2014) on the study of war at Oxford.

[18] Wilkinson, *The University and the Study of War*, pp. 11–12.

[19] Ibid., p. 13.

[20] Ibid., pp. 22, 21–8; see Strachan, 'The Study of War at Oxford 1909–2009', pp. 208–10; I am grateful to Professor Sir Hew Strachan for discussing Wilkinson's impact at Oxford with me.

[21] Wilkinson, *The University and the Study of War*, p. 28.

[22] Ibid., p. 10.

are acts of force or violence with a political aim. They are acts of State. Apart from these common characteristics, wars differ almost infinitely one from another.'[23] Wilkinson believed that 'The origin of wars lies in the conflict of policies ... [and] the time to weigh the possibilities of conflict is when the national policy is taking shape.'[24] Military history was required to understand national policy. The principal value of the resulting 'theory of war lies in the insight which it gives into war's true nature, [and] the knowledge to which it leads ... produces men fit to direct a war'.[25] These ideas defined his scope and method of study.

Almost twenty years earlier Wilkinson had noted that 'the theory can never have an independent existence; it must always' be connected with historical study and practice.[26] He advocated studying the 'Theory of War, with special reference to Napoleon and Moltke', and the French and German schools of military thought, along with courses like 'Arming a Nation, illustrated from the French Revolution Armies', and in 1914, 'First Lessons in War'.[27] 'If we can come to appreciate Napoleon and Moltke', he told his students in the Michaelmas term, 1912, 'we shall probably attain to as clear an insight into the reality of war as we are capable of acquiring', and of 'the nature of armies [and navies] and the causes of victory and defeat'.[28] In the years following 1914, Wilkinson lectured frequently on war and strategy to many audiences, but by 1916 the demands of fighting a war of attrition left few with any time for the reflective study of military history or the theory of war. Wilkinson abandoned his scheduled courses at Oxford to focus on 'historical studies and writing'.

Wilkinson's works during this period reflect this effort to study the theory of war. He wrote three chapters for Sir Adolphus William Ward's history of Germany, 1815–90, handling the wars of German unification of 1864, 1866 and 1870–71, where he praised Moltke for understanding the relationship between strategy and policy, the commander and the statesman.[29] Published in 1915, *The French Army before Napoleon* was based on lectures given at Oxford about the origins of modern strategy and command. In the summer of 1918, Wilkinson was invited to deliver the Lees Knowles lectures on military history at Cambridge and in November of that year he gave five lectures, published later as *The Defence of Piedmont 1742–48*, which he 'considered as the source of Napoleon's strategic

---

[23] Ibid., p. 13.
[24] Ibid., p. 20.
[25] S. Wilkinson, *Government and the War* (London, 1918), p. 173.
[26] S. Wilkinson, *The Brain of an Army*, p. 181, in Andrew Lambert (ed.), S. Wilkinson, *The Brain of an Army, The Command of the Sea, The Brain of the Navy* (Aldershot, 1992).
[27] J.L. Myres, *The Provision for Historical Studies at Oxford* (Oxford, 1915), pp. 24–5; S. Wilkinson, *First Lessons in War* (London, 1914), Oxford lectures became a textbook on tactics for officers.
[28] Spenser Wilkinson Notebooks, National Army Museum, Ogilby Trust, NAM 68-07-358-1: Navy blue notebook, titled 'Campaigns in Italy, Lectures Michaelmas Term, 1912'.
[29] Wilkinson to Vice-Chancellor, 26 June 1919, University Archives, UR 6/HMC/1, file 1; A.W. Ward and S. Wilkinson, *Germany, 1815–1890*, Volume II: *1852–1871* (Cambridge, 1917).

methods'. He demonstrated 'the debt of Napoleon as a general to his French predecessors of the eighteenth century', whose campaigns he had studied.[30] *The Rise of General Bonaparte* was the last in this trilogy of volumes on the origins of Napoleon's professional learning and his principles of war.[31] A lucid analysis of the relation between the theory of war and national policy, Wilkinson's *Government and the War* offered an important critique of the British government's conduct of the First World War.[32] According to *Punch Magazine* it 'entitled its author to be described as the British Clausewitz'.[33] Indeed, Wilkinson consistently had echoed Clausewitz's main arguments and thought that officers 'needed a broader education in the relationship between war and policy'.[34] 'The mistakes made between 1914 and 1919', he argued in *British Aspects of War and Peace*, were caused by 'an insufficient acquaintance of our Generals with the principles of national policy, and of our statesmen with the principles of what for want of a better name may be called international dynamics'.[35] The institutions tasked with the study of war should not neglect the knowledge of war as 'the employment of force by the State'.[36]

While at Oxford, Wilkinson established a method for the study of war, which along with the important work by Mahan and Sir Julian Corbett, shaped the development of a broader conception of strategy, moving from purely naval or military methods to something resembling national strategy.[37] Wilkinson developed his earlier ideas in lectures at Oxford on the theory of war, and applied them to assessments of fighting the First World War in his journalism, first for the *Morning Post*, then the *Westminster Gazette* and finally *The Times*, where Sims regularly read them.

Admiral William Sims and the Study of War at the Naval War College

Sims was born to American parents in Canada in 1858. His family moved to Pennsylvania from Ontario four years before he joined the US Naval Academy

---

[30] Wilkinson to Vice-Chancellor, 26 June 1919, University Archives, UR 6/HMC/1, file 1; Spenser Wilkinson, *The French Army before Napoleon* (Oxford, 1915); S. Wilkinson, *The Defence of Piedmont, 1742–48* (Oxford, 1927), Preface.
[31] S. Wilkinson, *The Rise of General Bonaparte* (Oxford, 1930).
[32] S. Wilkinson, *Government and the War* (London, 1918).
[33] *Punch Magazine*, 5 June 1918, Senate House Library, University of London, Caroline Elizabeth Playne Papers, MS1112/1.
[34] Strachan, 'The Study of War at Oxford 1909–2009', pp. 216–17; Wilkinson, *The University and the Study of War*, pp. 25–6.
[35] S. Wilkinson, *British Aspects of War and Peace* (London, 1920) pp. 61–2; also cited in Strachan, 'The Study of War at Oxford 1909–2009', pp. 208–9.
[36] Wilkinson to Vice-Chancellor, 26 June 1919, University Archives, UR 6/HMC/1, file 1; Wilkinson, *The University and the Study of War*, pp. 25–6; Strachan, 'The Study of War at Oxford 1909–2009', pp. 208–9.
[37] See H. Strachan 'The Lost Meaning of Strategy', *Survival*, vol. 47, no. 3 (Autumn 2005), pp. 33–54; see also, H. Strachan, *The Direction of War: Contemporary Strategy in Historical Perspective* (Cambridge, 2013).

in 1876. Graduating in 1880, he had an uneventful career at sea. In 1896 he was appointed US naval attaché in Paris, from where he studied the navies of the European powers. Sims was assigned to the China station in 1900, from where he reported flaws in US ship design and deficiencies in American naval gunnery. His assessments and innovations earned Sims the patronage of President Theodore Roosevelt, who in 1902 recalled him to be the US Navy's Inspector of Target Practice, a position he held until 1909. During this period Sims led major reforms in naval gunfire with the introduction of the continuous aim system, developed while on the China station with Captain Percy Scott, Royal Navy. In 1906 Sims challenged Mahan on battleship design and the utility of the newly launched *Dreadnought*, arguing that the development made American warships obsolete. Sims's advocacy was a success, and his appointment as Roosevelt's naval aide in November 1907 coincided with Congressional support for the construction of *Dreadnought*-type battleships. In recognition, Roosevelt rewarded Sims in 1909 with command of the battleship USS *Minnesota*.[38]

Sims arrived at the Naval War College in the summer of 1911 questioning the purpose of his assignment. The Summer Conference convinced him of the value of his work. As one of the first students to take part in the new 'long course' from 1911 to 1912, and then as a member of the staff through to June 1913, he enthused about what that study offered the 'practical naval officer'.[39] In completing the 'long course' thesis 'Policy in its Relation to War' Sims read a considerable amount, including Wilkinson, whom he quoted, showing a good grasp of his main arguments:

> The placing of an army on a war footing and its transport to a frontier are political acts of the gravest moment. They are therefore usually controlled almost as much by political as by military considerations, and it is impossible rightly to appreciate this without taking into account the political circumstances by which they are affected.[40]

Sims demonstrated the point long made by Wilkinson that 'the statesmen should have an adequate knowledge of the nature of war, and the military men who are charged with the making and the executing of the strategic plans should be well informed' by foreign politics.[41] 'The whole conduct of war should', Sims noted, 'be based upon plans the strategic objective of which is to gain the definite aims

---

[38] E.E. Morison, *Admiral Sims and the Modern American Navy* (Cambridge, MA, 1942); B. Little and K. Hagan, 'Radical, but Right: William Sowden Sims (1858–1936)', in J.B. Hattendorf and B.A. Elleman (eds), *Nineteen-Gun Salute* (Newport, RI, 2010); B.F. Armstrong, ed., *21st Century Sims: Innovation, Education, and Leadership for the Modern Era* (Annapolis, 2015).

[39] Morison, *Admiral Sims and the Modern American Navy*, pp. 287–93; Naval War College Archives, RG 4, Publications, Box 12, Folder 9, William S. Sims, 'Naval War College Principles and Methods Applied Afloat', August 1914 and Box 1, Folder 9, William S. Sims, 'The Practical Naval Officer', December 1919.

[40] NWC Archives, RG 13, Student Theses, Box 1, W.S. Sims, 'Policy in its Relation to War', 1911–12, p. 14.

[41] Ibid., p. 21.

of the policy involved.'[42] The students clearly were 'well acquainted' with Wilkinson's books. The entirety of Sims's Planning Staff in London during the war consisted of Naval War College graduates. The leading members of this group, Dudley W. Knox and Harry E. Yarnell, read and cited Wilkinson in their 'Policy' essays, as did most others during this period.[43]

Educational Questions, Correspondence and Reform

In 1917 Sims was appointed Commanding Officer, US Naval Forces in European Waters. While in London he regularly read Wilkinson's commentaries in *The Times*. By the Armistice in 1918, Sims had become an American naval hero. He requested to be appointed as President of the Naval War College, which offered, he thought, the greatest opportunity for making a difference to the navy.[44] Wilkinson had reached the same conclusion about the importance of educational reform. He wrote a series of articles in *The Times*, 'Reconstruction and the Army', which addressed the failures in the conduct of the First World War and called for a reorientation of officer education to focus on the theory of war. Any theory must be based on the 'experience gained during the War', and on military history, and there was a need to reconstitute 'the Imperial General Staff as the organ of the science of war and the art of command'.[45] 'The brain of an army, its university, is a General Staff for the cultivation of the science of war,' Wilkinson argued, and 'together with a Staff College' should educate officers in military history and the theory of war.[46] Wilkinson continued: 'among the officers of the Army there were none who had enjoyed the best training given by the Universities', and a 'means must be found of linking up what should be the brain of the Army with the Universities'.[47] This requirement was urgent because general pacifications were rarely permanent and preparation against the possibility of 'fresh wars' was essential. Indeed, as Wilkinson wrote, '[the need] for self-defence against unexpected challenge[s] seems to me to be as great as ever'.[48]

These arguments for the reform of military education greatly interested Sims, who on 24 December 1918 wrote to Wilkinson to request a meeting.[49] Wilkinson immediately told Sims of his 'willingness' to discuss his ideas on 'education for

---

[42] Ibid., p. 23.
[43] Hattendorf, *Sailors and Scholars*, pp. 79, 86–91; NWC Archives, RG 13 Student Theses, Box 1, W. D. Knox, 'Policy: Its Relation to War and Preparations for War', 1912–13, p. 2 and H.E. Yarnell, 'Policy: Its Relation to War and Preparation for War', 1913–14, pp. 5–6.
[44] Hattendorf, *Sailors and Scholars*, pp. 112–13.
[45] Spenser Wilkinson newspaper cuttings, Bodleian Library, vol. 40, pp. 44–5, 48, articles in the *Sunday Times*, 15 December 1918, 22 December 1918 and 29 December 1918, titled 'Reconstruction and the Army'.
[46] *Sunday Times*, 22 December 1918, 'Reconstruction and the Army', Wilkinson newspaper cuttings, vol. 40, p. 45.
[47] Ibid.
[48] *Sunday Times*, 29 December 1918, 'Reconstruction and the Army', Wilkinson newspaper cuttings, vol. 40, pp. 45, 48.
[49] Sims to Wilkinson, 24 December 1918, Wilkinson Papers, 13/43/1.

Officers for the Navy', sending along his pamphlet 'The Secret of the Sea', which explained his view of strategy and sea power. Sims agreed with those ideas 'most thoroughly'.[50] Wilkinson invited Sims to three lectures in January 1919 on the 'reconstruction of the British military system', which were published as *British Aspects of War and Peace*. Sims responded by inviting Wilkinson to his hotel apartment in London to discuss with his staff 'the lessons of the war'.[51] At a weekend visit to Oxford in February 1919, they had discussed a range of subjects related to officer education and the study of war. Sims wrote to Wilkinson to say 'how very much [he] was interested in [his] visit', while his aide, Commander J.V. Babcock emphasised that '[he] was very much interested in all that [he] saw and heard'.[52] Wilkinson made a lasting impression on Sims. He later invited Wilkinson to his daughter's wedding, but ill health prevented him attending.[53] The ideas presented in Wilkinson's 'Reconstruction and the Army', reinforced by their conversations in London and Oxford, guided some aspects of Sims's reforms at the Naval War College.

Sims wanted every officer at the Naval War College to study the art of war, with an emphasis on the relationship between policy, strategy and sea power. 'Brains ... trained in the art of command and coordinated effort' were essential if sea power was to be useful for national defence.[54] Sims's reforms aimed to shape those brains by first ensuring the War College was clearly defined as an educational institution and not a planning staff resource, and second, by having respected knowledgeable teaching chairs in strategy and tactics. This work had to be supplemented by a coherent policy and method of study, which required the employment of academic experts able to maintain contact with the university world and continuity in shaping the courses.[55] With these reforms and a rigorous curriculum, the mission of the Naval War College was 'to study the principles of warfare as enunciated by the great masters of the art, [and] to develop the practical application of these principles to war on the sea under modern conditions'.[56] The comparison with Wilkinson's remit at Oxford to study military history and the theory of war, 'with special reference to the conditions of modern warfare', is noteworthy.[57] While Wilkinson could only 'dream of an Oxford School of War

---

50 Sims to Wilkinson, 27 December 1918, Wilkinson Papers, 13/43/2; S. Wilkinson, *The Secret of the Sea* (London, 1895) copy in Wilkinson Papers, 13/63.
51 Wilkinson, *British Aspects of War and Peace* (London, 1920); Sims to Wilkinson, 11 January 1919, Wilkinson Papers, 13/43/3.
52 Sims to Wilkinson, 17 February 1919 and 19 February 1919, Wilkinson Papers, 13/43/4–5; and J.V. Babcock to Wilkinson, 20 February 1919, Wilkinson Papers, 13/43/6.
53 Wilkinson to Scammell, 30 June 1932, copy in Wilkinson Papers, 13/68; original in Scammell Papers, Box 1: Wilkinson told Scammell, 'I should like to see the Admiral again.'
54 Sims to Secretary of the Navy, 15 January 1919, quoted in Vlahos, *The Blue Sword*, p. 58, and in Hattendorf, *Sailors and Scholars*, p. 113.
55 Hattendorf, *Sailors and Scholars*, pp. 113–14.
56 NWC Archives, RG 4 Publications, Box 2, Folder 13, 'U.S. Naval War College Course outline', 8 September 1921: W.W. Phelps quoting Sims, p. 2.
57 Wilkinson, *The University and the Study of War*, p. 21; see Hattendorf, 'War History at Oxford', and Strachan, 'The Study of War at Oxford 1909–2009'.

developing', Sims established a college of war which broadly resembled that proposed by Wilkinson and the fellows at All Souls. This 'establishment of the College on a permanent foundation' rested on Sims's decision 'to bring into the College certain educational features from civil life',[58] thereby linking it to the universities, an idea developed by reading, corresponding and in discussion with Wilkinson.

Wilkinson in Student Theses and Staff Lectures

The reformed Naval War College shaped the minds of its students before the Second World War. Officers were required to complete a selected course of military reading in order 'to learn and reflect on the established, fundamental principles of warfare'.[59] In his opening address, 'The Practical Naval Officer', delivered to the first 'full course' in December 1919, Sims stressed the value of education in preparing officers for command. He suggested six preliminary readings on 'the knowledge that [to him was] essential to success in war'. Wilkinson's *The Brain of the Navy* was placed first on a list that included Mahan's *Naval Strategy*, Corbett's *Some Principles of Maritime Strategy* and Clausewitz's *On War*.[60] 'We consider it very valuable', Sims wrote to Wilkinson in 1922, '[for] not only learning the principles of the art of warfare, but practicing them to such an extent that [naval officers] will be able to apply them with the necessary facility.'[61] As Sims confirmed in an earlier letter to Wilkinson, 'many of your books are in constant use at the Naval War College and are widely quoted in naval writings'.[62] Indeed, many staff lectures encouraged students to study Wilkinson's works carefully and student theses frequently referenced his arguments.

Students were required to write theses in four areas: policy, strategy, tactics and command. The theses would form collectively 'a treatise on the Art of War'.[63] In the thesis on policy completed for the strategy department, which examined the US position in the Far East, students most commonly quoted Wilkinson, Clausewitz and Major Stewart L. Murray, whose introduction to Clausewitz, *The Reality of War*, included a foreword by Wilkinson. In particular, Wilkinson's *War and Policy* was lectured to, read and discussed by all students until at least the late 1920s. Wilkinson's clear writing style enabled the students to easily understand the connection between strategy and sea power and, since Wilkinson was

---

[58] Morison, *Admiral Sims and the Modern American Navy*, p. 474.
[59] Hattendorf, *Sailors and Scholars*, p. 134.
[60] NWC Archives, RG 4 Publications, Box 1, Folder 9, Opening Address, 'The Practical Naval Officer' W.S. Sims, 2 December 1919, p. 32; later published W.S. Sims, 'The Practical Naval Officer', U.S. Naval Institute *Proceedings*, vol. 47, no. 4 (April 1921), pp. 525–6; and reprinted in Armstrong (ed.), *21st Century Sims*, pp. 75–100.
[61] Sims to Wilkinson, 2 October 1922, Wilkinson Papers, 13/43/10.
[62] Sims to Wilkinson, 18 March 1922, Wilkinson Papers, 13/43/7.
[63] NWC Archives, RG 4 Publications, Box 2, Folder 13, 'U.S. Naval War College Course outline', 8 September 1921, p. 5; See Hattendorf, *Sailors and Scholars*, pp. 119–22 and 125–34 on the reorganised College curriculum.

The Teaching of Strategy and Sea Power, 1909–1927

the leading Anglo-American transmitter of Clausewitz, his works helped them attain a clear appreciation of the relationship between war and policy.[64]

In addition to Sims, several prominent staff members singled out Wilkinson's intellectual sophistication. The head of the strategy department, Captain Reginald R. Belknap, told students in his 1922 lecture, 'The Study of Strategy':

> in reading on strategy, some one or more works should be read with deliberation, in order to get the authors' true meaning ... Though several books may be read rapidly in order to get a wide range of views on some particular topic, the understanding of principles which is derivable from the works of Murray, Mahan, Corbett, Von der Goltz, Wilkinson, Clausewitz, Foch, can be realised only by painstaking study.[65]

Belknap's lecture on strategy outlined the 'requisites for the broad study of the art of war'. Quoting Wilkinson, Belknap wrote that the purpose of the students' study at the Naval War College was to think through 'all the problems of war, so that the principle[s] of strategy ... become incorporate[d] with the fibre of [their] mind[s]'.[66] In another lecture, Belknap reminded students citing Wilkinson that 'The policy of a nation must of course bear some relation to its strength, which depends upon its resources and the excellence of its administration.'[67]

Students were induced to read Wilkinson in order to understand policy in its relation to war, and they repeatedly quoted his most Clausewitzian statements: 'War is a means to an end and nothing more; it is a phase of policy in action ... the political purpose dominates everything.'[68] This impact was supported further in 1923 when Commander Harold R. Stark prepared and had distributed to his fellow students an edited volume of extracts from the forty-seven major books, including those by Clausewitz, Corbett, Darrieus, Daveluy and Wilkinson, on the reading courses for policy, command, strategy and tactics. From *War and Policy* Stark extracted Wilkinson's principal ideas derived from the history of war, including an important reminder for students writing their policy theses:

> The separation of military from political history ... is attended with grave disadvantages. It divorces in thought things which in reality and by nature go together. War is political action. It arises from political conditions, it ends in political conditions.[69]

---

[64] NWC Archives, RG 13, Student Theses, Box 7 in particular; S.L. Murray, *The Reality of War: An Introduction to Clausewitz with a Note by Spenser Wilkinson* (London, 1909); see C. Bassford, *Clausewitz in English: The Reception of Clausewitz in Britain and America 1815–1945* (Oxford, 1994) for Murray and Wilkinson on Clausewitz.

[65] NWC Archives, RG 4 Publications, Box 12, R.R. Belknap Lecture, 'The Study of Strategy', 9 August 1922, pp. 5–6; later published R.R. Belknap, 'The Study of Strategy', USNI *Proceedings*, vol. 49, no. 1 (January 1923).

[66] Ibid., pp. 1, 6–8.

[67] NWC Archives, RG 4 Publications, Box 2, R.R. Belknap Lecture, 'The Strategy Department of the War College', p. 5.

[68] NWC Archives, RG 13 Student Theses, Box 4, W.T. Cluverius, 'Policy Thesis', 1921, p. 3.

[69] NWC Archives, RG 17 Staff Studies, Box 1, H.R. Stark, 'Extracts from Books Read in Connection with War College Reading Courses', 1923 in two volumes: see, Volume II: H–Z, pp. 174–9 for Wilkinson, quote on p. 174.

Stark later would demonstrate this sophisticated understanding of national strategy as the Chief of Naval Operations from 1939 to 1942, as did his classmates, among them Chester W. Nimitz.

It is no coincidence that during Sims's presidency students regarded quoting Wilkinson as a thesis requirement. Yet significantly, this practice continued to a greater or lesser degree throughout the interwar period. Student theses regularly included a reference to Wilkinson. In his 1924 policy thesis, Charles P. Snyder (later President of the Naval War College, 1937–39) made more references to Wilkinson than any other source, quoting him at length ten times in a twenty-page paper.[70] Snyder worried that few American politicians had given any thought to the connection between American national interests and national strategy, 'the appreciation of which', as Wilkinson had noted, 'is the fundamental condition of success in the competition between states'.[71] Snyder wrote:

> To paraphrase Wilkinson, the business of the Government is therefore in the first place so to direct American action that the greater part of mankind may be satisfied with the way the United States plays its part, and in the mean time maintain a Navy strong enough to defeat any other.[72]

Student assessments of American policy largely mirrored Wilkinson's criticism of earlier British policy.

Rear Admiral William V. Pratt's term as President of the Naval War College 'emphasized and expanded upon the vision which Sims had charted in 1919'.[73] Sims's influence 'can be directly traced to the 1930s through Harris Lanning' and his three-year term as president from 1930 to 1933.[74] Wilkinson continued to be referenced throughout the 1930s. In 1932, Commander Ernest G. Small's lecture on thesis writing asked students to 'recall the title of a book "War and Policy" by Spenser Wilkinson'. 'This author implies in the very title that policy is a factor in war,' Small emphasised.[75] Rear Admiral John Halligan and Captain Ernest J. King are two notable examples of the numerous students who referenced Wilkinson's works during this period.[76] Students were still reading Wilkinson in 1935[77] and staff presentations included his works as late as 1938. As Professor John Hattendorf

---

[70] NWC Archives, RG 13 Student Theses, Box 7, C.P. Snyder, 'Policy Thesis', 1924, pp. 2–5, 8–9, 12–13, 18.
[71] Ibid., p. 12.
[72] Ibid., p. 18.
[73] Hattendorf, *Sailors and Scholars*, p. 133.
[74] Ibid., p. 143.
[75] NWC Archives, RG 14 Faculty and Staff Presentations, Box 4, Ernest G. Small Lecture, 'How to Write a Thesis: With Particular Reference to One Entitled "The Influence of the National Policy on the Strategy of a War"', 5 July 1932, p. 3.
[76] NWC Archives, RG 13 Student Theses, Box 9, J. Halligan, 'The Inter-Relation in War of National Policy, Strategy, Tactics and Command', 1931, pp. 3, 9–10, 12–13, 22 and E.J. King, 'The Influence of the National Policy on the Strategy of a War', 1932, p. 35.
[77] NWC Archives, RG 13 Student Theses, Box 10, M.S. Bennion, 'The Relationship Between the National Policy and Strategy of Great Britain', 1935.

noted, 'By this time the college had also come to follow a clear philosophy of the role of armed forces in the affairs of the state,' which was reflected in Captain C.W. Magruder's 1938 lecture 'Policy and Warfare', when he told students that:

> As for drifting into war, <u>Wilkinson</u> in WAR AND POLICY said: From a purpose which is plain and simple you may get a well-conducted war; from a purpose about which you are not clear you never can ... The starting-point of a good war is, therefore, a purpose necessary to your State and clearly understood by your statesmen.[78]

Conclusion

The historiography of the Naval War College, the famous 'War Plan Orange' and the War in the Pacific, places a heavy intellectual emphasis on Luce, Mahan, Clausewitz and Moltke, quite rightly, but Wilkinson had a strong intellectual influence on the Naval War College between 1919 and 1927, and, moreover, the interwar period as a whole.

By consulting Wilkinson, Sims's reforms turned the Naval War College into an effective organisation for teaching strategy and sea power and preparing students for future staff work.[79] By carefully reading Wilkinson, students developed a good understanding of the relation between sea power, strategy and policy. By studying Wilkinson as a transmitter of Clausewitz, students became familiar with the main principles of his theory of war and gained a broader conception of strategy, which became common in this period.

The connection between Sims and Wilkinson should be central in our understanding of the early development of modern professional military and civilian university education on war and strategy. The Naval War College led the study of grand strategy and national policy in the United States. These ideas were present in Wilkinson's writings and teaching methods, which resembled strategic studies. Although the Oxford 'school of war' was stillborn in the 1920s, through the consistent analysis of Wilkinson's arguments and methods in policy theses and staff lectures, the Naval War College came to approach the study of war, policy and strategy from a similar strategic studies perspective. The Naval War College graduates gained a sophisticated understanding of the interrelationship of policy and strategy. As Hattendorf notes, 'When the United States entered World War Two, every flag officer qualified to command at sea, but one, was a graduate of the Naval War College, and had become accustomed to think in terms it had established.'[80]

---

[78] Hattendorf, *Sailors and Scholars*, p. 154; NWC Archives, RG 14 Faculty and Staff Presentations, C.W. Magruder Lecture, 'Policy and Warfare', 8 December 1938, p. 16.
[79] Hattendorf, *Sailors and Scholars*, pp. 153–5.
[80] Ibid., p. 161.

19

Naval Intellectualism and the Imperial Japanese Navy

KEIZO KITAGAWA

In 1943, Admiral Koshiro Oikawa,[1] President of the Japanese Naval War College, told Professor Iwao Koyama of Kyoto University gravely that 'Now Japan is at war with the maritime nations, the United States and the United Kingdom. There were many reasons to enter the war, but I believe one of the main reasons was that in educating officers of the Imperial Navy and Army, we put too much emphasis on the techniques and technologies of battle.'[2]

Oikawa admits the failure of higher education in the Japanese Navy, which focused on battle rather than on war. The education was based on memorisation rather than on creativity and originality, and tended to suppress flexible thinking. But it is not fair to judge the officers of the Showa era (1925–89) in isolation; we have to consider how the Japanese Navy had evolved since the days of its creation in the 1860s. The failure of naval higher education was not simply an institutional or educational problem, but sprang from the lack of an 'intellectual attitude'. The purpose of this chapter is to explore the root causes of this failure, from the foundation of the Imperial Japanese Navy, up to 1905 when it triumphed over the Russian Navy.

In the same period, the US Navy was also in the process of modernisation. Its higher education system was shaped by Commodore Stephen B. Luce, who 'taught the Navy to think, to think about the Navy as a whole'.[3] That is, he defined a system of naval professional thinking, and a method of teaching it. In this chapter, this intellectual system is referred to as 'Naval Intellectualism'. Among Luce's many achievements, the establishment of the US Naval War College in Newport, Rhode Island to teach the art and science of war, was the key to a revolution in military higher education.

This chapter's key term is therefore 'naval intellectualism'. To understand this concept, I first examine the evolution of the US Navy's intellectual posture in the late nineteenth century, which guided the rise of the US Navy in the twentieth century. Having defined 'naval intellectualism', I then examine how, or whether,

---

[1] In Japan, surnames come first: this chapter uses Western style, forenames first.
[2] Yuzuru Sanematsu, *Kaigun wo kiru* (Tokyo, 1982), p. 13.
[3] B.A. Fiske, 'Stephen B. Luce, An Appreciation', *Proceedings of the US Naval Institute*, xliii, no. 9 (September 1917), pp. 1935–40.

the Imperial Japanese Navy produced an intellectual leader like Luce, and whether it generated and transmitted a comparable intellectual approach. In other words, I propose that the differences between the US Navy, the Japanese Navy and other modern navies are explained by their intellectual approaches.

The US Navy and the Challenge of Luce

In the post-Civil War era the US as a nation looked inward rather than overseas. The US Navy had about 700 warships during the Civil War, but declined to only 48 in 1880. Society was not favourable to the military, and the navy was isolated from politics and society, both intellectually and physically.[4] Accordingly, morale and career prospects in the navy were at rock bottom. Unlike Britain, the US did not yet possess extensive foreign colonies, so the role of the navy was limited to coastal defence and commerce raiding.[5] This did not begin to change until in 1883 Congress authorised the construction of the 'ABCD' ships, the first of the 'New Navy'.

In these unrewarding years, one officer was working on the intellectual development of the US Navy. His name was Stephen B. Luce, and he has been described by Professor Hattendorf as the 'intellectual leader of the New Navy'.[6] Luce entered the US Navy in 1841 at the age of fourteen. After sea training, he studied from 1848 to 1849 at the US Naval Academy, established in Annapolis in 1845. Luce lived in a unique period of history in that he was trained both traditionally as a midshipman at sea, and through systematic shore education, both in sail and in steam. By the 1870s he was experienced at sea and on shore, familiar with networks inside and outside the navy, especially in Congress. Luce retired in 1889 and, until his death in 1917, he was a constant contributor to many professional journals, writing textbooks and systematising US naval and maritime education.

Led by Luce, a band of reforming officers undertook the transformation of the US Navy. They had two objectives. First, to develop the navy into a true profession by making the naval officer the practitioner of a purely naval art, not merely an application of some civilian art or science. Second, to ensure for the officer a place in public esteem and a voice in the conduct of national affairs.[7] Among their achievements, the establishment of the US Naval War College (USNWC) at Newport in 1884 had undoubtedly the most influence on the history of the US Navy and other navies. They had to fight both technicism and amateurism to show why naval officers needed to understand strategy and international relations.

---

[4] S.P. Huntington, *Soldier and State* (Cambridge, 1957), p. 127.
[5] Eiichi Aoki, *Sea Power no Sekaishi 2* (Tokyo, 1983), p. 283.
[6] J.B. Hattendorf, 'Stephen B. Luce: Intellectual Leader of The New Navy', in James C. Bradford (ed.), *Quarterdeck to Bridge: The Two Centuries of American Naval Leaders* (Annapolis, 1997), pp. 201–18.
[7] R. Spector, *Professors of War: The Naval War College and the Development of the Naval Profession* (Honolulu, 2005, reprinted from 1977 version), p. 11.

Before the USNWC, all similar military higher education institutions provided technical education, rather than educating the future staff officers and leaders.

Luce especially emphasised the use of history to derive general principles. In order to solve the many problems of the US Navy, he took the following paths. Firstly, he laid stress on a broad education especially in the liberal arts. He relied on the pragmatic thinking which flourished in nineteenth-century America. He borrowed from Helmuth von Moltke his General Staff system, in particular the methodology of the 'applicatory system'. This had three parts: the estimate of the situation, the writing of orders, and the evaluation of the plan through staff rides and map problems. Luce utilised all these three aspects in creating the curriculum of the US Naval War College. In short, Luce assumed that the most profound qualification of the military professional was intellectual. Moreover, Luce was a staunch believer in the existence of principles of warfare.[8] Luce's intellectual attitude was geared to thinking and problem-solving methodology, rather than to memorising the answers to problems.

Luce was important, but for most readers Alfred T. Mahan will be better known, and his book *The Influence of Sea Power upon History, 1660–1783*, published in 1890. But it was Luce who encouraged Mahan and identified him as a writer rather than a seagoing naval officer. Luce was Mahan's mentor; without him Mahan might have made no great mark on history. Mahan's research method was based on Luce's philosophy of exploring the principles of warfare.

The reformers' efforts led to the creation not only of the US Naval War College, but also of other institutions. The first was the US Naval Institute (USNI), created by a group of reform-minded officers gathered at Annapolis in 1873 as a forum for the exchange of ideas among its members. What is valuable about it to this day is its private organisation, with membership open to anybody interested in the naval service. In order to nourish intellectualism the USNI started its journal *Proceedings* in 1874, and later established the Naval Institute Press for professional publications. One characteristic of the *Proceedings* was to encourage young members to write articles, to which it awarded prizes.

A second important institution was the Office of Naval Intelligence (ONI). The ONI was the first military intelligence organisation in the US, created in 1882, two years before the USNWC. Luce supported the ONI as a link between the USNWC and the navy, and as the key enabler of naval organisational reform.[9] Both the USNWC and the ONI were recognised as important to the success of the Spanish–American War in 1898. The ONI's 'estimate of the situation' derived from the 'applicatory system' taught by the USNWC.

From these intellectual habits of the late nineteenth-century US Navy, 'naval intellectualism' can be defined by three characteristics:

---

[8] J.I. Alger, *The Quest of Victory* (Westport, 1982), p. 89.
[9] J.M. Dorwart, *The Office of the Naval Intelligence: The Birth of America's First Intelligence Agency 1865–1918* (Annapolis, 1979), p. 23.

1. Putting intellectual qualifications as the most important for the military profession.
2. Stressing problem-solving methodology and research and development, with a commitment to learning the art and science of war.
3. A positive interaction with academic research outside the navy, presenting naval thinking and accepting criticism.

The Dawn of the Imperial Japanese Navy and the Birth of Professionalism
Here I consider whether the Imperial Japanese Navy (IJN) created a similar attitude of 'naval intellectualism'. The period known in Japanese history as *Sakoku*, with the country closed to foreigners except the Chinese and the Dutch, lasted from the early seventeenth century until 1854, when Commodore Matthew C. Perry of the US Navy's East India Squadron signed the Treaty of Kanagawa, which opened official relations with Japan. The Tokugawa Shogunate swiftly established the Nagasaki Naval School (*Nagasaki Kaigun Denshu Sho*) in 1855, and it was taken over by the new Japanese government upon the Meiji Restoration in 1868. The government established the army and the navy in the same year. The school was renamed the Naval Training School (*Kaigun Soren Jo*) in 1869, then the Imperial Japanese Naval Academy (*Kaigun Heigakko*) in 1876.

In the 1870s when Japan entered the modern naval world the era of steam and steel had already begun, but was still in its early days. This gave the Imperial Japanese Navy some materiel advantages. Firstly, thanks to the *Sakoku* policy, Japan did not have much of a tradition of a sailing navy and adopted the screw propeller from the beginning. At the same time it adopted steel hulls and turret-mounted guns. Thus the Japanese Navy was able to introduce the most advanced technology of the time. Lacking sufficient industrial capabilities, the IJN relied mainly on British-built warships until the early 1900s, including the well-known IJNS *Mikasa*, flagship of Admiral Heihachiro Togo at the Battle of the Sea of Japan (Tsushima) on 27 May 1905.

Until the 1880s, the IJN's main means of acquiring foreign professional expertise were the *oyatoi gaikokujin* (contracted foreign advisors), and Japanese officers sent to study overseas. The Japanese Navy employed 182 foreign advisors over the Meiji era (1868–1912). Among them were 130 British, 16 US, 12 French, 6 Dutch, 2 Swiss and 1 Russian. Britain exceeded all other counties because the War Ministry decided in 1870 that the Japanese Navy would follow the model of the Royal Navy. The first British Naval Mission, led by Captain Edward Horsey, Royal Marine Artillery, taught gunnery. The second mission in 1873 was headed by Commander Archibald Douglas. Douglas is still well remembered among Japanese naval officers for teaching the Royal Navy's traditions of order and discipline. Also, from 1869 to 1907, the Japanese Navy sent 150 students, mainly to Britain, to study subjects ranging from navigation and engineering to music.

From its foundation, the Japanese Navy emphasised education, especially for officers. In education like technology it took advantage of being a late-comer. Shore-based modern education was installed from the beginning, with the comprehensive engineering training needed for a steam navy.[10] The Imperial Japanese Naval Academy, initially established in Tokyo, moved to Etajima ('the Dartmouth of Japan') in 1888. Tracing back to the Tokugawa government, Japan already started educating naval officers ashore in 1855, only ten years after the foundation of the US Naval Academy in Annapolis. From the early days naval education was provided in collaboration with civilian institutions. While the Naval Academy educated executive officers, in the later Naval Engineering Academy the engineering education was provided by civilian universities.[11]

The first superintendent of the Naval Academy, Admiral Sumiyoshi Kawamura, reported to the Meiji Emperor in 1871 that warships could be purchased with money, but if the Japanese Navy's first priority was educating capable naval officers, within fifteen years it could be world class.[12] Kawamura listed only a few essential requirements. Firstly, to operate a highly technical navy required highly skilled professionals recruited without any social class barrier. Secondly, Kawamura called for a wide range of skills from navigation to international law – that is, a comprehensive capability. Thirdly, Kawamura expected the education of the professional officers to take a long time. What is surprising is that the foundation of the Naval Academy in 1869 predates the creation of the Ministry of the Navy in 1872, when the War Ministry was divided.

Lieutenant Commander Gonnohyoe Yamamoto (later admiral and Prime Minister) wrote in 1880 that there is no social class in intellectualism; study and research are the most important qualifications of a naval officer.[13]

Challenges for the Modern Navy

The Japanese Navy started without experiencing the age of sail, but until the 1880s it faced problems in adapting to the modern world. There was a technological gap between the modern naval powers and its own capability. The fundamental technological foundations of Japan were still weak. The priorities for weapons systems were unclear. Debate continued between advocates of battleships and torpedo boats. Tactics were immature. Commander L.P. Willan from the Royal Navy was hired by the Navy Ministry from 1876 to 1882 to teach tactics. He wrote four basic tactical documents for the Japanese Navy which were translated into Japanese. By today's standards, they were merely tactical manoeuvres, but they gave the Japanese Navy hints for the development of its own tactical thinking.

However, the fundamental problem for the Japanese Navy was strategic ambiguity. Since the Meiji Restoration of 1868, *fukoku kyohei* ('rich nation, strong country') was the national objective, and Japanese foreign policy was to become involved in continental Asian affairs to exploit competition among the Western

---

[10] Aoki, *Sea Power no Sekaishi 2*, p. 342.
[11] Minoru Nomura, *Nihon Kaigun no Rekishi* (Tokyo, 2002), p. 16
[12] Eitaro Tamura, *Kawamura Sumiyoshi, Nakamura Kuranosuke Den* (Tokyo, 1944), p. 172.
[13] Kaigun Daijin Kanbo, *Yamamoto Gonnohoe to Kaigun* (Tokyo, 1927), p. 31.

powers. But how the navy was to be involved in continental diplomacy was unclear. An offensive naval strategy implied a battle fleet, but a defensive naval strategy would suggest more mobile small torpedo boats. Unfortunately, national strategy was not determined in the 1880s, so the Japanese Navy prepared for both.

It was in 1887 that the Japanese Navy started its own tactical experiment. In January that year, Sub-Lieutenant Hayao Shimamura (later Admiral of the Fleet) wrote *Kaigun Senjutsu Dai Ippan* ('Fundamentals of Naval Tactics'). On 1 June, naval exercise procedures were formalised and in the same summer, the Naval Staff and the Standing Fleet conducted thirty days of experiment at Shimizu. During this month, individual ships practised battle preparations and the fleet as a whole tried combat manoeuvres. But the underlying tactical thinking was still the work of a few individuals, since there was no higher academic institution for organisational development and research.

One development to note is the birth of a discussion forum for naval officers. It was called *Suiko-sha* (*suiko* means noblemen's friendship); it was a sort of gentlemen's club, established in 1876 for naval officers and higher Navy Ministry civilians. The purpose of the club was threefold: to foster friendship among members; to research naval art and science; and to organise sporting events. There were twenty members of the academic committee. Their mission was to 'cover all aspects of naval matters and publish the proceedings'.[14] The *Suiko-sha* held a monthly meeting for academic discussion. They published the journal *Suiko Zatsushi* (1887 to 1890), renamed *Suiko sha kiji* (1890–1945). The proceedings of the monthly meetings were printed in the journal, which covered strategy, gunnery, torpedoes, shipbuilding, seamanship, navigation, marine engineering, economics, law and medicine.

The forum guaranteed free discussion, but the journal was distributed only to its members. Most of the influential senior officers belonged to the *Suiko-sha* and read the journal. That meant that discussions in the forum easily influenced the policy of the Naval Staff, but there was limited interaction and criticism between the staff and the society.

In 1886, Navy Minister Judo Saigo directed the naval education committee for officers and midshipmen to modernise officer education in leadership and technology. Minister Saigo visited the United Kingdom and other modern naval countries on fact-finding tours. In 1887, he made a report to Prime Minister Hirofumi Ito, remarkable for proposing higher education for officers, and inviting foreign officers to provide it. Saigo stated that the progress of naval technology depended on the progress of academic achievement. Navy Vice-Minister Sukenori Kabayama also made a fact-finding tour to the UK and other countries immediately after Saigo's in 1887. Saigo's trip concentrated more on technology and industry, but Kabayama focused on personnel matters and education.

---

[14] Suiko kai, 'Suiko 100 nen gaishi (13) Suiko sha kisoku no hensen I', *Suiko*, no. 284 (March 1977), p. 14.

Kabayama was especially impressed by the US Naval War College in Newport, Rhode Island. In his report, names such as Mahan on naval history and strategy and Little on the war game were mentioned. Kabayama was particularly interested in the atmosphere of self-study, the well-stocked library and the academic freedom of the institution.[15]

In the late nineteenth century, there were two types of naval higher education institutions. One type, such as the Marine-Akademie of Germany established in 1873 and the Royal Naval College in Greenwich in 1873, provided technical education. Their main objective was to re-educate the officers of the sailing navy to teach the steam navy. The other type was an institution like the US Naval War College to teach the advanced 'art and science of war'.

Japan established a Naval War College in 1888 in Tokyo in order to teach advanced academic studies under the strong leadership of Navy Minister Saigo. The Japanese Army had already established a War College in 1883 to produce staff officers according to the Prussian General Staff system. The difference between the two services was obvious. The army had fought a civil war with the local enemies of the Meiji state in the 1870s, and understood the importance of capable commanders and staff officers. The navy, however, had made little logistical contribution to the battles. In the navy, a staff officer was considered a job anyone could do without special training.[16]

Navy Minister Saigo was the founder of the Naval War College, and the greatest contributor to it was Captain John Ingles of the Royal Navy. He was invited and lived in Japan between 1887 and 1893. As mentioned earlier, British naval higher education was then considered the best modern technical education. Accordingly, Ingles advised Saigo of the importance of mathematics and physics.[17] His advice was well taken, because in the 1880s the Japanese Navy's modern equipment came from foreign countries and understanding it was the first priority. In the early curriculum, the lack of tactics and strategy is obvious. Nevertheless, the officers educated by Ingles such as Tomosaburo Sato, Tetsutaro Sato, Keisuke Okada and others fought well in the Sino-Japanese War of 1894–95. It was after the war that intellectual reform took place in the Japanese Navy.

The Foundation of the Modern Navy: Intellectual Mechanism

The Sino-Japanese War ended in a decisive Japanese victory on 17 April 1895. It was the fruit of the Japanese Navy's modernisation effort throughout the 1870s and 1880s. The naval battles of this war were the first fought by all-steam ships armed with torpedoes. But problems arose during the war. There were four points to be improved. Experience now showed the technologies and force structure the navy needed to adopt. One of the lessons of the war was that torpedoes were only

---

[15] Yamamoto-haku dennki hensankai, *Hakushuaku Yamamoto-haku den Jou* (Tokyo, 1937), pp. 156–60.
[16] Toshio Yoshida, *Kaigun Sanbo* (Tokyo, 1992), p. 117.
[17] Hiroshi Shinohara, *Kaigun Sosetsushi* (Tokyo, 1986), p. 348.

effective at short range, especially against enemy ships in port. In the first night torpedo attack in history Japanese Navy torpedo boats sank four Chinese ships in Weihaiwei in February 1895. With the improvement of torpedo capability and tactics, the navy thought torpedo boats could be used in the open sea.[18] The navy chose major combatants to build up the fleet in the light of experience. After the war, the navy planned *Roku roku kantai* ('Six battleships, six cruisers') as the basis of the fleet completed in 1902. The development of indigenous technology did not keep up with the naval build-up against the emerging Russian threat. Japan still had to rely on foreign technology.

Secondly, the tactics had to be improved. The Sino-Japanese War was the first modern naval gunfire battle, with no use of the ram. The Japanese Navy won through the combination of firepower and manoeuvre. But for the manoeuvres, the Japanese Navy only used the simple single column. The fleet's ability to manoeuvre was still at a basic level, and it had to conduct extensive manoeuvre exercises before the war.

Thirdly, the direction of strategy needed to improve. Immediately after the war in 1895 six guiding principles were adopted. Japanese warships were to be superior in both offence and defence. The fleet was to be ready to encounter Russian fleets. The 'Six Six Fleet' was to be the basic unit, with support ships. Regional logistical bases were to be established. The Naval War College was to be expanded and the Naval Academy improved. Most importantly battleships became the centre of the expanded fleet, and Russia was determined as the adversary. With the selection of battleships as its main strength, the navy chose an offensive strategy and moved towards sea control.

Fourthly, the capabilities of the officers needed many improvements. For this reason the new policy stressed education, especially of senior officers. Junior officers could be produced in numbers in a short time, but senior officers and commanders cannot be improvised. It was for the Naval War College to respond with a plan of naval higher education.

To improve all four aspects, the Japanese Navy was fortunate to have Toshiatsu Sakamoto. He can be considered as the Luce of Japan. Sakamoto studied in France between 1884 and 1888, and had experience working in the Naval Staff and as an instructor at the Naval War College. Sakamoto made a trip to Europe in 1896 and then wrote a report on the reform of the Naval War College. Among naval historians around the world, Saneyuki Akiyama the tactician and Tetsutaro Sato the strategist are famous. But it was Sakamoto who selected them and encouraged them to write. When Sakamoto died in 1941 at the age of eighty-three, his student Admiral Kantaro Suzuki, who was the Prime Minister to end the war in 1945, said, 'Sakamoto nourished the naval spirit and educated the people through the education of the navy; we are indebted to him.'[19]

---

[18] Shigetato Yoshimatsu, 'Teikoku Kaigun Senjutsu kenkyu no soshi to sono hatten no keii', *Yushu*, xvii, no. 5 (May 1930), p. 36.
[19] Azan Ota, *Danshaku Sakamoto Toshiatsu Den* (Tokyo, 1942), p. 2.

Sakamoto and Reform

The Naval War College was closed during the Sino-Japanese War. The College did not fully contribute to the victory in terms of operations, because most of the tactics were evolved by individuals like Ingles and Shimamura, and by experiment in the fleet. So the role of Sakamoto was to move the organisation from individual knowledge to organisational knowledge. In Sakamoto's report, he recommended putting emphasis on history, naval operations and naval policy. Also he recommended basing education not on lectures, but on student initiative. Sakamoto's recommendation changed the Naval War College from an advanced technical institution into the brain of the Japanese Navy. The first graduates of the new system graduated in 1898. Sakamoto used a very similar method to the Applicatory System which made students think and plan, followed by actual manoeuvring exercises. Sakamoto taught the Japanese Navy to think in the same way as Luce did the US Navy.

How did Sakamoto reform the College? Shimamura became the leading instructor in tactics of the newly reformed College. He reflected his experience of the war to the classroom, and also involved the fleet in creating tactical problems for the students. Sakamoto gathered instructors not only from the navy but also from the army to teach strategy and tactics. The most notable instructor was Saneyuki Akiyama, staff officer to the Combined Fleet commanded by Admiral Heihachiro Togo, whose mastery of tactics led to the decisive victory over the Russian Baltic Fleet on 27 May 1905. Akiyama's ideas of naval battle were incubated in the College between 1903 and 1905. Akiyama tried to enrol in the US Naval War College in 1897, but he was not accepted because of the classified nature of the College's work in those days. But Akiyama was fortunate to observe the Spanish–American War. He learnt of the closure of the harbour from the US Navy, and applied the lesson to close Port Arthur during the Russo-Japanese War of 1904–5. In addition to bright Japanese officers, Sakamoto tried to invite instructors from overseas such as Mahan, but none was successful. The Japanese Navy now had to stand on its own feet intellectually.

Sakamoto tried to use the War College for the organisational reform of the navy, drawing his principle from the 1895 Directive. To be a coherent navy, Sakamoto taught the navy to be a learning organisation. Among many contributions, his War College developed the *Kaisen Youmu Rei* (Naval Warfare Order) promulgated in 1901. The *Kaisen Youmu Rei* included modern operational planning and execution procedures, an 'estimate of the situation' along with tactical procedures. Its origin was the graduating projects of the students back in 1898. It was initially a methodology rather than a set of principles, but it later turned into the bible of the navy and led the inflexibility of the Japanese Navy until 1945. Along with the *Kaisen Youmu Rei*, in 1902 the College issued the *Heigo Gaisetsu* (Dictionary of Terms) in order to standardise the definitions of terms. Now the Japanese Navy acquired official definitions of 'art and science of war', 'strategy', 'operation' and 'tactics'. Also the *Sensaku* (Battle Procedures) were first created in 1901 and revised in accordance with the *Kaisen Youmu Rei*. So the seeds of victory in the Sea of Japan were sowed in these documents and following war games and exercises.

Prior to the Russo-Japanese War, the Japanese Navy therefore had organic cooperation among the Navy Staff, the fleet and the educational institutions. The most effective organisation was the *Kaigun Kyouiku Honbu* (Navy Education Headquarters) created in 1900, which directly depended on the Navy Minister. All the authorities concerned with the education and training of the navy were the responsibility of this headquarters. The remarkable mechanism of the organisation was integrated all the educational commands and improved communications among the commands.

Conclusion

I would like to conclude with the 'Naval Intellectualism' of the Imperial Japanese Navy. As you have read, all the characteristics of the concept were present in the Japanese Navy. So what was their intellectual attitude?

1. They regarded the intellectual as the most important qualification for the military profession – but in practice 'intellectual' tended to be interpreted as technical.
2. They put emphasis on their problem-solving methodology and on research and development, using an organisational learning posture dedicated to the 'art and science of war'. But without a comprehensive philosophy and methodology, intellectual systems such as the applicatory system did not flourish. Consequently, individual wisdom was not easily converted into organisational wisdom. That would be one of the reasons why the *Kaisen Youmu Rei* became the bible of the organisation.
3. The practice of positive interaction with academic research outside the navy, including the acceptance of criticism, was very limited. Intellectual interactions among naval officers were very active, but the discussion stayed within the organisation, which stifled the criticism so important for intellectual advancement.

These limitations of the Japanese Navy were influenced by its lack of experience of a navy under sail, and the urgency it felt to become a modern navy to confront the threats around Japan. So the Japanese Navy adopted modern technology and tactical thought without fully understanding the background, that is, why. So how did these characteristics affect the twentieth-century Japanese Navy?

The Japanese Navy was a professional organisation which perfected the setting of goals. But without a solid intellectual methodology, the organisation never fully became a learning organisation and became extremely conservative. This shows the importance of both deductive and inductive ways of thinking. The Japanese Navy understood battle, but not war, and this led to its defeat in the Second World War.

20

History and Navies: Defining a Dialogue

JAMES GOLDRICK

The relationship of naval historians with the contemporary navy is a discussion we need to have. Arguably, it is part of a wider question as to the relationship which naval historians should have to *all* the services. Past conversations about the interactions between the military and historians have too often been conducted within a context that relates much more to the concerns of the army than the navy, and for that reason the dialogue has been limited and incomplete. Indeed, much of the paradigm of what is described as 'Professional Military Education' (PME) is that of a combat arm officer of the army. Naval historians may not always have been sufficiently active in making military (that is, land warfare) historians aware of the wider dimensions of the PME problem – although John Hattendorf's quiet voice has been one of the most effective in attempting to restore the balance. It is also true, however, that naval officers have not been particularly successful in making their voices heard within what passes for inter-service discourse on PME matters.

There is more to do. There is much within the PME debate that is relevant to the navy, but also much that is left out. Far too much of PME and the role of history within it is about the management and direction of conflict on land and the relationships between policy makers and military leaders, rather than the wider problems associated with the management and direction of organisations and of technology in peace as well as war. There is something here of C.P. Snow's 'Two Cultures' because it may be partly driven by an aversion, however unconscious, to the complexities of technology in favour of the emotional satisfactions of human relationships. But if you are going to understand navies, you have to cover both – and more.

There are other contemporary problems with the naval profession with which historians may be able to help. They relate not only to naval form, but naval function. In many ways, they are the same problems being faced by other complex organisations in the contemporary world, but the nature of navies and the difficulty, to use modern management terms, of assessing their outputs makes their challenges even greater.

Navies need help to understand their function, and the requirement for that assistance becomes all the more critical when, as in much of the last fifteen years, the strategic attention of many nations is diverted away from the maritime domain. Because navies are about so much more than the application of lethal force and because so much of what they are about is out of sight of both decision-makers and electorates (and sometimes out of sight of themselves), it is easy for them to become caught up with the short term, in both policy and operations, at the expense of their abiding functions. A recent example is the way that the Royal Navy allowed itself and its people to become excessively committed to the conflict in Afghanistan through a justifiable but misdirected desire not only to be 'in on the action', but to support the war effort as such. This may well have contributed significantly to the Royal Navy taking its eye off the national maritime security problem, which in turn contributed to some of the 'relevance deprivation' syndrome that has been apparent in the Royal Navy of the last decade – and to the policy vacuum which allowed such extraordinary decisions as the removal of the airborne maritime patrol capability from the British order of battle, as well as acceptance of a naval manpower establishment which is much too small for the job. Historians need to help the navy and, in this case, the air force as well, keep their eye on the whole.

Historians also need to do more to force navies and other contemporary organisations to get their record keeping in order. History begins now. The nature of modern information systems and decision-making has passed the point where construction of any kind of a coherent narrative of events, let alone analysis, is becoming practically impossible without determined, targeted and consistent effort. Historians need to be involved as early as possible, even if their initial focus is solely upon the identification and preservation of key material. In *The Rules of the Game*, Andrew Gordon made the point that the British flagship in the 1982 conflict in the Falklands processed over 170,000 signals in little more than ten weeks, 62,000 of which (one every 107 seconds) called for 'flag action'.[1] This was before the era of PowerPoint and, even more significant, of command and control being conducted in 'Chat Rooms'. The reality is that the archival record for the last fifteen years of military and naval activity does not exist in a form that is in any way logical, coherent or accessible. Historians need to be making their voices heard about this appalling deficiency.

It is not only in operations that historians have to be involved as early as possible. They also should be forging effective alliances with archivists and information managers in relation to decision-making on policy, force structure and a host of other matters. In this regard, naval historians also need to converse more with the engineers and technologists in naval service, as well as with the other 'back room' elements. When contemplating the failures or near-failures of complex acquisitions, for example, it is all too often clear that wheels have been reinvented or basic mistakes made which have been made before. The author asserted a decade ago to the Society for Military History's annual conference that, without these efforts, the overload of information and data was such that the military were in danger of losing their recent past and of losing any chance of achieving a coherent understanding of that past. This point has been passed – we

---

[1] A. Gordon, *The Rules of the Game: Jutland and British Naval Command* (Annapolis, MD, 1996), p. 584.

have to recover what can be recovered from the wreckage, and conversations and alliances with information managers about what is going on need to happen *now*.

Furthermore, the changing demography of navies is exacerbating the problem. Navies have always been inherently practical and 'experience based'. They tend to be suspicious of theory and of anything which cannot be related directly to the task at hand. This means that they are largely reliant upon having a sufficient number of wise, long-serving personnel to act as their corporate memory. Such personnel are becoming increasingly rare, as much later entries and much shorter periods of service for officers become more common. The walls surrounding the fortress of the recent past within which too many naval personnel have always been trapped are becoming even thicker and moving ever inward.

There are also problems of – or, rather, with – historians that can make it difficult for them to relate effectively with the naval service. The first may be a result of the system of education which culminates in the doctorate of philosophy. Given the very early specialisation inherent in the English education system, the effect may be most acute in this country. It is what can be described as a fixation on 'the single cause'. The tight focus of a thesis topic can develop a mindset which creates a tendency to impose a priority for a particular issue on the wider analysis without sufficient regard to the actual place of that issue within the naval whole – or, indeed, of whatever 'whole' is being considered. In reality, the greater the responsibilities and the experience of decision-makers, the greater their suspicion of such 'single causes' and those who propound them. Historians need to be very wary of this tendency and seek every opportunity to extend their own knowledge and understand the wider connections, social, political, financial and technological. In this context, Nicholas Rodger's insistence that his monumental work should be a *naval history of Britain* and not a *history of the British Navy* is absolutely the right approach.

It may seem odd to accuse historians, of all people, of having difficulties with chronology, but this is a problem of which the author has become increasingly aware after returning to study the 1914–15 period at sea. It is particularly apparent when examining technological change and its effects on strategy and operations. *Conscious* hindsight is not actually the problem. It is the *unconscious* hindsight that is implicit in much of what is written about the navies of the period, including the author's own early work. The problem, for the naval officer – or public servant involved in the management of the navy – is that this discredits much historical analysis when it is compared, consciously or otherwise, with their own experience of the uncertainties and confusions of aligning resources to both current and future capability. The reality is that 1914 was a foreign country from 1910 – and even from 1912. But, to change L.P. Hartley's aphorism, it is not just that they did things differently there at each time, but that they also had different things to deal with – and those different things had different relationships. This remains a reality for contemporary decision-makers. The year 2014 is different from 2012. On the other hand, historians can also help avoid what has been termed the 'parochialism of the present' which marks much contemporary decision-making. The past matters.

Avoiding the taint of unconscious hindsight and conveying complexity are all the more important because historical studies constitute the *only* source of insights we can hope are not in some way 'cooked'. Many of the world's armed forces are placing increasing emphasis on simulation and gaming, on scenarios and futures. The horrendous costs of real-world operations and training – particularly the impossibility of testing complex systems at high combat load – mean that this will only increase. It is absolutely vital work, but the pressures that always exist in any organisation mean that we can never completely trust the conclusions of what are inherently artificial products. Even when there has been no conscious effort to 'situate the appreciation' to achieve desired results, subconscious limitations inevitably confine the conclusions. This problem has been aired extensively in the United States in the context of experimentation. Thorough historical studies provide the best means to check that such future efforts are, if not on the right track, at least asking the right questions. Historians can help inoculate navies against the excesses of the social scientists, but they also need to protect them against the assumption that virtual realities are actual realities.

In their engagement with navies, historians also should focus on their own analysis and not on their disputes with other historians. Compelling, comprehensive and thorough arguments clearly made in their own right will stimulate naval audiences. *Ad hominem* 'rants' aimed at the demolition of another's thesis will not.

The word 'thorough' covers another point as well. Good naval history demands the very highest standards of historical research, but having high standards is more than about reading and archival work. It is very much about extending your own understanding in every way that you can. For example, if historians are going to write about naval operations, they need to go to sea, and if they are going to write about the development of naval capability they need to go to sea. This is not to suggest that they need to become qualified mariners or serve in the navy – the author has said elsewhere and asserts again that he has learned much more about navies from historians than from other naval officers. There are such things as imagination and insight and the best historians possess these qualities in high degree. Yet, imagination and insight need to be fed by sheer hard work, while they can be encouraged, indeed galvanised, by a touch with the real world. Few can manage to grasp the silver lining from the disaster of world conflict that saw Garrett Mattingly gain the experience of naval operations that illuminated his work on the Spanish Armada. But, just as military historians make every effort to walk the actual battlefields of which they write, so should naval historians seek opportunities to experience both the environment and the ships. In thinking about the First World War, for example, even a ferry ride across the North Sea or Baltic can do something to understand the difficulties of operating in those seas – and it is always worthwhile seeing if you can get up to the bridge for a couple of watches. Navies, it must be said, also should do a lot more to take historians to sea when they can.

Operational and capability historians need to work even harder at understanding the mechanics of naval operations and of naval support and development in the last century. This is not easy, but the much greater sophistication apparent in the recent treatment of the era of the Revolutionary and Napoleonic Wars at sea and ashore gives a good example of not only what can be achieved, but how it can be achieved. There needs to be some comprehension of the practicalities of movement, of position finding, of communications and of shooting and of everything that supported those activities. This can sound like 'train spotting', but it is not. The idea is to spend some time in the engine driver's cabin, not just on the railway station platform. For example, if you are going to write about naval operations in the era of coal, a day with one of the few remaining coal-powered vessels, now usually in museum or heritage fleet service, would well repay you. So would a visit to a coal mine. This is not a claim to automatic understanding deriving from naval or merchant service, however extensive. Unconscious assumptions of one's own expertise can lead one equally astray – the 'further' past is indeed a foreign country, even to a person who may have extensive practical experience of an intermediate period.

Finally, historians need to do history for its own sake. It is true that even historians must eat. A certain amount of work has to be done to pay the rent – anniversaries are always the cause of increased popular interest and thus of a livelier market for historical products – and such work is not invalid just because of its origin, as many of the products of the Nelson Bicentenary demonstrate. Similarly, there is value when historians are asked to examine particular issues. Navies need the benefit of such expertise and directed analysis. In Australia, for example, some excellent work was done for our army on the historical performance of tanks as close support for infantry – work that contributed significantly to important force structure decisions.

But historians should go where *they* want to go, not just where they think the navy wants them to go. A good example of such work that may end in helping contemporary decision-makers contemplate their own challenges in a different way is Jeremiah Dancy's analysis on the manning of the Royal Navy. There are so many parallels to the manning problems that were being faced more than two hundred years ago with those of 2014 that naval manpower planners and recruiters would be well repaid by reading his work. It may even be that navies need to consider funding for naval historical research in the same way that scientific organisations manage theirs. A healthy science organisation, no matter how 'applied' its mission, will always retain a certain proportion of its resources for 'blue skies' research, however tenuous its connection with the concerns of the present day.

There may be something Clausewitzian in what the author is seeking in and from historians – the possession of a necessary 'genius' based on deep and wide understanding of the subject and a familiarity with complexity, with friction and, perhaps above all, with the realisation that what *can* go wrong, *will*. A realisation that generates that certain sympathy with the poor bastards doing the work at the time that marks the best histories and thus the best historians. After all, did not Thomas Carlyle suggest that 'genius' is the 'transcendent capacity of taking trouble'? It is the possession of a deep understanding of both the specific and the general and the ability to point to key issues without overemphasising

History and Navies: Defining a Dialogue

them which should distinguish the naval historian who seeks to interact with the contemporary naval service – and which will cause the naval service, however fitfully, to listen.

It can be done and this brings us back to the nature of the dialogue. We need to ensure that naval history, very much in the way that Corbett tried to use it, is part of the formal military professional educational curriculum. But historians also need to produce work that, while remaining intellectually credible, is aimed at wider audiences, including the tired officers who may want to read just one serious book during their holidays. Historians also need to press the navy to come to their conferences. Too many will be too busy, but some may come and what they learn may function as the mould spore in the Petrie dish. On two occasions the author has seen chiefs of his own navy – and neither was particularly historically minded – alter their programmes to extend their time after opening our biennial naval history conference in Australia because of the quality of the keynote speaker and his insights into complex problems. What is more, there was evidence in later months that some part of their thinking on contemporary problems had been influenced by that experience.

One other example, on the lines of Rudyard Kipling's short story 'Regulus' from *The Complete Stalky & Co* will suffice. When the author was responsible for Australia's maritime security operations, Border Protection Command experienced a period of conducting multiple arrests of illegal foreign fishing vessels. The result of this effort was that the number of incursions dropped away and the patrol boats were left to patrol up and down the boundary line two hundred nautical miles offshore. They started to get bored. When they complained about this, the command's naval operations officer decided to respond. He had studied history with the University of New South Wales at the Australian Defence Force Academy. Without needing to consult his admiral (who obtained a copy by other means), the young commander sent an eloquent email rocket to the commanding officers with a direction to understand that they were conducting a blockade in reverse; that they should go and read some history about the realities of naval operations and their unremitting and lengthy nature; that it was their duty as COs to keep their crews focused and happy in such circumstances – and that they had better dry their eyes and get on with it. As 'Stalky's' schoolmaster declares, 'You see. It sticks. A little of it sticks among the barbarians.'

21
Teaching Navies Their History

GEOFFREY TILL

The last chapter by James Goldrick has made a number of important points. First, it stressed that it is wholly appropriate for this book to end on the subject of how best to bring their history home to navies because it is so important both for them and for the historians who produce it. It argued that history helps explain to navies what they are for and to some extent at least how they should set about their business. Second, navies need to be receptive to the past, to preserve and process the records (or what these days passes for records) of what they have done to build a bank of experience for the future. They need to nurture the declining number of long-serving professional practitioners who actually *had* that experience and are willing to talk about it if they only had the encouragement to do so, and the appropriate outlets (neither of which, as an aside, I believe they currently do).

Naval historians can help in all this of course, but it is good to be reminded of some of the things that historians must do in order to perform that function effectively. They should think of things 'in the round' – to pay due regard to context and to avoid narrow fixations on mono-causal explanations. They need to understand the technological and logistical realities, what it is actually like to *be* at sea. Hence the particular value of ex-sailors (like James Goldrick himself, and indeed John Hattendorf) who are also historians. They also need to avoid unconscious hindsight and to sympathise with their subjects who clearly could not enjoy its advantages.

The chapter ended with the encouraging conclusion that all this can be done and that properly encouraged, proper history can 'stick' amongst the barbarians. This argument could go further. My own experience at the Royal Naval Colleges of Dartmouth and Greenwich and the Joint Services Command and Staff College at Shrivenham is that the 'barbarians' actually quite often *like* being 'stuck' with naval history, provided it is 'what it says on the tin' – namely real, honest objective analysis of the naval past, not a threadbare academic covering for proselytising. We historians are pushing on an open door, or should be. The long and generally depressing story of the Royal Navy's neglect and/or misuse of its own really rather spectacular history unfortunately makes this caveat necessary.[1]

---

[1] For an excellent summary of this, see H. Dickinson, 'Teaching Naval History', in Peter Hore (ed.), *Dreadnought to Daring: 100 Years of Comment, Controversy and Debate in The Naval Review* (Barnsley, 2012), pp. 284–98.

This brief chapter will be restricted to the addition of a few supporting points from my experience in British service education, points which are, I should hasten to say, in no way to be construed as official policy. First I would like to return to the point that navies need to understand their function. This isn't easy, these days. The potential tasks of navies have expanded and grown more complex (and, in parentheses, even more important as well – as the burgeoning navies of the Asia-Pacific region so amply demonstrate). It is no longer 'just' a question of properly understanding the war-fighting and deterrent war-prevention roles analysed by the likes of Mahan and Corbett at the beginnings of the last century, as they are affected by the international, technological and social realities of this one. That is difficult enough.

What is worse, is that to these have been added a whole series of non-traditional, 'post-modern' (there's a real labelling difficulty here!) tasks associated with Maritime Security (with capital letters) – dealing with drug runners, trafficking in illegal migrants, international terrorism, humanitarian action, disaster relief, environmental protection, search and rescue, capacity-building, security sector reform – and so it goes on and on. In many cases, arguably, early and effective engagement in these so-called 'Phase 0' activities will head off the need to exercise traditional war-fighting skills later on.[2] But preparing for what the UK military currently calls 'contingency' is a complicated business.[3]

One problem in the pursuit of guidance in making such difficult decisions about relative operational priorities is that of having to 'see through a glass darkly', as St Paul put it. It is uniformly and intrinsically difficult for foreign ministries, treasuries or defence and naval staffs to predict the future or to gauge its requirements. This is well exemplified by the problems that all navies face these days in getting their 'kit' because both the lead times normally required to produce sophisticated naval weapons, sensors and platforms and their probable service life are likely to be very long. Rear Admiral Thomas Rowden US Navy dramatically illustrated the point in early 2014 by pointing out that most ships of the US Fleet of 2034 are either already at sea or in advanced design stages.[4] This, together with rising costs and reducing budgets makes the acquisition of naval materiel intrinsically difficult.

One set of victims of the procurement process, taking a leaf out of Jane Austen's book, recently remarked: 'It is a truth universally acknowledged, that defence equipment acquisition is one of the most challenging of human activities ... a uniquely demanding bureaucratic morass littered with military, technological, economic and political pitfalls.'[5] Future-oriented procurement strategies tend to suffer badly from the unpredictability of the future economic, budgetary and

---

[2] US Army, 'Army Support to Security Cooperation' FM3–22, Jan. 2013, pp. 3–1.
[3] For a US view on this, see US *Naval War College Review*, Summer 2012.
[4] R. Adm. T. Rowden, 'Building the Surface Fleet of Tomorrow', *Proceedings of the USNI*, Jan. 2014.
[5] K. Hambleton, I. Holder and D. Kirkpatrick, 'Ten Chronic Challenges in UK Defence Acquisition', *Defence Studies*, xiii, no. 3 (2013), pp. 361–71.

strategic environment. All too frequently, this 'development risk' produces cycles of boom-and-bust which make sustained planning over, say, a thirty-year period, almost impossible for manufacturers and their customers. Typically, this will result in constant delays, cost increases and iterative tinkering with the original specification – and eventually in the failure or chronic delay of the programme in ways which means that the navy tends to acquire new materiel in a piecemeal, opportunistic way rather than as part of an overall strategic plan and in a manner which may undermine its capacity to perform its present roles, let alone its future ones. No navy has shown itself immune to such pressures and constraints; all navies need to be encouraged to think about how best to get round, if not to overcome, such difficulties.

Another problem is that to some extent, at least, the requirements of these possible 'contingency tasks' conflict with those of the more familiar war-fighting ones. The cost of one Type 45 Destroyer for example could generate any number of offshore patrol vessels. The more people train for things like the detection and apprehension of drug runners, the less they can train for anti-submarine operations. Given that resources are finite, choices have to be made.

Nor do Mahan and Corbett seem to have much guidance to offer on such matters. Worse still, all of these requirements are constantly changing; a force at sea might well find itself having to respond across the whole spectrum of challenges at the same time, especially as events take over to confound initial expectations about the nature of the mission. But for the moment, at least, British defence planners can be reasonably certain of just two things. First, the continuing value of the naval contribution to a basically expeditionary strategy. Second, the particular value of the naval flexibility that allows navies to cover the full spectrum of conflict – delivering everything from bombs to babies.

This is clearly an ambiguous, confusing and frankly sometimes demoralising situation. But can naval history help? If history is basically processed experience, the first issue to consider is whether, from the naval point of view, it has been *properly* processed, and this leads to a few more preliminary general and probably obvious observations about the 'processing' process itself which need to be made. First, although history does not repeat itself – it rhymes. As Michael Howard reminded us back in 1961, there are patterns: 'wars still resemble each other more than they resemble any other human activity'.[6] Naval students, it would seem, should know those patterns, but in their search for what the Russians call the 'norms' of military experience, they need to be helped to spot the *differences* as well as the similarities between their situation and the processed past.

Second, as John Hattendorf has reminded us,[7] historians need to recognise that their subject doesn't end in 1945, or with the close of the Cold War (if it has!). History is yesterday as well. This poses evidential problems of course. Analysis

---

[6] M. Howard, 'The Use and Abuse of Military History', *Journal of the RUSI*, cvii (February 1962), pp. 4–8.

[7] J.B. Hattendorf, *Talking About Naval History: A Collection of Essays* (Newport, RI, 2011), pp. 137–8, 151–2.

has therefore to be preceded by the availability of primary material. In any case, much of what in the past would have produced survivable paper copies (or much less survivable photostats) now only appears as transitory emails, chat in chat rooms and so on. Since 'recovering the unrecorded past'[8] is at least as important as it was, tomorrow's historians and their naval students will need their twenty-first-century skills as well as the more traditional ones employed by yesterday's historians.[9]

Third, naval history should remind students of the importance of *context* and so it should be designed to encourage a wider view of the impact of the international, technological, social, financial background to their operations. 'Was the Gallipoli campaign lost on the beaches of the peninsula or around the conference table in London?' is the sort of question we should be getting them to think about if they are to understand not only the purpose, planning and conduct of operations but the management of defence more widely. As an aside, it is hard to think of an approach better designed to encourage reflection about the three levels of war – tactical, operational and strategic – and the manner in which they interact. Encouraging students to track the consequences of the strategic decision-making process in London all the way down to the deficiencies in preparation on the landing beaches (such as the lack of sufficient medical facilities, water supply and so forth) and then to follow the tactical consequences back up through the hierarchy of decision to those ultimately responsible can hardly fail to help develop a more rounded understanding of military operations.

Assuming that past experience *is* properly processed in this way, we return to the question of how producing and teaching 'good' naval history might help. The answer to this reflects the existence of the two different sides of naval history, namely, firstly as a quarry of potentially relevant material and ideas and, secondly, as an intellectual process.

The Power of Example from the Processed Past

First then, naval history is a source of innumerable examples of the way things have been done in the past. For all the historian's reluctance to think of the 'lessons' of history, or even their 'norms', the past is a source of previous experience which might well help present practitioners in comparable but not identical situations better to understand their problems and to think through what they should do to solve them.[10] Looking at something like the sinking of the *Prince of Wales* and *Repulse* in December 1941, for example, teaches us all sorts of things about the need for inter-service cooperation, sustainable balances between resources and commitments, not underestimating your adversary – and so on. For all its

---

[8] Lord Acton, *Lectures on Modern History* (London, 1930), p. 349.
[9] G. Hughes, 'Iranophobia: The Dangers of Forgetting Operation Telic', *Journal of the RUSI*, clvii, no. 6 (December 2012), pp. 54–60.
[10] M. Howard, *The Lessons of History* (Oxford, 1991), ch. 1.

dangers, not least the evident danger of 'myth-making',[11] there is much to be said for the simple notion of seeing the past as providing previous examples of the problems of the present and the future.

The point can perhaps be best exemplified by reverting to the problems of naval procurement already discussed. While the past is another country, today's planners in the defence procurement field are facing problems and issues that are not that dissimilar from those faced by their predecessors. Those responsible for the design and procurement of today's *Queen Elizabeth*-class aircraft carriers can hardly fail to have been aware of the demoralising experience of their predecessors in the 1960s. This second time around, at the broadest level, the need to be sufficiently clear about the projected roles of the ship, to keep unavoidable inter-service competition down to manageable limits and not to get too far away from what would seem to be financially viable in the circumstances of the time all seem to have been hoisted in.[12] The difficulty of their task clearly provides an incentive for 'growing the smart customer' and it is hard to avoid the conclusion that study of the way in which such difficulties were handled in the past will provide at least some guidance for the present and the future.

Another area in which history as processed experience – a source of example – can be argued to have something to offer is in the area of leadership. Leadership of course varies enormously in its character and its function. On the face of it, the kind of leadership required to command in battle is not necessarily the same as that required to lead a design team in a submarine-acquisition project or to run a shore establishment. But is that true? Again looking at past examples of these kinds of leadership should at the very least encourage discussion and increase understanding of this otherwise very slippery concept.[13]

The list of areas like this in which naval history as processed experience can provide helpful examples could of course go on almost indefinitely, but there's another aspect to history as a quarry of explanatory material as well.

History as the Background to Now
Secondly, the past is prologue – it helps to explain how we have got to where we are today, and therefore to understand the present rather better and from that to design sensible policies for the future.[14] Take, for example, the modern Western concern for maintaining the freedom of navigation for warships. Naval activity is, and always has been, framed by contemporary interpretations of the law; understanding the background to those changing interpretations is an essential part

---

[11] Howard, 'The Use and Abuse of Military History'.
[12] No doubt, once the records have been made available future historians will be engaging in exercises in detailed contrast and comparisons between these two case studies!
[13] C. Steele, 'Don't Give up the Ship: The Continuing Need for Naval History in the Education of Young Leaders of Character (An American Perspective), *Naval Review* (February 2011), pp. 21–5.
[14] Hattendorf, *Talking About Naval History*, p. 272.

of the professional sailor's intellectual kit-bag, or at least should be, if they are to hold their own in the expressions of differences of opinion at sea, and to help define operational priorities.

At the moment, the US and other Western navies are trying to defend the basic notion of the freedom of navigation against a continentalist tide that is seeking, in effect, to 'territorialise' the sea by insidiously extending their jurisdiction more and more over what was once regarded as the high seas. This accounts for the very dangerous near collision of the USS *Cowpens* and a Chinese destroyer in the South China Sea in December 2013. The defence of the freedom of navigation, most particularly of warships, requires us really to understand the issues, what's at stake in other words, and how the world has got into this situation. Knowing what the UN Convention on the Law of the Sea (UNCLOS) says for example about the rights of warships in other people's Exclusive Economic Zones is not enough, because the wording of the Convention (being a political bargain) has enough ambiguity in it to allow (just about, and at a stretch) different interpretations and there are strong reasons why some countries should seek to exploit, or even ignore, vague or unhelpful provisions of UNCLOS altogether. International law, after all, is nothing more than political agreements that apply to a certain time and place – and is susceptible to change through subsequent state practice. As one of its leading experts has remarked:

> The history of the law of the sea has been dominated by a central and persistent theme – the competition between the exercise of governmental authority over the sea and the idea of the freedom of the seas. The tension between these has waxed and waned through the centuries, and has reflected the political, strategic, and economic circumstances of each particular age.[15]

For this reason, simply 'knowing' and enforcing the law is not enough. What Western navies ought to be doing as well is not just pontificating about what the law says on the freedom of navigation for warships but explaining why upholding it is a good thing, in fact for everyone. This can't just be left to lawyers. Only naval history can show us exactly why this apparently arcane principle is important enough to risk lives for, and all concerned need to know it, not least those whose lives might in the present or future be in question because of it.

Naval History as an Intellectual Exercise
The second angle on the value of naval history for professional military education is not as a source of data, material and example, but more as an intellectual discipline that encourages the development of thinking analytical and very possibly behavioural skills, that should help make students 'smarter'. As a former Commandant at the Joint Services Command and Staff College (JSCSC) used

---

[15] D.P. O'Connell, quoted in J. Kraska, *Maritime Power and the Law of the Sea: Expeditionary Operations in World Politics* (Oxford, 2011), p. 1.

to say, the modern airman, soldier and sailor have to respond to perhaps unprecedented levels of strategic ambiguity. They have to improvise creatively like jazz musicians around a central theme, instantly responding to changes set by others. No more can they fall back on the laboriously choreographed musical scores set by the kind of constantly rehearsed operational plans that characterised, for example, the Cold War.[16] Hence the need for what is gruesomely described as the 'end-state' of a student at the JSCSC: 'to have developed a mind that is flexible and able to analyse and conceptualise in a military context in order to make timely and logical decisions in all types of subsequent appointments'.[17]

To cope with a complex and often bewildering future those students will need the capacity to *analyse* incomplete and ambiguous data. They need to be able to think through problems, and most importantly to keep thinking them through, long after their staff course, or indeed their latest operation, has ended. They need to be 'independent learners'. These are some of the so-called 'golden threads' that, as educators, we historians need to develop in students. First a *continuing* interest in the naval past and its developing relationship with the naval present and the naval future. Some at least of what's taught in one year's Staff Course must have a limited shelf-life because the world moves on. We have to encourage students to develop the independent interest and habits of thought, and of continuing enquiry, that animate the best historians. This helps produce that very necessary characteristic that some call 'insight'.[18]

Charles Darwin indeed reminds us it was not necessarily the strongest but the most adaptable that won the evolutionary race. Naval history should help develop an openness of mind to uncomfortable ideas that confound and upset the student's own emerging conclusions. This really amounts to an early acceptance of the notion that there is no final and complete answer to anything. To paraphrase Napoleon, we have to tie knots and carry on, progressing to what my own mentor, Bryan Ranft, used to call 'a higher level of ignorance'.

In this, naval history can help, or maybe it should help, to elevate thinking from the empirical to the conceptual – from the concerns of the tactical-technological nitty-gritty of yesterday's or today's battle to that wider, shaping context that links the levels of war and conflict. But let me be clear, both the empirical and the conceptual are necessary parts of the mix. We should not however allow the perpetual fascination with the drums and smoke of battle to obscure the more abstract realities that in many cases determine outcomes. Naval history, in short, can and should help us understand the critical business of strategy and policy-making.[19]

---

[16] Air Vice-Marshal B. Burridge, 'Post-Modern Military Education: Are We Meeting Challenge?' *Defence Studies*, i, no. 1 (Spring 2001).

[17] Unsurprisingly, this is closely in line with the definition of 'Understanding' to be found in the UK Joint Doctrine (JDP 04), p. 2–1.

[18] Spartacus, 'Command and Leadership: A Rational View', *British Army Review*, cvi (April 1994).

[19] L. Milevski, 'Revisiting J.C. Wylie's Dichotomy of Strategy: The Effects of Sequential and

This is a much more widely practised activity than often realised. For example, the design teams developing the Royal Navy's Type 26 Global Combat Ship or those responsible for shaping the navy's training programmes at its various schools adopt, process and help create strategic thinking, in a continuous iterative cycle of reflection and action. It is quite likely that in many cases they do not realise they are doing it! Internet bloggers and the young naval enthusiasts who come together to create online think tanks like the Center for International Maritime Security (CIMSEC), on the other hand, do so quite consciously, aiming to study the past as a guide to the future, and their influence undoubtedly will seep out in all directions.

For all that, unfortunately, a sizeable constituency of thought in the UK reacted to what they considered to be Britain's frankly embarrassing Strategic Defence and Security Review of 2010 with the fear that the country is no longer capable of 'doing' strategy, an impression apparently confirmed in their minds at least by the experience of the later stage of the second Iraq and Afghanistan wars. This concern was initially triggered by the outgoing Chief of the Defence Staff, Air Chief Marshal Sir Jock Stirrup's address to the Royal United Services Institute (RUSI) in December 2009, where he claimed that Britain had lost the 'habit' of making strategy:

> But one thing that's struck me in my present role, and that I think requires urgent action over the next year, is the degree to which we seem to have lost an institutionalised capacity for, and culture of, strategic thought. I'm not saying that we don't have people who can think strategically, or that we haven't evolved a proper strategic basis for our actions. But we've seized on ability where we've found it, and as a result our formulation of strategy has been much harder than should have been the case. We've been hunter/gatherers of strategic talent, rather than nurturers and husbandmen.[20]

It was followed up through a series of inquiries by the House of Commons Public Administration Select Committee ('who does national strategy' etc.) and highly critical articles from a large number of academics. Their concerns were reinforced by the uncertain consequences of Britain's engagement in the Iraq and Afghanistan wars. The suggestion was that the UK had not thought through what its involvement in these wars was supposed to achieve, nor its requirements, nor its likely consequences. While the urgency of the need to cut government expenditure and to require the Ministry of Defence to start filling in the 'black hole' in its finances offers some excuse for the failings of the Strategic Defence and Security Review (SDSR), this is less true of Britain's operational failings. These are hard to explain except in terms of the speed of events to which the UK feels it must respond (which allows insufficient time for consultation and strategic reflection)

Cumulative Patterns of Operations', *Journal of Strategic Studies*, xxxv, no. 2 (April 2012), pp. 223–42.

[20] Air Chief Marshal Sir Jock Stirrup, Chiefs of Staff lecture at the RUSI, 3 December 2009, at https://www.rusi.org/cdslectures.

and, perhaps, the lack of defence experience amongst the political class. Nor is the quality of the advice offered ministers by the military exempt from academic and insider criticism.[21]

Nor, sadly, is this inability to 'do strategy' all that uncommon. A good case can be made that it applied to both the Germans and especially the Japanese in the Second World War, who managed to combine tactical and operational brilliance with a strategic insouciance in a manner which now appears quite breathtaking.

So, once again, how can history help? Such help probably lies much less in the delivery of 'the facts', or answers and prescriptions for the future, than in identifying the questions about strategy that those conducting it, or those trying to understand it, should ask. A brilliant recent review of four very good books about the causes of the First World War (a subject one might think exhaustively studied for a century now) concluded that 'they did not even come close to agreeing … [and that] historical consensus on the causes of the First World War appears no closer than it was 50 or 75 years ago, nor does it appear that a shared view will ever be achieved … This means we must be both cautious and humble when generalising about war and peace and making policy recommendations based on our understanding of the conflict.'[22] Much the same, if on a less elevated plane, could still be said about interpretations of the course and consequence of the Battle of Jutland and a host of other such familiar naval subjects. Lawrence Freedman, in his recent magisterial book on strategy, makes the same point.[23] The intrinsic diversity and ambiguity of our subject – the conduct of military operations, not least at sea – means that it is very easy to get things fundamentally wrong but sadly hard to get them right. Analysing past examples to see whether we can work out *why* some things went well and some did not should at least identify the questions we, or anyone trying to do strategy or make policy in the naval realm, should be asking. In this, the process of naval history – the analysis of data and the testing of hypotheses – is more important than the product – the answers. The journey, in other words, can be more useful than the destination.

While this is true of all types of history, its obvious salience for sailors, given the undeniable continuities of operations at sea over the centuries, means that naval history is particularly useful from this regard. The point was made, earlier in this chapter, that naval students usually rather enjoy doing naval history – or at least freely concede that engaging in a modicum of historical research is worthwhile. Much the same applies to strategists and policy-makers. By the time they have reached such elevated positions, they have engaged with history, absorbing views about the relevance of the past, even if through a process of osmosis. Either consciously or unconsciously they use history as a guide to future policy in a

---

[21] M. Clarke, ed., 'The Afghan Papers: Committing Britain to War in Helmand 2005–6', *Whitehall Paper* No. 77 (2011).
[22] F.J. Gavin, 'History, Security Studies, and the July Crisis', *Journal of Strategic Studies*, xxxvii, no. 2 (2014), pp. 319–31.
[23] L. Freedman, *Strategy: A History* (Oxford, 2013), p. 104.

whole variety of ways.[24] Some of these can indeed be wholly misleading both as conclusions about what happened in earlier times and/or as a guide to future ones. For this reason, some historians seek to insulate their discipline from the contaminating fingers of strategists and policy-makers and would have nothing to do with their world. Whether naval historians like it or not, however, naval students, strategists and policy-makers *will* go on using history as a guide to future behaviour. That being the case, it is plainly the duty of naval historians to do their best to help them by ensuring that what they deliver is accessible and as valid as both processed experience and as an intellectual discipline as they can. They owe this to the future as much as to the past.

---

[24] These have been thoroughly explored by W. Inboden in 'Statecraft, Decision-Making, and the Varieties of Historical Experience: A Taxonomy', *Journal of Strategic Studies*, xxxvii, no. 2 (2014), pp. 291–318.

Afterword

The word 'strategy' is a relatively recent import into Western languages, first appearing in English in the early nineteenth century (though it was in use in French rather earlier) as a direct rendering of the Greek word meaning 'generalship'. For much of that century it was usually applied to the battlefield, meaning something close to the modern 'tactics', and it was not often applied to war at sea. Julian Corbett at the end of the century was the first to publish on the strategy of naval warfare, and he deliberately avoided the term 'naval strategy' as being too limited and parochial. The proper strategy for a naval power, he maintained, was a 'maritime strategy', one embracing both services and all arms. Since Corbett's time, 'strategy' has come to be applied ever more widely. It has long been casually used to refer to almost any sort of systematic or wide-ranging planning, not necessarily having any connection with war. In universities today a 'professor of strategy' is more likely to be studying business or economics than warfare.[1] Even within a military context, 'strategy' has long outgrown its original meaning. In its modern sense it is not so much the art of the general as the art of the General Staff. It covers the whole organisation and management of war.

John Hattendorf has long taught and studied strategy in the broadest of senses. His published work ranges as widely in time and space and treatment as any one scholar could go in a single lifetime (if not several), but the focus of his work has always been on the proper employment of armed forces, especially navies. As befits a Professor of History seated in that most intellectual of naval establishments the US Naval War College, he has taken a particular interest in the study and teaching of naval warfare, in the ways in which navies think, learn, and act on what they have learnt. Naturally and properly, his instrument and theirs has been history. The present slips constantly between our fingers; the future, which it would be so convenient to know, is regrettably inaccessible; only the past (recent or distant) yields a great bank of evidence with which to study navies and the conduct of war at sea.

The essays presented here range over five hundred years of history from the Pacific to the North Atlantic, and they discuss topics as varied as naval officer education and the role of private industries in war efforts. Some of these contributions deal with the strategy of war at sea in the obvious military sense, but others range over almost every aspect of the organisation of war, dealing as much with ideas and attitudes as with activities and events. We learn about the deflection of strategy by such factors as politics and inter-service rivalry. We see how

---

[1] For example the Harvard Business School has a Strategy Unit which 'studies firms as competitors in an economic landscape'.

navies selected and trained their officers and ratings, and the social as well as intellectual tests they had to pass. Here are studies of the problems and opportunities of command and control, of diplomacy and international disputes, of technology, logistics and supply. A particular focus of several contributors is on the intellectual context of naval war, the professional thinking of navies and the sources from which they drew. It is not astonishing to see how the Imperial Japanese Navy borrowed ideas from the West; some will be more surprised to discover how much the US Naval War College owed to All Souls. The diversity of subjects and approaches is a tribute to John's own wide-ranging interests and contributions to historical scholarship.

N.A.M. Rodger
All Souls College, Oxford

A Bibliography of Books, Articles and Reviews Authored, Co-authored, Edited or Co-edited by John B. Hattendorf 1960–2015

1960
'Prize Winning Essay: "My True Security – The American Way"', *Western Springs Citizen* (28 April 1960), Pt 2 [unpaginated p. 13].

1964
A Dusty Path: A Pictorial History of Kenyon College (Gambier, OH: Kenyon College Reveille, 1964).

1966
'*O'Brien*'s Odyssey: One Destroyer's Duty in the Seventh Fleet', by Commander C.S. Christensen and Ensign J.B. Hattendorf. Photography by Ensign M.R. Hamilton, *Our Navy: The Navyman's Magazine*, vol. 61, no. 9 (September 1966), pp. 2–4, 60.

1971
'Sir Julian Corbett on the Significance of Naval History', *American Neptune*, vol. xxxi, no. 4 (October 1971), pp. 275–85. Revised and reprinted in *Naval History and Maritime Strategy: Collected Essays*, 2000), pp. 77–89.
'Technology and Strategy: A Study in the Professional Thought of the U.S. Navy, 1900–1916', *Naval War College Review* (November 1971), pp. 25–48; Reprinted in B.M. Simpson, ed., *War, Strategy Maritime Power* (New Brunswick, NJ: Rutgers University Press, 1977), pp. 111–38, and revised and reprinted in *Naval History and Maritime Strategy: Collected Essays*, 2000), pp. 29–57.
'Research in the Mahan Library: A Long Lost Farragut Letter is Rediscovered', *Naval War College Review*, xxiv (December 1971), pp. 97–9.

1972
Review of E.B. Potter, *Naval Academy History of the U.S. Navy*, *The Naval War College Review* (January 1972), p. 90.

1973
Review of Christopher McKee, *Edward Preble: A Naval Biography*, *The Naval War College Review* (March–April 1973), p. 81.
Review of J.R. Powell, *Robert Blake, General-at-sea*, *The Naval War College Review* (July–August 1973), pp. 84–6.

1974
Review of John Alden, *The American Steel Navy*, *The Naval War College Review* (January–February 1974), p. 93.

1975
The Writings of Stephen B. Luce, edited with Rear Admiral John D. Hayes, USN. Naval War College Historical Monograph series, no. 1 (Newport: Naval War College Press, 1975. Reprinted 1977, 1993).

1976
'The American Navy in the World of Franklin and Jefferson, 1775–1826', in Brian Bond and Ian Roy (eds), *War and Society* (London: Croom-Helm, 1976), vol. II. [This is the text of a lecture given at the British Museum, London, on 17 October 1975 in connection with the exhibition *The World of Franklin and Jefferson*.]

1977
Review of Julian Gwynn, *The Royal Navy and North America: The Warren Papers, 1732–1736*, *The Naval War College Review* (Summer 1977), p. 143.

1978
Review of Geoffrey Bennett, *Trafalgar*, *The Naval War College Review* (Winter 1978), p. 94.
Review of Brian Ranft, ed., *Technical Change and British Naval Policy 1860–1939*, *The Naval War College Review* (Spring 1978), p. 129.

1979
Review of Hans Delbrück, *History of the Art of War within the Framework of Political History*, vol. I, *Antiquity*, *The Naval War College Review* (Winter 1979), pp. 104–5.
Review of Berault Stuart, Seigneur d'Aubigny, *Traite sur l'Art de la Guerre*, *The Naval War College Review* (January–February 1979), p. 122.
Review of Martin van Creveld, *Supplying War*, *The Naval War College Review* (January–February 1979), p. 123.
Review of D.A. Baugh, *Naval Administration 1715–1750*, with M. Collinge, *Office Holders: Navy Board, 1660–1832*, *The Naval War College Review* (March–April 1979), pp. 116–17.
Review of P. Aubrey, *The Defeat of James Stuart's Armada*, *The Naval War College Review* (November–December 1979), p. 103.
Review of D. Elliot, *Maritime History: A Preliminary Handlist to the Collection in the John Carter Brown Library*, *The Naval War College Review* (November–December 1979), p. 109.
Review of G.W. Keaton and G. Schwarzenberger, *The Year Book of World Affairs, 1979*, *The Naval War College Review* (November–December 1979), p. 113.

1980
Register of the William L. Mullin Papers (Newport: Naval War College, Naval Historical Collection, 1980).
'The Machinery for the Planning and Execution of English Grand Strategy in the

War of the Spanish Succession', in R.M. Love, Jr, *New Sources and Changing Interpretations of Naval History: Proceedings of the Third Naval History Symposium* (New York: Garland, 1980).
'Swedish Naval Defense in the 1980s', *Naval War College Review* (January–February 1980), pp. 22–34.
Review of N.A.M. Rodger, *The Admiralty*, The *Naval War College Review* (March–April 1980), p. 124.
Review of C.L. Symonds, *Navalist and Anti-Navalists*, The *Naval War College Review* (May–June 1980), p. 129.
Review of Giuseppe Fioravanzo, *A History of Naval Tactical Thought*, The *Naval War College Review* (July–August 1980), p. 116.
Review of David Maland, *Europe at War, 1600–1650*, The *Naval War College Review* (July–August 1980), p. 219.
Review of R.E. Johnson, *Far China Station*, The *Naval War College Review* (July–August 1980), pp. 117–18.
Review of J.G. Wells, *Whaley: The Story of HMS Excellent*, The *Naval War College Review* (September–October 1980), p. 116.
Review of O.A. Cooke, *The Canadian Military Experience*, The *Naval War College Review* (September–October 1980), pp. 103–4.
'The Rakoczi Insurrection in English War Policy, 1703–1711', *Canadian American Review of Hungarian Studies*, vol. vii, no. 2 (Fall 1980), pp. 91–102.

1981

Register of the William McCarty Little Papers (Newport: Naval War College, Naval Historical Collection, 1981).
Review of R.G. Albion, *Makers of Naval Policy*, The *Naval War College Review* (January–February 1981), pp. 94–6.
Review of R. Johnson, *Defense by Ministry*, The *Naval War College Review* (January–February 1981), pp. 110–11.
Review of Geoffrey Till, *Air, Power and Royal Navy*, The *Naval War College Review* (March–April 1981), pp. 124–5.
Review of Hans Delbrück, *History of the Art of War within the Framework of Political History*, vol. II: *The Germans*, The *Naval War College Review* (March–April 1981), pp. 109–11.
Review of John Horsfield, *The Art of Leadership in War*, The *Naval War College Review* (May–June 1981), pp. 117–19.
Review of William N. Still, Jr, *American Sea Power in the Old World*, The *Naval War College Review* (July–August 1981), pp. 122–3.
Review of Barry Gough, *Distant Dominion*, and Glynn Baratt, *Russia in Pacific Water 1715–1825*, The *Naval War College Review* (September–October 1981), pp. 113–15.
Review of P.E. Coletta, *A Bibliography of American Naval History*, The *Naval War College Review* (September–October 1981), pp. 115–16.

1982

'Notes for a Guide to Western Historical Manuscripts in Singapore', *Journal of the History Society National University of Singapore* (1982/83), pp. 69–78.

'American Thinking on the Theory of Naval Strategy, 1945–1980', in Geoffrey Till (ed.), *Naval Strategy in the Nuclear Age* (London: Macmillan, 1982).

'Some Concepts in American Naval Strategic Thought, 1940–1970', in J.J. Bartell, *The Yankee Mariner and Sea Power* (Los Angeles: University of Southern California Press, 1982), pp. 93–108.

Review of J. Robertson, *Australia at War 1939–1945*, *The Journal of Southeast Asian Studies*, vol. 13, no. 1 (1982), pp. 210–12.

'Note: Some British and American Sailors' Tombstones in Penang, Malaysia', *The Mariner's Mirror*, vol. 68, no. 3 (August 1982), pp. 325–6.

Review of A. Marder, *Old Friends, New Enemies*, *The Journal of Strategic Studies*, vol. 5, no. 3 (September 1982), pp. 443–5.

1983

On His Majesty's Service: Observations of the British Home Fleet from the Diary, Reports, and Letters of Joseph H Wellings, Assistant US Naval Attaché, London, 1940–41. Naval War College Historical Monograph series, no. 5 (Newport: Naval War College Press, 1983). Reprinted 1993.

Review of W. Y'Blood, *Red Sun Setting*, *The Journal of Southeast Asian Studies*, vol. 14, no. 1 (1983), pp. 204–5.

Review of I.C. McGibbon, *Blue Water Rationale: The Naval Defense of New Zealand*, *The Journal of Southeast Asian Studies*, vol. 14, no. 1 (1983), pp. 206–7.

Review of James Leutze, *A Different Kind of Victory*, *The Journal of Southeast Asian Studies*, vol. 14, no. 2 (1983), pp. 449–52.

Review of Marwyn S. Samuels, *Contest for the South China Sea*, *The Mariner's Mirror*, vol. 69 (1983), p. 217.

'English Grand Strategy and the Blenheim Campaign, 1704', *The International History Review*, vol. 5, no. 1 (February 1983), pp. 3–19.

Review of David Howarth, *The Voyage of the Armada: The Spanish Story*, *The Naval War College Review* (March–April 1983), pp. 89–90.

'Note: H.M.S. *Redpole* at Christmas Island', *Mariner's Mirror*, vol. 69, no. 2 (May 1983), p. 199.

1984

Sailors and Scholars: The Centennial History of the Naval War College (Newport: Naval War College Press, 1984) with B. Mitchell Simpson III and John R. Wadleigh. Chinese translation (Taipei: Operations and Planning Advisory Committee, Republic of China Navy, 1994).

Two Beginnings: A History of St. George's Church, Tanglin (Singapore: St George's Church, 1984).

'Luce's Idea of the Naval War College', *Naval War College Review* (September–October 1984), pp. 35–43. Revised and reprinted in *Naval History and Maritime Strategy: Collected Essays*, 2000), pp. 17–28.

'Purpose and Contribution in Editing Naval Documents: A General Appreciation', in *Editing Naval Documents: An Historical Appreciation* (Washington, DC: Naval Historical Center, Department of the Navy, 1984), pp. 43–61. Revised and reprinted in *Naval History and Maritime Strategy: Collected Essays*, 2000), pp. 91–108.

'Benbow's Last Fight: Documents Relating to the Battle of Cape Santa Marta, August 1702', in N.A.M. Rodger (ed.), *Naval Miscellany* (London: Naval Records Society, 1984), vol. 5.

Review of James Neidpath, *The Singapore Naval Base*, *The Journal of Southeast Asian Studies*, vol. 15, no. 1 (1984), pp. 195–7.

Review of G.A. Horridge, *The Lashed-Lug Boat of the Eastern Archipelagos*, *The Journal of Southeast Asian Studies*, vol. 15, no. 1 (1984), pp. 203–4.

Review of David B. Quinn and Alison M. Quinn, *The English New England Voyages*, *Terræ Incognitæ*, vol. 16 (1984), pp. 94–6.

1985

'Stephen B. Luce', in Roger J. Spiller (ed.), *Dictionary of American Military Biography* (New York: Greenwood, 1985), vol. 2, pp. 668–70.

'Editor's Introduction' and notes to Charles Nordhoff, *Man-of-War Life* (Annapolis: Naval Institute Press, 1985). Classics of Naval Literature series.

Review of James Bradford, *Command Under Sail*, *Journal of the Early Republic*, vol. 5 (1985), pp. 544–5.

Review of Jürgen Rohwer, *Axis Submarine Successes, 1939–45*, *The Naval War College Review* (January–February 1985), pp. 120–2.

Review of D.M. Schurman, *Education of a Navy*, *The Naval War College Review* (March–April 1985), pp. 116–17.

Review of Theodore Ropp, *History and War*, *The Naval War College Review* (July–August 1985), pp. 108–9.

'English Governmental Machinery and the Conduct of War, 1702–1713', *War and Society*, vol. 3, no. 2 (September 1985), pp. 1–22.

Review of Henry Denham, *Inside the Nazi Ring*, *The Naval War College Review* (September–October 1985), pp. 118–19.

Review of Piers Mackesy, *War Without Victory*, *The Naval War College Review* (November–December 1985), pp. 114–16.

1986

A Bibliography of the Works of Alfred Thayer Mahan, Naval War College Historical Monograph series, no. 7 (Newport: Naval War College Press, 1986). Compiled with sister-in-law Lynn C. Hattendorf. Reprinted 1990, 1993.

'Med sjövinden till Newport', *Forum Navale*, no. 41 (1986), pp. 3075. [In Swedish, jointly authored with father-in-law Gunnar Sundell on the first Swedish naval officers to come to the Naval War College.]

'Note: A Special Relationship: The Royal Navy and the U.S. Naval War College', *Mariner's Mirror*, vol. 72, no. 2 (1986), pp. 200–1.

Review of Robert Putnam, *Early Sea Charts*, *Terræ Incognitæ*, vol. 18 (1986), pp. 112–13.

Review of S. George West, *A List of the Writings of Charles Ralph Boxer*, *Terræ Incognitæ*, vol. 18 (1986), pp. 113–14.

Review of C.R. Boxer, *Portuguese Conquest and Commerce in Southern Asia*, *Terræ Incognitæ*, vol. 18 (1986), pp. 113–14.

Review of William S. Dudley, *The Naval War of 1812*, *The Mariner's Mirror*, vol. 72, no. 2 (1986), p. 236.

Review of Edward L. Beach, *The United States Navy: 200 Years*, *The Mariner's Mirror*, vol. 72, no. 4 (1986), p. 492.
Review of Hubert Moinville, *Naval Warfare Today and Tomorrow*, *The Naval War College Review* (January–February 1986), pp. 96–7.
Review of Malcolm Murfett, *Fool Proof Relations*, *The Journal of Southeast Asian Studies*, vol. 17, no. 1 (March 1986), pp. 192–3.
Review of Brian Lavery, *The Ship of the Line*, *The Naval War College Review* (March–April 1986), pp. 118–19.
Review of Linda and Marsha Frey, *A Question of Empire: Leopold I and The War of the Spanish Succession, 1701–1705*, *The Hungarian Studies Review* (Spring 1986), pp. 53–4.
'Note: Naval Memorials in Singapore Cathedral', *Mariner's Mirror*, vol. 72, no. 2 (May 1986), pp. 150–1.
Review of Margaret Rule, *Mary Rose*, *The Naval War College Review* (May–June, 1986), pp. 128–31.
Review of Stephen and Elizabeth Usherwood, *The Counter Armada*, *The Naval War College Review* (May–June, 1986), pp. 128–31.
Review of Myron Smith, *Battleships and Battlecruisers*, *The Naval War College Review* (Autumn 1986), p. 148.
Review of Edward L. Beach, *The United States Navy: 200 Years*, in U.S. Naval Institute *Proceedings* (October 1986).

1987

England in the War of the Spanish Succession: A Study of the English View and Conduct of Grand Strategy, 1702–1712. Outstanding Dissertations in Modern European History, series eds William H. McNeill and Peter Stansky (New York: Garland Publishing, 1987).
Register of the Alfred Thayer Mahan Papers (Newport: Naval War College, Naval Historical Collection, 1987).
'Résumé of the Eighth International Seapower Symposium', *Ninth International Seapower Symposium: Report of the Proceedings of the Conference: 26–28 October 1987* (Newport: Naval War College, [1988]), pp. 6–10.
Review of Captain L.R.W. Beavis, *Passage: From Sail to Steam*, *Terræ Incognitæ*, vol. 19 (1987), p. 85.
Review of Louis Allen, *The Burma War*, *The Journal of Southeast Asian Studies*, vol. 18, no. 2 (1987), p. 331.
Review of Hans Delbrück, *History of the Art of War within the Framework of Political History*, vol. III: *The Middle Ages*, *The Naval War College Review* (Spring 1987), pp. 108–9.
Review of Keith Bird, *German Naval History*, *The Naval War College Review* (Summer 1987), pp. 118–19.
Review of Philip Ziegler, *Mountbatten*, *The Naval War College Review* (Winter 1987), pp. 127–8.
Review of Andrew Rothstein, *Peter the Great and Marlborough*, *Albion*, vol. 19, no. 4 (1987), pp. 625–7.

1988

'Admiral Sir George Byng and the Cape Passaro Incident, 1718: A Case Study in the Use of the Royal Navy as a Deterrent', in *Guerre et Paix 1660–1815* (Vincennes: Service Historique de la Marine, 1988), pp. 19–38.

'International Naval Co-operation and Admiral Richard G. Colbert: The Intertwining of a Career with an Idea', in W.A.B. Douglas (ed.), *The RCN in Transition: Challenge and Response, 1910–1985* (Vancouver: University of British Columbia Press, 1988), ch. 12. Revised and reprinted in *Naval History and Maritime Strategy: Collected Essays*, 2000), pp. 161–85. Further revised and reprinted as 'Admiral Richard G. Colbert: Pioneer in Building Global Maritime Partnerships', *Naval War College Review*, vol. 61, no. 3 (Summer 2008), pp. 109–30.

Review of Marcus Rediker, *Between the Devil and the Deep Blue Sea: Merchant Seamen and the Anglo-American Maritime World, 1700–1750*, The Washington Post Book World (March 1988), p. 6.

'The Evolution of the Maritime Strategy, 1977–1988', *Naval War College Review* (Summer 1988), pp. 7–28. Revised and reprinted in *Naval History and Maritime Strategy: Collected Essays* (2000), pp. 201–28.

'NATO's Policeman on the Beat: The Standing Naval Force, Atlantic, 1968–1988', *U.S. Naval Institute Proceedings* (September 1988), pp. 66–71, with Commander Stan Weeks. Revised and reprinted in *Naval History and Maritime Strategy: Collected Essays* (2000), pp. 187–200.

'Series Editors' Introduction' by John B. Hattendorf and Wayne P. Hughes, Jr., Classics of Sea Power series (Annapolis: Naval Institute Press, 1988):
- Corbett, Julian Stafford, *Some Principles of Maritime Strategy* (1911), facsimile edition with an introduction by Eric J. Grove.
- Fiske, Bradley Allen, *The Navy as a Fighting Machine* (1916), with an introduction by Wayne P. Hughes.

Review Article: 'A Harmonic in Some Divers Writing on British Naval History', *The Naval War College Review* (Winter 1988), pp. 125–33, included reviews of: Andrew Lambert, *Battleships in Transition*; Barry Gough, *Gunboat Frontier*; David Cordingly, *Nicholas Pocock*; Brian Ranft, *Ironclad to Trident*; N.A.M. Rodger, *The Wooden World*, and Bernard Semmel, *Liberalism and Naval Strategy*.

'The Protestant Wind', *The Cruising Association Bulletin*, vol. 27, no. 4 (December 1988), pp. 150–1.

1989

Maritime Strategy and the Balance of Power: Britain and America in the 20th Century. Co-edited with Robert S. Jordan (London: Macmillan in association with St Antony's College, Oxford; New York: St Martin's, 1989). Chinese translation (Taipei: Operations and Planning Advisory Committee, Republic of China Navy, 1994).

The Evolution of the U.S. Navy's Maritime Strategy, 1977–1987. The Newport Papers classified series, no. 6 (Newport: Naval War College Press, 1989).

'The English Royal Navy', in Robert P. Maccubbin and Martha Hamilton-Phillips (eds), *The Age of William III and Mary II: Power, Politics and Patronage 1688–1702: A Reference Encyclopedia and Exhibition Catalogue* (Williamsburg: The College of William and Mary, 1989), pp. 127–32.

'An Outline of Recent Thinking on the Theory of Naval Strategy', *Tidskrift i Sjöväsendet*, no. 1 (1989), pp. 55–65.
'The Hattendorf-Jarvis Family', in Bill Smythe (compiler and ed.), *A Place Called Portage: A Collection of Memories by Those who Experienced the Development of a Place called Portage from 1912–1989* (Manistee, MI: J.B. Publications, 1989), pp. 109–12.
'Series Editors' Introduction' by John B. Hattendorf and Wayne P. Hughes, Jr., Classics of Sea Power series (Annapolis: Naval Institute Press, 1989):
- Wegener, Wolfgang, *The Naval Strategy of the World War* (1929), trans. Holger H. Herwig, with an introduction by Holger H. Herwig.
- Wylie, J.C., *Military Strategy: A General Theory of Power Control* (1967), with an introduction by John B. Hattendorf. Reprinted in paperback, Naval Institute Press, 2014. Introduction revised and reprinted in *Naval History and Maritime Strategy: Collected Essays* (2000), pp. 137–59.

'War at Sea', in Noble Frankland (ed.), *The Encyclopedia of Twentieth Century Warfare* (London: Mitchell Beazley, 1989), pp. 129–42.
Review of G. Modelski and W. Thompson, *Sea Power in Global Politics 1494–1993*, *Naval History* (Spring 1989), p. 61.
'New Books in Reprints in Naval History', *The Naval War College Review* (Spring 1989), pp. 148–55. Nineteen short notices.

1990

The Limitations of Military Power: Essays Presented to Norman Gibbs on his 80th Birthday. Co-edited with Malcolm H. Murfett (London: Macmillan; New York: St Martin's Press, 1990).
'Stephen B. Luce', in James Bradford (ed.), *Admirals of the New Steel Navy: Makers of American Naval Tradition* (Annapolis: Naval Institute Press, 1990), pp. 3–23.
'Series Editors' Introduction' by John B. Hattendorf and Wayne P. Hughes, Jr., Classics of Sea Power series (Annapolis: Naval Institute Press, 1990):
- Colomb, P.H., *Naval Warfare: Its Ruling Principles and Practice Historically Treated*, 2 vols (1891), with an introduction by Barry M. Gough.
- Makarov, Stepan Osipovich, *Discussion of Questions in Naval Tactics* (1898), trans. John B. Bernadou, facsimile edition with an introduction by Robert B. Bathurst.

Review of Michael Palmer, *Origins of the Maritime Strategy: American Naval Strategy in the First Postwar Decade*, *The Naval War College Review* (Spring 1990), pp. 123–5.
'The Anglo-American Way in Maritime Strategy', *Naval War College Review* (Winter 1990), pp. 90–9. Revised and reprinted in *Naval History and Maritime Strategy: Collected Essays* (2000), pp. 109–20.
'The Bombardment of Acre, 1840: A Case Study in the Use of Naval Force for Deterence', in Edward Freeman (ed.), *Les empires en guerre et paix, 1793–1860: Journées franco-anglaises d'histoire de la marine, Portsmouth, 23–26 mars 1988* (Vincennes: Service Historique de la Marine, 1990), pp. 205–23.
'1588: An Armada of Books', *The Naval War College Review* (Summer 1990), pp. 113–21. [Review article of thirteen books published in connection with the 400th anniversary of the Armada, 1588, including Corbett, *Drake and the Tudor Navy*; Corbett, *Papers Relating to the Navy during the Spanish War*; Fernandez-Armesto,

Spanish Armada; Kemp, *Campaign of the Spanish Armada*; Laughton, *State Papers*; Martin and Parker, *Spanish Armada*; Mattingly, *The Armada*; Padfield, *Armada*; Rodger, *The Armada in the Public Records*; Rodriguez-Salgado, *Armada, 1588–1988*; Rowse, *Froude's Story of the Armada*; Whiting, *Enterprise of England*; Wernham, *Expedition of Sir John Norris and Sir Francis Drake to Spain and Portugal, 1589.*]

'Recollections of My Parents: Rear Admiral and Mrs. Alfred T. Mahan', by Lisle Mahan, ed. John B. Hattendorf, *Naval War College Review* (Autumn 1990), pp. 81–97.

1991

'Series Editors' Introduction' by John B. Hattendorf and Wayne P. Hughes, Jr., Classics of Sea Power series (Annapolis: Naval Institute Press, 1991):
- Mahan, Alfred Thayer, *Mahan on Naval Strategy: A Selection of Essays by Alfred Thayer Mahan*, ed. John B. Hattendorf, with an introduction by John B. Hattendorf.

The Influence of History on Mahan: The Proceedings of the Mahan Centenary Conference, ed. John B. Hattendorf. Naval War College Historical Monograph series, no. 9 (Newport: Naval War College Press, 1991). Reprinted 1993; Chinese translation (Taipei: Operations and Planning Advisory Committee, Republic of China Navy, 1994).

'Alliance, Encirclement, and Attrition: British Grand Strategy in the War of the Spanish Succession', in Paul M. Kennedy (ed.), *Grand Strategies in War and Peace* (New Haven: Yale University Press, 1991), pp. 11–29 with notes on pp. 186–8.

Review of Clark G. Reynolds, ed., *Global Crossroads and the American Seas; History and the Sea: Essays on Maritime Strategies*, *The Naval War College Review* (Spring 1991), pp. 137–8.

'Recent Books', unsigned notes on William Cogar, *New Interpretations in Naval History*; J.J. Colledge, *Ships of the Royal Navy*; Brian Lavery, *Nelson's Navy*; C.R. Pennell, *Privacy and Diplomacy in 17th c. North Africa*; J.H. Pryor, *Geography, Technology and War*; C. Bayly, *Atlas of the British Empire*; J. Franklin, *Navy Board Ship Models*, all in *The Naval War College Review* (Spring 1991), pp. 164–72.

'Naval Warfare under Sail', *The Naval War College Review* (Summer 1991), a series of reviews of the following books: Jean Bodriot, *The Seventy-Four Gun Ship*, pp. 94–5; Patrick Crowhurst, *The French War on Trade*, pp. 95–6; J. Byrn, *Crime and Punishment in the Royal Navy*, pp. 96–7; David Syrett, *The Royal Navy in American Waters, 1775–1783*, pp. 97–8; Nicholas Tracy, *Navies, Deterrence, and American Independence*, pp. 98–9; Jonathan Coad, *The Royal Dockyards, 1690–1850*, pp. 100–1; Donald Shomette, *Raid on America*, pp. 101–2; Chester Starr, *The Influence of Seapower on Ancient History*, pp. 102–3; Robert Louis Stevenson, *St. Ives*, pp. 103–4.

Review of Brian Ranft, ed., *The Beatty Papers*, vol. 1, *The Naval War College Review* (Autumn 1991), pp. 132–4.

Review of Piri Reis, *Kitab-i Bahriye*, *AACAR Review* [Association for the Advancement of Central Asian Research], vol. iv, no. 2 (Fall 1991).

Review of H. Colvin and J.S.G. Simmons, *All Souls, an Oxford College and its Buildings*, *Oxford: The Journal of the Oxford Society*, vol. xliii, no. 2 (December 1991), pp. 94–5.

1992

Eleventh International Seapower Symposium: Report of the Proceedings of the Conference: 6–9 October 1991, ed. John B. Hattendorf (Newport: Naval War College Press, 1992).

'Résumé of the Tenth International Sea Power Symposium', in *Eleventh International Seapower Symposium: Report of the Proceedings of the Conference: 6–9 October 1991* (Newport: Naval War College Press, 1992).

'Sea Power as Control: Britain's Defensive Naval Strategy in the Mediterranean, 1793–1815', in *Français et Anglais en Méditerranée de la Révolution française à l'indépendance de la Grèce (1789–1830)* (Vincennes: Service Historique de la Marine, 1992), pp. 203–20.

'Series Editors' Introduction' by John B. Hattendorf and Wayne P. Hughes, Jr., Classics of Sea Power series (Annapolis: Naval Institute Press, 1992):
- *Sound Military Decision* (1942 edn), facsimile edition with an introduction by Frank M. Snyder.

Contributed to the revision of C.P.B. Jefferys, *Newport: A Short History* (Newport: Newport Historical Society, 1992), and with further revisions, published as *Newport: A Concise History* (Newport: Newport Historical Society, 2008).

'Maritime History Series', John B. Hattendorf, series editor (Delmar, NY: Scholars' Facsimiles & Reprints for the John Carter Brown Library, 1992):
- Anghiera, Pietro Martire d', et al., *The history of travayle in the West and East Indies* (1577), facsimile edition with an introduction by Thomas R. Adams.
- Cà da Mosto, Alvise, *Questa e una opera necessaria a tutti li naviga[n]ti* (1490), together with Pietro Martire d' Anghiera, *Libretto de tutta la navigatione de Re de Spagna* (1504), facsimile editions with an introduction by Felipe Fernández-Armesto.
- Cortés, Martín, *Arte of navigation* (1561), facsimile edition with an introduction by D.W. Waters.
- Medina, Pedro de, *L'Art de Naviguer* (1554), facsimile edition with an introduction by Carla Rahn Phillips.
- Davis, John, *The seamans secrets* (1663), facsimile edition with an introduction by A.N. Ryan.
- Gentleman, Tobias, *Englands way to win wealth, and to employ ships and mariners* (1614), together with Robert Kayall, *The trades increase* (1615); Dudley Digges, *The defence of trade* (1615); Edward Sharpe, *Britaines busse* (1615), facsimile editions with an introduction by John B. Hattendorf.
- Gemma, Frisius, *De principiis astronomiae & cosmpographiae* (1553), facsimile edition with an introduction by C.A. Davids.
- Varthema, Lodovico de, *Die ritterlich un[d] lobwirdig Rayss* (1515), facsimile edition with an introduction by George Winius.

Review of Richard P. Stebbins, *The Career of Herbert Rosinski* and Evelyn Cherpak, *Register of the Herbert F. Rosinski Papers*, *The Naval War College Review* (Winter 1992), pp. 127–8.

Review of William B. Cogar, comp., *Dictionary of Admirals of the U.S. Navy*, vol. 1, *The Naval War College Review* (Spring 1992), pp. 144–5.

Review of Christopher McKee, *A Gentlemanly and Honorable Profession*, *The William and Mary Quarterly*, 3rd ser., vol. 49, no. 3 (July 1992), pp. 566–8.

Review of H.J.M.W. Peters, *The Crone Library*, *The Naval War College Review* (Summer 1992), pp. 157–8.
Review of Edward Freeman, ed., *Les empires en guerre et paix, 1793–1860*, *The Naval War College Review* (Autumn 1992), p. 144.
Review of Richard Harding, *Amphibious Warfare in the 18th Century*, *Albion*, vol. 24, no. 4 (Winter 1992), pp. 655–6.

1993

British Naval Documents 1204–1960, ed. John B. Hattendorf, R.J.B. Knight, A.W.H. Pearsall, N.A.M. Rodger and Geoffrey Till. Publications of the Navy Records Society, vol. 131 (London: Navy Records Society, 1993).
Mahan is Not Enough: Proceedings of the Corbett–Richmond Conference, ed. with James Goldrick (Newport: Naval War College Press, 1993).
'Seapower', in Trevor N. Dupuy (ed.), *International Military and Defense Encyclopedia* (Washington and New York: Brassey's (US), Inc., 1993), vol. 5, pp. 2378–83.
'Maritime History Series', John B. Hattendorf, series editor (Delmar, NY: Scholars' Facsimiles & Reprints for the John Carter Brown Library, 1993):
- *Shipbuilding Timber for the British Navy. Parliamentary Papers, 1729–1792*, facsimile edition with an introduction by R.J.B. Knight.
- *Marine Architecture: Directions for carry on a Ship* (1739), facsimile edition with an introduction by Brian Lavery.
- Bontekoe, Willem Ysbrandz, *Die vier und zwantzigste Schiffahrt* (1648), facsimile edition with an introduction by Augustus J. Veenendaal, Jr.
- Hacke, William, *A collection of original voyages* (1699), facsimile edition with an introduction by Glyndwr Williams.
- Pownall, Thomas, *The Administration of the Colonies* (1769), facsimile edition with an introduction by Daniel A. Baugh and Alison Gilbert Olson.
- Seller, John, *Practical Navigation* (1680), facsimile edition with an introduction by Michael Richey.
- Veer, Gerrit de, *The true and perfect description of three voyages* (1609), facsimile edition with an introduction by Stuart M. Frank.
- Vossius, Isaak, *A treatise concerning the motion of the seas and winds* (1677), facsimile edition with an introduction by Margaret Deacon.

Review of William B. Cogar, comp. *Dictionary of Admirals of the U.S. Navy*, vol. 2: *1901–1918*, *The Naval War College Review* (Winter 1993), pp. 145–7.
Review of K.R. Andrews, *Ships, Money & Politics*, *The Naval War College Review* (Summer 1993), p. 173.
Review of C. McKee, *A Gentlemanly and Honorable Profession*, *The Naval War College Review* (Summer 1993), p. 176.
Review of Robert Love, Jr., *History of the U.S. Navy, 1775–1991*, in U.S. Naval Institute *Proceedings* (August 1993), pp. 99–100.
Review of William Honan, ed., *Fire When Ready, Gridley*, *The Naval War College Review* (Autumn 1993), p. 152.
'The Decision to Close Rhode Island Bases in 1973', in Rhode Island Historical Society, *What a Difference a Bay Makes* (Providence, RI, 1993), pp. 104–6. Revised and reprinted in *Newport History*, *Newport History*, vol. 79, no. 262 (2010), pp. 54–65.

'"We Have Met the Enemy and They Are Ours": The Naval War of 1812', *Documentary Editing*, 15 (September 1993), pp. 57–60. [A review article on William S. Dudley et al., eds, *The Naval War of 1812*.]

Review of Robert L. O'Connell, *Sacred Vessels*, *The Mariner's Mirror*, vol. 79, no. 4 (November 1993), pp. 497–8.

'Sea Battle', *Gunji Shigaku*, vol. 29, no. 3 (December 1993), p. 1 [in Japanese, a one-page introduction to a special number on this theme.]

1994

Twelfth International Seapower Symposium: Report of the Proceedings of the Conference: November 1993, ed. John B. Hattendorf (Newport: Naval War College Press, 1994).

Ubi Sumus?: The State of Naval and Maritime History, ed. John B. Hattendorf (Newport: Naval War College Press, 1994).

'Résumé of Eleventh International Sea Power Symposium', in *Twelfth International Seapower Symposium: Report of the Proceedings of the Conference: 7–10 November 1993* (Newport: Naval War College Press, 1994), pp. 7–10.

'Introduction' with D.M. Schurman to Sir Julian Corbett, *Maritime Operations in the Russo-Japanese War* (Annapolis: Naval Institute Press, 1994), pp. v–xiv.

'Maritime Conflict and the Laws of War: An Historical Outline', in Sir Michael Howard, George Andreopoulos and Mark Shulman (eds), *Laws of War* (New Haven: Yale University Press, 1994), pp. 98–115, with notes 247–50.

'Series Editors' Introduction' by John B. Hattendorf and Wayne P. Hughes, Jr., Classics of Sea Power series (Annapolis: Naval Institute Press, 1994):
- Castex, Raoul, *Strategic Theories* (1931–39), trans. and ed. Eugenia C. Kiesling, with an introduction by Eugenia C. Kiesling.

'Maritime History Series', John B. Hattendorf, series editor (Delmar, NY: Scholars' Facsimiles & Reprints for the John Carter Brown Library, 1994):
- *Saint Barthélemy and the Swedish West India Company: A Selection of Printed Documents, 1784–1814*, facsimile editions with an introduction by John B. Hattendorf.

Review of N.A.M. Rodger, *The Insatiable Earl*, *Journal of Military History*, vol. 58, no. 2 (April 1994), pp. 322–3.

Review of Jan Glete, *Navies and Nations*, *International History Review*, vol. xvi, no. 2 (May 1994), pp. 345–7.

Review of Sigurd H. Trumpy, ed., *Naval Prints from the Beverley R. Robinson Collection*, *The Naval War College Review* (Summer 1994), pp. 166–7.

Review of Donald A. Yerxa, *Admirals and Empire*, *The Naval War College Review* (Autumn 1994), p. 136.

1995

Doing Naval History: Essays Toward Improvement, ed. John B. Hattendorf (Newport: Naval War College Press, 1995).

A Sea of Words: A Companion to the Seafaring Novels of Patrick O'Brian. With Dean H. King and Worth Estes (New York: Henry Holt, 1995; second edition [revised and expanded], 1997; third edition [revised and expanded], 2000).

'Prince Louis of Battenberg', in Malcolm Murfett (ed.), *The First Sea Lords and British Naval Policy: From Fisher to Mountbatten* (New York: Praeger, 1995), pp. 75–90

'The Battle off Cape Passaro, 1718', in Eric Grove (ed.), *Great Battles of the Royal Navy* (London: Arms and Armour Press, 1995), pp. 64–70.

'Toulon', 'Malaga', 'Vigo', in Linda and Marsha Frey (eds), *The Treaties of the War of the Spanish Succession: An Historical and Critical Dictionary* (Westport, CT: Greenwood Publishing, 1995), pp. 261–3, 437–40, 473–6.

'The Struggle with France, 1689–1815', in J.R. Hill (ed.), *The Oxford Illustrated History of the Royal Navy* (Oxford: Oxford University Press, 1995), ch. 4, pp. 80–119. Reprinted with corrections in paperback, Oxford University Press, 2002.

'Maritime History Series', John B. Hattendorf, series editor (Delmar, NY: Scholars' Facsimiles & Reprints for the John Carter Brown Library, 1995):
- Burchett, Josiah, *A Complete History of the Most remarkable Transactions at Sea* (1720), facsimile edition with an introduction by John B. Hattendorf.
- Faleiro, Francisco, *Tratado del espehera y del arte del marear* (1535), facsimile edition with an introduction by Timothy Coates.

'Maritime Strategy for the 21st Century', in Greg Mills (ed.), *Maritime Strategy for Developing Countries* (Johannesburg: South African Institute of International Affairs and Lancaster: University of Lancaster Centre for Defence and International Security Studies, 1995), ch. 2, pp. 38–48.

'Alfred Thayer Mahan and American Naval Theory', in Keith Neilson and Jane Errington (eds), *Navies and Global Defence: Theories and Strategy* (Westport, CT: Praeger, 1995), ch. 3, pp. 52–67. Revised and reprinted in *Naval History and Maritime Strategy: Collected Essays* (2000), pp. 59–75.

Review of Brian Tunstall, *Naval Warfare in the Age of Sail*, *The Naval War College Review* (Winter 1995), pp. 161–2.

Review of Derek Howse and N.J.W. Thrower, eds, *A Buccaneer's Atlas*, *The Naval War College Review* (Summer 1995), pp. 144–5.

Review of J.M. Haas, *A Management Odyssey*, *American Historical Review*, vol. 100, no. 5 (December 1995), pp. 1568–9.

1996

Maritime History, vol. 1: *The Age of Discovery*, ed. John B. Hattendorf (Malabar, FL: Krieger Publishing, 1996).

Thirteenth International Seapower Symposium: Report of the Proceedings of the Conference: 5–8 November 1995, ed. John B. Hattendorf (Newport: Naval War College Press, 1996).

Harbors and High Seas: A Map Book and Geographical Guide to the Aubrey-Maturin Novels of Patrick O'Brian, by Dean H. King with John B. Hattendorf (New York: Henry Holt, 1996; second edition [revised and expanded], 1999; third edition [revised and expanded], 2000).

'Series Editors' Introduction' by John B. Hattendorf and Wayne P. Hughes, Jr., Classics of Sea Power series (Annapolis: Naval Institute Press, 1996):
- Callwell, C.E., *Military Operations and Maritime Preponderance: Their Relations and Interdependence* (1905), facsimile edition with an introduction by Colin S. Gray. 'Admiral Spruance as War College President', Naval War College *Foundation Notes*, no. 27 (Spring 1996), pp. 8–9.

Review of Cole Kingseed, *Eisenhower and the Suez Crisis of 1956*, *The Naval War College Review* (Summer 1996), pp. 153–4.

'Stephen B. Luce: Intellectual Leader of the New Navy', in James Bradford (ed.), *Quarterdeck, Bridge and Pentagon: Two Centuries of American Naval Leadership* (Annapolis: Naval Institute Press, 1996), pp. 203–18.

Review Essay: 'The War Diary of the German Naval Staff, 1939–1945', *Documentary Editing*, 18 (September 1996), pp. 58–62. [A review article on Werner Rahn et al., eds, *Kriegstagebuch der Seekriegsleitung, 1939–1945*.]

Review of Erik Goldstein and John Maurer, eds, *The Washington Conference*, *International History Review*, vol. xviii, no. 4 (November 1996), pp. 948–50.

1997

Every Man Will Do His Duty: An Anthology of First Hand Accounts from the Age of Nelson. With Dean H. King (New York: Henry Holt, 1997).

Maritime History, vol. 2: *The Eighteenth Century and the Classic Age of Sail*, ed. John B. Hattendorf (Malabar, FL: Krieger Publishing, 1997).

'Sea Warfare', in Charles Townshend (ed.), *The Oxford Illustrated History of Modern Warfare* (Oxford: Oxford University Press, 1997), pp. 213–27. Republished in paperback under the title *The Oxford History of Modern War* (Oxford: Oxford University Press, 2000), pp. 245–61. New updated edition (Oxford: Oxford University Press, 2005), pp. 245–61.

'What is a Maritime Strategy?', in David Stevens (ed.), *In Search of a Maritime Strategy: The Maritime Element in Australian Defence Planning Since 1901*. Canberra Papers on Strategy and Defence, no. 119 (Canberra: Strategic and Defence Studies Centre, The Australian National University, 1997), pp. 5–18. Revised and reprinted in *Naval History and Maritime Strategy: Collected Essays* (2000), pp. 229–40.

'Sea Power and Sea Control in Contemporary Times', *Journal of the Australian Naval Institute*, 23 (April–June 1997), pp. 15–20. Revised and reprinted in *Naval History and Maritime Strategy: Collected Essays* (2000), pp. 253–65.

Review of W. Calvin Dickinson and Eloise R. Hitchcock, comps, *The War of the Spanish Succession, 1702–1713: A Selected Bibliography*, *Journal of Military History*, vol. 61, no. 3 (July 1997), pp. 610–11.

'From the Hill' [Remarks on receiving an honorary degree], *Kenyon College Alumni Bulletin*, vol. 20, no. 1 (Summer/Fall 1997), pp. 12–13, 55.

'Great Ships and Grand Strategy: England, 1400–1700', in Martine Acerra (ed.), *L'invention du vaisseau de ligne, 1450–1700*. Collection Kronos, 24 (Paris: SPM, 1997), pp. 167–81.

'Review Essay: A Dutch Door to Europe, 1702–1720', *Documentary Editing*, 19 (September 1997), pp. 57–61. [A review article on A.J. Veenendaal, ed., *De Briefwisseling van Anthonie Heinsius, 1702–1720*.]

Review of N.A.M. Rodger, ed., *Naval Power in the 20th Century*, *International History Review*, vol. xix, no. 4 (November 1997), pp. 932–3.

1998

Fourteenth International Seapower Symposium: Report of the Proceedings, 2–5 November 1997, ed. John B. Hattendorf (Newport: Naval War College Press, 1998).

America and the Sea: A Maritime History, by Benjamin W. Labaree, Edward W. Sloan, John B. Hattendorf, William M. Fowler, Jr, Jeffrey Safford and Andrew German (Mystic, CT: Munson Institute, 1998). John Lyman Book Award for the Best Book in American Maritime History, 1998.

John Robinson's Account of Sweden, 1688. Karolinska Förbundets Årsbok, 1996 (Stockholm: Karolinska Förbundet, 1998).
Review of Tyrone Martin, *A Most Fortunate Ship: A Narrative History of Old Ironsides*, *The Naval War College Review* (Winter 1998), pp. 168–9.
'Forget the *Maine:* Navies in the Modern World', *Culturefront: A Magazine of the Humanities*, 7 (Spring 1998), pp. 83–6.
'Résumé of the Thirteenth International Seapower Symposium', *Fourteenth International Seapower Symposium: Report of the Proceedings, 2–5 November 1997*, ed. John B. Hattendorf (Newport: Naval War College Press, 1998), pp. 5–12.
'Joshua Slocum: The First Solo Circumnavigator', *The Log of Mystic Seaport*, vol. 50, no. 1 (Summer 1998), pp. 23–5. [Vignette reprinted from *America and the Sea*.]
'The American Friends of the Hakluyt Society: Annual Report 1997–8', *The Hakluyt Society: Annual Report and Statement of Accounts for 1997* (London: The Hakluyt Society, 1998), pp. 11–12.
'The Admirals', in Steven Weingartener (ed.), *The Greatest Thing We Have Ever Attempted: Historical Perspectives on the Normandy Campaign*. Cantigny Military History series (Wheaton, IL: Cantigny First Division Foundation, 1998), pp. 106–11.
'Introduction', to Christopher Lloyd, *Lord Cochrane: Seaman, Radical, Liberator.* Heart of Oak series (New York: Henry Holt, 1998).
'Rear Admiral Charles Stockton, The Naval War College and the Law of Naval Warfare', in Leslie C. Green and Michael N. Schmitt (eds), *The Law of Armed Conflict: Into the Next Millennium*. International Law Blue Book series, vol. 71 (Newport: Naval War College Press, 1998), pp. xvii–lxxii.
'U.S. Navy, 1941–1993', in Robin Higham and Donald J. Mrozek (eds), *A Guide to the Sources of U.S. Military History: Supplement IV* (North Haven, CT: Archon Books, 1998), pp. 378–90.
'The Battle of Manila Bay', in Jack Sweetman (ed.), *Great American Naval Battles* (Annapolis: Naval Institute Press, 1998), pp. 175–97. John Lyman Book Award for the Best Book in American Naval History, 1998.
Review of Ann Savours, *The Voyages of the* Discovery, *Terræ Incognitæ*, vol. 30 (1998), p. 132.

1999

Naval Policy and Strategy in the Mediterranean: Past, Present, and Future, ed. John B. Hattendorf (London: Frank Cass & Co., 1999).
'Theodorus Bailey', 'William Caperton', 'Napoleon Collins', 'Stephen B. Luce', 'Silas Stringham', in John A. Garraty and Mark C. Carnes (eds), *American National Biography* (Oxford and New York: Oxford University Press, 1999), vol. 1, pp. 899–900; vol. 4, pp. 357–8; vol. 5, pp. 255–6; vol. 14, pp. 94–6; vol. 21, pp. 30–1.
'The American Friends of the Hakluyt Society: Annual Report 1997–8 [1998–9]', in *The Hakluyt Society: Annual Report and Statement of Accounts for 1998* (London: The Hakluyt Society, 1999), pp. 19–20.
'Geschichte und technologisher Wandel: Das Studium der Marinegeschichte in der US-Marine 1873–1890', in *Seemacht und Seestrategie im 19. und 20. Jahrhundert. Im Auftrag des Militärgeschichtlichen Forschungsamtes herausgegeben von Jörg Duppler* (Hamburg, Berlin and Bonn: E.S. Mittler & Shon, 1999), pp. 105–20. In German;

revised and published in English in *Naval History and Maritime Strategy: Collected Essays* (2000), pp. 1–16.

'Foreword' to Alexander Boyd Hawes, *Off Shore Soundings: Aspects of the Maritime History of Rhode Island* (Chevy Chase, MD: Posterity Press, 1999), pp. ix–xi. Honorable Mention: John Lyman Book Award for U.S. Naval and Maritime History, 1999.

'Introduction' to Joseph Conrad, *The Rover: A Novel*. Heart of Oak Sea Classics series (New York: Henry Holt & Co., 1999), pp. xi–xvii.

'Maritime History Series', John B. Hattendorf, series editor (Delmar, NY: Scholars' Facsimiles & Reprints for the John Carter Brown Library, 1999):
- Taisnier, Joannes, trans. Richard Eden, *A very necessarie and profitable booke concerning navigation* (1579?), facsimile edition with an introduction by John Parker.
- Zimmermann, Peter Carl, *Reise nach Ost- und West-Indien* (1771), with *Journaal, van het Oost-Indische Schip Blydorp* (1734) and *Rampspoedige reys-Bexchriving, ofte Journaal van's Ed: Oostindische Compagnies Schip Blydorp* (1735), facsimile editions with an introduction by Roelof van Gelder.

Review of Chris Madsen, *The Royal Navy and German Naval Disarmament, 1942–1947*, *The Mariner's Mirror*, vol. 85, no. 1 (1999), p. 95.

Review of N.A.M. Rodger, *The Safeguard of the Sea*, *International History Review*, vol. xxi, no. 1 (March 1999), pp. 138–40.

Review of Jack Sweetman, *The Great Admirals*, *The Naval War College Review* (Spring 1999), pp. 168–70.

Review of Mark Shulman, *Navalism and the Emergence of American Sea Power, 1882–1894*, *The Naval War College Review* (Summer 1999), pp. 168–70.

Review of Roger Morriss, *Cockburn and the British Navy in Transition: Admiral Sir George Cockburn, 1772–1853*, *Journal of Military History*, vol. 63, no. 3 (July 1999), pp. 722–3.

Review of Joseph A. Maiolo, *The Royal Navy and Nazi Germany, 1933–39*, *The Naval War College Review* (Autumn 1999), pp. 159–60.

Review of Michael Thwaites, *Atlantic Odyssey*, *Oxford: The Journal of the Oxford Society*, vol. li, no. 2 (November 1999), pp. 43–5.

'The U.S. Naval War College, Newport, Rhode Island', *Oxford: The Journal of the Oxford Society*, vol. li, no. 2 (November 1999), pp. 18–20.

2000

Naval History and Maritime Strategy: Collected Essays (Malabar, FL: Robert Krieger Publishing Company, 2000).

'Foreword' to William H. White, *A Press of Canvas: A Novel. Volume One in the War of 1812 Trilogy* (St Michaels, MD: Tiller Publishing, 2000), pp. 8–11.

'American Strategies in the Pacific War', in John Crawford (ed.), *Kia Kaha: New Zealand in the Second World War* (Auckland, New Zealand: Oxford University Press, 2000; paperback edition, 2002), pp. 36–48. Reprinted in *Naval History and Maritime Strategy: Collected Essays* (2000), pp. 121–35.

'Stephen B. Luce' and 'Sea Power', in William E. Simons (ed.), *Professional Military Education in the United States: A Historical Dictionary* (Westport, CT: Greenwood Press, 2000), pp. 176–9; pp. 289–91.

'Die Ursprünge des Spanischen Erbfolgkrieges [The Origins of the War of the Spanish Succession]', in Bernd Wegner (ed.), *Wie Kriege entstehen: Zum historischen Hintergrund von Staatenkonflikten.* = Krieg in der Geschichte, Bd 4 (Paderborn: Verlag Ferdinand Schöningh Gmbh, 2000; second edition, 2003), pp. 109–44. In German.

'Sir George Rooke (1650–1709) and Sir Cloudesley Shovell (1650–1707)', in Richard Harding and Peter Lefevre (eds), *The Precursors of Nelson: Admirals and the Development of the Royal Navy* (London: Chatham Publishing, 2000), pp. 48–78.

'Horatio Bridge', 'Monitor and Merrimack' and 'Charles Nordhoff the Elder', in Gil Gidmark (ed.), *An Encyclopedia of American Literature of the Sea and the Great Lakes* (Westport, CT: Greenwood Press, 2000), pp. 51–2, 297–8, 326–7.

Review of Richard Buel, Jr, *In Irons: British Naval Supremacy and the American Revolutionary Economy*, *Journal of Imperial and Commonwealth History*, vol. 28, no. 1 (January 2000), pp. 168–9.

Review of Rear-Admiral Raja Menon, *Maritime Strategy and Continental Wars*, *The American Neptune*, vol. 60, no. 3 (Summer 2000), pp. 336–7.

Review of Frank Kitson, *Prince Rupert: Admiral and General-at-Sea*, *RUSI Journal* [The Royal United Services Institute], vol. 145, no. 3 (June 2000), p. 76.

Review of J.R. Bruijn, *Varend Verleden*, *The Mariner's Mirror*, vol. 86, no. 3 (August 2000), pp. 349–50.

Review of Pablo Pérez-Malláina, *Spain's Men of the Sea: Daily Life on the Indies Fleets in the Sixteenth Century*, and A.J.R. Russell-Wood, *The Portuguese Empire, 1415–1808: A World on the Move*, *Journal of World History*, vol. 11. no. 2 (Fall 2000), pp. 384–7.

'A Contribution to the Discussion about NASOH', *NASOH Newsletter*, vol. 24, no. 2 (Fall 2000), pp. 4–5.

Review of Paul Butel, *The Atlantic Ocean*, *The Mariner's Mirror*, vol. 86, no. 4 (November 2000), pp. 479–81.

Review of Andrew Lambert, *The Foundations of Naval History*, *Sea History*, no. 95 (Winter 2000–1), p. 00.

2001

Semper Eadem: A History of Trinity Church in Newport, 1698–1998 (Newport: Trinity Church, 2001).

'The Caird Lecture, 2000: The Anglo-French Naval Wars (1689–1815) in Twentieth Century Naval Thought', *Journal for Maritime Research* (June 2001) http://www.jmr.nmm.ac.uk/jmr_new_articles.htm#caird2000. Reprinted in *Talking About Naval History: A Collection of Essays* (2010).

'Charles XII' and 'United States: Armed Forces: Navy', in Charles Messenger (ed.), *Reader's Guide to Military History* (London and Chicago: Fitzroy Dearborn Publishers, 2001), pp. 90–1 and 604–5.

'The Experience of the Spanish–American War and its Impact on Professional Naval Thought', in Edward J. Marolda (ed.), *Theodore Roosevelt, the U.S. Navy, and the Spanish–American War* (London and New York: Palgrave, 2001), pp. 61–80.

Review of D.M. Schurman, *Imperial Defence, 1868–1887*, *Defence Studies: The Journal of the Joint Services Command and Staff College*, vol. 1, no. 2 (Summer 2001), pp. 147–8.

Review of Pertti Luntinen, *The Imperial Russian Army and Navy in Finland*, *International Journal of Maritime History*, vol. xiii, no. 3 (June 2001), pp. 355–6.

Review of David McCullough, *John Adams*, in U.S. Naval Institute *Proceedings*, vol. 127 (September 2001), pp. 82–4.

'Review Essay: Closing the Dutch Door', *Documentary Editing*, 23 (September 2001), p. 59. [A review of A.J. Veenendaal, ed., *De Briefwisseling van Anthonie Heinsius*, vol. xix.]

2002

War at Sea in the Middle Ages and the Renaissance, ed. John B. Hattendorf and Richard W. Unger (Woodbridge and Rochester, NY: Boydell and Brewer, 2002).

Michel Vergé-Franceschi, ed., *Dictionnaire d'histoire maritime*, ed. Collection Bouquins (Paris: Editions Robert Laffont, 2002) [sixteen entries:]

Arleigh Burke, p. 258; George Dewey, p. 482; Samuel F. Dupont, p. 516; David Glasgow Farragut, p. 595; William F. Halsey Jr, p. 723; H. Kent Hewitt, p. 741; John Paul Jones, pp. 803–4; Ernest J. King, p. 814; Stephen B. Luce, pp. 890–1; Matthew Fontaine Maury, pp. 954–5; Oliver Hazard Perry, p. 1123; David Dixon Porter, p. 1173; Hyman Rickover, pp. 1246–7; William S. Sims, p. 1337; Raymond Spruance, p. 1353.

Spencer Tucker, ed., *Naval Warfare: An International Encyclopedia* (New York: ABC-Clio, 2002) [thirty-eight articles, totalling 17,500 words]:

Albion, Robert G. (1896–1983), vol. 1, pp. 18–19; HMS *Association*, 1701–14, vol. 1, pp. 60–1; Benbow, John (1653–1702), vol. 1, p. 114; Burrows, Montagu (1819–1905), vol. 1, p. 166; Byng, Sir George (1663–1733), vol. 1, pp. 168–9; Cape Passaro, Battle of, 1718, vol. 1, p. 186; Cartagena, Battle of, 1708, vol. 1, p. 196; Chappell, Howard I. (1901–75), vol. 1, pp. 203–4; Colbert, Richard C. (1915–73), vol. 1, pp. 234–5; Cooper, James Fenimore (1789–1851), vol. 1, p. 255; Corbett, Sir Julian (1854–1922), vol. 1, pp. 258–9; Eccles, Henry E. (1898–1986), vol. 1, p. 348; Gambier, James, first Baron (1756–1833), vol. 2, p. 422; Goodrich, Casper (1847–1925), vol. 2, pp. 441–2; Hayes, John D. (1902–91), vol. 2, pp. 484–5; Knox, Dudley W. (1877–1960), vol. 2, pp. 584–5; Laughton, Sir John Knox (1830–1915), vol. 2, pp. 613–14; Leake, Sir John (1656–1720), vol. 2, pp. 616–17; Luce, Stephen B. (1827–1917), vol. 2, p. 640; McCarty Little, William (1845–1914), vol. 2, p. 666; Morison, Samuel E. (1887–1976), vol. 2, p. 710; Mountbatten, Prince Louis of Battenberg (1854–1921), vol. 2, pp. 716–17; Naval War College, vol. 2, p. 737; Oppenheim, Michael (1853–1915), vol. 2, p. 773; Paullin, Oscar (1868–1944), vol. 2, pp. 788–9; Richmond, Sir Herbert (1871–1946), vol. 3, p. 854; Rooke, Sir George (1650–1709), vol. 3, p. 860; Rosinski, Herbert (1903–62), vol. 3, p. 862; Santa Marta, Battle of, 1702, vol. 3, p. 886; Shovell, Sir C. (1650–1707), vol. 3, pp. 923–4; Spanish Succession, War of (1702–14), vol. 3, pp. 951–3; Stockdale, James (1923–), vol. 3, pp. 971–2; Stockton, Charles (1845–1924), vol. 3, pp. 972; Taylor, Henry (1845–1902), vol. 3, pp. 1004–5; Turner, Stansfield (1923–), vol. 3, pp. 1045–6; Vélez Málaga, 1704, vol. 3, pp. 1070–1; Vigo Bay, 1702, vol. 3, pp. 1080–1; Wylie, J.C. (1911–93), vol. 3, pp. 1121–2.

'"To Aid and Assist the Other": Anglo-Dutch Cooperation in Coalition Warfare at Sea, 1688–1714', in Jan A.F. de Jongste and A.J. Veenendaal Jr (eds), *Anthonie*

Heinsius and the Dutch Republic, 1688–1720: Politics, Finance, and War (The Hague: Institute for Netherlands History, 2002), pp. 177–98. Reprinted in *Talking About Naval History: A Collection of Essays* (2010).
Review of Jan Glete, *Warfare at Sea, 1500–1650*, *International History Review*, vol. xxiv, no. 1 (March 2002), pp. 126–8.
Review of Bernard D. Cole, *The Great Wall at Sea: China's Navy Enters the Twenty-First Century*, *The China Quarterly*, 172 (December 2002), pp. 1071–2.
'The Origins of Aquidneck's Anglican Parishes', *The Evangelist* [St John's Church, Newport, Rhode Island] (December 2002), pp. 6–7.
'The Conundrum of Military Education in Historical Perspective', in Gregory C. Kennedy and Keith Neilson (eds), *Military Education: Past, Present, and Future* (Westport, CT, and London: Praeger Publishers, 2002), pp. 1–12.

2003

The Boundless Deep: The European Conquest of the Seas, ca. 1450–ca. 1830: Catalogue of an Exhibition of Original Sources on Maritime History from the John Carter Brown Library (Providence: John Carter Brown Library, 2003).
'The Uses of Maritime History in and for the Navy', *Naval War College Review*, lvi (Spring 2003), pp. 13–38. Edward S. Miller History Prize, Naval War College Press, for the 2003 Publishing Year. Reprinted in the *International Journal of Naval History*, vol. 2, no. 2 (August 2003) http://ijnhonline.org/volume2_number1_Apr03/article_hattendorf_uses_apr03.htm. Reprinted in Andrew Lambert, ed., *Naval History, 1850–Present*. International Library of Essays on Military History (London and Burlington, VT: Ashgate, 2007), vol 2. Reprinted in *Talking About Naval History: Collected Essays* (2010).
'The Englishmen Abroad: Professor John Hattendorf Charts the Emergence of the Maritime Book from its Earliest Origins in the 15th Century', *Antiquarian Book Review*, vol. 30, no. 3, issue 337 (April 2003), pp. 24–8.
'L'histoire maritime et son enseignement à l'étranger: 4. Aux États-Unis', *Chronique d'histoire maritime*, 50 (April 2003), pp. 19–22.
'Foreword' to Christopher M. Bell and Bruce Elleman, eds, *Naval Mutiny in the Twentieth Century* (London: Frank Cass, 2003), pp. xv–xviii.
'Luce, Mahan, and the Founding of the Naval War College', in M. Hill Goodspeed (ed.), *U.S. Navy: A Complete History* (Washington: Naval Historical Foundation, 2003), pp. 256–7.
'The French Connection in Newport During the American Revolution: An Overview', *Newport History*, vols 72–3, nos. 249–50 (Fall 2003–Spring 2004), pp. 5–11.

2004

The Evolution of the U.S. Navy's Maritime Strategy, 1977–1987. Newport Paper, no. 19 (Newport: Naval War College Press, 2004).
Newport, the French Navy, and American Independence (Newport: Redwood Press, 2004). Revised and corrected edition (Newport: Redwood Press, 2005).
'The Sea as an Arena for Conflict', in Daniel Finamore (ed.), *Maritime History as World History* (Gainesville: University Press of Florida, 2004), pp. 130–9.
'The US Navy and the "Freedom of the Seas", 1775–1917', in R. Hobson and

T. Kristiansen (eds), *Navies in Northern Waters 1721–2000*. Naval Policy and History series, no. 26 (London: Frank Cass, 2004), pp. 151–74.

H.C.G. Matthew and Brian Harrison, eds, *Oxford Dictionary of National Biography* (Oxford: Oxford University Press, 2004). Research Associate of the *Oxford DNB* [twenty-two articles:]

Benbow, John (1653–1702), vol. 5, pp. 52–8
Berkeley, James, third earl of Berkeley (1680–1736), vol. 5, pp. 379–80
Burchett, Josiah (1666?–1746), vol. 8, pp. 728–30
Byng, George, viscount Torrington (1663–1733), vol. 9, pp. 309–13
Churchill, George (1654–1710), vol. 11, pp. 601–3
Churchill, John, first duke of Marlborough (1650–1723), vol. 11, pp. 607–33
Cutts, John, baron Cutts of Gowran, Ireland (1661–1707), vol. 14, pp. 850–4
Griffith, Richard (d. 1719), vol. 23, pp. 973–4
Herbert, Arthur, earl of Torrington (1647–1716), vol. 26, pp. 654–8
Jennings, Sir John (1664–1743), vol. 30, pp. 19–20
Leake, Sir John (1656–1720), vol. 32, pp. 973–8
Mitchell, Sir David (1650–1710), vol. 38, pp. 397–8
Mordaunt, Charles, third earl of Peterborough (1658–1735), vol. 39, pp. 13–21
Robinson, John (1650–1723), vol. 47, pp. 360–4
Rooke, Sir George (1650–1709), vol. 47, pp. 689–94
Savage, Richard, fourth Earl Rivers (1660–1712), vol. 49, pp. 78–81
Sergison, Charles (1654–1732), vol. 49, pp. 777–8
Shovell, Sir Clowdisley (1650–1707), vol. 50, pp. 441–6
Smith, Thomas (d. 1708), vol. 51, pp. 337–8
Walton, Sir George (1665–1739), vol. 57, pp. 201–201
Webb, John Richmond (1667–1724), vol. 57, pp. 842–5
Wright, Lawrence (d. 1713), vol. 60, pp. 468–70

'Les États-Unis et les mutations de la puissance maritime au xxe siècle', in Christian Buchet, Jean Meyer and Jean-Pierre Poussou (eds), *La puissance maritime*. Collection Histoire-Maritime (Paris: Presses de l'Université Paris-Sorbonne, 2004), pp. 577–96. In French. English text published in *Talking About Naval History: A Collection of Essays* (2010).

'Anglo-Dutch Naval Wars', in Jonathan Dewald (ed.), *Europe 1450–1789: Encyclopedia of the Early Modern World* (New York: Charles Scribners' Sons division of Thomson-Gale, 2004), vol. 1, pp. 63–6.

'Halsey, William Frederick, Jr. (1882–1959)', in *The World Book* (New York, 2004), vol. 9, p. 28; reprinted in editions 2005 and after, vol. 9, pp. 27–8.

Review of Joel Hayward, *For God and Glory: Lord Nelson and His Way of War*, *Journal of Military History*, vol. 68, no. 1 (January 2004), pp. 252–3.

Review of Marsden Hordern, *King of the Australian Coast: The Work of Phillip Parker King in the Mermaid and Bathurst, 1817–1822*, *Itinerario: International Journal on the History of European Expansion and Global Interaction*, vol. 28, no. 2 (2004), p. 175.

Review of Patrick J. Speelman, *Henry Lloyd and the Eighteenth Century Military Enlightenment*, *Albion*, vol. 36, no. 1 (Spring 2004), pp. 141–2.

Review of Steven Dick, *Sky and Ocean Joined: A History of the U.S. Naval Observatory*, *The Naval War College Review*, vol. lvii, no. 3/4 (Summer–Autumn, 2004), pp. 171–2.

Sixteenth International Seapower Symposium: Report of the Proceedings, 26–29 October 2003, ed. John B. Hattendorf (Newport: Naval War College Press, 2004).
Review of Louis Sicking, *Neptune and The Netherlands, 1488–1558*, *International Journal of Maritime History*, vol. 16, no. 2 (December 2004), pp. 406–8.

2005
'The Cold War at Sea: An International History', Lyle Goldstein, John Hattendorf and Yuri Zhukov, guest eds, *Journal of Strategic Studies*, vol. 28, no. 2 (April 2005), pp. 151–439.
'Le livre maritime dans le monde Anglophone, 1770–1850', in Annie Charon, Thierry Claerr and François Moureau (eds), *Le livre maritime: Édition et diffusion des connaissances maritimes (1750–1850)* (Paris: Presses de l'Université Paris-Sorbonne, 2005), pp. 59–68. In French.
'Our Naval Heritage is in Danger', in U.S. Naval Institute *Proceedings*, vol. 130/12/1,222 (December 2005), pp. 64–8. Reprinted in *Talking About Naval History: A Collection of Essays* (2010).
'Deutschland und die See: Historische Wurzeln deutscher Seestreitkräfte bis 1815', in Werner Rahn (ed.), *Deutsche Marinen im Wandel: Vom Symbol nationaler Einheit zum Instrument internationaler Sicherheit*. Beiträge zur Militärgeschichte, Band 63 (Munich: R. Oldenbourg Verlag, 2005), pp. 17–40. In German.
'Letters from Overseas: From our Correspondent in the USA', *Newsletter of the Society for Nautical Research*, no. 57 (February 2005), pp. 13–14.
'In Memoriam John Allen Gable, 1943–2005: Some Memories from Four Decades of Friendship', *Theodore Roosevelt Association Journal*, vol. xxvi, no. 2 (2005), pp. 14–15.
'"In a Far More Thorough Manner"', *Naval History*, vol. 19, no. 2 (April 2005), pp. 38–43. Revised and reprinted in *Talking About Naval History: A Collection of Essays* (2010).
'Stephen B. Luce: Scholarship' and 'Alfred Thayer Mahan: Professionalism', in Lt Col. Joseph J. Thomas (ed.), *Leadership Embodied: The Secrets of Success of the Most Effective Navy and Marine Corps Leaders* (Annapolis: Naval Institute Press, 2005), pp. 35–8, 51–4.
'Nelson Afloat: A Hero Among the World's Navies', in David Cannadine (ed.), *Admiral Lord Nelson: His Context and Legacy* (London: Palgrave Macmillan, 2005), pp. 160–86. Reprinted in *Talking About Naval History: A Collection of Essays* (2010).
'Introduction' to Alexander Stillwell, ed., *The Trafalgar Companion* (Oxford: Osprey Publishing, 2005), pp. 8–5, with footnotes at p. 213.
'The Naval War College Museum in Founder's Hall, at Fort Adams, and in the Navy', and 'Battle of Trafalgar', *Naval War College Foundation: Members Only Newsletter*, vol. 14 (November 2005), pp. 7, 12.

2006
Seventeenth International Seapower Symposium: Report of the Proceedings 20–23 September 2005 (Newport: U.S. Naval War College, 2006).
U.S. Naval Strategy in the 1990s: Selected Documents. Newport Paper, no. 27 (Newport: Naval War College Press, 2006).
Trafalgar and Nelson 200: Catalogue of an Exhibition of Rare Books, Maps, Charts,

Prints, Models, and Signal Flags Relating to Events and Influences of the Battle of Trafalgar and Lord Nelson (Newport: Naval War College Museum, 2006). Printed in a limited edition of thirty numbered and signed copies; published on the internet at http://www.usnwc.edu/About/NWC-Museum.aspx.

Register of the Schlie Family Papers. Register No. 36 (Newport: Naval War College, Naval Historical Collection, 2006).

'Foreword' to Bruce A. Elleman and S.C.M. Paine, eds, *Naval Blockades and Seapower: Strategies and Counterstrategies, 1805–2005* (London and New York: Routledge, 2006), pp. viii–xx.

Review of Edgar F. Puryear, *American Admiralship: The Moral Imperatives of Naval Command, Journal of Military History,* vol. 70, no. 2 (April 2006), pp. 557–8.

Review of Jeremy Black, *The British Seaborne Empire, The Naval War College Review,* vol. lv (Summer 2006), pp. 156–7.

'Part and Parcel of a Nation's Totality', review essay on N.A.M. Rodger, *Command of the Ocean, The Naval War College Review,* vol. 59, no. 4 (Autumn 2006), pp. 134–6.

2007

The Oxford Encyclopedia of Maritime History (4 vols, Oxford and New York: Oxford University Press, 2007). John B. Hattendorf, editor-in-chief and author of 'Introduction' and the articles on: Astronomers and Cosmographers; Atlantic Ocean: North Atlantic; North Atlantic Navies; Constable, John; Chartered Companies: Northern Europe; Discipline and Punishment: Galley Discipline and Punishment; Fiction: Naval Novel; Fishing Vessels; Gibraltar, Strait of; Mahan, Alfred T.; Naval Logistics before 1850; Newport, Rhode Island; Rivers, Canals, and Inland Waterways; Stockton, Charles H.; Suez Canal.

American Library Association-Dartmouth Medal, 2008.

North American Society for Ocean History – John Lyman Book Award for Reference Works.

Association of American Publishers Professional and Scholarly Publishing Division Award for Excellence in Multivolume Reference/Humanities and Social Sciences – Honorable Mention.

Library Journal Best Reference of 2007.

U.S. Naval Strategy on the 1970s: Selected Documents, Newport Paper, no. 30 (Newport: Naval War College Press, 2007).

'Globalization and Navies: Some Considerations for Naval Theory', in Ravi Vohra and Devbrat Chakraborty (eds), *Maritime Dimensions of a New World Order* (New Delhi: Anamaya Publishers on behalf of the National Maritime Foundation, 2007), pp. 32–51. Reprinted in *Talking About Naval History: A Collection of Essays* (2010).

Review of Robert J. Allison, *Stephen Decatur: American Naval Hero, 1779–1820, International History Review,* vol. xxix, no. 2 (June 2007), pp. 370–1.

Review of Richard Harding, *Naval History, 1680–1850, International Journal of Maritime History,* vol. xix, no. 2 (December 2007), pp. 505–6.

Review of Randolph Cock and N.A.M. Rodger, eds, *A Guide to the Naval Records in the National Archives of the UK, International Journal of Naval History,* vol. 6, no. 3 (December 2007) http://ijnhonline.org/volume6_number3_dec07/review_cock_rogers_hattendorf_dec07.html.

"'Whither with Nelson and Trafalgar: A Review Article on the Bicentenary Scholarship on the Nelson Era', *Journal for Maritime Research* (December 2007). Reprinted with revisions and additions in *Talking About Naval History: A Collection of Essays* (2010).

2008

U.S. Naval Strategy in the 1980s: Selected Documents, ed. John B. Hattendorf and Peter M. Swartz Newport Paper, no. 33 (Newport: Naval War College Press, 2008).

Command of the Sea: Catalogue of an Exhibition of American Naval Art from the U.S. Naval Academy Museum, the U.S. Navy Art Collection, and the U.S. Naval War College Museum Displayed at the Newport Art Museum, Newport, Rhode Island, 6 June–12 August 2007 (Newport: The Naval War College Museum, 2008). Printed in a limited edition of thirty numbered and signed copies. Published on the internet at http://www.usnwc.edu/About/NWC-Museum.aspx.

Register of the Papers of Admiral of the Fleet Sir James Hawkins, Whitshed, Bart., G.C.B., Royal Navy. Register no. 34; Manuscript Collection 279 (Newport: Naval Historical Collection, Naval War College, 2008).

'Silas Duncan', 'William Lynch' and 'James Spotts', in David Tatham (ed.), *Dictionary of Falklands Biography (including South Georgia)* (Ledbury: ABC Print, 2008), pp. 203, 347–8, 512–13.

'L'expédition particulière de 1780–1781 une opération jointe et combine', *Bulletin de la Société Archéologique du Vendômois* (2008) , pp. 66–73. In French.

'L'expédition particulière of 1780–1781 as a joint and combined operation', *Bulletin de la Société Archéologique du Vendômois* (2008), pp. 74–80. Reprinted in *Talking About Naval History: A Collection of Essays* (2010).

'Foreword' to *Naval Coalition Warfare: From the Napoleonic War to Operation Iraqi Freedom*, ed. Bruce A. Elleman and S.C.M. Paine (London: Routledge, 2008), pp. xvi–xviii.

'El mar frente a la costa en la teoría y la praxis: la guerra de 1812', in A. Guimerá Ravina and Jose Mariá Blanco Núñez (coords), *Guerra Naval en la Revolución y el Imperio: bloqueos y operaciones anfibias, 1793–1815* (Madrid: Marcial Pons Historia, 2008), pp. 405–25. In Spanish; English text published in *Talking About Naval History: A Collection of Essays* (2010).

'Les Americans et la guerre sur mer (1775–1783)', in Olivier Chaline, Philippe Bonnichon and Charles-Philippe de Vergennes (eds), *La France et l'Indépendance américaine* (Paris: Presse de l'Université Paris-Sorbonne, 2008), pp. 131–51. In French.

Review of Michael Whitby, Richard H. Gimblett and Peter Haydon, *The Admirals: Canada's Senior Naval Leadership in the Twentieth Century*, *Journal of Military History*, vol. 72, no. 1 (January 2008), pp. 257–8.

Review of Eric Gruber von Arni, *Hospital Care and the British Standing Army, 1660–1714*, *English Historical Review*, vol. cxxiii (February 2008), pp. 208–9.

Review of Admiral James L. Holloway, IIII, USN (ret.), *Aircraft Carriers at War: A Personal Retrospective of Korea, Vietnam, and the Soviet Confrontation*, *The Naval War College Review*, vol. 61, no. 2 (Spring 2008), pp. 141–3.

'The Sinking of the Galleon *San José* on 8 June 1708: An Exercise in Historical Detective Work', by Carla Rahn Phillips, John B. Hattendorf and Thomas R. Beall, *Mariner's Mirror*, vol. 94, no. 2 (May 2008), pp. 176–87.

Review of Jamel Ostwald, *Vauban under Siege: Engineering Efficiency and Martial Vigor in the War of the Spanish Succession*, English Historical Review, vol. cxxiii (August 2008), pp. 1041–3.

Review of Francisco Bettencourt and Diogo Ramado Curto, eds, *Portuguese Oceanic Expansion, 1400–1800*, The Naval War College Review, vol. 61, no. 3 (Summer 2008), pp. 148–9.

Review of Rockwell Stensrud, *Newport: A Lively Experiment*, New England Quarterly, vol. 81, no. 3 (September 2008), pp. 538–40.

Review of Roland, Bolster and Keyssar, *The Way of a Ship: America's Maritime History Revisited, 1600–2000*, International Journal of Maritime History, vol. xx, no. 2 (December 2008), pp. 392–4.

2009

International Seapower Symposium XVIII: Report of the Proceedings 17–19 October 2007, ed. John B. Hattendorf with John W. Kennedy (Newport: Naval War College Press, 2009).

'Foreword' to Gary J. Ohls, *Somalia ... From the Sea*, Newport Papers, no. 34 (Newport: Naval War College Press, 2009).

'Foreword' to Evelyn Cherpak, ed., *Three Splendid Little Wars: The Diary of Joseph K. Taussig, 1898–1901*. Naval War College Historical Monograph series, no. 16 (Newport: Naval War College Press, 2009).

Faces of the Naval War College: An Illustrated Catalogue of the U.S. Naval War College's Collection of Portrait Paintings and Busts (Newport: Naval War College, 2009). Also published on the internet in .pdf format at http://www.usnwc.edu/About/NWC-Museum.aspx.

Review of H.W. Dickinson, *Educating the Royal Navy: Eighteenth- and Nineteenth-Century Education for Officers*, Journal of Military History, vol. 73, no. 3 (July 2009), pp. 945–6.

Review of Roger Parkinson, *The Late Victorian Navy*, The Naval War College Review, vol. 62, no. 4 (Autumn 2009), pp. 171–2.

Review of Geoffrey Till, ed., *The Development of British Naval Thinking*, Journal of Military History, vol. 73, no. 4 (October 2009), pp. 1332–4.

Review of Susan Rose, ed., *The Naval Miscellany, volume VII*, International Journal of Maritime History, vol. xxi, no. 2 (December 2009), pp. 443–4.

2010

Nineteen-Gun Salute: Case Studies of Operational, Strategic, and Diplomatic Naval Leadership during the 20th and Early 21st Centuries, ed. John B. Hattendorf and Bruce A. Elleman (Newport: Naval War College Press, 2010).

'Navies, Strategy, and Tactics in the Age of de Ruyter', in J.R. Bruijn, *Michiel De Ruyter* (Rotterdam: Karawansary, 2010). Reprinted in *Talking About Naval History: A Collection of Essays* (2010).

Talking About Naval History: A Collection of Essays (Newport: Naval War College Press, 2010).

International Seapower Symposium XIX: Report of the Proceedings, ed. John B. Hattendorf with John W. Kennedy (Newport: Naval War College Press, 2010)

'Seekrieg' in Friedrich Jaeger, ed., *Enzyklopädie der Neuzeit* [1450–1850]' (Stuttgart: J.B. Metzler Verlag im Auftrag des Kuturwissenschaflitchen Instituts Essen, 2010), Band 11, pp. 1012–13.

'Here's for a Coriolis Effect in Maritime History', *Coriolis: An Interdisciplinary Journal of Maritime History*, vol. 1, no. 2 (April 2010) http://ijms.nmdl.org/index.

Review of Andrew D. Lambert, John Beeler, Barry Strauss and John B. Hattendorf, 'The Neglected Field of Naval History? A Forum', *Historically Speaking*, vol. 11, no. 4 (September 2010), pp. 9–19.

Review of Jan Glete, *Swedish Naval Administration, 1521–1721*, *Northern Mariner*, vol. 21, no. 4 (October 2010), pp. 421–2.

Review of William S. Dudley, ed., *Troubled Waters*, *International Journal of Maritime History*, vol. xxii, no. 2 (December 2010), pp. 345–6.

Review of M.K. Barritt, *Eyes of the Admiralty: J.T. Serres – an Artist in the Channel Fleet, 1799–1800*, *The Naval War College Review*, vol. 63, no. 1 (Winter 2010), pp. 167–8.

2011

The Way of a Ship: An Essay on the Literature of Navigation Science along with Some American Contributions to the Art of Navigation, 1519–1802, by Lawrence C. Wroth. Revised versions, edited with a foreword by John B. Hattendorf (Providence: The John Carter Brown Library, 2011).

Talking About Naval History: A Collection of Essays. Naval War College Historical Monograph series, no. 19 (Newport: Naval War College Press, 2011).

'Educating Leaders at the Naval War College: The Inspiration and Continuing Relevance of the Founder's Vision', in John E. Jackson and Carla McCarthy (eds), *Naval War College: The Navy's Home of Thought* (Tampa, FL: Faircountmedia group, Inc., 2011), pp. 12–19.

'Navies, Strategy, and Tactics in the Age of de Ruyter [1607–1676)', in J.R. Bruijn (ed.), *De Ruyter: Dutch Admiral* (Rotterdam: Karawansary, 2011). Reprinted in *Talking About Naval History: Collected Essays* (2010).

'Toponymy of Herschel Island (Qikiqtaryuk), Western Arctic Coast, Canada', by Christopher Burn and John B. Hattendorf, *Arctic*, vol. 64, no. 4 (December 2011), pp. 459–64.

'Maritime History Today', *Perspectives on History*, vol. 50, no. 2 (February 2012), pp. 34–6.

'Place Names', by Christopher Burn and John B. Hattendorf, in Charles R. Burn, *Herschel Island Qikiqtaryuk: A Natural and Cultural History of Yukon's Arctic Island* (University of Calgary Press for Wildlife Management Advisory Council (North Slope), 2012), pp. 22–9.

'George Washington's Navy', in Edward G. Lengel (ed.), *A Companion to George Washington* (Chichester: Wiley-Blackwell, 2012), pp. 302–19.

'The United States Navy in the Twenty-first Century: Thoughts on Naval Theory, Strategic Constraints and Opportunities', *The Mariner's Mirror*, vol. 97, no. 1 (February 2011), pp. 00–0.

'Foreword' to Bruce A. Elleman and S.C.M. Paine, *Naval Power and Expeditionary Warfare: Peripheral Campaigns and New Theatres of Naval Warfare* (London: Routledge, 2011), pp. xii–xiii.

'Foreword' to Bruce Elleman, *High Seas Buffer: The Taiwan Patrol, 1950–1979.* Newport Paper, no. 38 (Newport: Naval War College Press, 2012), pp. xiii–xiv.

'Foreword' to Craig C. Felker and Marcus O. Jones, eds, *New Interpretations in Naval History: Selected Papers from the Sixteenth Naval History Symposium Held at the United States Naval Academy 10–11 September 2009.* Naval War College Historical Monograph, no. 20 (Newport: Naval War College Press, 2012), pp. ix–x.

Review of Richard Palmer and Michelle Brown, eds, *Lambeth Palace Library: Treasures from the Collection of the Archbishops of Canterbury, Anglican & Episcopal History,* vol. 80, no. 1 (March 2011), pp. 94–6.

Review of Eric Dietrich-Berryman et al., *Passport Not Required, Naval History,* vol. 25, no. 2 (April 2011), p. 76.

Review of Jeremy Black, *Naval Power, The Mariner's Mirror,* vol. 97, no. 2 (May 2011), pp. 84–5.

Review of George Shelvocke, *A Voyage Around the World, Terræ Incognitæ,* vol. 43 no. 2 (September 2011), pp. 183–4.

Review of Richard Harding, *The Emergence of Britain's Global Naval Supremacy: The War of 1739–1748, Journal of Military History,* vol. 75, no. 4 (October 2011), pp. 1288–90.

Review of Sam Willis, *The Admiral Benbow, TLS [London Times Literary Supplement],* no. 5664 (21 October 2011), p. 34.

Review of N.A.M. Rodger, *Essays in Naval History from Medieval to Modern, The Naval War College Review* (Autumn 2011), pp. 00–0.

2012

Marlborough: Soldier and Diplomat. Protagonists of History in International Perspective, vol. 2. (Rotterdam: Karwansaray Publishing, 2012).

'An External Audit', in Captain Peter Hore, RN (ed.), *From Dreadnought to Daring: 100 Years of Comment, Controversy, and Debate in The Naval Review* (Barnsley: Seaforth Publishing, 2012), pp. 427–38.

A Memoir of My Professional Life: Scholar Diplomat and University Administrator, by Charles Ray Ritcheson, as told to John B. Hattendorf (private printing of seventeen copies, 2012).

'The War Without a Loser' [a review essay], *The Wall Street Journal* (Saturday/Sunday 28–9 January 2012), pp. C5–C6

Review of John Laurence Busch, *Steam Coffin: Captain Moses Rogers and the Steamship Savannah Break the Barrier, The Naval War College Review* (Winter 2012), pp. 173–5.

Review of Don R. Gerlach with George E. DeMille, *Samuel Johnson of Stratford in New England, 1696–1772, Anglican & Episcopal History,* vol. 81, no. 1 (March 2012), pp. 87–8.

Review of Roger Morriss, *The Foundations of British Maritime Ascendancy: Resources, Logistics and the State, 1755–1815, Journal of Military History,* vol. 76, no. 3 (July 2012), pp. 865–7.

Review of C.I. Hamilton, *The Making of the Modern Admiralty, Journal of Modern History,* vol. 84, no. 4 (December 2012), pp. 958–60.

2013

International Seapower Symposium XX: Report of the Proceedings 19–21 October 2011, ed. John B. Hattendorf and John W. Kennedy (Newport: Naval War College Press, 2013).

Sailors and Scholars: The History of the Naval War College, 1884–2012 (Newport: Naval War College, 2013). Second edition, revised and expanded.

'Rhode Island, the War of 1812, and Oliver Hazard Perry', in *Oliver Hazard Perry: The Hero of Lake Erie*. [Checklist of Items in Exhibition] *July 3 2013–January 31, 2014*. (Newport, RI: Redwood Library & Athenaeum, 2013), pp. 4–8.

'Naval War College', in G. Kurt Piehler and M. Houston Johnson (eds), *Encyclopedia of Military Science* (Thousand Oaks, CA: Sage Publishing, 2013), pp. 949–52.

'The War of 1812: A Perspective from the United States', in Tim Voelker (ed.), *Broke of the Shannon and the War of 1812* (Barnsley: Pen and Sword Books, 2013), pp. 1–15.

'What is a Maritime Strategy?', in Justin Jones (ed.), *A Maritime School of Strategic Thought for Australia: Perspectives*. Sea Power series, no. 1 (Canberra: Sea Power Centre, 2013), pp. 19–28.

'La formation et les missions de la marine continentale américaine', in Olivier Chaline (ed.), *Les marines de la guerre de l'Indépendance américaine* (Paris: Presse de l'Université Paris-Sorbonne, 2013), pp. 79–106.

Review of Jason R. Musteen, *Nelson's Refuge: Gibraltar in the Age of Napoleon*, *The Historian*, vol. 75, no. 1 (2013), pp. 206–7.

Review of Alexis Catsambis, Ben Ford and Donny L. Hamilton, eds, *The Oxford Handbook of Maritime Archaeology*, *The Naval War College Review* (Winter 2013), pp. 132–3.

'The Third Alan Villiers Memorial Lecture. The Naval War of 1812 in International Perspective', *Mariner's Mirror*, vol. 99, no. 1 (February 2013), pp. 5–22.

'The Third Alan Villiers Memorial Lecture. The Naval War of 1812 in International Perspective', *The Naval Review*, vol. 101, no. 1 (February 2013), pp. 31–8 [abbreviated version without footnotes].

'The Third Alan Villiers Memorial Lecture. The Naval War of 1812 in International Perspective', *The Journal of the Britannia Naval Research Association*, vol. 5, no. 3 (February 2013), pp. 56–66.

Review of J.W. Middendorf II, *Potomac Fever*, *The Naval War College Review* (Spring 2013), pp. 126–7.

'The 80-Gun Ship-of-the-Line *Duc de Bourgogne*', *Nautical Research Journal*, vol. 58, no. 2 (Summer 2013), pp. 141–2.

Review of J.-M. Van Hille, *Dictionnaire des marins francs-maçons*; J.-P. Zanco, *Dictionnaire des ministres de la marine 1689–1958*, *The Naval War College Review* (Summer 2013), pp. 152–3.

'Modèle du *Duc de Bourgogne* vaisseau de 80 canons réalisé à la demande de l'American Naval War College Museum de Newport (U.S.A.)', *Neptunia: Revue des Amis du Musée National de la Marine*, no. 270 (June 2013), pp. 44–5.

'Civil War Navies: A Review Essay' [on Craig L. Symonds, *The Civil War at Sea* and James M. McPherson, *War on the Waters*], *Historically Speaking: The Bulletin of the Historical Society*, vol. xiv, no. 3 (June 2013), pp. 22–3. Jack Miller Center Prize for the Best Essay on military or diplomatic history to appear in *Historically Speaking* in 2013.

Review of *Fish and Ships! Food on the Voyages of Captain Cook*, *Terræ Incognitæ*, vol. 45, no. 2 (October 2013), pp. 153–4.

What is a Maritime Strategy? Soundings Papers–No. 1. October 2013. http://www.navy.gov.au/media-room/publications/soundings-papers-october-2013

2014

'Rear Admiral Henry E. Eccles and the "Lessons of Suez" Gleaned at the U.S. Naval War College, 1956–1968' (Paris: Publications de la Sorbonne, 2014, pp. 539–56). Also published in *Talking About Naval History: A Collection of Essays* (2010).

'L'idée d'espaces maritimes et côtiers dans la pensée navale aux États-Unis depuis 1970', in Jean de Préneuf, Eric Grove and Andrew Lambert (eds), *Entre terre et mer: L'occupation militaire des espaces maritimes et littoraux* (Paris: Economica, 2014), pp. 109–22.

Kenyon College Class of 1964: Fifty Years On, compiled by John B. Hattendorf (Gambier, OH: Kenyon Alumni Affairs Office, 2014).

'Entretien: Mahan et Luce aux sources de la stratégie navale américaine', *Défense & Sécurité Internationale*, Hors-série no. 33 (December 2013–January 2014), pp. 28–32.

Review of Jerker Widen, *Theorist of Maritime Strategy*, *Journal of Startegic Studies*, vol. 37, no. 1 (January 2014), pp. 165–7.

Forum: [on the first twenty-five years of the *International Journal of Maritime History*] 'Naval History', *International Journal of Maritime History*, vol. 25, no. 1 (February 2014), pp. 104–9.

Review of John Lewis Gaddis, *George F. Kennan*, The *Naval War College Review* (Winter 2014), pp. 152–4.

'The Idea of a "Fleet in Being" in Historical Perspective', *Naval War College Review*, vol. 67, no. 1 (Winter 2014), pp. 43–60. Also: 'The Idea of the "Fleet in Being" and the War of the American Revolution' [in French], in Olivier Chaline, Phillippe Bonnichon and Charles-Philippe de Vergennes (eds), *Les marines de la guerre d'Indépendance Américaine*, vol. II: *Les aspects opérationnels* (Paris: Presse de l'Université Paris-Sorbonne, forthcoming).

Review of Ann Savours, *The Voyages of the* Discovery: *The Illustrated History of Scott's Ship*, *Terræ Incognitæ*, vol. 46, no. 1 (April 2014), pp. 61–2.

Review of Jonathan Dull, *American Naval History*, *The Historian*, vol. 76, no. 2 (Summer 2014), pp. 353–4.

'The Naval War College and Fleet Admiral Nimitz's "Graybook"', *Newsletter of the Naval Order of the United States*, vol. xxiv, no. 7 (Summer 2014), pp. 12–15.

'Saving Nimitz's "Graybook"', *Naval History*, vol. 28, no. 3 (June 2014), pp. 48–51.

'A City by and for the Sea: Naval History Has Long Been Intertwined with Newport's', by John B. Hattendorf and John Kennedy, *Celebrate Newport, Rhode Island. 375th Anniversary 1639–2014. A special publication of the* Newport Daily News, [10] June 2014, p. 26.

'Changing American Perceptions of the Royal Navy Since 1775', *International Journal of Naval History*, vol. 11, no. 1 (July 2014).

Review of Grant Tapsell, ed., *The Later Stuart Church, 1660–1714*, *Anglican and Episcopal History*, vol. 83, no. 3 (September 2014), pp. 332–4.

Review of James Rentfrow, *Home Squadron: U.S. Navy on the North Atlantic Station*, *Naval History*, vol. 28, no. 6 (October 2014), pp. 68–9.

'The International Newport Connection and International Student Sponsorships' [Interview], in David F. Manning with Joel L. Sokolsky, *Global Arms of Sea Power: The Newport Connection* (n.p.: CreateSpace Independent Publishing Platform, 2014), pp. 44–5.

'Commonwealth Navies as Seen by the United States Navy, 1910–2010', *The Northern Mariner/Le Marin du Nord*, vol. xxiv, nos. 3–4 (July–October 2014), pp. 157–75.

2015

'Knox Awardee Roundtable', *Pull Together: Newsletter of the Naval Historical Foundation* (Winter 2014–15), pp. 7–8.

Review of James Davey and Richard Johns, *Broadsides: Caricature and the Navy, 1756–1815*, *The Mariner's Mirror*, vol. 101, no. 1 (2015), pp. 95–6.

TwentyFirst International Seapower Symposium: Report of the Proceedings 16–19 September 2014, ed. John B. Hattendorf and John W. Kennedy (Newport: Naval War College, 2015).

Review of Jan Lemnitzer, *Power, Law, and the End of Privateering*, *Naval War College Review*, vol. 68, no. 2 (Spring 2015), pp. 139–40.

'The Naval Historian and his Library: An Interview with John Hattendorf', by Lieutenant Commander Christopher Nelson, USN. War on the Rocks website, posted on 21 April 2015. http://warontherocks.com/2015/04/the-naval-historian-and-his-library-an-interview-with-john-hattendorf/.

Review of Rodney K. Watterson, *Whips to Walls: Naval Discipline from Flogging to Progressive Era Reform at Portsmouth Prison*, *Historical New Hampshire*, vol. 69, no. 1 (Summer 2015), pp. 75–6.

'L'histoire maritime, l'histoire de la science de la navigation et l'Oxford Encyclopedia of Maritime History', *Revue d' Histoire Maritime*, no. 20 (2015/1), pp. 195–203.

'Friends and Allies from the War: Collegial Scholarship on the Era of the War of the Spanish Succession', in [Jannie Veenendaal-Barth, Dirk Veenendaal and Matthijs Veenendaal, compilers], *Bibliografie ter Gelegenheid van de 75e Verjaardag van Augustus J. Veenendaal, Jr. (Guus Veenedaal)* (Rotterdam: Karwansaray Publishers, 2015), pp. 18–24.

Forthcoming and Works in Progress

The Battle of Trafalgar. Great Battles: Memory, Culture, and History, series editor, Sir Hew Strachan (Oxford: Oxford University Press, 2017).

Naval Force and Peacetime Coercion: Case Studies from British Naval History on the Peacetime Use of Naval Force for Coercive Diplomacy, 1700–1878.

The Journal of Admiral Sir George Rooke, 1700–04, ed. John B. Hattendorf (London: Navy Records Society, forthcoming).

'North America as a Theatre of Conflict and Imperial Competition during the War of the Spanish Succession, 1701–13', in Matthias Pohlig and Michael Schaich (eds), *The War of the Spanish Succession: New Perspectives* (Oxford: Oxford University Press, forthcoming).

Putting Cargoes Through: The U.S. Navy at Gibraltar, 1917–1919, by Vice Admiral Albert P. Niblack, edited with an introduction by John B. Hattendorf (Gibraltar: Calpe Press, forthcoming).

Charles XII: Warrior King (Rotterdam: Karawansary, 2016).
Stephen B. Luce: A Biography (forthcoming).
To the Java Sea: Selections from the Diary, Letters and Reports of Henry E. Eccles, 1940–42, ed. John B. Hattendorf (Newport: Naval War College, forthcoming). Historical Monograph series.
U.S. Naval Strategy, 2001–2010: Selected Documents, ed. John B. Hattendorf and Peter M. Swartz (forthcoming).
A Seven Years' War Diary, by Lieutenant William Bamford, 35th Regiment, British Army (forthcoming).
The Society of the Cincinnati in the State of Rhode Island and Providence Plantations (Society of the Cincinnati, forthcoming).
The Military Correspondence of the Duke of Marlborough and Prince Eugene of Savoy.
'Les bases de la marine américaines en Europe depuis la révolution industrielle' (Paris: Service Historique de la Défense). Also published in *Talking About Naval History: A Collection of Essays* (2010).
'Admiral Benbow's Description of the West Indies, 1699'.
'*Influence of Sea Power upon History, The* (1890, Mahan)' and ' Navy', in Edward J. Blum (ed.), *Dictionary of American History, Supplement: America in the World, 1776 to the Present* (Farmington Hills, MI: Charles Scribner's Sons, forthcoming).

Index

References to figures are shown in *italics*. References to tables are shown in **bold**. References to footnotes consist of the page number followed by the letter 'n' followed by the number of the note, e.g. 115n14 refers to footnote no. 14 on page 115.

'ABCD' ships 227
Aboukir, HMS 120
Aboukir Bay, battle of (1798) 89
Achilles' strategy 99
Addington, Henry, 1st Viscount Sidmouth 92
Admiral Graf Spee (German ship) 175
Admiral Scheer (German ship) 176
Afghanistan war
   and 'doing' strategy 249–50
   and Royal Navy 237
air power
   and Britain's island identity 209–12
   post-1919 period 110
   and WWI 171
   and WWII 173
   see also Royal Air Force (RAF)
aircraft carriers ('flat tops')
   1919–39 interwar period 126, 127
   and capital ships 171, 172–3, 175, 177, 178
   and procurement process 246
Ajax (French ship) 25
Akeleye, Samuel 34
Akiyama, Saneyuki 233, 234
Albion, Robert G. 2
Alcalá Galiano, Dionisio 104
Alcedo y Bustamante, José 104
Aldridge, D. 54n24
Algerian corsairs 100
Algiers
   and Balearic Islands privateers 104
   French offshore bombardments of (1682–83) 38
   and Spain 100, 104–5
All Souls College, Oxford 2, 5, 222, 253
America and the Sea: A Maritime History 3, 8
American Civil War 115, 206, 227
American War of Independence (1775–1783)
   and Britain 106–7
   and Impress Service 53

   influence of sea power on 110
   and quarterdeck manpower problem 68, 70, 71
   and Spain 102, 105, 106–7
   and strategy seen from the quarterdeck 20, 21–2, 26
Americas, and Spanish Navy's strategy 101–2, 106–7
Amery, Leo 133–4
Amiens, Peace of (1802) 73, 75
Amsterdam
   admiralty 76, 78, 84, 86, 87
   private navy 84
Anglo-Dutch Wars
   First Anglo-Dutch War (1652–54) 80, 84, 85, 134, 192
   Fourth Anglo-Dutch War (1780–84) 79, 81, 84, 87, 134
   Second Anglo-Dutch War (1665–67) 50, 79, 80, 84, 134
   Third Anglo-Dutch War (1672–74) 45, 50, 80, 84, 134
Anglo-German Naval Agreement (1935) 126, 149
Anne, Queen of England 32, 51
Antelope, HMS (50-gun) 94
'applicatory system' methodology 228, 234, 235
archival record keeping 237–8
Archivo del Museo Naval (AMN) 10, 17
Archivo General de Simancas (AGS) 10
Arethusas (British light cruisers) 146, 147
Argus, HMS 126
Ark Royal, HMS 126, 127
armateurs 44, 45–6
   see also privateering
arms control *see* Indian Ocean and arms control in the 1970s (Peter John Brobst)
Asquith, Herbert, 1st Earl of Oxford and Asquith 216
Assmann, Heinz 166–8
Aston, George 195

asymmetrical warfare 120
The Atlantic
  and Spanish Navy's strategy 106–7
  see also Americas
The Atlantic in strategic perspective of Hitler and his Admirals, 1939–1944 (Werner Rahn)
  differing thinking of Hitler and Naval War Staff 159
  fighting Britain 160–1, 162, 164, 168
  fighting in North Africa 132, 161, 163, 166
  fighting the Soviet Union 161–2, 164, 168
  fighting the United States 161–3, 164, 168
  'Fortress Europe' directive (Nov. 1943) 166
  Hitler's doubts about possible victory 166–7
  Hitler's negative impact on the decision-making process 167–8
  submarine warfare (U-boat war) 162, 163, 164–5
  survival warfare 163–4
  time factor in German strategy 160
atomic weaponry see nuclear weapons
Audacious, HMS 120
Australia, and Indian Ocean security strategy 187
'Avalanche, Operation' (1943) 172

Babcock, J.V. 213n3, 221
"Backfire" (Soviet bombers) 189
Bacon, Sir Reginald Hugh Spencer 205
'Bagration, Operation' (1944) 132
Baldwin, Stanley 148, 211
Balearic Islands privateers 104
Ballard, George 146–7
ballistic missile submarines, and security in Indian Ocean 182, 189
Barbarossa (pirate) 11
Barbary corsairs 11, 82, 83, 84, 85
Barceló, Antonio 104
Barfleur-La Hougue, battles of (1692) 40, 47
Barfoed, Niels Lavritzen 28, 29, 30, 31
Barker, Edward 68
Bart, Jean 29, 46
Battenberg, Louis Alexander of, Prince 146, 147
Battle of Britain (1940) 212
Battle of Normandy (1944) 167
Battle of the Atlantic (1939–45) 129, 130–1, 173
Battle of the Pacific (1941–45) 132–3, 136–7

Battle Procedures (*Sensaku*) 234
battlecruisers and Royal Navy on eve of WWI (Matthew S. Seligmann)
  controversy over battlecruisers 138
  first battlecruiser and motive for building them 139–40
  first three battlecruisers' deployment to North Sea 140–1
  move to Mediterranean and 'North Sea Problem' 141–5
  use of battlecruisers in North Sea mixed squadrons 146–7
  see also capital ship, Royal Navy and British strategy from WWII to 1950s (Tim Benbow)
Bayly, Lewis 192, 195, 197
Bazán, Don Álvaro de, Marquis of Santa Cruz 11, 14, 15, 16
Beachy Head (or Bévéziers), battle of (1690) 38–9, 47
Beatty, David Richard, 1st Earl Beatty 122, 124, 145, 147
Beeler, John 205
Belknap, Reginald R. 223
Bell, Christopher 142
Benbow, Tim 7–8, 169
  see also capital ship, Royal Navy and British strategy from WWII to 1950s (Tim Benbow)
Beresford, Charles William de la Poer, 1st Baron Beresford 194
Bethell, Sir Alexander Edward 194, 197
Bévéziers (or Beachy Head), battle of (1690) 38–9, 47
Biblioteca Nacional de España (BNE) 10
Bigot, Sébastien-François, vicomte de Morogues 22
Bismarck (German ship) 136, 172, 175
Bismarck, Otto von 115
Blackburn, David 74
Blake, Robert 111
Blériot, Louis 210
Bonaparte, First Consul
  and Franco-Spanish alliance 103
  see also Napoleon
Bonrepaus, François d'Usson, marquis de 40
Borodino, battle of 135
Boscawen, Edward 20–1
Bowen, James 68
Breslau (German ship) 120
Britain
  American War of Independence 106–7
  Anglo-Danish Incident (1694) 28–30, 33
  Anglo-Danish Incident (1695) 30–1, 33
  Anglo-Danish Incident (1800) 35–6

Index

Anglo-German Naval Agreement (1935) 126, 149
Anglo-Swedish incident (Battle of Orford Ness, 1704) 31–2, 33
Channel, claim for sovereignty in 33
Channel neutral trade treaties 29
Committee of Imperial Defence (CID) 192, 194, 199–200
competition between forces (1937–41) 148, *149*
courtesy battles and relations with Denmark/Sweden 28
Crimean War (1853–56) 115
Danish Navy, capture of (1807) 36
Danish tactics against British trade convoys (1807) 94
diplomatic realignments (1885–1905) 117
enemy privateers 89, 95–6, 135
English pirates 82
Entente Cordiale 139
fort-building programmes 91, 205
geography of wars at sea 111–12, 118–19
Hitler's views on defeating Britain 159, 160–1
Japanese Navy, British foreign advisors to 229, 230, 232
Martello towers 91, 205
Navy Act (1758) 53
'North Sea Problem' (1912–1914) 142–7
Pax Britannica and naval predominance 113–15
Pax Britannica at an end 116–19
post-WWI sea power 125, 126, 128
and Spain 98–9, 100–1, 102–3, 107
and Spain over Gibraltar 105–6
Strategic Defence and Security Review (2010) 249–50
Talents ministry (1806) 97
taxation, finance and war 112–13
Two-Power Act (Naval Defence Act, 1889) 115
WWI naval operations 119–24
and WWII German strategy 160–1, 162, 164, 168
WWII naval operations 129–32
WWII strategy and United States 161
see also Anglo-Dutch Wars; battlecruisers and Royal Navy on eve of WWI (Matthew S. Seligmann); capital ship, Royal Navy and British strategy from WWII to 1950s (Tim Benbow); Danish and Swedish flag disputes with the British in the Channel (Jakob Seerup); Indian Ocean and arms control in the 1970s (Peter John Brobst); Royal Air Force (RAF); Royal Navy; Royal Navy and grand strategy, 1937–41 (George C. Peden)
Britannia Royal Naval College, Dartmouth 242
British army (1937–41)
  competition with Royal Navy 148
  expenditure data *149, 153*
  Inskip defence review 151, 152, 154
British defensive strategy at sea in war against Napoleon (Roger Knight)
  characteristics of British defence strategies 88–9
  early British victories against France (1790s) 89
  fear of French invasion and anti-invasion measures 89–91
  hostilities shifted northward 91–2
  industrial capacity and warship-building output 92–3
  Keith's fleet's defensive campaigns 94–5
  navy's convoying role 95–7
  political divisions and success of British strategy 97
British national identity and sea power (Duncan Redford)
  background and issues 201–3
  concept of identity 203–4, 212
  island identity
    and air power 209–12
    and free trade liberalism 207–9
    and security 205–6, 212
    and sense of moral superiority 207
    and starvation threat 206–7
    and submarine warfare 208–9
British naval administration and lower-deck manpower problem in 18th century (J. Ross Dancy)
  background and issues 49–50
  manning practices 50–1, 53–4
    Royal navy manpower in 18th century *52*
  press (or impressment) practice 54–6, 58, 61–3
    ages of pressed men *60*
    factored seamen and petty officer recruitment *55*
    seamen and petty officer ratings *57*
    volunteer seamen ages and rating *59*
  see also impressment (or the press)
British naval administration and quarterdeck manpower problem in 18th century (Evan Wilson)
  background and issues 64–5

lieutenants vs masters 65–8
oversupply of lieutenants 68, 70–1, 73, 74–5
  estimate of lieutenants' positions by rate **71**
  lieutenants' commissions and successful exams (1775–1805) *69*
  ratio of number of officers to positions available *72*
  shortage of masters 73–4, 75
British Naval Documents (1204–1960) 8
Brobst, Peter John 7, 179
  see also Indian Ocean and arms control in the 1970s (Peter John Brobst)
Brock, Osmond de 198
Brown University 2
Bruijn, Jaap R. 6, 7, 76
  see also Dutch Navy in early modern times (Jaap R. Bruijn)
Budde, Ole 34
Burleigh, William Cecil, 1st Baron Burleigh 88
Burridge, B. 248n16
Butler, Thomas 31–2
Byron, John 23, 25

Callaghan, Sir George 144–5, 147
Cambridge History of the First World War (J. Winter, ed.) 120n20
Camperdown, battle of (1797) 89, 111
Cape Spartel, battle of (1782) 105
Cape St Vincent, battle of (1797) 89, 111
capital ship, Royal Navy and British strategy from WWII to 1950s (Tim Benbow)
  definition and issues 169–70
  First World War 170–1
  Second World War 172–3
  post-WWII period 174–7
  summary and conclusion 177–8
  see also battlecruisers and Royal Navy on eve of WWI (Matthew S. Seligmann); Royal Navy and grand strategy, 1937–41 (George C. Peden)
Carlyle, Thomas 240
carriers see aircraft carriers ('flat tops')
Cartagena records 17–18
Carter, James ("Jimmy") Earl, Jr. 188
Casablanca military directives (WWII) 131
Castries, Scipion de 26
Center for International Maritime Security (CIMSEC) 249
Chaline, Olivier 19
  see also strategy from the quarterdeck in 18th-century French Navy (Olivier Chaline)

Chamberlain, Neville 148, 153, 154
Channel
  British claim for sovereignty in 33
  Channel neutral trade treaties 29
  see also Danish and Swedish flag disputes with the British in the Channel (Jakob Seerup)
Charles Galley (English ship) 30–1
Charles I, King of Spain (Charles V, Holy Roman Empire) 11, 14, 76, 81
Charles II, King of England 50
Charles V, Holy Roman Emperor (Charles I, King of Spain) 11, 14, 76, 81
Charles XI, King of Sweden 31, 33
Charles XII, King of Sweden 31, 32, 33
Château-Renault, François-Louis Rousselet, marquis de 47
Chatfield, Ernle, 1st Baron Chatfield 150
Cheng Ho (or Zheng He) 113
Chesapeake (or Virginia Capes) battle of (1781) 25, 26
China
  USS *Cowpens* and Chinese destroyer near collision (2013) 247
  see also Sino-Japanese War (1894–95)
Christiansborg (Danish ship) 33–4
Churchill, Winston
  First Lord (WWI) 121, 142, 146, 198
  First Lord (WWII) 128, 130, 154, 173
  on Jellicoe 122
  on unrestricted submarine warfare 208–9
Churruca, Cosme 104
chusma (oarsmen) 12
Clausewitz, Carl von
  and Corbett 191, 195–6, 198, 199
  societal/political factors and theory of war 201–2
  and U.S. Naval War College 222–3, 225
  and Wilkinson 215, 218, 225
Cobden, Richard 207–8
Cochrane, Thomas, 10th Earl of Dundonald 55, 113
Colbert, Jean-Baptiste 37–8, 39, 40, 41–2, 43, 45, 47–8, 112
Colbert, Jean-Baptiste Antoine see Seignelay, Jean-Baptiste Antoine, marquis de
Colley, Linda 203–4, 205n16
Collingwood, Cuthbert, 1st Baron Collingwood 112
Colomb, Philip Howard 191
Committee of Imperial Defence (CID) 192, 194, 199–200
conferences
  'Doing Naval History' (Conference, Yale, 1994) 3

Index

'The Influence of History on Mahan' (U.S. Naval War College, 1991) 3
'Mahan is not Enough' (Conference, U.S. Naval War College, 1992) 3
'Ubi Sumus? The State of Naval and Maritime History' (Conference, Yale, 1993) 3
Conflans, Hubert de Brienne, comte de 20n3, 21, 22
Constellation, USS 1–2
Continental System (or Blockade) 97, 112, 135
'contingency tasks' 243, 244
contracted foreign advisors (*oyatoi gaikokujin*) 229
convooien en licenten 77, 81
convoying
  British Navy 95–7, 123
  Dutch Navy 81–7
    'Memento Convoying' (Cornelis van Kerchem) 85–6
Cooper, Duff, Viscount Norwich 152
Copenhagen, battle of (1801) 66, 112
Corbett, Sir Julian
  in A. Lambert's essay
    autobiographical details 190–1, 194
    The Campaign of Trafalgar 194, 196
    England in the Seven Years' War 193
    'Green Pamphlet' 193, 197
    lectures 191–3
    Maritime Operations of the Russo-Japanese War 195, 196
    Some Principles, aim and main arguments 194–7
    Some Principles, publication and reception 197–200
  'Mahan is not Enough' (Conference, Naval War College, 1992) 3
  on 'maritime' vs 'naval' strategy 252
  and naval history 241
  in P .Kennedy's essay
    Corbett's main theory 110, 134
    and sea power by eve of WWII 127
    and sea power in Napoleonic Wars 135
    and sea power in WWI 120, 123, 136
    and sea power in WWII 130, 136
  on sea power and societal/political factors 201
  and Sims 199, 222
  and study of war 218
  and U.S. Naval War College 197, 199, 223
  on War of the Spanish Succession 191
Coronel, battle of (1914) 119
corsairs and pirates
  Algerian corsairs 100
  Barbary corsairs 11, 82, 83, 84, 85
  English pirates 82
  Irish pirates 82
  North African corsairs 104
  see also privateering
courtesy battles, and England's relations with Denmark/Sweden 28
Cowpens, USS 247
Crecy, HMS 120
Crimean War (1853–56) 115
Cunningham, Sir John 174–5

Daily Express, on British security and air warfare developments 211
Daily Mail
  'air-mindedness' campaign 211
  on Britain 'no longer an island' 210
  on British sea supremacy (1909) 206
Dancy, J. Ross 7, 8, 49, 240
  see also British naval administration and lower-deck manpower problem in 18th century (J. Ross Dancy)
Danish and Swedish flag disputes with the British in the Channel (Jakob Seerup)
  Anglo-Danish Incident (1694) 28–30, 33
  Anglo-Danish Incident (1695) 30–1, 33
  Anglo-Danish Incident (1800) 35–6
  Anglo-Swedish incident (battle of Orford Ness, 1704) 31–2, 33
  how to avoid saluting battles 32–6
Dardanelles campaign, 18 March 1915 battle 121
Darnell, Benjamin 6, 8, 37
  see also guerre de course under Louis XIV (Benjamin Darnell)
Darrieus, Gabriel 195, 223
Dartmouth (Britannia Royal Naval College) 242
Darwin, Charles 248
Daveluy, René 195, 223
D-Day operation (1944) 132, 172
Deane, Captain of HMS *Stirling Castle* 28, 30
Declaration of Paris (1856) 208
Defence Requirements Committee (DRC) fleet (Royal Navy), vs New Standard fleet 152, 155–8, **156**
Denmark
  Anglo-Danish Incident (1694) 28–30, 33
  Anglo-Danish Incident (1695) 30–1, 33
  Anglo-Danish Incident (1800) 35–6
  British capture of Danish Navy (1807) 36
  Channel neutral trade treaties 29

courtesy battles and Anglo-Danish relations 28
Danish tactics against British trade convoys (1807) 94
decision to avoid Channel with warships 32–3
navy's saluting traditions and customs 34–5
wars with Dutch Republic 80
see also Danish and Swedish flag disputes with the British in the Channel (Jakob Seerup)
d'Enville, duc *see* La Rochefoucauld, Louis-Alexandre de, duc d'Enville (or d'Anville)
d'Estaing *see* Estaing, Charles-Henri, comte d'
d'Estourmel *see* Estourmel, Constantin-Louis d' (Commandeur d'Estourmel)
Deutschland (German ship, renamed *Lützow*) 176
Dickinson, H. 242n1
Dictionary of Terms (*Heigo Gaisetsu*) 234
Diego Garcia (US military base) 185, 186, 187, 188, 189
Diligence, HMS 96
Dilke, Charles Wentworth, 2nd Baronet 215
directieschepen 84, 87
Doenitz, Karl *see* Dönitz, Karl
Dogger Bank, battle of (1781) 78
Dogger Bank, battle of (1915) 122
Dogger Bank French naval expedition (1691) 46
'Doing Naval History' (Conference, Yale, 1994) 3
Dönitz, Karl 131, 163, 165
Doria, Andrea 10, 14
d'Orves, comte *see* Estienne d'Orves, Thomas, comte d'
d'Orvilliers *see* Orvilliers, Louis Guillouet, comte d'
Douglas, Archibald 229
Douhet, G. 171
Dover, Western Heights fortification 91
Doyle, Arthur Conan, 'Danger! Being the Log of Captain John Sirius' (short story) 207
'Dragoon, Operation' (1944) 172
DRC (Defence Requirements Committee) fleet (Royal Navy), vs New Standard fleet 152, 155–8, **156**
Dreadnought battleships 115, 117, 219
Drury-Lowe, Sidney 198
Du Bois de La Motte, Emmanuel-Auguste de Cahideuc, comte 20, 21, 22
Duffy, Michael 93n22

Dunkirk privateers 76–7, 82, 83, 86
Dupree, A. Hunter 2
A Dusty Path (anthology) 1
Dutch East India Company 86, 87
Dutch Navy, adoption of English ship saluting customs 35
Dutch Navy in early modern times (Jaap R. Bruijn)
 16th century 76–7
 Dutch context 77–9
 Navy as a battle force 79–81
  numerical strength of leading navies in 17th and 18th centuries **80**
 Navy's convoying task 81–6
  'Memento Convoying' (Cornelis van Kerchem) 85–6
 summary and conclusion 86–7
Dutch Republic
 convooien en licenten 77, 81
 creation of 76–7
 directieschepen 84, 87
 dissolution of 84, 85
 General Insurance Company idea 83–4
 gleuser (special advisor on ship) 86
 Great Fishery (*Grote Visserij*) 82, 83, 86
 Lesser Fishery (*Kleine Visserij*) 82, 83
 Ordinances of Navigation (1550 and 1551) 82
 and Seven Years' War (1756–63) 79
 and War of the Spanish Succession 78, 79, 80, 84, 86
 wars with Denmark, Sweden and Portugal 80
 see also Dutch Navy; Dutch Navy in early modern times (Jaap R. Bruijn); Netherlands
Dutch War of Independence (or Eighty Years' War, 1568–1648) 76, 78, 82, 83, 84, 86–7
Dutch Wars *see* Anglo-Dutch Wars; Franco-Dutch War (1672–78)

East India Company (Dutch) 86, 87
East Indiamen 86
Edward I, King of England 33
Eighty Years' War (or Dutch War of Independence, 1568–1648) 76, 78, 82, 83, 84, 86–7
Eisenhower, Dwight D. 132
El Alamein, battles of (1942) 163
Elias, N. 10n4, 12n16, 15n30
Elizabeth I, Queen of England 88
Eller, Ernest M. 2
England *see* Britain
English identity

vs British identity 202, 207
  see also British national identity and sea power (Duncan Redford)
Entente Cordiale 139
Enterprise, USS 185
Enville, duc d' *see* La Rochefoucauld, Louis-Alexandre de, duc d'Enville (or d'Anville)
equipment acquisition (naval procurement) 243–4, 246
Escaño, Antonio de 104
Essex, USS 133
Essex-class fleet carriers 133
Estaing, Charles-Henri, comte d' 20, 21, 23, 25
Estienne d'Orves, Thomas, comte d' 21–2
Estourmel, Constantin-Louis d' (Commandeur d'Estourmel) 22
Exclusive Economic Zones 247

Falkland Islands
  battle of the Falklands (1914) 119–20, 202
  Falklands Conflict (1982) 237
Fantasque (French frigate) 23
First Anglo-Dutch War (1652–54) 80, 84, 85, 134, 192
First of June, battle of (or Glorious First of June, 1794) 68, 89, 111
First World War *see* World War I (1914–18)
Fisher, John ("Jackie"), 1st Baron Fisher
  and battle of the Falkland Islands (1914) 119–20
  and battlecruisers 138, 139–40, 141
  and Corbett 193–4, 196, 198, 199
  faith in new technology 117
Fiske, B.A. 226n3
Fiske, USS 2
flag disputes *see* Danish and Swedish flag disputes with the British in the Channel (Jakob Seerup)
Flanders, convoying 81
'flat tops' (aircraft carriers) *see* aircraft carriers ('flat tops')
Floridablanca, José Moñino y Redondo, conde de 102
Foch, Ferdinand 223
Forbes, George 67
Forbin, Claude de 46
Ford, Gerald 186
'Fortress Britain' school of military strategy 205
'Fortress Europe', and WWII German strategy 165–6
Fotheringham, Thomas 66
Fourth Anglo-Dutch War (1780–84) 79, 81, 84, 87, 134
Fox, Charles James 97
France
  Algiers, offshore bombardments of (1682–83) 38
  capital-ship building programmes (1880s) 115–16
  Channel neutral trade treaties 29
  Crimean War (1853–56) 115
  defeat by Prussians (1871) 39
  Dogger Bank naval expedition (1691) 46
  Entente Cordiale 139
  Genoa, offshore bombardments of (1684) 38, 41
  Ireland, expedition to (1798) 90
  jeune école naval theorists 39
  navy, numerical strength of leading navies in 17th and 18th centuries **80**
  Ordonnances pour les Armées navales (1689) 37
  Palamós, capture of (1694) 47
  post-WWI sea power 125, 128
  règlement (October 1674) 45
  Smyrna convoy, attack of 46, 84
  and Spain 99, 100–1, 102, 103
  and Spain during French Revolutionary Wars 106, 107
  and Spain in Gibraltar 105–6
  Spitsbergen naval expedition (1692) 46
  taxation, finance and war 112
  Tripoli, offshore bombardments of (1685) 38
  WWII naval operations 130
  see also British defensive strategy at sea in war against Napoleon (Roger Knight); French Revolutionary Wars (1792–1802); *guerre de course* under Louis XIV (Benjamin Darnell); Napoleonic Wars (1802–15); strategy from the quarterdeck in 18th-century French Navy (Olivier Chaline)
Franco-Dutch War (1672–78) 38, 45, 80
free trade liberalism, and Britain's island identity 207–9
Freedman, Lawrence 5, 6, 99, 250
freedom of navigation, vs 'territorialising' the sea 247
French Revolutionary Wars (1792–1802)
  and British defence strategies 88, 89
  and British fear of French invasion 90
  and British fort-building programme 205
  and British Navy 91
  and impressment system 49, 54, 61, 62
  influence of sea power on 109, 110, 111–13, 134

and quarterdeck manpower problem 70, 71
and Spain 106, 107
see also Napoleonic Wars (1802–15)
Freya (Danish frigate) 35–6
Friesland,
  admiralty 76
  see also Dutch Navy in early modern times (Jaap R. Bruijn); Dutch Republic
Froude, J.A. 207
fukoku kyohei ('rich nation, strong country') 230

galleys see Spanish noblemen as galley captains (Carla Rahn Phillips)
García, Don see Toledo y Osorio, García Álvarez de
Garland, HMS 96
Gavin, F.J. 250n22
Genoa, French offshore bombardments of (1684) 38, 41
Germany
  Anglo-German Naval Agreement (1935) 126, 149
  capital ships, building of (after 1936) 126
  capital ships, fate of during WWII 175–6
  German Navy, building of new 116, 117–19
  German Navy, post-WWI 125
  and inability to 'do strategy' in WWII 250
  Marine-Akademie 232
  Tirpitz's naval laws 115
  wars of unification 115
  WWI naval operations 119–24, 170
  WWII naval operations 129–32
  WWII U-boats 162, 163, 164–5, 172, 173, 209
  see also The Atlantic in strategic perspective of Hitler and his Admirals, 1939–1944 (Werner Rahn)
Gibbs, Norman 2
Gibraltar
  British-Spanish conflict over 105–6
  and geography of wars at sea 111
  'Great Siege' of (1779–82) 105
Gleason, Phillip 203
Glete, Jan 41, 77–8, **80**
gleuser (special advisor on ship) 86
Glorious First of June (or First of June, battle of, 1794) 68, 89, 111
Gneisenau (German ship) 176
Gneisenau, August Graf Neidhardt von 113
Goeben (German ship) 120
Goldrick, James 124n28, 236, 242
see also history and navies (James Goldrick)
Goltz, Colmar von der 223
Gordon, Andrew 122n25, 237
Gorshkov, Sergei 181, 188–9
Goussencourt, chevalier de 24
Grasse, François Joseph Paul, comte de 21, 23, 24, 107
Gravina, Federico 104
Gray, Colin 184n23, 201–2
guerre de course, and battlecruiser controversy 138
guerre de course under Louis XIV (Benjamin Darnell)
  expansion and contraction of Colbertian fleet 37–8
  from *guerre d'escadre* to *guerre de course* 38–41
  reasons for strategic shift 41–4
  strategic 'shift' and naval policy 45–8
guerre d'escadre 39, 41, 45, 46
  see also *guerre de course* under Louis XIV (Benjamin Darnell)
Guichen, Luc Urbain de Bouëxic, comte de 22–3, 25–6
Guimerá, Agustín 5, 98
  see also Spanish Navy's offensive strategy, 1763–1808 (Agustín Guimerá)
gunboats
  and British campaigns against Napoleon 94–5
  and 'Great Siege' of Gibraltar (1779–82) 105
Gyldenløve (Danish ship) 28, 29–30

Habsburg regime, in the Netherlands 76, 86, 89
Halligan, John 224
Halpern, P.G. 123n26
Hankey, Maurice, 1st Baron Hankey 150
Hanover, and British crown 89
Harding, Richard 107
Hartley, L.P. 238
Hattendorf, John B.
  bibliography 255–84
  career 1–3
  Festschrift 5, 98
  historian and ex-sailor 242
  honours and awards 4
  on Luce 227
  on naval history 244
  and Professional Military Education (PME) 236
  on Royal Navy's decline in 1930s 148, 155

scholarly work 2, 3–4, 8, 252, 253
and U.S. Naval War College 2, 3, 222, 225
Hattendorf Prize for Maritime History (U.S. Naval War College) 4, 5
Hatton, Ragnhild 3
Heath, Edward 180, 183
Heigo Gaisetsu (Dictionary of Terms) 234
Hermes, HMS (aircraft carrier) 155
Hipper (German cruiser) 130
Hipper, Franz Ritter von 122
history and navies (James Goldrick)
  chronology and 'parochialism of the present' 238
  historians' need to go to sea 239–40
  history for its own sake 240
  nature of dialogue between historians and navies 241
  naval functions 236–7
  Professional Military Education (PME) 236
  record keeping 237–8
  'single causes' fixation 238
  social scientists and virtual realities 239
  see also teaching navies their history (Geoffrey Till); teaching of strategy and sea power, 1909–27 (Paul M. Ramsey)
Hitler, Adolf
  and Anglo-German Naval Agreement (1936) 126
  on defeating Britain 159, 160–1
  on fighting the United States 161–2
  on 'German living-space' 163–4
  on the German people's 'life-and-death struggle' 168
  his helplessness re. the United States 162
  his negative impact on the decision-making process 167
  his reaction to the 1944 assassination attempt 167–8
  his recognition of the failure of his strategy 168
  on possibility of losing the war 166–7
  on submarine warfare in the Atlantic 165
  see also The Atlantic in strategic perspective of Hitler and his Admirals, 1939–1944 (Werner Rahn)
Hobsbawm, E. 114
Hogue, HMS 120
Holland
  admiralty 76
  Channel neutral trade treaties 29
  convoying 81, 82
  naval expenses 81
  see also Dutch Navy in early modern times (Jaap R. Bruijn); Dutch Republic
Holloway, John 94
Holst, Johan Christopher 33–4
Hong Kong harbour 125
Hood, Samuel, 1st Viscount Hood 112
Horsey, Edward 229
Howard, Sir Michael 151–2, 200n56, 244, 246n11
Howe, Richard, 1st Earl Howe 68, 102, 105, 195
Huet de Froberville, Barthélémy 25

identity *see* British national identity and sea power (Duncan Redford)
Illustrious-class fleet carriers 126
Imperial Japanese Naval Academy (*Kaigun Heigakko*) 229, 230, 233
Imperial Japanese Navy and naval intellectualism (Keizo Kitagawa)
  background and issues 226–7
  birth of naval intellectualism (U.S. Navy and Luce) 227–9
  birth of professionalism in Japanese Navy 229–30
  challenges of modern navy 230–2
  foundation of modern navy and intellectual mechanism 232–3
  Sakamoto and Reform 234–5
  summary: Japanese naval intellectual 235
impressment (or the press)
  assumptions of current scholarship 49–50
  need for during War of the Grand Alliance 50–1
  Regulating Captains and Impress Service 51, 53, 61–2
  rendezvous 54–5
  seamen vs landsmen 56, 58, 61
  statistics 54, 56
    ages of pressed men *60*
    factored seamen and petty officer recruitment *55*
    seamen and petty officer ratings *57*
    volunteer seamen ages and rating *59*
  statutory protections against 58
  see also British naval administration and lower-deck manpower problem in 18th century (J. Ross Dancy)
Indefatigable, HMS 141
Indian Ocean and arms control in the 1970s (Peter John Brobst)
  British interests and security policy 179–81
  Naval Arms Limitation Treaty (NALT) 188
  Soviet threat 181–3, 188–9

Soviet threat and British arms control debates 183–4, 187–9
United States' position 184–8, 189
Industrial Revolution, impact of on warfare 110, 114
Inflexible, HMS 13, 120
'The Influence of History on Mahan' (Conference, Naval War College, 1991) 3
Ingles, John 232, 234
Inskip, Thomas, 1st Viscount Caldecote, Inskip defence review 150–4
intellectual exercise, naval history as 247–51
intellectualism *see* Imperial Japanese Navy and naval intellectualism (Keizo Kitagawa); naval intellectualism
Intrepid, USS 133
Invincible, HMS 120
Invincible-class battlecruisers 117, 140
Iowa-class battleships 133
Iraq war, and 'doing' strategy 249–50
Ireland
    French expedition to (1798) 90
    Martello towers 91
Irish pirates 82
'Ironclad, Operation' (1942) 172
Italy
    capital-ship building (after 1936) 126
    post-WWI sea power 125, 128
    WWII naval operations 130
Ito, Hirofumi 231

Jackson, Thomas 197
James, William 94–5
James II, King of England 47, 50
Japan
    capital-ship building (after 1936) 126
    fukoku kyohei ('rich nation, strong country') 230
    Heigo Gaisetsu (Dictionary of Terms) 234
    and inability to 'do strategy' in WWII 250
    Kaigun Heigakko (Imperial Japanese Naval Academy) 229, 230, 233
    Kaigun Kyouiku Honbu (Navy Education Headquarters) 235
    Kaisen Youmu Rei (Naval Warfare Order) 234, 235
    Naval War College 232, 233, 234
    oyatoi gaikokujin (contracted foreign advisors) 229
    post-WWI sea power 125, 128
    Roku roku kantai ('Six battleships, six cruisers') 233
    Sensaku (Battle Procedures) 234
    Showa era (1925–89) 226

Suiko-sha (naval officers' club) 231
    and Washington and London naval treaties 149
    WWII British naval and air operations against 154–6, 158
    WWII naval operations 132–3
    see also Imperial Japanese Navy and naval intellectualism (Keizo Kitagawa); Russo-Japanese War (1904–06); Sino-Japanese War (1894–95)
Jellicoe, John, 1st Earl Jellicoe 120, 122, 123, 124, 132, 136
Jersey, HMS 30
Jervis, John, 1st Earl of St Vincent 108
jeune école naval theorists 39
Joint Services Command and Staff College, Shrivenham 242, 247–8
Jomini, Antoine-Henri 191, 195, 196, 198, 199
Jonquière, Jacques-Pierre de Taffanel, Marquis de la Jonquière 22
Juel, Just 30, 31
Junta de Galeras 14–16
Jutland, battle of (1916) 122–3, 138, 170, 250

Kabayama, Sukenori 231–2
Kaigun Heigakko (Imperial Japanese Naval Academy) 229, 230, 233
Kaigun Kyouiku Honbu (Navy Education Headquarters) 235
Kaisen Youmu Rei (Naval Warfare Order) 234, 235
Kawamura, Sumiyoshi 230
Keith, George Keith Elphinstone, 1st Viscount Keith 91–2, 93–4
Kennedy, Edward 186
Kennedy, Paul 5, 109
    see also sea power and three great global wars (Paul Kennedy)
Kenyon College 1
Keppel, Augustus 25
Kerchem, Cornelis van, 'Memento Convoying' 85–6
King, Ernest J. 3, 214, 224
King George V-class battleships 126
Kipling, Rudyard, 'Regulus' short story 241
Kissinger, Henry 185, 186–7
Kitagawa, Keizo 226
    see also Imperial Japanese Navy and naval intellectualism (Keizo Kitagawa)
Knight, Roger 5, 6, 88
    see also British defensive strategy at sea in war against Napoleon (Roger Knight)
Koyama, Iwao 226

Krabbe, Peter Greis 35

La Clue-Sabran, Jean-François de 20–1
La Galissonnière, Roland-Michel Barrin, Marquis de La Galisonière 20
La Hougue, battle of (1692) 40, 47
La Rochefoucauld, Louis-Alexandre de, duc d'Enville (or d'Anville) 20, 21, 22
Lagos, battle of (1693) 46
 see also Smyrna convoy
Lambert, Andrew, D. 190
 see also Corbett, Sir Julian
Lambert, N. 121n22, 191n4
Langley, USS 126
Lanning, Harris 224
last- en veilgelden 77, 81
law of the sea 246–7
Le Bailly, Sir Louis 189
leadership, and naval history 246
League of Nations 125, 136
Lehman, John 186–7
Leipzig, battle of (1813) 135
Lenin, Vladimir 124
Lepanto, battle of (1571) 9, 10, 11, 14, 18
Lescure (ensign) 25
Levine, Alan J. 160n4
Lewin, Terence, Baron Lewin 188, 189
Lewis, Michael 66
Leyte Gulf, battle of (1944) 133
licenten (permissions) 77
lieutenants (Royal Navy)
 vs masters 65–8
 oversupply of 68, 70–1, 73, 74–5
  estimate of lieutenants' positions by rate **71**
  lieutenants' commissions and successful exams (1775–1805) *69*
  ratio of number of officers to positions available *72*
Lindormen (Danish ship) 30–1
Little, William McCarty 232
Liverpool, Robert Banks Jenkinson, 2nd Earl of Liverpool 97
Lloyd George, David 124
London Naval Treaty (1930) 125, 149
long nineteenth century, and chronological 'naval' subcategories 114
Longman, Charles 197, 198–9
Louis XIV, King of France
 and Colbertian navy 37, 38, 39, 41, 42–3
 death of and end of French pursuit of hegemony in Europe 78
 lack of interest in naval affairs 40
 naval policy 45, 47, 48
 and William III's Grand Alliance 88

Louis XV, King of France 21
Louisbourg, reconquest of 20, 22
Lubert, Louis de 42
Luce, Stephen B. 214, 225, 226–9, 234
Ludendorff, Erich 123
Lusaka conference of non-aligned nations (1970) 183
Lusitania, RMS 140
Lützow (German ship, previously named *Deutschland*) 176

Machiavelli, Niccolò 10n4
Mackesy, Piers 3
Mackinder, Sir Halford 110, 120, 123, 124–5, 133–4, 215n13
Macnemara, Jean-Baptiste 20, 21
Madden, Charles 147
Magruder, C.W. 225
Mahan, Alfred Thayer
 and analysis of sea power 110, 134
  by eve of WWII 127
  in Napoleonic Wars 111, 112, 113, 134
  in WWI 123, 135
  in WWII 136
 conferences on (U.S. Naval War College, 1991 and 1992) 3
 vs. Corbett 191, 196, 199
 historian and officer 2
 vs *jeune école* theorists 39
 and Kabayama 232
 and Luce 228
 on Russian naval presence in Persian Gulf 179
 on sea power and 'national character' 201, 202, 204
 and Sims 219, 222
 and study of war 218
 and U.S. Naval War College 111, 214, 223, 225
'Mahan is not Enough' (Conference, Naval War College, 1992) 3
Malaga, battle of (1704) 78
Manchester Guardian, and Spenser Wilkinson 215
Mandler, Peter 203
Marine-Akademie 232
Maritime Security 243
Marne, battle of the (1914) 121
Martello towers 91, 205
Martin, Thomas Byam 94
masters (Royal Navy)
 vs lieutenants 65–8
 shortage of 73–4, 75
Mattingly, Garrett 239

Mauretania, RMS 140
May, Henry 191
Mazarredo, José de 98, 102, 103
Mehemet Ali (or Muhammad Ali Basha) 113
Melville, Henry Dundas, 1st Viscount Melville 93
Mercer, William 73, 74
Mikasa, IJNS 229
Militärgeschichtliche Forschungsamt 3
Milner, Alfred, 1st Viscount Milner 216
Minnesota, USS 219
Missiessy, Édouard-Thomas de Burgues, comte de 91
Missouri, USS 137
Mitchell, Billy 126
Møen (Danish frigate) 34
Moll, K. 109n2
Moltke, Helmuth von, the Elder 217, 225, 228
Montgomery, Bernard Law, 1st Viscount Montgomery of Alamein 132
Monumenta Germaniae Historica 1
Moore, Graham 66, 95
Moorer, Thomas 182, 189
Morgan-Owen, D. 143n12
Morison, Elting E. 222n58
Morocco, and Spain 100, 104–5
Morogues *see* Bigot, Sébastien-François, vicomte de Morogues
Muhammad Ali Basha (or Mehemet Ali) 113
Munich conference (1938) 148, 154
Munson Institute of Mystic Seaport 2
Murray, Stewart L. 222, 223
mutinies, Nore and Spithead mutinies (1797) 62

Napoleon
    British fear of invasion from 89–90, 91
    as First Consul Bonaparte and Franco-Spanish alliance 103
    Gneisenau on 113
    'to tie knots and carry on' 248
    on ubiquity of Royal Navy 113
    and Wilkinson's views on theory of war 217–18
    see also Napoleonic Wars (1802–15)
Napoleonic Wars (1802–15)
    and British fort-building programme 205
    and British use of gunboats 94–5
    and British use of impressment 62
    Continental System (or Blockade) 97, 112, 135
    influence of sea power on 109–10, 111–13, 134, 135
    and quarterdeck manpower problem 70, 71, 73
    see also British defensive strategy at sea in war against Napoleon (Roger Knight); French Revolutionary Wars (1792–1802)
National Service League 206
National University of Singapore 3
Naval Arms Limitation Treaty (NALT), Indian Ocean 188
Naval Destroyer School 2
naval functions 236–7, 243
naval history
    as intellectual exercise 247–51
    see also history and navies (James Goldrick); teaching navies their history (Geoffrey Till); teaching of strategy and sea power, 1909–27 (Paul M. Ramsey)
Naval History Division (Washington) 1–2
naval intellectualism
    concept 226
    and Imperial Japanese Navy 235
    and social class 230
    and U.S. Navy 228–9
    see also Imperial Japanese Navy and naval intellectualism (Keizo Kitagawa)
naval procurement 243–4, 246
Naval War College *see* United States Naval War College
Naval War College (Japan) 232, 233, 234
Naval Warfare Order (*Kaisen Youmu Rei*) 234, 235
navalism 125, 136, 191, 205–6
Navarino, battle of (1827) 113
Navy Education Headquarters (*Kaigun Kyouiku Honbu*) 235
Navy League 202, 210
Nelson, Horatio, 1st Viscount Nelson 70, 92, 111, 112, 122, 135, 140, 197
Nelson Bicentenary 240
'Neptune, Operation' (1944) 132
Netherlands
    Habsburg regime 76, 86, 89
    see also Dutch Navy; Dutch Navy in early modern times (Jaap R. Bruijn); Dutch Republic; Dutch War of Independence (or Eighty Years' War, 1568–1648)
New Standard fleet (Royal Navy), vs DRC (Defence Requirements Committee) fleet 152, 155–8, **156**
Newbolt, Henry 197
Nimitz, Chester William 133, 214, 224
Nine Years' War (1688–97) 28, 38, 41, 43, 80, 81

nineteenth century *see* long nineteenth century
Nixon, Richard 185
Noailles, Anne-Jules, 2ème duc de 47
Nootka crisis (1790) 70, 71, 107
Nore and Spithead mutinies (1797) 62
North Africa, and WWII German strategy 132, 161, 163, 166
North African privateering 100, 104–5
'North Sea Problem' (1912–1914) 142–7
Northcliffe, Alfred Charles William Harmsworth, 1st Viscount Northcliffe 211
nuclear weapons
    and Britain's island identity 212
    and claims of armed services 137

oarsmen (*chusma*) 12
O'Brien, USS 1
O'Connell, D.P. 247n15
Odysseus' strategy 99
Office of Naval Intelligence (ONI) 228
officers *see* lieutenants (Royal Navy)
Oikawa, Koshiro 226
Okada, Keisuke 232
Öland (Swedish ship) 31, 32
Opium Wars 115
Orford Ness, battle of (Anglo-Swedish incident, 1704) 31–2, 33
Orves, comte d' *see* Estienne d'Orves, Thomas, comte d'
Orvilliers, Louis Guillouet, comte d' 25, 26
Osterhammel, J. 112, 115
Ostfriesland (German ship) 175
other, concept of the 203–4
Ottley, Charles 192, 193, 194, 198
Ottoman Empire, and Spain 100
'Overlord, Operation' (1944) 167, 173
Oxford Dictionary of National Biography 3
Oxford Encyclopedia of Maritime History 3
Oxford 'school of war' 225
    see also University of Oxford
oyatoi gaikokujin (contracted foreign advisors) 229

Palamós, French capture of (1694) 47
Palermo, battle of (1676) 38
Pallas, HMS, recruiting poster for 55
Palmerston, Henry John Temple, 3rd Viscount Palmerston 208
parochialism of the present, and contemporary decision-making 238
Patton, George S. 132
Pauly, Mr (Danish resident in London) 30
Pax Britannica
    and Britain's naval predominance 113–15
    at an end 116–19
Peden, George C. 6, 7, 148
    see also Royal Navy and grand strategy, 1937–41 (George C. Peden)
'Pedestal, Operation' (1942) 130
Pembroke College, Oxford 2, 3
Peninsular War (1808–14) 99
Perceval, Spencer 97
Perry, Matthew C. 229
'Phase 0' activities 243
Philip II, King of Spain 9, 10, 11–12, 14, 15, 76, 88, 113
Phillips, Carla Rahn 6, 9
    see also Spanish noblemen as galley captains (Carla Rahn Phillips)
Phillips, Sir Thomas "Tom" 150, 151, 152, 153, 154, 155, 157, 158
pirates and corsairs
    Algerian corsairs 100
    Barbary corsairs 11, 82, 83, 84, 85
    English pirates 82
    Irish pirates 82
    North African corsairs 104
    see also privateering
Pitt, William, the Younger 92
Polaris submarines 182
Pontchartrain, Jérôme Phélypeaux, comte de 40
Pontchartrain, Louis Phélypeaux, comte de 40, 42, 43, 46, 47
Portal, Charles, 1st Viscount Portal of Hungerford 173
Portland, William Cavendish-Bentinck, 3rd Duke of Portland 97
Portugal
    and Spain 100, 102, 107
    wars with Dutch Republic 80
Poseidon submarines 182, 189
Pratt, William V. 224
press (press gangs) *see* impressment (or the press)
Prince of Wales, HMS 132, 154–5, 158, 176, 245
privateering
    abolition of (1856) 208
    Balearic Islands privateers 104
    Dunkirk privateers 76–7, 82, 83, 86
    England's enemy privateers 89, 95–6, 135
    and *guerre de course* 39, 44, 45–6, 48
    North African privateering and Spain 100, 104–5
    see also pirates and corsairs
Professional Military Education (PME) 236
Psilander, Gustaf von 31, 32, 33

quarterdeck
    definition 64
    see also British naval administration and quarterdeck manpower problem in 18th century (Evan Wilson); strategy from the quarterdeck in 18th-century French Navy (Olivier Chaline)
Queen Elizabeth-class aircraft carriers 246

Raeder, Erich 159n3, 160–2, 165n16
Rahn, Werner 159
    see also The Atlantic in strategic perspective of Hitler and his Admirals, 1939–1944 (Werner Rahn)
Rajalihn (Swedish captain) 33
Ramsay, Bertram Home 132
Ramsey, Paul M. 213
    see also teaching of strategy and sea power, 1909–27 (Paul M. Ramsey)
Ranft, Bryan 196, 248
Rawlinson, Henry Seymour, 1st Baron Rawlinson 193
record keeping 237–8
Redford, Duncan 7, 201
    see also British national identity and sea power (Duncan Redford)
'relevance deprivation' syndrome, and Royal Navy 237
rendezvous (seamen's recruitment) 54–5
Repington, Charles à Court 206
Repulse, HMS 132, 154–5, 158, 176, 245
'rich nation, strong country' (*fukoku kyohei*) 230
Richmond, Sir Herbert 2, 3, 169n1
Ritcheson, Charles 1
Roberts, Frederick Sleigh, 1st Earl Roberts 215
Rodger, N.A.M. 4, 8, 89n4, 238, 252–3
Rodney, George Brydges, 1st Baron Rodney 107, 122
Rohwer, J. 129n33
Roku roku kantai ('Six battleships, six cruisers') 233
Rome, extent of sea power 113
Roosevelt, Franklin D. 162
Roosevelt, Theodore 219
Rowden, Thomas S. 243
Royal Air Force (RAF)
    Bomber vs. Coastal Command 173, 174–5, 176
    competition with Royal Navy 148, 155, 156–8
        expenditure data *149, 153*
    Inskip defence review 150–1, 152, 153, 154

Vickers Virginia bomber force 211
    see also air power
Royal Naval Academy 70
Royal Naval College (1806) 70
Royal Naval College, Greenwich 232, 242
Royal Naval War Course 191, 192, 193, 194, 198, 199
Royal Navy
    1806 *Regulations and Instructions* 36
    and Afghanistan conflict 237
    airborne maritime patrol capability, removal of 237
    and Britain's island identity 205–6, 209–10
    and British rejection of unrestricted submarine warfare 208–9
    capital ships, building of (after 1936) 126
    capital ships, fate of during WWII 176
    Napoleon on ubiquity of 113
    numerical strength of leading navies in 17th and 18th centuries **80**
    'relevance deprivation' syndrome 237
    ship saluting customs 34–5
    Spithead and Nore mutinies (1797) 62
    Two-Power Standard 115, 116
    War Plan G.U. (1909) 140–1
    see also battlecruisers and Royal Navy on eve of WWI (Matthew S. Seligmann); British naval administration and lower-deck manpower problem in 18th century (J. Ross Dancy); British naval administration and quarterdeck manpower problem in 18th century (Evan Wilson); capital ship, Royal Navy and British strategy from WWII to 1950s (Tim Benbow); Royal Navy and grand strategy, 1937–41 (George C. Peden)
Royal Navy and grand strategy, 1937–41 (George C. Peden)
    competition for funds with army/RAF 148
        expenditure data *149, 153*
    Inskip defence review 149–54
    naval operations against Japan 154–6, 158
    Navy's support for Anglo-German Naval Agreement (1935) 149
    New Standard vs DRC fleet 152, 155–8, **156**
    reduced capacity of shipbuilding industry 157–8
Ruckert, Frederick 67
Russell, Edward, 1st Earl of Orford 40, 47
Russell, Thomas McNamara 94
Russia

capital-ship building programmes (1880s) 115–16
numerical strength of leading navies in 17th and 18th centuries **80**
see also Soviet Union
Russo-Japanese War (1904–06) 139, 191, 192, 195, 196, 234
Ruyter, Michiel de 78

Saigo, Judo 231, 232
Saints, battle of the (1782) 107
Sakamoto, Toshiatsu 233–4
Salomon, Richard G. 1, 4
saluting battles *see* Danish and Swedish flag disputes with the British in the Channel (Jakob Seerup)
Santa Cruz, Marquis of *see* Bazán, Don Álvaro de, Marquis of Santa Cruz
Sato, Tetsutaro 232, 233
Sato, Tomosaburo 232
Saumarez, James, 1st Baron de Saumarez 112
Scammell, J. Marius 214
Scharnhorst (German ship) 136, 175
Scheer, Reinhard 122
Schiønning, Peter 35
Schlieffen, Alfred von 118
  Schlieffen Plan 119
Schmidt (envoy from the *Öland*) 31–2
Schurman, Don 190n2
Scott, C.P. 215
Scott, Percy Moreton, 1st Baronet 219
Sea Beggars (Protestant rebels) 76
the Sea of Japan (or Tsushima), battle of (1905) 229, 234
sea power and three great global wars (Paul Kennedy)
  1793–1815: French Revolutionary and Napoleonic Wars 111–13
  1815–1914: interwar period 113–19
  1914–1918: World War I 119–24
  1919–1939: interwar period 124–8
  1939–1945: World War II 128–34
  background and issues 109–11
  concluding thoughts 134–7
Second Anglo-Dutch War (1665–67) 50, 79, 80, 84, 134
Second Hundred Years' War 49
Second World War *see* World War II (1939–45)
Seerup, Jakob 6, 28
  see also Danish and Swedish flag disputes with the British in the Channel (Jakob Seerup)
Seignelay, Jean-Baptiste Antoine, marquis de 37, 38, 40, 47
Seligmann, Matthew S. 138
  see also battlecruisers and Royal Navy on eve of WWI (Matthew S. Seligmann)
Sensaku (Battle Procedures) 234
Seven Years' War (1756–63)
  and Dutch Republic 79
  and impressment system 51, 58, 61, 62
  influence of sea power on 110, 134
  and strategy seen from the quarterdeck 22, 26
Shakespeare, William, 'sceptre'd isle' quote 202
Shimamura, Hayao 231, 234
ships *see* aircraft carriers ('flat tops'); battlecruisers and Royal Navy on eve of WWI (Matthew S. Seligmann); capital ship, Royal Navy and British strategy from WWII to 1950s (Tim Benbow); submarine warfare; *individual ships/types of ships*
Shovell, Sir Cloudesley 28, 29–30, 35
Showa era (1925–89) 226
Sims, William S.
  autobiographical details 218–19
  collaboration with Wilkinson 213–14, 220–2
  and Corbett 199, 222
  quoting Wilkinson 219–20
  and U.S. Naval War College 218–20, 221–2, 224, 225
  works
    'Policy in its Relation to War' (student thesis) 219–20
    'The Practical Naval Officer' 222
'single causes' fixation 238
Sino-Japanese War (1894–95) 232–3, 234
'Six battleships, six cruisers' (*Roku roku kantai*) 233
Six Day War (1967) 180–1
Slade, Edmond 192, 197, 198
Slessor, Sir John Cotesworth 174
Slesvig (Danish ship) 33
Small, Ernest G. 224
Smith, John 73, 74
Smith, Sidney 94
Smyrna convoy, French attack (1693) 46, 84
Snow, C.P. 236
Snyder, Charles P. 214, 224
Society for Military History 237
Solano y Bote, José de 23
Somerville, Sir James 155
Somme, battle of (1916) 123
Souchon, Wilhelm Anton 118, 120
Soviet Union
  Indian Ocean naval presence 179–80,

181–3, 188–9
  British position 183–4, 187–9
  United States position 189
Operation Bagration (1944) 132
post-WWI fleet 174–5
and WWII German strategy 161–2, 164, 168
see also Russia
Spain
  and Algiers 100, 104–5
  and American War of Independence 102, 105, 106–7
  and the Americas 101–2, 106–7
  and Britain 98–9, 100–1, 102–3, 107
  and Britain over Gibraltar 105–6
  and France 99, 100–1, 102, 103
  and France during French Revolutionary Wars 106, 107
  and Morocco 100, 104–5
  navy, numerical strength of leading navies in 17th and 18th centuries **80**
  and North African privateering 100, 104–5
  and Ottoman Empire 100
  and Portugal 100, 102, 107
  wars with Dutch Republic 80
  see also Spanish Navy's offensive strategy, 1763–1808 (Agustín Guimerá); Spanish noblemen as galley captains (Carla Rahn Phillips)
Spanish Navy's offensive strategy, 1763–1808 (Agustín Guimerá)
  defensive vs offensive strategy 98–9
  Spanish interests and strategy 99–102
  Spanish Navy's grounds for offensive strategy 102–4
  specific naval operations
    The Atlantic 106–7
    Trafalgar campaign 107–8
    Western Mediterranean and the Strait of Gibraltar 104–6
Spanish noblemen as galley captains (Carla Rahn Phillips)
  galleys and recruitment difficulties 9–10
  García de Toledo on disadvantages of service
    biographical details 10–11
    financial disadvantages 11–12, 14
    inadequate crew and officers 12–13
    risks of dishonour 13–14
  Junta de Galeras on recruitment of noblemen
    experience and skills 14–15
    financial incentives 15–16
  late 17th-century Cartagena records

deterioration and remaining books 17
  noblemen's ranks and incomes 17–18
Spanish-American War (1898) 191, 228, 234
Spavens, William 62
Spee, Maximilian Reichsgraf von 118, 119
Spencer, George John, 2nd Earl Spencer 70
Spithead and Nore mutinies (1797) 62
Spitsbergen French naval expedition (1692) 46
Stalin, Josef 136
Stark, Harold R. 214, 223–4
Stead, W.T. 115n14
Stephens, W.J. 55
Stevenson, Robert Louis 207
Stirling Castle, HMS 28, 29–30
Stirrup, Graham Eric, Baron Stirrup 249
strategy
  and book's contributions 5–8, 252–3
  evolution of concept 252
  inability to 'do strategy' 249–50
  Lawrence Freedman's definition 5, 6
strategy from the quarterdeck in 18th-century French Navy (Olivier Chaline)
  secrecy and strategy in theory and practice 19–22
  senior officers expressing views 22–4
  understanding strategy from the quarterdeck 24–7
Sturdee, Frederick Charles Doveton, 1st Baronet 143–4, 145, 146, 202
submarine warfare
  advent of and merchant shipping 170
  ballistic missile submarines and security in Indian Ocean 182, 189
  British rejection of unrestricted submarine warfare 208–9
  German U-boats 162, 163, 164–5, 172, 173, 209
  Soviet submarine numbers (1940s) 174–5
Suffren, Pierre André, bailli de Suffren 21, 23, 24
Suiko Zatsushi (later *Suiko sha kiji*) journal 231
Suiko-sha (naval officers' club) 231
Sumida, Jon 138
Sundell, Berit 3
Superpowers 128, 134
Suzuki, Kantaro 233
Sweden
  1695 men-of-war regulations 31
  Anglo-Swedish incident (Battle of Orford Ness, 1704) 31–2, 33
  Channel neutral trade treaties 29
  courtesy battles and Anglo-Swedish

relations 28
  decision to avoid Channel with warships 32–3
  navy's saluting traditions and customs 34–5
  wars with Dutch Republic 80
  see also Danish and Swedish flag disputes with the British in the Channel (Jakob Seerup)
Symcox, G. 43

Tannenberg, battle of (1914) 121
Taranto, battle of (1940) 172
'tarpaulins' 66
Taylor, A.J.P. 123
teaching navies their history (Geoffrey Till)
  background and issues 242–5
  history as background to now 246–7
  naval history as intellectual exercise 247–51
  power of example from processed past 245–6
  see also history and navies (James Goldrick); teaching of strategy and sea power, 1909–27 (Paul M. Ramsey)
teaching of strategy and sea power, 1909–27 (Paul M. Ramsey)
  collaboration between Sims and Wilkinson 213–14
  Spenser Wilkinson
    and study of war at Oxford University 215–16
    teaching history, strategy and theory of war 216–18
  William Sims
    and study of war at U.S. Naval War College (NWC) 218–20
  Wilkinson and Sims: education questions and reform 220–2
  Wilkinson in NWC student theses and staff lectures 222–5
  see also history and navies (James Goldrick); teaching navies their history (Geoffrey Till)
theory of war
  Oxford 'school of war' 225
  Wilkinson's views on 216–18
  see also naval intellectualism
Third Anglo-Dutch War (1672–74) 45, 50, 80, 84, 134
Thirty Years' War (1618–48) 110
Thornborough, Edward 94
Till, Geoffrey 169n1, 242
  see also teaching navies their history (Geoffrey Till)

Tirpitz (German ship) 172, 175–6
Tirpitz, Alfred von 115, 117, 118, 119
Togo, Heihachiro 229, 234
Toledo y Osorio, García Álvarez de 10–14
'Torch, Operation' (1942) 172
Torrington, Arthur Herbert, 1st Earl of Torrington 38–9
Tourville, Anne Hilarion de Costentin, comte de 40, 46–7
Town-class cruisers 126
Trafalgar, battle of (1805) 89, 104, 107–8, 111, 135
Treaty of Kanagawa (1854) 229
Treaty of London *see* London Naval Treaty (1930)
Treaty of Paris (1763) 99
Treaty of Versailles (1783) 107
Treaty of Washington *see* Washington Naval Treaties (1921–22)
Tripoli, French offshore bombardments of (1685) 38
Troubridge, Ernest 197–8
Tsushima (or the Sea of Japan), battle of (1905) 229, 234
Turner, Stansfield M. 2
Twelve Years' Truce (1609–21) 83
Two-Ocean Navy Act (United States, 1940) 126
Two-Power Standard 115, 116
Type 26 Global Combat Ship 249
Tyrwhitt, Reginald Yorke, 1st Baronet 122

'Ubi Sumus? The State of Naval and Maritime History' (Conference, Yale, 1993) 3
U-boat war (WWII) 162, 163, 164–5, 172, 173, 209
  see also submarine warfare
UN Convention on the Law of the Sea (UNCLOS) 247
United States
  American Civil War 115, 206, 227
  capital-ship building (after 1936) 126, 131, 133–4
  Diego Garcia military base 185, 186, 187, 188, 189
  Indian Ocean security strategy 180, 182, 184–8, 189
  International Seapower Symposia 4
  post-WWI sea power 125, 126
  Spanish-American War (1898) 191, 228, 234
  Two-Ocean Navy Act (1940) 126
  US Navy and Luce 226–9
  US Navy on Indian Ocean and arms

control 185
US Navy's strategic focus 177
USS *Cowpens* and Chinese destroyer near collision (2013) 247
Vinson-Tramell Act (1940) 126
and WWI 120–1, 123, 124
and WWII 131–4
and WWII British strategy 161
and WWII German strategy 161–3, 164, 168
see also American War of Independence (1775–1783); The Atlantic in strategic perspective of Hitler and his Admirals, 1939–1944 (Werner Rahn)
United States Naval Institute (USNI) 228
United States Naval War College
and Akiyama 234
and Corbett 197, 199, 223
creation and purpose 190, 227–8
and Hattendorf 2, 3, 222, 225
Hattendorf Prize for Maritime History 4, 5
and Kabayama 232
and Luce 227–8
and Mahan 111, 214, 223, 225
and Sims 218–20, 221–2, 224, 225
and Sims' correspondence with Wilkinson 213–14
Wilkinson in student theses and staff lectures 222–5
University of Oxford
All Souls College 2, 5, 222, 253
Pembroke College 2, 3
and Spenser Wilkinson 215, 216–18
Utrecht, Peace of (1713) 81, 87

Vauban, Sébastien Le Prestre, Seigneur de 44, 45
Vickers Virginia bombers 211
Vietnam War 1, 2
Vinson-Tramell Act (United States, 1940) 126
Virginia Capes (or Chesapeake) battle of (1781) 25, 26

Wachtmeister (Swedish ship) 29–30
Walpole, Robert, 1st Earl of Orford 112
Walterloo, battle of (1815) 135
War of American Independence *see* American War of Independence (1775–1783)
War of the Austrian Succession (1740–48) 22, 51, 53
War of the Grand Alliance (1689–1697) 50–1

War of the Spanish Succession (1701–14)
Corbett on 191
and the Dutch Republic 78, 79, 80, 84, 86
and the French navy 47
Hattendorf's thesis subject 2, 8
War Plan G.U. (1909) 140–1
Ward, Sir Adolphus William 217
Washington Naval Treaties (1921–22) 125, 149, 184n23, 210
Waterloo, battle of (1815) 111
Wegener, Wolfgang 129–30
Weir, William Douglas, 1st Viscount Weir 158
Wellington, Arthur Wellesley, 1st Duke of Wellington 96, 97, 112
Western Mediterranean, and Spanish Navy's strategy 104–5
Whitlam, Gough 187
Widen, J. 190n2
Wildt, David de 78
Wildt, Job 78
Wilkinson, H. Spenser
autobiographical details 215
collaboration with Sims 213–14, 220–2
journalism 215, 218, 220
main works and themes 215–16
quoted by Sims 219–20
teaching history, strategy and theory of war at Oxford 216–18
in U.S. Naval War College student theses and staff lectures 222–5
works
The Brain of an Army 215
The Brain of the Navy 214, 215, 222
British Aspects of War and Peace 221
The Command of the Sea 215
The Defence of Piedmont (1742–48) 217
The French Army before Napoleon 217
Government and the War 218
Imperial Defence 215
'Reconstruction and the Army' 221
The Rise of General Bonaparte 218
'The Secret of the Sea' 221
'The University and the Study of War' 216, 218n34, 218n36, 221n57
War and Policy 215, 222–3, 224, 225
Willan, L.P. 230
William, Prince, Duke of Gloucester and Edinburgh 70
William III, King of England 50, 51, 80, 88
Wilson, Arthur Knyvet, 3rd Baronet 141–2, 197
Wilson, Evan 7, 8, 64

see also British naval administration and quarterdeck manpower problem in 18th century (Evan Wilson)
Wilson, Harold 180, 182, 187
Wilson, Robert 66
Wilson, Woodrow 124
Winter, J. 120n20
Witt, Jan de, Grand Pensionary of Holland 78, 80
Worcester, HMS 31
World War I (1914–18)
   British defence strategies 88
   Cambridge History of the First World War (J. Winter, ed.) 120n20
   capital ships in Royal Navy, role of 170–1
   lack of historical consensus on causes of 250
   sea power, influence of on 109, 110, 119–24, 134, 135–6
   see also battlecruisers and Royal Navy on eve of WWI (Matthew S. Seligmann)
World War II (1939–45)
   capital ships in Royal Navy, role of 172–3
   Casablanca military directives 131
   five main campaigns 128–9
   'Fortress Europe' 165–6
   and inability to 'do strategy' 250
   sea power, influence of on 109, 128–34, 136–7
   see also The Atlantic in strategic perspective of Hitler and his Admirals, 1939–1944 (Werner Rahn); Royal Navy and grand strategy, 1937–41 (George C. Peden)

X1 cruiser submarine 209

Yamamoto, Gonnohyoe 230
Yorktown, USS 133
Young, William 91
Ypres, battle d' (1915) 121

Zeeland
   admiralty 76, 86
   convoying 81, 82
   see also Dutch Navy in early modern times (Jaap R. Bruijn); Dutch Republic
Zeepaard (Dutch ship) 85–6
Zeppelins 211
Zheng, He (or Chen Ho) 113

Tabula Gratulatoria

John W. Adams
Alan M. Anderson
Commander Benjamin Armstrong,
  US Navy
Captain Michael Barritt, Royal Navy
Larry Bartlett
Richard M. Bateman
Henry L.P. Beckwith
John Beeler
Tim Benbow
Peter and Ingrid Bentley
Hans Christian Bjerg
Colonel Hugh Boscawen,
  Coldstream Guards, British Army
Pelham G. Boyer
James C. Bradford
Peter John Brobst
Captain Nicholas Brown,
  US Navy (Ret.)
Jaap R. Bruijn
Sebastian Bruns
Anne and Rod Burgess
J. Revell Carr
Olivier Chaline
Vice Admiral John N. Christenson,
  US Navy
Ann Veronica Coats
Theodore Crackel
Lieutenant Commander Thomas J.
  Cutler, US Navy (Ret.)
J. Ross Dancy
Benjamin Darnell
J.D. Davies
Timothy J. Demy
W.A.B. Douglas
Zisis Fotakis
Robert D. Foulke
William M. Fowler, Jr

Gabriela A. Frei
Mark J. Gabrielson
Captain and Mrs James F. Giblin, Jr,
  US Navy (Ret.)
Richard H. Gimblett
Karla Goins
Rear Admiral James Goldrick,
  Royal Australian Navy (Ret.)
Captain Herbert Graubohm,
  German Navy (Ret.)
Agustín Guimerá-Ravina
Alan J. Guy
Linda and Richard Hall
Richard Harding
Anna Hattendorf and Frank Doyle,
  with Freja, Porter and Levi Doyle
George G. Herrick
Beatrice Heuser
J. David Hilton
Rolof Baron van Hövell tot Westerflier
Rear Admiral P. Gardner Howe, III,
  US Navy
Alan James
Rear Admiral Nils-Ove Jansson,
  Royal Swedish Navy
Ida Christine Jørgensen
Commander and Mrs Thomas B.
  Keefer, US Navy (Ret.)
Commander John W. Kennedy,
  US Navy (Ret.)
Paul Kennedy
Faye Kert
Dean King
Captain Keizo Kitagawa, Japan
  Maritime Self-Defense Force
Roger Knight
Andrew D. Lambert
Margarette Lincoln

Carnes Lord
Patrick M. Malone
Jorge Semedo de Matos
Captain Robert E. McCabe,
    US Navy (Ret.)
A.B. McLeod
Robert M. Meyer
Guillermo J. Montenegro
Joseph Moretz
Nicholas Murray
Kristina and Tommy Nasser, with
    Hannah and Max Nasser
Lieutenant Colonel Charles P.
    Neimeyer, US Marine Corps (Ret.)
Rear Admiral Roger T. Nolan,
    US Navy Reserve (Ret.)
Rear Admiral Leif Nylander,
    Royal Swedish Navy (Ret.)
Colonel Gary J. Ohls,
    US Marine Corps (Ret.)
Robert O'Neill
Lincoln Paine
Sarandis Papadopoulos
Jonathan Parkinson
George C. Peden
Ingrid and Jason Peters, with Hazel and
    Olivia Peters
Lieutenant Commander Lawrie Phillips,
    RD, TD, Royal Naval Reserve
Admiral Arun Prakash,
    Indian Navy (Ret.)
Virginia Preston
Nicholas C. Prime
Captain Werner Rahn,
    German Navy (Ret.)
Carla Rahn Phillips
Paul M. Ramsey
Duncan Redford
Seán T. Rickard, US Navy
Captain John A. Rodgaard,
    US Navy (Ret.)
N.A.M. Rodger

Vice Admiral and Mrs Ronald A.
    Route, US Navy (Ret.)
Captain Robert C. (Barney) Rubel,
    US Navy (Ret.)
Lars U. Scholl
Jakob Seerup
Matthew S. Seligmann
Joshua M. Smith
Craig L. Symonds
Geoffrey Till
Nicholas Tracy
Sir Rick Trainor and Marguerite
    Dupree
Heath Twichell
Lieutenant Colonel and Mrs Ronald
    Vanden Dorpel, US Air Force (Ret.)
Augustus J. Veenendaal
Admiral Nirmal Verma,
    Indian Navy (Ret.)
Richard and Gail Verplank
Captain Lars Wedin,
    Royal Swedish Navy (Ret.)
Nathan E. White, Jr
Thor and Gerdur Whitehead
Captain Robert N. Whitkop,
    US Navy (Ret.)
J.G. Willard
Kathleen Broome Williams
Simon Williams
Evan Wilson
Z. Vance Wilson
James Wittenburg
Lars Ericson Wolke
Donald Yerxa

The Cumberland Society
Ike Skelton Combined Arms Research
    Library
Naval Order of the United States
Naval Order of the United States:
    Florida First Coast Commandery
Naval Order of the United States:
    San Francisco Commandery

Lightning Source UK Ltd.
Milton Keynes UK
UKOW06n0254230617
303904UK00002B/135/P